Weapons Proliferation
and World Order

Weapons Proliferation and World Order

After the Cold War

Brad Roberts

Kluwer Law International

The Hague / London / Boston

A C.I.P. Catalogue record for this book is available from the Library of Congress

ISBN 90-411-0205-1

Published by Kluwer Law International,
P.O. Box 85889, 2508 CN The Hague, The Netherlands.

Sold and distributed in the U.S.A. and Canada
by Kluwer Law International,
675 Massachusetts Avenue, Cambridge, MA 02139, U.S.A.

In all other countries, sold and distributed
by Kluwer Law International,
P.O. Box 85889, 2508 CN The Hague, The Netherlands.

Printed on acid-free paper

Table of Contents

Introduction

MAKING SENSE OF the new currents and dynamics of international security after the Cold War is no small challenge. Analysts and pundits have made a fetish first of the new world order and more recently of the new world disorder. But debate about the foreign policy crises of the moment has generally served only as a substitute for exploration of the deeper currents of international security poliitics in the 1990s. The purpose of this study is to explore some of those deeper currents.

Its focus is weapons proliferation. Between its emergence as an issue of international concern in the 1940s and the end of the Cold War, proliferation sat at the margins of the security agenda. But a wake-up call was sounded with the Persian Gulf War of 1991 and the discovery of Iraq's advanced nuclear weapons program as well as its stockpiles of chemical and perhaps biological weapons, and ballistic missiles, and its large defense industrial base well stocked by international suppliers. Not least among the discoveries was Saddam Hussein's apparent willingness to exploit these proliferation assets for purposes of national aggrandizement. Proliferation-related issues have hardly left the world stage since then. Iraq has been joined in the debate by the breakup of the Soviet Union and questions about the fate of its nuclear arsenal, as well as nuclear-related foreign policy problems in the Middle East, Far East, and South Asia.

These events hinted at the changing nature of the proliferation subject and thus the necessity for a fresh look at it. But the more probing that inquiry, the more it will reveal that proliferation reflects other and even more profound realities in the international system. Its military features suggest something of the new challenges to peace and security in the interstate system. Its technical features reflect something about the changing capacity of states to act in the world. Its political features reveal a number of fundamental changes in the nature of the international political system and the likely pattern of future relations among states. Put differently, the weapons proliferation subject is a window through which to examine the sources of order and disorder in the post–Cold War era.

This way of thinking about proliferation implies that what governments choose to do about proliferation will be one of the principal determinants of the future world order. Indeed, the 1990s represent a moment of trial—and opportunity—for policy. The task of this analysis is to calibrate the problem at this juncture in world affairs. It seeks to identify both the risks associated with proliferation and the new potential for cooperation it creates.

Despite the new prominence of proliferation and its utility as a vehicle for understanding the post-cold war security agenda, it is a subject cluttered by much old thinking and many conventional wisdoms. Scratch beneath the surface of discussion about proliferation and one often finds that people invoke an understanding of the subject firmly rooted in the 1960s and 1970s: the focus is almost exclusively on nuclear weapons; all proliferation is decried as dangerous and destabilizing; and nonproliferation is prescribed as the antidote.

Accordingly, this study has as a central purpose a fundamental rethinking of the weapons proliferation subject. It begins in chapter 1 with a conceptual review of the prevailing model of proliferation and its application in public policy. This chapter describes the emergence of the proliferation problem in the early Cold War decades and traces the development of basic ideas about the problem that, despite their Cold War foundations, continue to dominate current thinking. It reviews debates within the strategic studies discipline about stability, arms control, deterrence, conflict, and order for their impact on the proliferation subject. The discussion underscores as well the challenges confronting that discipline as the twentieth century draws to a close.

Chapter 2 begins with a simple question: Working with a clean slate, what are the essential features of the proliferation problem as it exists in the 1990s? Research for this analysis draws on a wide variety of unclassified sources of information to create as complete a picture as possible. Different categories of items are identified and assessed: nuclear, chemical, and biological weapons; delivery systems including both ballistic and cruise missiles; conventional weapons; and the defense industrial base. The picture that emerges is of a multifaceted proliferation dynamic, with many features ignored by most scholars and some of the most important badly misunderstood.

If chapter 2 offers essentially a technical review of the proliferation subject, chapter 3 turns to its political and economic dimensions. It explores systemic features related to the interstate system, the traditional security dilemma, and political and economic development in terms of their importance for the future orientation of states toward their weapons potential. This chapter includes an assessment of the end of the Cold War in terms of its impact on proliferation. It reveals a number of trends, some in conflict with one another, that intersect to make predictions difficult.

Chapter 4 poses a number of questions about proliferation's implications. Will the world be more or less secure in an era of the proliferation of high-leverage weapons and the diffusion of military industrial competence? Will proliferation's impact be felt as a marginal influence in the world system or will it affect core institutions and processes? Cold-war-vintage thinking in the academic community is defined and analyzed—and found to be increasingly threadbare. Those in search of simple answers to these questions will be disappointed by the complexities revealed.

The final chapter turns to policy questions. What impact can policy reasonably be expected to have on proliferation in today's environment? What new departures in policy are necessary? The chapter identifies the central tasks of policy and reviews the instruments of policy suitable to those tasks. It concludes with an assessment of progress made in recent years in meeting new challenges and of the prospects for future progress. The line of argument is informed by a concern with what Barbara Tuchman, in her *March to Folly,* describes as the "woodenheadedness" of leaders who throughout history have all too often rigidly maintained existing policies despite clear evidence of the need to move in new directions. There is no better example of outdated thinking, the spent utility of inherited policy approaches, and the risks associated with misunderstanding than the subject of weapons proliferation. Traditional nonproliferation policies are growing not only increasingly ineffective but also counterproductive and dangerous. I coin a new term to encompass a comprehensive new approach to the challenge: antiproliferation. Discussion under this rubric focuses on both the ability and the will to acquire weapons and draws attention to those world order tasks required by proliferation.

The genesis of this volume merits a note of explanation. The author was drawn to the project after a decade's work on the proliferation and control of chemical and biological weapons. This work revealed the dynamics of proliferation and the politics of control to be more complex than imagined by those working solely on the nuclear dimension. It also generated a certain frustration with the rigid approaches of the nuclear nonproliferation community, its marked unwillingness to question old assumptions, its defensiveness in the face of new challenges, and its complacency about the durability of the international political bargain embodied in the Nuclear Non-Proliferation Treaty (NPT). The chemical and biological subjects reveal proliferation to be merely a symptom of a relatively permissive technology environment, in which a relatively large number of states have such weapons within their national competence because developmental processes have contributed to a growing trivialization of barriers against them. Such weapons offer high leverage to those possessing them, not unlike that of nuclear weapons, but not exactly like it either. Moreover, to control such weapons requires major departures in arms control approaches and policy, not the least of which is the necessity to take into consideration a world in which power is diffusing and multilateral negotiations are as much about agreeing to an allocation of rights and responsibilities in the world as about specific technologies. In discussing these issues with people in both in the United States and overseas, the author found a widespread interest based on the conviction that the thinking of the traditional nonproliferation community is increasingly idiosyncratic and anachronistic. Hence the thinking reflected here.

This study began as a book project in the aftermath of the Persian Gulf War and the breakup of the Soviet Union. With the advice and encouragement of Godfried van Benthem van den Bergh and Jan Zielonka, it transmuted into a doctoral dissertation under their joint sponsorship in Holland. I owe them a large debt of gratitude, not just for the original notion of a mid-career Ph.D., but also for the benefits of intellectual growth and rigor that go with such endeavors. I have been fortunate indeed to have such excellent tutors, mentors, and friends. I also owe a debt of gratitude to the team of Dutch colleagues assembled by them to evaluate my work.

This volume would not have been possible without the assistance and support of many other people as well. An early version of the manuscript was given in-depth review by Victor Utgoff, Joseph Pilat, and C. Raja Mohan, whose reactions and insights significantly enriched my own thinking. Many of the arguments included here have been honed as a result of long-running dialogue with others working in the field; although individuals are too numerous to mention, I would like particularly to acknowledge and thank Michael Moodie. Some of that dialogue occurred in my former role as editor of *The Washington Quarterly*, where the privileged opportunity to interact with thought-provoking analysts contributed greatly to my own intellectual development. A word of thanks is also in order to Amos A. Jordan and Zbigniew Brzezinski, former colleagues whom I credit for a certain habit of strategic thought and discipline. Lastly, special thanks are due to two talented individuals with whom I worked at *The Washington Quarterly* and who were critical to the book in your hands: Yoma Ullman, whose gift as a text editor is manifest again in the pages of this book, and James Rutherford, whose eye for production detail helped produce a volume of which I can be proud.

BRAD ROBERTS

Washington, D.C.
September 1, 1995

Chapter 1

Proliferation and the End of the Cold War

WEAPONS PROLIFERATION HAS emerged in the 1990s from the shadows of the Cold War as a preeminent problem of international security. The interest of the research community in the subject has been rekindled after a long lull, leading to a detailed examination of separate pieces of the proliferation puzzle. Policymakers have rediscovered the stakes in halting proliferation, thus reenergizing their cooperative nonproliferation efforts. The heightened salience of the issue in the post–Cold War era was perhaps best expressed in a communiqué issued by the permanent members of the United Nations (UN) Security Council at the conclusion of their January 1992 summit, in which they declared the proliferation of unconventional weapons to be a threat to international peace and security (code words for justifying the use of force), and committed themselves to concerted follow-up actions to strengthen nonproliferation approaches.[1]

What is the nature of this problem that has emerged out of the shadows? How does it connect to the larger subject of order and disorder in the international system? Where does it fit into the post–Cold War international security agenda? To find answers to these questions, this chapter offers a conceptual review of the prevailing model of proliferation and its application in public policy. It begins with a description of the emergence of the proliferation problem in the early

---

1   See UN Security Council Resolution on proliferation: Note by the President of the Security Council, UN document S/23500 (January 31, 1992).

Cold War decades and then traces events of recent years in terms of their relevance for the proliferation subject. One of the principal conclusions of this historical review is that conventional wisdoms about weapons proliferation are rooted in the strategic realities of an era now passed. The chapter then turns to an exploration of those roots. It considers a variety of intellectual debates within the strategic studies discipline and their impact on the prevailing understanding of proliferation. This review underscores the connection between the weapons proliferation subject and the much broader debate about the nature of world order.

The Emergence of the Proliferation Problem

Concern about the spread of nuclear weapons emerged as an early priority in the nuclear era. It was one of the factors that led to the Baruch Plan at the end of World War II to establish some form of international control over this revolutionary new weapon. But the Baruch Plan lapsed, international control was not established, and the march toward a nuclearization of the relationship among the victors in World War II began. In the 1950s, the Atoms-for-Peace program of U.S. President Dwight D. Eisenhower was motivated in significant measure by the desire to safeguard the ongoing diffusion of fissile materials and atomic technology while securing the benefits of the peaceful uses of such technology. In 1957 the International Atomic Energy Agency (IAEA) was established in Vienna to assist countries with their peaceful nuclear energy programs in exchange for their acceptance of inspections and safeguards to prevent weapons development programs. But the safeguards regime was slow to be adopted internationally, and even many of its supporters doubted whether it could stand alone as a bulwark against proliferation.

The term "proliferation" itself entered the public policy lexicon in the late 1950s and early 1960s, against the backdrop of the deepening Cold War confrontation and the emerging nuclear balance of terror.[2] At this time, the world was locked firmly in a sharp confrontation between an expansionist Soviet Union driven by a Marxist-Leninist ideology and a United States committed to

---

2   Albert Wohlstetter, "Nuclear Sharing: NATO and the N+1 Country," *Foreign Affairs*, Vol. 39, No. 3 (April 1961), pp. 355–387.

containment of Soviet power and to the strengthening of an international system based on self-determination and free trade. Each side was arming itself with ever larger arsenals of first atomic and then thermonuclear weapons, and those weapons were being distributed to ever more numerous parts of their force structures, including both advanced long-range delivery systems and short-range tactical systems. International alliances in support of these strategies had come into existence, with some states seeking membership while others struggled either not to be coopted into the East–West competition—or exploited it to extract political or economic goods. This was also a time when strategic studies was beginning to emerge as a rubric under which to examine the behavior of states interacting under the threat of nuclear Armageddon.

The United States and the Soviet Union were concerned to solidify their power and protect their alliances. But in the West there was also a recognition that meeting the Soviet threat in Europe and elsewhere by reliance purely on conventional means of warfare would be prohibitively expensive. Thus nuclear weapons and issues of nuclear strategy emerged at the core of the security approach of the superpowers. The superpowers were also concerned to maintain the stability of the alliance systems and to prevent their disruption by nuclear weapons acquisition by allied states such as Germany or Japan. The West especially also desired to coopt challengers to the international status quo into a binding legal framework of obligations. A related concern that came into clearer focus in subsequent decades was the risk that nuclear war between regional adversaries allied to opposing superpowers could escalate into direct nuclear exchange between East and West, thus creating a shared interest in dampening the risks of so-called catalytic war.

In much of the world, decolonization was accelerating the decay of long-standing structures of international relations. The term "Third World" was coined at this time to distinguish the industrial democracies and the countries of the Communist world (the first two worlds, respectively) from the less developed and postcolonial rest of the world. The term masked, however, substantial differences among the countries of Asia, Africa, and Latin America, both in terms of their level of development and of their orientation to questions of international security and politics.

Among many countries, there was much interest in the peaceful uses of nuclear power. Some countries were also interested in the military applications of nuclear technologies, including states in the developed world such as Sweden and

Switzerland, as well as states in the developing world, such as Israel.[3] Many countries were also concerned about the implications for national, regional, and global security if nuclear weapons were to proliferate to a larger number of countries. In the 1950s and 1960s some analysts predicted that 15 to 20 states, if not more, would possess nuclear weapons by the 1970s, with perhaps substantially larger numbers by the turn of the century.[4]

The UN was laboring to carry out its mandate to promote peace and development, with more efficacy than its League of Nations predecessor but with less impact than its founders had envisioned. The hope that it would emerge as a reliable instrument of collective security had long since been dashed by the East–West clash on the Security Council, except when the Council could act at the margins of international affairs. But as a forum for international dialogue and debate, it gave expression to both the ambitions of peoples around the world, especially those newly free of colonial relations, and the fears of many about the Cold War confrontation.

The almost singular focus on nuclear weapons naturally carried over into the work of the UN to promote disarmament. This effort had its genesis in World War I and the belief of many that the arms industries of the newly industrialized powers and the associated trade in armaments were among the primary causes of that war. The result was a series of international negotiations in the 1920s and 1930s to initiate controls on weapons in pursuit of general and complete disarmament, a project that collapsed in the late 1930s but resumed under UN auspices after World War II. For some particularly concerned countries of the Third World, such as Yugoslavia and Indonesia, these negotiations became primarily a forum for challenging the distribution of power internationally, although these countries were hardly alone in seeking to exploit the nuclear disarmament movement to advance political interests. As Avi Beker has argued:

---

3 For a discussion of the restraint shown by some nuclear-capable states in this era, see George H. Quester, "Unilateral Self-Restraint on Nuclear Proliferation: Canada, Sweden, Switzerland, and Germany," in Bennet Ramburg, ed., *Arms Control Without Negotiation: From the Cold War to the New World Order* (Boulder, Colo.: Lynne Rienner Publishers, 1993), pp. 141–157.

4 Lewis A. Dunn, "Four Decades of Nuclear Nonproliferation: Some Lessons from Wins, Losses, and Draws," *The Washington Quarterly*, Vol. 13, No. 3 (Summer 1990), p. 6.

Disarmament was perceived as a major vehicle for the Third World in its attempt to get rid of the "law of the great powers" through disarmament of the superpowers and through reallocation of resources and power from them to the Third World....United Nations deliberations on disarmament served different factions. For the superpowers, and particularly during the cold war period, it provided a major forum for introducing disarmament proposals as part of East–West psychological maneuvers. For the smaller nations it could provide a consciousness-raising forum to express their fears and concerns over the perils of the nuclear arms race. For their part, members of the United Nations Secretariat, such as former Secretary General Dag Hammarskjöld, were convinced that, if the United Nations wants to be relevant to international politics, disarmament "must remain a central preoccupation of the United Nations."[5]

These features of the international environment of the first two postwar decades coalesced into a way of dealing with the nuclear proliferation problem that was quite specific. It had three elements: (1) a deep-seated fear of an increase in the risks of war as more countries acquired nuclear weapons, (2) a belief in the utility of an international agreement to structure a cooperative response to those risks, and (3) the consequent necessity of a bargain among the nuclear-weapon states and the nonweapon states concerning their respective rights and obligations. This concept of nonproliferation evolved within the diplomatic community from 1958 and 1961, as formulated by the UN General Assembly in a resolution proposed by Ireland in 1961 that paved the way for the negotiation of the Nuclear Non-Proliferation Treaty (NPT).[6]

The NPT was finally agreed in 1968 and entered into force in 1970. It is a political agreement born of the accommodation arrived at in the Cold War

---

5   Avi Beker, *Disarmament Without Order: The Politics of Disarmament at the United Nations* (Westport, Conn.: Greenwood Press, 1985), pp. 6, 32. The Hammarskjöld cite is from Brian Urquhart, *Hammarskjöld* (New York, N.Y.: Alfred A. Knopf, 1972), p. 332.

6   Mohamed I. Shaker, "The Nonproliferation Treaty Regime: A Rereading before 1995," in Joseph F. Pilat and Robert E. Pendley, eds., *Beyond 1995: The Future of the NPT Regime* (New York, N.Y.: Plenum Press, 1990), pp. 7–8.

context described above. The non-nuclear-weapon states forswore the right to acquire nuclear weapons in exchange for a commitment by the nuclear-weapon states (defined as those that had manufactured and exploded a nuclear explosive device prior to January 1, 1967) to make progress toward comprehensive arms control and nuclear disarmament measures while also cooperating on the use of nuclear materials, technologies, and expertise for peaceful purposes.[7] This exchange of promises proved a workable political bargain in an era of sharp confrontation between East and West, because the non-nuclear-weapon states recognized the futility of requiring immediate nuclear disarmament by superpowers locked in sharp confrontation. An understanding of the regime as being founded on a political bargain appears to have receded in the decades since its negotiation, but this bargain remains its preeminent feature.

The NPT is the cornerstone of the nuclear nonproliferation regime, but it is also only one of many elements. The IAEA safeguards system, already in place before the NPT came into being, assumed greater prominence as a tool for detecting and deterring the diversion of nuclear materials from peaceful to weapons purposes when it became an instrument of NPT enforcement. Security assurances (although not formal guarantees) were also provided, in the form of a UN Security Council resolution deeming nuclear aggression, or the threat of such aggression, to require immediate action by the Security Council, especially its permanent members. States supplying nuclear materials and technology on the international market met regularly and informally, first under the aegis of the Zangger Committee and then the Nuclear Suppliers' Group, to coordinate their efforts to prevent the diversion of their exports from licit to illicit activities—the dominance of this market by a few advanced countries willing to work in coordination and the relatively esoteric nature of the commodities themselves (fissile fuels and weapons technologies) offered considerable leverage in support of the nonproliferation goal. As noted above, regional alliances also played an important role in diminishing the incentives of states in regions of insecurity to acquire nuclear weapons. These elements all came to reinforce one another significantly.

---

7   U.S. Arms Control and Disarmament Agency, *Arms Control and Disarmament Agreements: Texts and Histories of the Negotiations*, 1990 ed. (Washington, D.C.: ACDA, 1990), pp. 89–106.

Although the regime was created at a time of widespread expectation that the coming decades would bring an inevitable accretion of nuclear-weapon states, the worst case has not come to pass. In its first two decades, the regime had to contend with a number of significant holdouts, principally France, China, Israel, India, Pakistan, Argentina, Brazil, and South Africa. It struggled with doubts about the diversion of nuclear assets from civilian to military purposes. But no state openly joined the ranks of the nuclear-weapon states, and a powerful norm against nuclear-weapons possession and use has operated in the international system to constrain the choices made by decision makers around the world. By the mid 1990s, the NPT has acquired more states parties than virtually any other major international treaty of the twentieth century. The significant commitment of the superpowers to nuclear nonproliferation was perhaps best demonstrated by their ability to act in relative concert over the years, and often at times of deep acrimony in their bilateral relations, to hinder nuclear weapons proliferation through joint diplomatic efforts and intelligence sharing.

The Nuclear Nonproliferation Model

This history has left as a legacy a certain way of thinking about proliferation as a problem of international security. Its basic elements are the following.

First, its focus is nuclear weapons. Nuclear weapons loomed large in the diplomatic and strategic communities of the 1950s and 1960s, and their massively destructive potential continues to give them exceptional weight as a currency of power and as a political and military concern. The spread of other types of military capability has not featured in the inherited way of thinking about proliferation. Conventional weapons flowed in substantial amounts through the international system during the Cold War. Such arms transfers were dominated by states that were permanent members of the UN Security Council and that generally viewed weapons transfers and sales as a legitimate instrument of influence as well as a way to dampen the demand for unconventional weapons.[8]

---

8   As Thomas Ohlson has noted, "so long as the confrontation between the two major blocs of
    the world has a global dimension, some of the developing countries in areas of high strategic
    interest for the major powers are in a position to extract arms supplies from the latter."
    Ohlson, *Arms Transfer Limitations and Third World Security* (Oxford: Oxford University Press

Perhaps this approach to conventional arms reflects the conventional arms trade of that time, in which the volume and quality of arms traded was markedly different from that of more recent decades. Perhaps it also reflects the predisposition of the analytical community to focus on the readily evident revolutionary aspects of the nuclearization of conflict to the detriment of thinking through the more subtle problems associated with non-nuclear proliferation. The fear of nuclear weapons, which went hand in hand with the promotion of nuclear industries, has also instilled an emphasis on proliferation as a problem of weapons and not of the larger capabilities of industry, science, engineering, and military competence that they represent.

Second, the inherited way of thinking views proliferation as detrimental to international security. It views it as a heresy to praise the virtues of nuclear proliferation for states beyond those that arrived first and formalized their rights in the NPT. Indeed, discussion of the implications of proliferation evokes from nonproliferation experts an almost theological view about international security and stability. The pejorative connotation of proliferation has reinforced a tendency to look at the problem in systemic terms and to evaluate proliferation as a global problem and not as a regional or national one.

Third, the model embraces policy responses that are global and discriminatory, establishing a different set of rights for the possessors and the nonpossessors, supported by measures to enforce a strict barrier between the so-called haves and the have-nots. There is a widespread belief within the nonproliferation community in the efficacy of these so-called strategies of denial and of their continued utility in the 1990s.

All of this is underpinned by a belief in the durability of the political bargain negotiated in the 1960s and indeed in the basic manageability of the proliferation dynamic. These beliefs have been reinforced by the experience of an expanding arms control agenda, first at the bilateral superpower level and later at the East–West level more broadly, in which Western decision makers have accustomed themselves to trading off the benefits of specific military capabilities for other advantages, whether of a military, political, or narrowly reciprocal nature.

---

for the Stockholm International Peace Research Institute, 1988), p. 42.

This model has dominated thinking not just in the policy community but among academics as well. Proliferation has been studied as a nuclear phenomenon almost exclusively, because thinking about the impact of nuclearization on great power relations has been imported into the study of developing countries. The issue has generally been conceived in systemic terms, which is to say in terms of the impact of proliferation on global, rather than regional or national, dynamics. The study of nonproliferation has focused on the attributes of the nuclear nonproliferation regime and its various legal and managerial aspects. Only at the margins of the field has there been much interest in the proliferation of conventional weapons, in distinctive regional and national patterns of proliferation, or in the political context within which the nonproliferation bargain was created.

Proliferation and the 1990s

Throughout the 1980s, the proliferation subject received scant policy and intellectual attention. Because no new state had openly joined the nuclear club, and because the 1980s held few of the debates of the 1960s about whether and how states might "go nuclear," a general complacency prevailed (despite the open secret of weapons programs in Iraq and Pakistan, among others).

This complacency was accentuated by the end of the Cold War. In the immediate aftermath of its victory in the Cold War, the West was in a mood of celebration and, in some quarters, triumphalism. Voters everywhere were ready to reap the benefits of the peace dividend by cutting now-irrelevant Cold War military capabilities. Dire problems of international security were being consigned to an era now past by prognosticators of the "end of history."

An alarming wake-up call was sounded by the confrontation with Iraq brought about by its annexation of Kuwait in August 1990. The military machine assembled by Saddam Hussein profoundly challenged many of the inherited wisdoms in the nonproliferation field. It demonstrated the salience of technical and political factors that simply had not received serious attention from either policymakers or academics.

At the nuclear level, the advanced state of Iraq's nuclear weapons program raised serious and far-reaching questions about the efficacy of the NPT, the IAEA, and indeed the entire nonproliferation regime. That program was assembled despite Iraq's professed adherence to the NPT and went undetected despite Iraq's compliance with associated IAEA safeguards declarations and inspections. The nonproliferation community seemed genuinely unprepared for a nuclear weapons development program that used technology deemed outdated in the more advanced countries.

But the non-nuclear elements of Iraq's arsenal held equal surprises for the nonproliferation community. Fear sometimes bordering on hysteria accompanied the recognition of Iraq's chemical and biological warfare capabilities. The near brush with those capabilities compelled analysts to confront the serious strategic consequences of their proliferation. It also brought clearly into focus the Western tendency to think of such weapons with conceptual models based on the strategic nuclear experience, and it was further helpful in generating a debate about the ways in which chemical, biological, and nuclear weapons differ in utility from one another.

Iraq's arsenal of SCUD missiles and advanced weapons and its substantial indigenous defense industrial infrastructure demonstrated the pernicious interconnection between an open international market in advanced defense-related goods and the capacity of developing countries to build their own military systems. Iraq's conventional arsenal also demonstrated the importance, but heretofore near impossibility, of a coordinated international response by states supplying advanced, non-nuclear technologies with military significance.

Saddam Hussein's willfulness in using his military assets, or threatening to do so, for purposes inconsistent with international standards set out in the UN Charter underscored the risks associated with Iraq's possession of such capabilities. The confrontation also revealed how substantially the dynamics of regional conflict had changed with the end of the Cold War, and how ill-attuned security experts schooled in the exigencies of the Cold War were to the strategic realities of the new era.

The response of the nonproliferation community to the realities revealed by Iraq was twofold. First, the research community sought to reap the resurgence of interest in their field by updating their analyses of proliferation trends. There appears to have been little in the way of fresh departures in the thinking of the nonproliferation community at this time. Instead, there was a marked tendency to employ constructs from the nuclear model to understand newly discovered parts of the problem. This led, for example, to an effort to assess the proliferation of chemical and biological weapons and missile delivery systems in terms imported directly from the nuclear domain. Some began to discover patterns and trends that had been slighted in the 1980s; for example, the confrontation between the United Kingdom and Argentina over the Falklands/Malvinas Islands in the South Atlantic a decade earlier came to be seen in a somewhat different light as an early warning of the threats posed by advanced military capabilities in the developing world.

Second, policymakers redoubled their efforts to promote strategies of denial. The emphasis on export controls and technology denial found new support among the advanced industrial democracies, which already in the mid-1980s had sought to expand these basic approaches into an ever larger number of militarily relevant technologies. The proliferation threat was also used in some Western quarters in a failed attempt to sustain military spending at Cold War levels.

If the Persian Gulf War was the wake up call, it was also fundamentally a sideshow to the larger international event of this era—the end of the Cold War. The collapse of the Soviet Union introduced the wholly novel proliferation problems associated with the breakup of a nuclear-armed state. More significantly from the proliferation perspective, the passing of the bipolar order raised profound questions about the order that would succeed it and the possibility that in the new strategic environment the incentives to proliferate would be substantially stronger. Thus, if the Persian Gulf War revealed something about the trends and faults of the nuclear nonproliferation model, the end of the Cold War touched on the fundamental premises of the nonproliferation project itself.

Concern about the future feasibility of nonproliferation arises from the fact that the Cold War provided a structure of international relations in which nonproliferation could be pursued largely as a subsidiary goal. The West's strategy of containment, the engagement of both superpowers in the security affairs of regional allies, and the joint fear of cataclysmic nuclear war arising from uncontrollable regional conflicts all served to narrowly constrain the tendencies toward proliferation except where superpower security assurances were not taken as credible or sufficient, as in the case of Israel, or where the international community had little leverage, as in the case of India. In this context, the NPT entailed a political bargain not easily abrogated by developing countries with client relations to the North and the IAEA was tasked simply with monitoring the declared activities of states. Nonproliferation outcomes in the international system thus depended heavily on the nature of the system. Specific nonproliferation policy tools were employed only at the margins, where the major powers had no sharply conflicting interests, as in South Africa (and there ineffectually).

After the Cold War, the international system no longer structures the choices of leaders of militarily ambitious states in the developing world in the way that it did in the past. The supposed will of the international community is still expressed in the spirit and body of the NPT. The strength of that will is only now being tested by post–Cold War crises of nuclear proliferation in Iraq, Ukraine, and North Korea. Whether that will can sustain the passing of the strategic era that gave birth to it remains a fundamental and unanswered question.

As discussed in more detail in a following chapter, the end of the Cold War may have a contrary effect on proliferation, weakening incentives to proliferate by permitting a resolution, or at least easing, of conflicts in regions where superpower competition was intense, as in the Middle East and South Asia. But among many in the nonproliferation community, a stark pessimism prevails. Planning for the military implications of failed nonproliferation strategies has emerged as a centerpiece of the debate in the United States and elsewhere about the nature of the military forces necessary for a post–Cold War world.

One of the primary features of international politics in the post–Cold War era is the difficulty leading states are having in conceiving the proper means and ends of their national and international security strategies. This is hardly surprising, given the deep uncertainty about the nature of the post–Cold War world order—indeed, of the primary dynamics and the roles of the principal players. But it is surely a mark of deep confusion about the nature of the proliferation problem that in the United States at least, under the Clinton administration, nonproliferation has essentially emerged as a substitute for international security policy, as an end in itself and not as a means to some larger end. If the experience of Clinton administration foreign policy is any guide, such policies pursued without some kind of strategic vision to inform choices among competing priorities is doomed to failure.

Addressing the Epistemological Problem

Thus the strategic realities prevailing in the 1990s have brought into focus the basic problems with the nonproliferation model described above.

First, its descriptive utility is limited, and increasingly so. The tendency in the nonproliferation community to focus on nuclear matters exclusively, or to view other parts of the proliferation subject through the nuclear lens, or to focus on weapons types and not strategic motives, distorts the non-nuclear aspects of proliferation and obscures the broader, ongoing redistribution of military power in the international system. Furthermore, as more analysts and policymakers have begun to work with the instrumentalities of nonproliferation and to strengthen their coercive aspects, the consensual aspects of the nonproliferation regime that underpinned strategies for the selective denial of weapons have fallen from view.

Second, its predictive utility is limited. A particular way of thinking about the behavior of states toward their nuclear competence has emerged, one that focused on the traditional security dilemma of states in an anarchic system; it is a way of thinking that nourishes fears about proliferation in an unstable era but also overlooks other types of state behavior in both the Cold War and post–Cold War eras. A way of thinking also developed about the efficacy of nonproliferation policy; the fact that no state openly joined the ranks of the nuclear-weapon states has reinforced a sense that strategies of weapons and technology denial are effective and can continue to be so. In parallel, a way of thinking about the consequences of proliferation also emerged in the Cold War, one that has not been tested in the light of new strategic realities. The models and theories of the behavior of states on issues related to proliferation—decisions to acquire, deploy, or use weapons, or to do none of these and instead pursue alternate strategies—appear to account for an ever smaller part of the experience base available to test those theories.

Third, the prescriptive utility of the Cold War–vintage proliferation model is also limited. The emphasis given to strategies of denial no longer encompasses the full range of policy mechanisms useful to halt, reverse, manage, or otherwise cope with weapons proliferation and its consequences. Instead, emphasis falls on fine-tuning old approaches and extending the nuclear nonproliferation effort to an ever broader set of international security problems. If policies are to be crafted that offer any meaningful promise of dealing with the proliferation problem as it exists in the post–Cold War era, a new understanding of the proliferation problem is necessary.

Thus, a fresh approach to the subject is required. In the chapters that follow, basic questions are posed about the study of proliferation and the making of public policy. What is the nature of the proliferation problem as it exists today? What factors will determine the future rate and character of proliferation? What are its implications, for both the international system and the efforts of governments to constrain it? Answers to these questions require casting the intellectual inquiry quite broadly, because the relatively narrow purview of the traditional academic inquiry into these matters fails to encompass enough of the new strategic dynamic. It is necessary to range across a wide variety of topics in the strategic studies discipline now that proliferation is moving from the periphery to the core of the field.

This is a particular challenge given the state of the discipline comprising the study of international relations and strategic and security affairs. As Joseph Nye and Sean Lynn-Jones have argued, this field suffers major intellectual problems, including inadequate basic theoretical work, ethnocentrism, and a lack of attention to history.[9] The problems they identified in 1987 have only become magnified with the end of the Cold War. In the study of proliferation in particular, there is a highly noticeable disjunction between a proliferation topic that is highly dynamic in political, economic, technical, and military terms and a conceptual arsenal that is largely static and outdated.

In analyzing proliferation, there is a tendency, for example, to continue to use basic definitions and terms firmly rooted in an era now past. Terms like "First," "Second," and "Third" worlds would appear to have lost their utility after the collapse of the second, Communist world; so too "East" and "West." Some in the erstwhile Third World do, however, continue to find the term suitable as a way to express shared historical experiences (in their emergence from colonial rule), common problems, and opposition to intervention.[10] Terms like "developed" and "developing" have come into increasing usage as replacements, but they mask the profound underdevelopment of many poor countries, as well as the economic

---

9   Joseph S. Nye and Sean M. Lynn-Jones, "International Security Studies: A Report of a Conference on the State of the Field," *International Security*, Vol. 12, No. 4 (Spring 1987), pp. 5–27.

10   As James O. C. Jonah has written, "Countries calling themselves 'Third World' believe that they are members of the grouping no matter what their economic performance....Fundamentally, one can say that the Third World is a state of mind....we should not be too surprised if the term 'Third World' is widely used even in a post–Cold War world." Jonah, "Critical Commentary: A Third World View on the Implications of Superpower Collaboration," in Thomas G. Weiss and Meryl A. Kessler, eds., *Third World Security in the Post–Cold War Era* (Boulder, Colo.: Lynne Rienner Publishers, 1991), p. 164.

imperative in the wealthier countries. "North" and "South" are substitute terms as well, but convey a coherence of world view and a degree of perceived shared interest only rarely in evidence. Terms like "renegade," "pariah," "rogue," and "backlash" are used to depict states that do not participate in global treaty regimes, masking large differences in their strategic orientations. Of course, until some greater coherence or consensus emerges within the study of relations among states in the post–Cold War era, analysts must rely on all of these terms, using them cautiously where necessary and precisely to convey a specific grouping.

But the larger methodological problem relates to the collection of concepts, models, and theories used to evaluate and prescribe policy in the area of weapons proliferation. The specific problem is the incomplete state of thinking as reflected in the unresolved debates among strategic analysts about a number of core issues in the understanding of international security affairs. In rethinking the proliferation field, it is important to recognize how these stillborn debates now shape thinking about the post–Cold War proliferation subject. As Benjamin Frankel has noted, "Too many students of the subject accept unreflectively the presuppositions that have undergirded the proliferation debate of the last two decades....Close scrutiny...reveals many of the proliferation debate's shibboleths to be nothing more than tired platitudes, unable to withstand critical examination."[11]

Three examples suffice. The first relates to the impact of proliferation on stability. The ostensible statistical correlation between an increasing number of nuclear-armed states and the likelihood of war nourished a sense that proliferation would contribute to instability in the international system. But two contrary views emerged. One held that selective proliferation to states facing threats to their very existence was necessary and probably stabilizing; hence the double standard that has emerged in dealing with Israel on the nuclear nonproliferation agenda. The other held that proliferation, by increasing the risks associated with war as well as its likelihood, could have the effect of changing the perception of states about the stakes of their conflict and over time promoting

---

11   Benjamin Frankel, ed., *Opaque Nuclear Proliferation: Methodological and Policy Implications* (London: Frank Cass, 1991), p. 1.

more peaceful and stable relations; hence the general acquiescence to the nuclearization of the relationship between India and Pakistan.[12]

Uncertainty about the impact of proliferation on stability reflected the incomplete debate about the effect of technological change on military relations among states and especially of the impact of arms races on stability.[13] There are two distinct schools of thought about the connection between the competitive acquisition of armaments and the propensity to war in relations among states. One school holds that arms races unfold according to an inexorable logic of their own and increase the likelihood that crisis will lead to war, especially as weapons are fielded that must be used or lost in the early phases of a conflict.[14] An opposite school holds that "the idea that arms races obey a logic of their own and can only result in war, is false...because it conceives the arms race as an autonomous process in which the military factor alone operates....arms races arise as the result of political conflicts, are kept alive by them, and subside with them."[15] In the 1990s, the movement toward military relations among states that

---

12   Kenneth N. Waltz, *The Spread of Nuclear Weapons: More May Be Better*, Adelphi Paper No. 171 (London: International Institute for Strategic Studies, 1981).

13   See Grant T. Hammond, *Plowshares into Swords: Arms Races in International Politics, 1840–1991* (Columbia, S.C.: University of South Carolina Press, 1993), and Donald MacKenzie, "Technology and the Arms Race: A Review," *International Security*, Vol. 14, No. 1 (Summer 1989), pp. 161–175.

14   See the chapter on "The Dialogue of Competitive Armament," in Thomas C. Schelling, *Arms and Influence* (New Haven, Conn.: Yale University Press, 1966), pp. 260–286. This viewpoint is supported by research findings indicating that disputes that led to war were preceded by arms races in 23 of 28 cases, while those disputes not preceded by an arms race terminated in war only 3 out of 71 times. See Michael D. Wallace, "Arms Races and Escalation," *Journal of Conflict Resolution*, Vol. 23, No. ? (March 1979), pp. 3–16.

15   Hedley Bull, *The Control of the Arms Race: Disarmament and Arms Control in the Missile Age* (London: Weidenfeld and Nicolson, 1961), pp. 7–8. See also Albert Wohlstetter, "Optimal Ways to Confuse Ourselves," *Foreign Policy*, No. 20 (Fall 1975), pp. 170–198, and Colin S. Gray, *Weapons Don't Make War: Policy, Strategy, and Military Technology* (Lawrence, Kan.: University of Kansas Press, 1993), chapter 3, "The Arms Race Metaphor," pp. 47–64. This view is supported by research findings indicating that a nation's military spending does not importantly affect its propensity to initiate or become involved in "militarized disputes." The authors conclude that military buildups are neither early warning indicators nor inducements of conflict on the basis of major power involvement in militarized disputes between 1816 and 1976. See Paul Diehl and Jean Kingston, "Messenger or Message: Military

had the potential to resort to unconventional weapons has begun to bridge these two perspectives, creating an element of consensus that the interaction of unconventional weapons deployments among states raises risks and decreases stability.

This tradition of thinking about technological change and force balances derives from a set of experiences in which the acquisition and deployment of weapons occurs openly, or at least is knowable and ultimately publicly understood. But the proliferation problem has been characterized by an additional form of behavior: weapons acquisition and deployment have occurred in secret, and uncertainty about actual behavior has been purposefully fostered so as to obscure actual capabilities and intent. As Frankel has argued, this problem of "opaque" nuclear proliferation raises a set of conceptual problems about the nature of stability that arises from the interaction of changing force postures and to which the existing conceptual arsenal has little to contribute. In particular, he notes,

> The two central institutions of the nuclear age—nuclear deterrence and the Non Proliferation Treaty—are founded on concepts borrowed from the visible proliferation universe. As such, they may not be suitable to deal with phenomena that defy the universe's underlying logic....it is possible to build pure fission weapons and have confidence in their operational reliability even without testing. In other words, the institution of non-proliferation is built on conceptual foundations borrowed from the universe of visible nuclear proliferation.[16]

Uncertainty about the impact of proliferation on stability also reflects the continuing effort to understand the impact of the nuclear revolution on international affairs. The emergence of nuclear weapons seems to have changed much in the way states, especially great powers, act in the world, but there is no agreement on exactly how or why, or whether the impact of nuclearization on the affairs of small powers will parallel the impact on the affairs of great powers,

---

Buildups and the Initiation of Conflict," *Journal of Politics*, Vol. 49, No. 3 (1987), pp. 801–813.

16   Frankel, *Opaque Nuclear Proliferation*, pp. 8, 10.

or whether the introduction of other unconventional weapons or advanced military capabilities will have some or all of the effects of nuclearization.[17]

A second example is the unresolved debate about strategic deterrence. Models of strategic deterrence are firmly rooted in the experience of the superpowers and especially of the United States in the Cold War. As Edward Luttwak has put it, "the Cold War and nuclear deterrence grew up together. Can the latter survive without the former?"[18]

There is a key unresolved question about whether strategic deterrence actually worked as advertised to prevent war. With the successful avoidance of nuclear war between East and West, there is among Western scholars a widespread sense that nuclear deterrence worked. But as yet too little is known about the history of Soviet strategic behavior to gauge whether and how the strategic posture of the United States and the West shaped specific choices at critical junctures. In addition, a contrary view has emerged that nuclear weapons were essentially irrelevant to the character of relations between the superpowers.[19] Moreover, deterrence theorists have been left with the problem of proving a negative, except to the degree history reveals behavior aimed at avoiding crises or the escalation of crises.[20] Of course, had deterrence broken down, an entirely different set of lessons would have emerged.[21]

---

17 See Godfried van Bentham van den Bergh, *Forced Restraint: The Nuclear Revolution and the End of the Cold War* (London: Macmillan, 1992); Robert Jervis, *The Meaning of the Nuclear Revolution: Statecraft and the Prospect of Armageddon* (Ithaca, N.Y.: Cornell University Press, 1989); and Michael Mandelbaum, *The Nuclear Revolution: International Politics Before and After Hiroshima* (New York: Cambridge University Press, 1981).

18 Cited in Lawrence Freedman, "Foreword," in Patrick J. Garrity and Steven A. Maaranen, eds., *Nuclear Weapons in the Changing World: Perspectives from Europe, Asia, and North America* (New York, N.Y.: Plenum Press, 1992), p. viii. Or as Freedman elsewhere puts it, "nuclear strategy had come to be associated with total war, and in the West at least, the age of total war was believed to be passing into history." Freedman, "Great Powers, Vital Interests, and Nuclear Weapons," *Survival*, Vol. 34, No. 4 (Winter 1994/95), p. 35.

19 John Mueller, "The Essential Irrelevance of Nuclear Weapons: Stability in the Postwar World," *International Security*, Vol. 13, No. 2 (Fall 1988), pp. 55–79. See also his book *Retreat from Doomsday: The Obsolescence of Major War* (New York, N.Y.: Basic Books, 1989).

20 Lawrence Freedman writes that "they have done so by arguing that nuclear weapons introduced a qualitative change into the risks of war and that both anecdotal and archival evidence supports the view that this was fully understood by the responsible political leaders

The experience of nuclear deterrence during the Cold War provides one model for thinking about the propensity to stability or war in times of strategic competition under the shadow of weapons of mass destruction. It is an instructive model, but it is only one model. To understand the dynamics of conflict relations in other parts of the world where proliferation has brought a new level of strategic interaction requires that this model be examined for unique characteristics and its utility assessed in different contexts. Among the factors that may in retrospect appear to have been important unique features of this model is the clearly bipolar nature of the confrontation and the apparent capacity of the decision makers on both sides to understand the consequences of their actions and to control effectively the various instruments of state power. In no regional conflict are there confrontations distinctly bipolar in character. In non-Western cultures the politics of strategy and conflict may be influenced by the experience and behavior of the West little if at all. Questions of the effective command and control of unconventional weapons in the developing world are largely unanswered, and they raise the specter of accidental or unauthorized use.

The third example is the unresolved debate about arms control.[22] The centrality of arms control to the East–West relationship over the last three decades has nurtured a widely held conviction that arms control was a valuable,

---

at the onset of the nuclear age and ever since." Freedman in "Foreword," p. ix.

21 Ted Galen Carpenter has argued that "because deterrence did not break down, U.S. officials may have learned some erroneous lessons. Instead of regarding non-proliferation and extended deterrence as useful (or at least tolerable) policies under a peculiar set of conditions, they assumed that both policies had enduring value to the point of being sacrosanct." Carpenter, "A New Proliferation Policy," *National Interest*, No. 28 (Summer 1992), p. 64.

22 Arms control is defined as all forms of military cooperation between potential enemies in the interest of reducing the likelihood of war, its scope and violence if it does occur, and the political and economic costs of being prepared for it. Six techniques have been used historically to further these objectives, including (1) limitation and reduction of weapons, (2) demilitarization, denuclearization, and neutralization, (3) regulating or outlawing specific weapons, (4) controlling arms manufacture and traffic, (5) laws of war, and (6) stabilizing the international environment through confidence- and security-building measures. See Richard Dean Burns, ed., *Encyclopedia of Arms Control and Disarmament* (New York, N.Y.: Charles Scribner's Sons, 1993).

indeed critical instrument of Western policy that helped to bring the Cold War to an end. As Emanuel Adler has written,

> During the first chapter of the nuclear age we have been able to take a few steps back from the abyss; arms control has been one of the tools that has kept us from falling over the edge. The development of arms control ideas and practice allowed nation-states to share expectations of proper action and to rationally calculate their choices according to a common understanding of the situation.[23]

This analysis generally fails to take account of the difficult challenges of verification and compliance that dogged the East–West arms control regime throughout the Cold War years or of the fact that the East–West agenda was but one part of a larger international disarmament effort that transcended the Cold War experience.

A contrary school of thought has long dismissed the usefulness of arms control to national strategy, arguing that where it is possible it is not necessary because the relations among states are generally peaceful, and where effective arms control is necessary it is not possible because of the adversarial relations among states that prevent the risk-taking and confidence-building that are the essence of negotiated arms restraint. Colin Gray puts it starkly: "The practice of arms control among states is unimportant, and the theory upon which the practice is based is wrong."[24] Hedley Bull and Steven E. Miller define the middle ground, respectively: Arms control "is relevant when tension is at a certain point, above which it is impossible and beneath which it is unnecessary."[25] "There is much evidence to suggest that arms control has been overrated as a path to peace."[26]

---

23 Emanuel Adler, "Arms Control, Disarmament, and National Security: A Thirty Year Retrospective and a New Set of Anticipations," in Adler, ed., *The International Practice of Arms Control* (Baltimore, Md.: Johns Hopkins University Press, 1992), p. 18.

24 Gray, *Weapons Don't Make War*, p. 173. See also Patrick Glynn, *Closing Pandora's Box: Arms Races, Arms Control, and the History of the Cold War* (New York, N.Y.: Basic Books, 1992).

25 Bull, *Control of the Arms Race*, p. 75.

26 Steven E. Miller, "Is Arms Control a Path to Peace?" in W. Scott Thompson and Kenneth M.

Moreover, the arms control tradition tends to focus on weapons as problems and sources of instability rather than on the underlying political context and the ways in which arms control choices influence that context. As one diplomat has put this connection, "The solution of the problem of disarmament cannot be found within the problem itself, but outside of it. In fact, the problem of disarmament is not the problem of disarmament. It really is the problem of the organization of the World Community."[27] Avi Beker puts it somewhat differently: "Disarmament cannot be dealt with as a self-contained process, disregarding the conditions of world order. In essence, disarmament is about the organization of power in the international community."[28]

Arms control played a central role in reducing the likelihood of war during the Cold War years because the process rather than the product of arms control took on important political functions in East–West relations, especially with the expansion of arms control into confidence- and security-building measures. The changing and expanding role of arms control in Russian–U.S. relations suggests the possibility that arms control might take new and different forms and purposes in different strategic environments. Future events may show that early definitions were too narrow and that arms control is nothing more than a shorthand for the range of cooperative activities that states might pursue in the security domain to manage the competitive acquisition of armaments. Weapons proliferation puts a premium on the exploration of alternatives to national self-reliance and accumulating ever more and ever more powerful weapons. This suggests the importance of looking beyond the form of arms control to its substance and purpose, classically defined in the early Cold War years by Thomas Schelling and Morton Halperin as being to reduce "the likelihood of war, its scope and violence if it occurs, and the political and economic costs of being prepared for it," and of evaluating these questions in light of new strategic realities.[29]

Jensen with Richard N. Smith and Kimber M. Schraub, eds., *Approaches to Peace: An Intellectual Map* (Washington, D.C.: U.S. Institute of Peace, 1991), p. 46.

27 Salvador de Madariaga, *Disarmament* (1929; reprint ed., New York, N.Y.: Kennikat Press, 1967), p. 56.

28 Beker, *Disarmament Without Order*, pp. 3–4.

29 In Thomas C. Schelling and Morton H. Halperin, *Strategy and Arms Control* (New York, N.Y.: Twentieth Century Fund, 1961), p. 2.

For this purpose, Western experience is applicable, but there is not a lot of evidence that the Western arms control community is able to translate and articulate the lessons of its experiences for decision makers in different environments. To date, such experts have expressed some urgency about adapting arms control tools to regional problems without also offering many concrete and realistic proposals for doing so.

Revisiting these basic questions requires also investigation of the broader history of arms control and disarmament measures for lessons of general utility. The history of multilateral arms control negotiations and measures deserves particular study, given its apparent ascendance in the post–Cold War era but its complete neglect in the arms control literature. Some understanding of the successes and failures of efforts that predate the Cold War would be particularly germane.[30]

The study of strategic relations among states has tended to cloud these issues by focusing almost exclusively on the adversarial relations between two large powers. Models have been developed to explain the behavior of such states in an anarchic international system and to predict their reliance on unilateral, meaning military, responses to uncertainty. Those models have done a good job of explaining why states acquire weapons and pursue strategies of national self-reliance, given the uncertainties of the international environment many confront.[31] But they have done a less satisfactory job in accounting for the

---

30 For a discussion of arms control efforts between World Wars I and II, see B. J. C. McKercher, *Arms Limitation and Disarmament: Restraints on War, 1899–1939* (Westport, Conn.: Praeger, 1992), and Caroline F. Ziemke, "Peace Without Strings? Interwar Naval Arms Control Revisited," *The Washington Quarterly*, Vol. 15, No. 4 (Autumn 1992), pp. 87–108. For a discussion of arms control efforts that followed wars, see United Nations, Institute for Disarmament Research, *From Versailles to Baghdad: Post-War Armament Control of Defeated States*, with the Graduate Institute of International Studies, Geneva, UNIDIR/92/70 (1992). One particularly interesting but unstudied aspect of the arms control record is the imposition of a ban on guided missiles in post–World War II peace treaties in an effort to prevent future deployments of V–2 type missiles, a ban that receded from memory as missile technologies evolved.

31 Robert Jervis describes a "spiral of international insecurity" by which the attempts of individual states to achieve security generates insecurity among their neighbors which, tending to believe the worst of each other, respond with unilateral measures of their own. The result of their collective actions is anarchy, a deepening spiral of insecurity, and the

behavior of medium-sized and smaller states[32] and for the fact that many states abandon weapons programs and choose to mix strategies of self-reliance with cooperative strategies with both allies and adversaries. Some fuller appreciation of these factors would be a useful addition to understanding the broader proliferation dynamic.[33]

In each of these examples, the problem of limited theory-building seems to combine with the problem posed by the limited historical experiences generally used in testing and refining those theories. Many of the theories that prevail in academic discussion in the 1990s may in fact be sufficiently developed, but they have been tested largely against Cold War–vintage nuclear experiences. Stability theories tend to focus on the open nuclearization of bilateral relationships. Arms race theories tend to focus only on dyadic relationships. Deterrence theories draw heavily on U.S. and Western experience during the Cold War. Arms control theories focus largely on the competitive behavior of the superpowers.[34] A broader understanding of historical experience will prove particularly useful as analysts look beyond Cold War experiences to the broader sweep of international affairs and the constants of state behavior.

Looking beyond these three examples, the end of the Cold War has helped bring into the open the debate at the core of the international relations discipline about the very nature of order and disorder in the international system. There is in fact no consensus about the nature of world order or the most efficient

---

impossibility of escape from this security dilemma. See Jervis, *Perception and Misperception in International Politics* (Princeton, N.J.: Princeton University Press, 1976), pp. 63–76.

32 Heinz Gaertner, *Challenges of Verification: Smaller States and Arms Control,* Occasional Paper Series No. 12 (New York, N.Y.: Institute for East–West Security Studies, 1989), pp. 1–2.

33 Bernard Brodie offers a cautionary note to the search for models of strategic behavior. He underscores the "inevitable limitations and imperfections of the scientific method in strategic analysis and decisionmaking....Most basic issues of strategy often do not lend themselves to scientific analysis...because they are laden with value judgements and therefore tend to escape any kind of disciplined thought." From Brodie, "The Scientific Strategists," in Robert Gilpin and Christopher Wright, eds., *Scientists and National Policy-Making* (New York, N.Y.: Columbia University Press, 1964), p. 253.

34 For a discussion of the way in which arms control theory "for the most part stood still and waited" during the end of the Cold War, see Ken Booth and Eric Herring, *Keyguide to Information Sources in Strategic Studies* (London: Mansell Publishing Ltd., 1994). Citation is from p. 114.

strategies for its achievement, and the debate on these subjects has only grown more wide-ranging with the passing of the bipolar era. Different traditions in the analytical community emphasize different solutions to the problems of international insecurity: Do the answers of the Congress of Vienna (balance of power), of 1919 and 1991 (punitive enforcement), of the 1920s and 1930s (general and complete disarmament), or of 1945 (collective security, political reform, and economic integration) remain relevant to the security agenda of the 1990s, and if so, how?

The end of the Cold War and the passing of the threat of global nuclear annihilation have raised hopes in the United States and elsewhere for the advent of a "new world order," in George Bush's famous words, based on the rule of law and the peaceful pursuit of shared prosperity and common responses to transnational challenges. There is much evidence beyond the end of the Cold War to suggest that global events are moving in this direction:

- an increasingly global economy based on both trade and investment and supported by communications and transportation technologies has come into being and its continued well-being is essential for the economies of most of the nations of the world;
- this globalizing economy has been buttressed by the dramatic near globalization of liberal political values over the last two decades;
- a transnational agenda related to the environment and public health has come into being with the population growth and industrialization of the twentieth century, and the state itself is ceding ever larger parts of its historical functions to non-state actors;[35]
- the great powers whose interests dominated global affairs for much of the twentieth century have retreated from the global scene and into domestic preoccupations;[36]

---

35   A challenge to the state has emerged with striking speed in the 1990s related to international criminal activities whose scope and reach has expanded greatly with advanced communications and data-processing technologies, as well as the drug culture prevalent in so many societies, developed and developing. See Phil Williams, "Transnational Criminal Organizations: Strategic Alliances," *The Washington Quarterly*, Vol. 18, No. 1 (Winter 1995), pp. 57–72.

36   As Lawrence Freedman has observed, "What distinguishes the contemporary international

- the problem of war has moved from the core to the periphery of the international system, meaning that war among the great powers is virtually unthinkable and wars of aggression between states are ever less frequent; in 1993, all major armed conflicts were intrastate.[37]

Such a new world order would represent a triumph of the interdependence school of international relations theory. Taking note of the increasing penetration of the state by subnational, supranational, and transnational actors, and of the declining relevance for international politics of the distribution of power internationally (with a concomitant rise in the importance of functional concerns), theoreticians have described the world order task as deepening patterns of integration while preserving such cooperation from disruptions from security concerns of marginal legitimacy.[38]

---

system from its predecessors is the lack of compelling expansionist motives for great-power intervention beyond their neighborhoods." Freedman, "Great Powers, Vital Interests, and Nuclear Weapons," p. 37.

37 See Peter Wallensteen and Karin Axell, "Major Armed Conflicts," in Stockholm International Peace Research Institute, *SIPRI Yearbook 1994: World Armaments and Disarmament* (Oxford: Oxford University Press for the Stockholm International Peace Research Institute, 1994), pp. 81–96. Wallensteen and Axell define major armed conflict as prolonged combat between the military forces of two or more governments, or of one government and at least one organized armed group, and incurring the battle-related deaths of at least 1,000 people during the entire conflict. They note also a marked increase in the percentage of intrastate conflicts that are about territory and independence rather than control of the central government. For a review of the period 1989–1993, see Peter Wallensteen and Karin Axell, "Conflict Resolution and the End of the Cold War, 1989–93," *Journal of Peace Research*, Vol. 31, No. 3 (August 1994), pp. 333–349. The predilection in the intellectual community to focus on the problem of interstate war has in fact obscured due attention to those forces that have caused the most killings during the twentieth century. Studies by Reinhard Rummel indicate that in contrast to the approximately 38.5 million people who have died in all of the wars of this century, an estimated 151 million people have been killed by 15 "megamurderers" running authoritarian states—exclusive of legitimate casualties in war. R. J. Rummel, *Death by Government* (New Brunswick, N.J.: Transaction Publishers, 1994).

38 Robert O. Keohane and Joseph S. Nye, *Power and Interdependence* (Boston, Mass.: Little, Brown, 1977). For a contemporary argument that the pundits of the new world disorder have slighted prevailing and durable patterns of international cooperation, see Paul W. Schroeder, "The New World Order: A Historical Perspective," *The Washington Quarterly*,

For this school of thought, proliferation is a vestige of a more anarchic past in world affairs that threatens to unsettle patterns of global economic and political interdependence. And proliferation is best dealt with by marginalizing it, meaning that the central world order task is deepening those patterns of cooperation and dealing with only the most egregious proliferants when their behavior is also predatory.

Another perspective on world order rallies around Gray's assertion that "if there is a golden rule in world politics it is to the effect that bad times return."[39] Adherents of this view argue that the amity among great powers is a matter of felicitous and temporary coincidence and that power remains the central principle of world order, especially military power. In support of such a worldview proponents note:

- the pattern of decay in many states that has precipitated an outburst of civil wars and heightened risks of anarchy in a number of regions of the world;[40]
- conversely, the continued prominence of the state as a generator of loyalty and as the primary governor of transnational processes;[41]
- the emergence of regional trading blocs within the global economy that may over time evolving into politico-military blocs;

Vol. 17, No. 2 (Spring 1994), pp. 25–43.

39 Colin S. Gray, "Villains, Victims, and Sheriffs: Strategic Studies and Security for an Interwar Period," *Comparative Strategy*, Vol. 13, No. 4 (October/November 1994), p. 354. See also Christopher Layne, "The Unipolar Illusion: Why New Great Powers Will Rise," *International Security*, Vol. 17, No. 4 (Spring 1993), pp. 5–51.

40 As Michael Howard has written, "One reason why there seems so little prospect [of a more orderly world developing] is because of the apparent disintegration of the nation-states, the building blocks of the old 'International Order.'" See Howard, "Tomorrow's International Order: The Role of the Nation State," in Theodore H. Winkler and Peter Ziegler, eds., *The World of Tomorrow* (Die Welt von morgen) (Stuttgart: Paul Haupt Berne, 1994), p. 19.

41 As Thomas G. Weiss has argued, "To argue that the state is a less effective actor than classical realists assume is very different from proposing that it has virtually left the stage. Saddam Hussein has reminded us that states still can become animated by grand strategies of predation. In so doing, however, he discovered that an immediate threat of armed attack is not the only challenge that can concentrate the energies of even so plural a polity as the United States." Weiss, ed., *Collective Security in a Changing World* (Boulder, Colo.: Lynne Rienner Publishers, 1993), p. 181.

- continued ideological ferment in parts of the developing and impoverished world that might in time generate new political fault lines of strategic significance;[42]
- profound questions about the future of reform in Russia and China as well as growing uncertainty about the will or ability of the other advanced industrial powers to offer world leadership that is both active and benign;
- a reading of strategic affairs in Central Europe, the Asia–Pacific, and the Middle East that highlights the continued importance of a balance of military forces for long-term prospects for peace and deepened integration.

Such a new world disorder would represent the triumph of the realist school of international relations theory. Arguing that the state remains the central unit of analysis in the global system, and that all states act at all times to maximize their power, not just as a means to an end but as a goal in itself, adherents of this view perceive security to be a limited resource that none can enjoy completely because states inevitably compete to advance their different national interests. For realists, military force remains both necessary and effective in an international system without a central monopoly on the use of force—that is, in an anarchic system, even if that system is not also chaotic.[43] And states face a basic security dilemma, as described by Glenn Snyder:

---

42 To quote Michael Howard again: "The further fear inevitably arises, that 'the West' as a whole, with its insolent wealth and its intrusive culture, will become for many of them [weak states that historically have used ideology to legitimize themselves] the adversary they need in order to establish their own authority and identity." "Tomorrow's International Order," p. 21.

43 See Hedley Bull, *The Anarchical Society: A Study of Order in World Politics* (New York, N.Y.: Columbia University Press, 1977); E. H. Carr, *The Twenty Years' Crisis, 1919–1939*, 2d ed. (London: Macmillan Press, 1946); Inis L. Claude, *Power and International Relations* (New York, N.Y.: Random House, 1962); Hans J. Morgenthau, *Politics Among Nations: The Struggle for Power and Peace*, 5th ed. (New York, N.Y.: Alfred Knopf, 1973); Kenneth N. Waltz, *Theory of International Politics* (Reading, Mass.: Addison-Wesley, 1979); Martin Wight, *Power Politics*, ed. Hedley Bull and Carsten Holbraad (London: Penguin Books and the Royal Institute of International Affairs, 1979); and Robert J. Lieber, *No Common Power: Understanding International Relations*, 2d. ed. (New York, N.Y.: HarperCollins, 1991).

Even when no state has any desire to attack others, none can be sure that others' intentions are peaceful, or will remain so; hence each must accumulate power for defense. Since no state can know that the power accumulation of others is defensively motivated only, each must assume that it might be intended for attack. Consequently, each party's power increments are matched by the others, and all wind up with no more security than when the vicious cycle began, along with the costs of having acquired and having to maintain their power.[44]

Realists recognize the existence of international cooperation but note the historical tendency of states to put their self-interests first whenever those interests conflict with larger collective interests. The self-help principle is thus the primary generator of national security and international disorder.[45]

At the core of the realist view of world politics is an understanding of the utility of force in international relations. As Edward A. Kolodziej and Patrick M. Morgan have observed, "for most of the history of international politics war was a regular, sometimes useful, and quite legitimate tool of statecraft. In some respects, it still is."[46] Its legitimacy has derived from its utility in protecting national integrity and independence and advancing national interests. Moreover, the capacity to inflict violence on others with military means has also been valued for the influence it exerts on the behavior of states in times other than

---

44 Glenn H. Snyder, "The Security Dilemma in Alliance Politics," *World Politics*, Vol. 36, No. ? (July 1984), p. 461. The original use of the term "security dilemma" was made by John H. Herz in his *Political Realism and Political Idealism* (Chicago: University of Chicago Press, 1951). See also Jervis, *Perception and Misperception in International Politics*, pp. 63–76.

45 But as Robert W. Tucker has argued, not even the passing of the self-help principle would necessarily bring about a more orderly international system. "It is the institution of self-help that must be changed if international society is to become increasingly egalitarian. But whereas the decline of self-help would signal a markedly more egalitarian international society, it would not necessarily promise a more *orderly* one. The erosion of self-help need not give rise to effective collective procedures....The hierarchical character of this society is the indispensable precondition for an order of sorts, defective though that order may be." Tucker, *The Inequality of Nations* (New York, N.Y.: Basic Books, 1977), pp. 169–170.

46 Edward A. Kolodziej and Patrick M. Morgan, eds., *Security and Arms Control, Vol. 2, A Guide to International Policymaking* (New York, N.Y.: Greenwood Press, 1989), p. xi.

war, whether for purposes of deterrence or blackmail. As Thomas Schelling has written,

> The bargaining power that comes from the physical harm a nation can do to another nation is reflected in notions like deterrence, retaliation and reprisal, terrorism and wars of nerve, nuclear blackmail, armistice and surrender, as well as in reciprocal efforts to restrain that harm in the treatment of prisoners, in the limitation of war, and in the regulation of armaments. Military force can sometimes be used to achieve an objective forcibly, without persuasion or intimidation; usually, though—throughout history but particularly now—military potential is used to influence other countries, their government or their people, by the harm it could do to them. It may be used skillfully or clumsily, and it can be used for evil or self protection, even in the pursuit of peace; but used as bargaining power it is part of diplomacy—the uglier, more negative, less civilized part of diplomacy—nevertheless, diplomacy. There is no traditional name for this kind of diplomacy...diplomacy of violence....Success to some extent, failure even more, is not an exclusively competitive notion; when violence is involved, the interests even of adversaries overlap. Without the overlap there would be no bargaining, just a tug-of-war.[47]

The debate about the utility of force in international affairs is in significant measure a reflection of the debate about the nature of power in the international system. The end of the bipolar nuclear confrontation has helped to reveal the increasing salience of sources of state power other than military ones, including both economic and political, and their relevance to the functioning of the global system.[48]

For this realist school of thought, proliferation is both a symptom and cause of anarchy and merely another reflection of the competitive nature of the interstate

---

47   Schelling, *Arms and Influence*, p. v–vi.

48   Joseph Nye defines "soft" power as a country's ability to use its cultural or ideological appeal to influence others. See Joseph S. Nye, Jr., *Bound to Lead: The Changing Nature of American Power* (New York, N.Y.: Basic Books, 1990).

system. And it is best dealt with through means such as alliances and military preparations that preserve a balance of power.

This debate about the underlying nature of world affairs has been dominated not just by the experiences of the Cold War but by the broader issues of war and peace in the twentieth century. As that century ends, and as the shadow cast by the Cold War recedes, it appears that the ongoing processes of change in the international system are substantial, raising questions about its very nature in future decades. The following changes appear particularly salient to questions of international security and the weapons proliferation subject.

In a striking departure from the previous history of the modern interstate system, that system has now fallen into a circumstance in which two different worlds exist, in the sense that relations among the industrialized and developed countries are completely pacified, meaning that war is virtually unthinkable among these states "as a continuation of policy by other means" (to invoke Clausewitz's term), whereas in other parts of the world war remains a legitimate instrument of policy. The great powers as not just balanced, they are pacified, and the resulting transnationalism that prevails among them is genuinely unprecedented in world affairs. But in other parts of the world, "zones of insecurity" prevail.[49] And it is the points of contact and friction between the two from which new global conflicts may emerge.

The tension between economic might and military trepidation among some of the most advanced countries casts doubt on the very notion of great powers as understood historically in world affairs. In some sense the great powers remain great, given their affluence, independence, and military prowess. But in another sense they are merely middle-rank or small powers, given their timidity about the use of force and their disengagement from large parts of the world where economic or political interests compel little or no attention. Luttwak has described a "debellicization" of Western societies, based on the passing of an era in which demographics made it possible to tolerate a system of interstate relations that drew on "expendable" young men; Luttwak argues accordingly that the range of circumstances in which Western publics are willing to support the use of force in diplomacy is growing ever more circumscribed.[50] This has

---

49   Max Singer and Aaron Wildavsky, *The Real World Order: Zones of Peace/Zones of Turmoil* (Chatham, N.J.: Chatham House Publishers, 1993).

reinforced the public commitment to create an international system in which the recourse to war is less necessary and frequent.[51]

To the degree a Western consensus remains on the role of force in international relations, it focuses on self-defense and collective security. The principle of self-defense is firmly established as a norm governing state behavior, as is the right to collective self-defense in answer to the aggression of others. As the Persian Gulf War suggests, there remains today some willingness to use force, essentially for enforcement purposes rather than narrow self-defense reasons and in support of the principle of collective security.

Thus it would be hasty to consign war to the history books. As one recent study of war in the international system concludes,

> if there truly were any doubts, events in the Persian Gulf in 1990–91 proved that the obituaries for war and military force were, at best, premature....The Persian Gulf war did prove that notwithstanding the fall of the Berlin Wall, the increased importance of economic power, and other transformations of the international order, military power still has relevance and utility.[52]

---

50 As Edward Luttwak has described it, "In our own times, the post-1918 delegitimation of war has progressed much further, sometimes reaching the ultimate stage that has been described as 'debellicization,' in which even defensive war is no longer deemed acceptable. Moreover, the widespread suspicion that the ship of state is fated by its very nature to be steered periodically into morally dubious but always deadly fights has engendered a novel countercollectivism, manifest, for example, in the refusal to credit the pronouncements of the state institutions in charge of foreign affairs, intelligence, and the armed forces." Luttwak attributes the term "debellicization" to Norman Podhoretz. Quoted in Thompson and Jensen, *Approaches to Peace*, p. 11. See also Edward N. Luttwak, "Where Are the Great Powers?" *Foreign Affairs*, Vol. 73, No. 4 (July/August 1994), pp. 23–28.

51 "[World War I] had the effect of directing much more attention to concerns and ideas that had been raised prior to 1914 and that have since become (with the help of World War II) central preoccupations in the field—the problem of devising an effective and stable deterrence system, the fear of weapons of mass destruction, deep concern about arms racing and arms transfers, systematic efforts at arms control, and suggestions that the decaying utility of force necessitated a less war-prone international system." Kolodziej and Morgan, *Security and Arms Control*, p. xii.

52 Ariel E. Levite, Bruce W. Jentleson, and Larry Berman, "Foreign Military Intervention in Perspective," in Levite, Jentleson, and Berman, eds., *Foreign Military Intervention: The*

The international system is defined today by a circumstance in which the problem of war continues to exist but where the use of war as an instrument of policy is held to quite different standards of legitimacy in different parts of the international system, with a strong propensity against war in the developed world and a continued reliance on war in parts of the developing world.

This bifurcation creates a powerful dilemma for the developed world. As Lawrence Freedman has observed,

> [T]his contraction of truly vital interests and the additions to the hazards of power projection have come to rest uneasily with an awareness that the equilibrium of the international system as a whole constitutes a vital interest of sorts. The evident limits on the ability of some states to defend themselves have reminded the former great powers of their traditional responsibility for managing the international system, even though this may require an involvement in conflicts that do not touch directly on their sovereignty or well-being.[53]

This dilemma is felt most keenly in the subject of collective security. Collective security processes and institutions remain a critical feature of the international security scene, perhaps more so than ever with the passing of the Cold War and with the declining will of the great powers to use force unilaterally. Yet the purview and promise of collective security seem to shrink regularly, given that declining will and the profusion of civil conflicts.

Collective security has evolved over recent centuries as a means to provide some element of order in an anarchic system, one more reliable than a simple balance of power because it does not depend as much on the durability or principled hegemony of the dominant powers. Its core principle is that states would join together to prevent any one of their number from using coercion to gain advantage. Aggression, by threatening the general peace and security, would be treated as a threat not just to the targeted state but to the larger community. The collective security system is one based not so much on the general

---

Dynamics of Protracted Conflict (New York, N.Y.: Columbia University Press, 1992), p. 308.

53   Freedman, "Great Powers, Vital Interests, and Nuclear Weapons," p. 39.

enforcement of law as on the maintenance of international peace. Underscoring the increasing demands on international institutions and leading states to devote forces to UN missions, UN Secretary General Boutros Boutros-Ghali has asserted that the end of the Cold War presages a resurgence in collective security.[54]

But clearly collective security principles have not removed the problem of war and aggression from the international system. Collective security has yet to live up to the aspirations of its most ardent supporters, because many nations must continue to weigh the likelihood of a collective response to their security challenges and to doubt the credibility of the promise of any such action. Whether the principle of collective security will grow stronger or weaker in the post–Cold War era, and whether it will continue to evolve as a result of the changing capacities to wage war in support of foreign policy goals, remain open questions.

Thomas Weiss has described the disjunction between the collective security notion and the world as it exists at the end of the twentieth century.

> The unadorned concept of collective security, extracted from the ethical baggage that sometimes overwhelms it, involves certain assumptions that conceivably no longer can be squared with international policies. It assumes a world in which every government is prepared to use force to gain its will; in that world, restraint evolves from anticipation of the results of superior power. It is a world regulated not by a hegemonic power but rather by a collection of free actors that avoid domination from outside. It is a decentralized world in which central decisional organs have little or no place. If there are rules, therefore, they develop from explicit or implicit individual consent and usage, not from deliberate legislation.[55]

Hence the growing interest within the policy community in alternative security concepts. These include common security, based on the view that "all

---

54   Boutros Boutros-Ghali, *An Agenda for Peace: Preventive Diplomacy, Peacemaking and Peace-Keeping* (New York, N.Y.: United Nations, 1992).

55   Weiss, *Collective Security in a Changing World*, pp. 3–5.

states, even the most powerful, are dependent in the end upon the good sense and restraint of other nations."[56] They also include comprehensive security, based on the view that economic and social development, the protection of human rights, and the promotion of good governance and democracy should be seen as security policies that complement and supplement military security.[57]

These divergent patterns of development and orientation to the use of force are accentuated by a second major change in the modern interstate system: regions have taken on far greater prominence in the organization of world affairs after the Cold War. And within these different regions, different types of order seem to prevail.

The Middle East and South Asia appear to be governed by the traditional rules of realism, given the clash of power that prevails, the continued salience of force in national power, and proliferation's significance in the regional security dynamic; the movement toward new forms of cooperation in both regions casts some doubt on the traditional realist interpretation, however. Latin America appears in contrast to be governed by a dynamic born of political and economic liberalism and civil-military reform. The Asia–Pacific appears to be governed by processes of economic integration and growing interdependence, albeit under the shadow of significant doubts about the long-term balance among the great powers engaged in the region. Africa represents a major part of the globe where none of these traditional schools of thought prevail, although there are many signs of a growing emphasis on political and economic liberalism and civil-military reform. Europe epitomizes the tension between the integrationist and realist schools, as revealed in the sharp debate about whether the future European order will best be secured through emphasis on the European Union (EU) or the North Atlantic Treaty Organization (NATO).

---

56 Palme Commission on Disarmament and Security Issues, *A World At Peace: Common Security in the Twenty-first Century* (Stockholm: The Palme Commission, 1989), pp. 6–7.

57 Such ideas are contained in Boutros-Ghali's *An Agenda for Peace* especially in the discussion of preventive diplomacy and peace-building, and in Gareth Evans, *Cooperating for Peace: The Global Agenda for the 1990s and Beyond* (Sydney: Allen and Unwin, 1993). For a review of alternative conceptions, see Robert C. Johansen, "Building World Security: The Need for Strengthened International Institutions," in Michael T. Klare and Daniel C. Thomas, *World Security: Challenges for a New Century*, 2d ed. (New York, N.Y.: St. Martin's Press, 1994), pp. 372–397.

The third major change is the growing force of multilateralism in world politics. Historically, multilateral institutions and processes operated at the margins of the international system and were tolerated or ignored by the great powers as they chose. Today, basic issues of regional and global security and of economic and political development can no longer be addressed by narrow national or bilateral mechanisms. Such mechanisms are not yet strong enough to command the sustained engagement of leading members of the international community or to long endure in the event of weakened commitment, but nor can those leaders afford to operate without them.[58]

Moreover, the prevailing pattern of multilateralism is not the pattern of old, which is to say, state-to-state-to-state interaction in intergovernmental forums. Rather, these multilateral processes increasingly involve myriad governmental and nongovernmental forces. Nongovernmental organizations are gaining unprecedented weight—and a formal role—in many international undertakings.[59] In the proliferation domain, nongovernmental organizations play especially important roles as watchdog and educator. In the commercial arena, business associations are playing an increasing role in negotiating the form and substance of oversight they receive in their international operations. Business also serves as the primary conduit of the diffusion of advanced technology.[60]

Cumulatively, these features of the contemporary international system reflect the fact that much more is changing in that system than simply the permutations wrought by the end of the Cold War. As J. Martin Rochester has observed,

---

58 Rosemary Righter, *Utopia Lost: The United Nations and World Order* (New York, N.Y.: Twentieth Century Fund Press, 1995).

59 Lester M. Salamon, "The Rise of the Nonprofit Sector," *Foreign Affairs*, Vol. 73, No. 4 (July/August 1994), pp. 109–122, and Peter J. Spiro, "New Global Communities: Nongovernmental Organizations in International Decision-Making Institutions," *The Washington Quarterly*, Vol. 18, No. 1 (Winter 1995), pp. 45–56.

60 On role of businesses as purveyors of advanced technology, see Richard A. Bitzinger, *The Globalization of Arms Production: Defense Markets in Transition* (Washington, D.C.: Defense Budget Project, December 1993), chart on page 13. See also J. D. Kenneth Boutin, "Structural Changes in the International Technology Order and Their Impact on the Strategic Environment of the 21st Century" (Paper presented to the International Studies Association/West conference, Phoenix, Arizona, November 5–7, 1992).

The question remains whether we are witnessing merely the end of the postwar era and the transformation of the international system back to the more normal historical pattern of full-blown multipolarity, in which case we can continue to rely on the state-centric paradigm and its focus on national interests, sovereignty, and international anarchy, or whether we are on the brink of a more fundamental and epic transformation, namely the unraveling of the very fabric of the Westphalian state system itself that has been the primary basis of human political organization for the past several centuries.[61]

This latter type of world, neither particularly orderly nor disorderly, but in flux, fits poorly into either camp identified above. Might it constitute a triumph of the neorealists, who believe essentially that military strength is the foundation for the integrationist ideal?[62] Or of the systems theorists, who emphasize the complex interaction of myriad units with myriad interests and the salience of structural features in international politics?[63] Or of the proponents of the world society model, who identify common problems, processes, and values as the primary drivers of world order?[64] Fortunately for the intellectual life of the discipline, but

---

61 J. Martin Rochester, *Waiting for the Millennium: The United Nations and the Future of World Order* (Columbia, S.C.: University of South Carolina Press, 1993), p. 238.

62 Robert O. Keohane, ed., *Neorealism and Its Critics* (New York, N.Y.: Columbia University Press, 1976). For a sharp critique of neorealism as "unhistorical, perhaps antihistorical," see Paul W. Schroeder, "Historical Reality vs. Neo-realist Theory," *International Security*, Vol. 19, No. 1 (Summer 1994), pp. 108–148.

63 Morton A. Kaplan, *System and Process in International Politics* (New York, N.Y.: John Wiley, 1957); and Klaus Knorr and Sidney Verba, eds., *The International System: Theoretical Essays* (Princeton, N.J.: Princeton University Press, 1961). For examples of the structural approach, see Karl W. Deutsch and J. D. Singer, "Multipolarity, Power Systems and International Stability," *World Politics*, Vol. 16, No. 3 (April 1964), pp. 390–406, and Johan Galtung, "A Structural Theory of Imperialism," *Journal of Peace Research*, Vol. 13, No. 2 (1971), pp. 81–94.

64 See Seyom Brown, "World Interests and the Changing Dimensions of Security," in Klare and Thomas, *World Security*, pp. 10–26; Richard A. Falk, *A Study of Future Worlds* (New York, N.Y.: Free Press, 1975); and Saul H. Mendlovitz, ed., *On the Creation of A Just World Order: Preferred Worlds for the 1990's* (New York, N.Y.: Free Press, 1975).

unfortunately for the search for tidy answers, each way of thinking penetrates only some part of the new reality.[65]

From these various perspectives, proliferation is yet one more reflection of the competing orders dominating world politics at the end of the twentieth century. And responding to the problems caused by proliferation constitutes one of the building blocks of future order.

Models are tools for explaining and predicting behavior or systemic outcomes and, in the international affairs discipline, none purports to capture the entirety of reality. But the debate about which model is the most valid gains special importance with the passing of the Cold War. Have patterns of interdependence and habits of transnationalism matured to the extent that new and enduring forms of state behavior have come into being, such that the twenty-first century will be characterized by a far more orderly system than the nineteenth or twentieth? Do issues of power, hard and soft, remain preeminent, such that too heavy an emphasis on interdependence will slowly corrode the foundations of the existing order? Should the developed and secure nations give emphasis in their foreign and security policies to commercial or military matters?

There is little in the proliferation subject to demonstrate that one or another of these schools of thought is the correct one for understanding contemporary international affairs. Indeed, the larger world is in such a state of flux that it would appear that each school has some utility in explaining some part of the proliferation subject and in prescribing useful actions. This suggests that the coming years will be fertile for theoretical debate in the international relations and strategic studies disciplines. But policy cannot await the outcome of this debate and has already forged ahead into uncharted territory, as will be seen in following chapters.[66]

---

65 See the introduction to Thompson et al., *Approaches to Peace*, for a review of the different approaches to the study of international conflict in the 1990s.

66 This gap between theory and action is a stubborn one—even and perhaps especially in the early atomic era, when major public policy decisions were taken in the virtual absence of any academic insights into the subject. See Alexander L. George, *Bridging the Gap: Theory and Practice in Foreign Policy* (Washington, D.C.: United States Institute of Peace, 1993), Part 1, pp. 1–30.

Conclusions

As proliferation has moved out from under the shadow of the Cold War, the historically rooted character of the prevailing way of thinking about it has become clearer. Because proliferation emerged as a subject of concern during the Cold War, the theories developed to understand it and the policies to manage it are also firmly rooted in that era. If theory is now to do its job of defining the problem and foreseeing its future, and if policy is to do a better job of shaping the problem in positive ways, then conventional wisdoms about proliferation must be reevaluated and updated.

Given the rapid changes in the structure and functioning of the international system, this is not an easy or straightforward task. Few of the past certainties endure in the 1990s. Yet rethinking the subject is imperative if policy is to continue to make a positive impact in the years ahead. In exploring these changes, it is essential also to identify the elements of continuity. As Martin Wight observed, "Basic changes occur in the structure of international politics...but it is only against the background of an understanding of what is permanent in that structure that we can recognize changes when they come or assess claims that they are basic."[67]

Whether there will be a renaissance in strategic studies that reinvigorates these debates and carries forward the task of theory-building and reconceptualization is uncertain. The early age of strategic studies, when the field generated many of the theories, models, and concepts still in use today, is long past.[68] On the other

---

67 Wight, *Power Politics*, p. 21.

68 That age is defined as the period from the mid-1950s to mid-1960s when a few dominant intellectuals committed to peace and stability established the intellectual agenda for the next 30 years, including among others Bernard Brodie, Morton Halperin, Herman Kahn, William Kaufman, Henry Kissinger, Klaus Knorr, Thomas Schelling, Glenn Snyder, and Albert Wohlstetter in the United States and Pierre Gallois and Michael Howard in Europe. See Booth and Herring, *Keyguide to Information Sources in Strategic Studies*. In 1983, two other authors observed that "strategic nuclear studies are barely three decades old, and yet one already perceives a sense of intellectual decline and theoretical exhaustion within the community of strategic analysts. One reads nostalgic recollections of a 'golden age' of strategic thought." From the "Introduction" by Kolkowicz and Intriligator in Bernard Brodie, Michael D. Intriligator, and Roman Kolkowicz, eds., *National Security and International Stability* (Cambridge, Mass.: Oelgeschlager, Gunn & Hain for the Center for

hand, the end of the Cold War has released the field from highly confining shackles.[69]

The result, so far, has been ambiguous. Two camps appear to have emerged in the academic world concerning the future of the strategic studies field. One camp argues that the passing of the high stakes nuclear contest between East and West, together with the ostensible pacification of great power relations, means that the genuinely important and interesting questions in the field have gone away. Hence the migration of some security studies specialists to new work in related fields such as preventive diplomacy and conflict resolution. For this camp, the old nuclear nonproliferation model may still be good enough.

The other camp argues that the passing of the Cold War means that its unique features no longer constrain the field of strategic studies, which has, as a result, become more rather than less interesting. Hence, for example, the fresh thinking on collective, cooperative, and comprehensive security in recent years and other signs of new theory-building and a broader reconceptualization of the field.[70] For this camp, the old model must be substantially revamped. If in the past proliferation was essentially an arms control problem at the margins of the international security agenda, today it has become a core issue of security and world order.

International and Strategic Studies, 1983), p. 1.

69   Stephen M. Walt, "The Renaissance of Security Studies," *International Studies Quarterly* 35 (June 1991), pp. 211–239; John Chipman, "The Future of Strategic Studies: Beyond Even Grand Strategy," *Survival*, Vol. 34, No. 1 (Spring 1992), pp. 109–131; and Brad Roberts, Stanton H. Burnett, and Murray Weidenbaum, "Think Tanks in a New World," *The Washington Quarterly*, Vol. 16, No. 1 (Winter 1993), pp. 169–182. See also Edward A. Kolodziej, "Renaissance in Security Studies? Caveat Lector!" *International Studies Quarterly*, Vol. 36, No. 4 (December 1992), pp. 421–438, for the argument that a renaissance is necessary but not much in evidence. See also Gray, *Weapons Don't Make War*, who argues provocatively that "nuclear age history does not prove the success, or even the viability, of the dominant ideas of modern Western strategic theory" (page 174).

70   See for example Janne E. Nolan, ed. *Global Engagement: Cooperation and Security in the 21st Century* (Washington, D.C.: Brookings Institution, 1994); Scott D. Sagan and Kenneth N. Waltz, *The Spread of Nuclear Weapons: A Debate* (New York, N.Y.: W. W. Norton & Company, 1995); John Mearsheimer, "The False Promise of International Institutions," *International Security*, Vol. 19, No. 3 (Winter 1994/95), pp. 5–49.

How quickly analysts work through the questions of stability, deterrence, arms control, conflict, order and disorder in a new era will impinge directly on the understanding of the proliferation problem that emerges and on the debate over how to respond to it. The following chapters, while focusing narrowly on the conceptual tasks of rethinking the proliferation subject, also attempt to set out some benchmarks on these larger questions.

Chapter 2

The New Technical Features of Proliferation

AS A POINT of departure for a new model of proliferation, the current technical features of the proliferation dynamic must be brought into clear focus. The Cold War–vintage model portrays a proliferation problem nuclear in character and limited to a relatively few states. Is this perception still valid? Working with a clean slate, what are the essential technical elements and contours of weapons proliferation as they exist today?[1] The new political features of the proliferation subject—and assessments of its changing implications—are examined in later chapters.

Unconventional Weapons

The term "unconventional weapons" has emerged as a short-hand to designate that category of weapons with effects on the battlefield, or against population centers, or on public and political perceptions, beyond those normally achieved by single weapon systems because of their potential use in ways that wreak mass,

---

[1] This survey uses a wide variety of sources in the open, unclassified literature to assemble a picture of the contemporary proliferation subject. It necessarily draws on incomplete, imperfect, and sometimes contradictory information. No comprehensive survey has been issued by any government, and what information governments have made available may also have been released for political purposes, thus raising questions about its accuracy. To the best of the author's knowledge, however, the sources used in this survey are credible and make reasoned judgments on the basis of available information.

virtually indiscriminate destruction. It is a shorthand for nuclear, chemical, and biological weapons.[2]

Nuclear Weapons

In the 1990s, the spread of nuclear weapons remains the pinnacle of proliferation concern. The acknowledged nuclear-weapon states include the United States, Russia, Britain, France, and China, all of which had exploded a nuclear device prior to 1965. With the breakup of the Soviet Union, four states inherited nuclear weapons (Russia, Ukraine, Belarus, and Kazakhstan), although the non-Russian republics have recognized Russia's status as the inheritor of the erstwhile Union's nuclear status and international nuclear obligations and they have begun to denuclearize accordingly.[3] Table 2–1 summarizes their nuclear status. South Africa also surprised many in 1992 with the announcement that it had possessed but then destroyed a half dozen atomic bombs.[4]

The set of countries of concern in the nuclear proliferation area has changed over the years. In the 1950s and 1960s, attention generally focused on advanced industrialized countries, such as Germany, Japan, Australia, and Sweden, with the potential to acquire nuclear weapons. In the years since, focus has shifted to countries in the Middle East, such as Iraq, Iran, Egypt, Saudi Arabia, and Israel; in Latin America, such as Argentina and Brazil; and in Asia, such as India, Pakistan,

---

2   In 1969, the United Nations designated atomic, chemical, and biological weapons to be weapons of mass destruction. United Nations, Report of the Secretary General, *Chemical and Bacteriological (Biological) Weapons and the Effects of Their Possible Use*, A/7575/Rev. 1, S/9292/Rev. 1 (1969).

3   Uncertainty remains about whether or how their pledges will be carried out. Ukraine in particular has been reluctant to relinquish the nuclear weapons on its soil for fear of potential Russian revanchism concerning Ukrainian independence and out of a hope that it can use its nuclear status to extract political and economic commitments from a West more interested in Russia than Ukraine. See William C. Potter, *Nuclear Profiles of the Soviet Successor States* (Monterey, Calif.: Monterey Institute of International Studies, 1993).

4   See Patrick Worsnip, "Bomb Admission Highlights Proliferation Threat," Reuters, March 24, 1993; Patrick Collings, "South African Admits to Having Constructed Nuclear Bombs," UPI, March 24, 1993; R. Jeffrey Smith, "South Africa's 16-Year Secret: The Nuclear Bomb," *Washington Post*, May 12, 1993, p. A–1; and David Fischer, "South Africa," in Mitchell Reiss and Robert S. Litwak, *Nuclear Proliferation after the Cold War* (Washington, D.C.: Woodrow Wilson Center Press, 1994), pp. 207–230.

Table 2–1
Nuclear Assets of the Soviet Successor States, 1992

	Armenia	Azerbaijan	Belarus	Estonia	Georgia	Kazakhstan	Kyrgyzstan	Latvia	Lithuania	Moldova	Russia	Tajikistan	Turkmenistan	Ukraine	Uzbekistan
Member, Nuclear Suppliers Group (NSG)											X				
Acceded to Nuclear Non-Proliferation Treaty		X		X				X	X		X				X
Nuclear Weapons			X			X					X			X	
Nuclear Power Reactor	a					X			X		X			X	
Nuclear Research Reactor			b		c	X		X			X			X	X
Nuclear Weapons Design											X				
Uranium Mining and Milling				X		X	X				X	X		X	X
Uranium Enrichment Capability											X				d
Fuel Fabrication Facility						X					X				
Plutonium Production and Handling						e					X				
Heavy Water Production	f										X	X		X	
Other NSG-Controlled Material						g					X			h	
Nuclear Research Center	X	X			X	X		X			X			X	X
Nuclear Test Site						X					X				

   a.   The two Armenian reactors were shut down in 1989 for safety reasons, but the Armenian government is planning to restart them despite local and international opposition.

   b.   The IRT–M Minsk reactor was shut down in 1988.

   c.   The IRT–M Tbilisi reactor was shut down in 1990.

   d.   A uranium research facility, of at least an experimental nature, possibly operated at Navoi during the 1970s and 1980s.

   e.   A hot cell is reportedly located at the Semipalatinsk test site.

   f.   Although one report of an Armenian heavy water site has appeared in print, there has been no additional confirmation.

   g.   The Ulbinsky Metallurgy Plant in Ust-Kamenogorsk produces beryllium and possibly zirconium.

   h.   Zirconium, hafnium, and ion exchange resins are produced in Ukraine at the Pridneprovsky Chemical Factory.

Taiwan, and North Korea. In the early 1990s, consensus has emerged in the West that the nuclear programs posing the most immediate and broadly destabilizing implications are those in Iraq, Iran, and North Korea. This shortlist is certain to evolve with time, as it has periodically in the past, to account for new or waning threats.

Much is guessed but little is known publicly about the degree to which any of the de facto powers have built small nuclear forces, or which of those with rumored programs have produced a nuclear explosive device. A general consensus exists that only Israel, India, and Pakistan have pursued a nuclear weapons capability to the point of having an arsenal of weapons, or at least of ready-to-assemble weapons, the so-called "bomb in the basement." As CIA director James Woolsey put it,

> As far as assembly is concerned, it is our estimate that at the present time both India and Pakistan have the capability to assemble the components of nuclear weapons, a small number of nuclear weapons within a very short period of time, and that the distinction between whether or not those weapons are in fact assembled or only able to be assembled within a few days is a very small distinction.[5]

By one estimate, Israel possesses on the order of 100 nuclear explosive devices, India up to 60 devices, and Pakistan 6 to 10.[6] Such estimates vary widely, given dependence on projections of the production of weapons-grade fuels or surreptitious acquisition. It is possible that these estimates are grossly inaccurate: some states may have stockpiled fissionable material without building large numbers of weapons; or they may have produced more weapons than estimates;

---

5 Statement by R. James Woolsey, director of central intelligence, Senate Committee on Governmental Affairs, February 24, 1993, p. 21.

6 For a regular, comprehensive review of developments related to nuclear proliferation, see the annual yearbooks of the Stockholm International Peace Research Institute. Cited here are *SIPRI Yearbook 1993: World Armaments and Disarmament* (Oxford: Oxford University Press for the Stockholm International Peace Research Institute, 1993) and *SIPRI Yearbook, 1992*. See also Leonard S. Spector with Jacqueline R. Smith, *Nuclear Ambitions: The Spread of Nuclear Weapons 1989–1990* (Washington, D.C.: Carnegie Endowment for International Peace, 1990).

or they may have built fewer or none, and manipulate only the perception of possible nuclear activities for the benefit of the doubt created about their capabilities.[7]

But nuclear proliferation is not an all-or-nothing proposition. It is best thought of as a process, with a number of steps along the way, beginning with a weapons development program and continuing with weapons testing; production; creation of a rudimentary nuclear force equipped with delivery systems and a small arsenal, with the appurtenances of effective command and control of those weapons; the enlargement and diversification of the nuclear arsenal, with possible emphasis on creation of a secure retaliatory capability; and the requisites of strategy and doctrine.[8] What is noteworthy about this proliferation "ladder" is the variety of ways it is scaled by states. The first nuclear states proceeded up it methodically and at large expense. Some states may pause at certain of its rungs, perhaps for a very long time, as apparently have those states that prefer to keep their bomb "in the basement" so as not to be the first to introduce nuclear

---

7   This survey of unconventional weapons proliferation is particularly vulnerable to the uncertainties described earlier arising from the use of open, as opposed to classified, information sources. Many states do not declare their programs of military acquisition and actively work to keep secret their advanced weapons capabilities, often in direct contravention of public declarations or commitments.

8   Benjamin Frankel has described a "proliferation ladder" very precisely: "(1) the establishment of a basic nuclear infrastructure (reactor, personnel); (2) the development of an infrastructure to produce weapon grade material (a separation plant for the production of plutonium, or uranium enrichment facility); (3) the acquisition of the technology and know-how to design, assemble, and manufacture the bomb; (4) a full-scale nuclear test followed by political declarations; (5) the development of the means to deliver nuclear weapons; (6) the promulgation of a nuclear doctrine that would provide guidelines and procedures to govern nuclear weapons within the country's overall security posture; (7) the building of a substantial nuclear arsenal to support the doctrine; and (8) deployment; the establishment of operational procedures to handle weapons, especially in crisis." Frankel, ed., *Opaque Nuclear Proliferation: Methodological and Policy Implications* (London: Frank Cass, 1991), pp. 17–18. See also Lewis A. Dunn, *Controlling the Bomb* (New Haven, Conn.: Yale University Press, 1982); Carnegie Task Force on Non-Proliferation and South Asian Security, *Nuclear Weapons and South Asian Security, Report* (Washington, D.C.: Carnegie Endowment for International Peace, 1988), pp. 7–8; and Rodney W. Jones, *Proliferation of Small Nuclear Forces* (Washington, D.C.: Center for Strategic and International Studies, Georgetown University, 1983).

weapons into a region (e.g., Israel and India). Some states may step back down a few rungs, as in the case of South Africa, which has destroyed its weapons and production facilities but not its general national competence to reassemble a program. Other states may jump ahead a rung or two, especially those capable of using computing capabilities to avert the need for weapons tests.

It is important also to note the difference between atomic (fission) weapons and thermonuclear (i.e., hydrogen) weapons, more advanced nuclear weapons with a far larger explosive yield. Only the United States, Russia, Britain, France, and China are thought to have thermonuclear capability, although the ranks may also include Israel. As John M. Deutch has observed, "The proliferation of thermonuclear capability is a long-range threat that differs quantitatively, not qualitatively, from the present threat of proliferation of fission devices."[9]

This proliferation process points to the existence of a pattern of vertical proliferation (accumulation) in contrast to that of horizontal proliferation (diffusion). The vertical process has numerous thresholds where states may opt to remain, or at least pause, as they calculate the consequences in terms of cost and benefit of going on to a new level of capability.

Another type of nuclear proliferation risk has come into sharper focus in the 1990s—so-called instant proliferation. This is a process by which states buy weapons on the international market, steal them from unwitting guardians, or inherit them from predecessor states, thus circumventing time-consuming and high-cost development programs. Related risks are that nuclear material or expertise may be shared across borders, whether illicitly or not.

This is in fact an old issue, if one recalls the concern in the 1970s about an Islamic bomb created through the pooled efforts of the Arab countries and Pakistan. But it has been given new impetus—and different risks and prospects—by the breakup of the Soviet military establishment. As noted above, this breakup led to the existence of three new nuclear-equipped states. But it has also raised grave questions about both the effective command and control of deployed weapons and the security and safety of nuclear weapons and materials stored in military depots. It has also raised questions about the possibility that scientists and technicians from the Soviet military-industrial complex might offer their expertise for hire to weapons producers in the developing world. So far at

---

9   John M. Deutch, "The New Nuclear Threat," *Foreign Affairs*, Vol. 17, No. 4 (Fall 1992), p. 123.

least, a variety of national and international programs, such as the U.S.–Russian Cooperative Threat Reduction Program undertaken to facilitate the safe and secure dismantlement of excess Russian nuclear capabilities, have proven salutory in addressing these questions.[10]

It is of course possible that other countries are engaged in nuclear weapons programs or may become so engaged in the future. Interest in nuclear weapons among states of the developing world has sometimes been strong; after India conducted its nuclear test in 1974, it was approached by more than a dozen countries requesting assistance with nuclear weapons programs.[11] As discussed in chapter 3 the prospects for a wider diffusion of nuclear weapons may have increased in recent years with the demise of the Cold War, the breakup of the Soviet Union, the heightening of tensions in the Middle East and South Asia, and the continuing problem in North Korea.[12]

On the other hand, no state has openly joined the nuclear club since the creation of the Nuclear Non-Proliferation Treaty (NPT) in 1968. Rather, South Africa, China, and France have recently joined the treaty, thereby strengthening its global credibility. Moreover, the accumulation of nuclear weapons by the former Soviet Union and the United States has been halted and deep cuts in existing stockpiles are being made, with the expectation that by the end of the decade those stockpiles will have been cut by more than two-thirds. These cuts have created pressure on the other nuclear powers to cease production and join in cuts. But their future is in some doubt given deepening concerns about Russia's ability to comply with its existing arms control commitments in the face of faltering political and economic reform.

This short survey of nuclear proliferation would not be complete without also pointing to the "rollback" of some nuclear programs. Over the decades some states with nuclear weapons development programs have abandoned them: for example, Sweden in the 1960s; South Korea in the 1970s; Argentina and Brazil in the 1980s; and South Africa most recently. This suggests that there is nothing

---

10   U.S. Congress, Office of Technology Assessment, *Proliferation and the Former Soviet Union,* OTA–ISS–605 (Washington, D.C.: GPO, September 1994).

11   Interview with an informed source, who also reported that India declined each request.

12   For a review of this argument and of the various programs discussed here, see Lewis A. Dunn, *Containing Nuclear Proliferation,* Adelphi Paper No. 263 (London: Brassey's for the International Institute for Strategic Studies, 1992).

inevitable about the future proliferation dynamic. Indeed, there is a very striking gap between expectations of the early atomic era that proliferation would have proceeded quite far by the end of the century and today's world, in which the number of nuclear weapon states, acknowledged and unacknowledged, remains small.

Chemical Weapons

Chemical weapons emerged in the 1980s as another major proliferation concern. The number of states allegedly possessing chemical weapons has grown steadily in recent decades, with approximately a doubling of states in the last three decades.[13] Six countries possessed or actively sought offensive chemical warfare (cw) capabilities from 1945 to 1960, 7 in the 1960s, about 13 in the 1970s, and about 16 by 1984.[14] In 1990, one senior U.S. official described the problem as follows:

> at least fourteen countries outside of NATO and the Warsaw Pact
> currently have an offensive chemical warfare capability. Many of
> these nations are likely to assist other countries in developing
> offensive capabilities as well. Ten more nations are believed to be
> either developing (or are suspected of seeking) an offensive cw
> capability.[15]

---

13 Testimony by the director of U.S. naval intelligence, Rear Admiral Thomas A. Brooks, to the Subcommittee on Seapower, Strategic, and Critical Materials of the House Armed Services Committee, March 7, 1991. See also U.S. Congress, House of Representatives, Committee on Armed Services, *Countering the Chemical and Biological Weapons Threat in the Post-Soviet World*, Report of the Special Inquiry into the Chemical and Biological Threat, February 23, 1993 (Washington, D.C.: GPO, 1993). This section is drawn from Brad Roberts, *Chemical Disarmament and International Security*, Adelphi Paper No. 267 (London: Brassey's for the International Institute for Strategic Studies, 1992); and Roberts, "Controlling Chemical Weapons," in Jonathan Dean and David Koplow, guest editors, "Symposium on World Security and Weapons Proliferation," *Transnational Law & Contemporary Problems*, Vol. 2, No. 2 (Fall 1992), pp. 435–452.

14 See "Implications of Soviet Use of Chemical and Toxin Weapons for U.S. Security Interests," *Chemical and Engineering News*, February 25, 1985, about a leaked U.S. national intelligence estimate.

15 Brooks testimony of March 7, 1991.

That official identified those that "probably possess" chemical weapons as China, Egypt, India, Iran, Iraq, Israel, Libya, Myanmar, North Korea, Pakistan, South Korea, Syria, Taiwan, and Vietnam. He also identified Indonesia, Saudi Arabia, South Africa, and Thailand as countries that "may possess" such weapons.

Because the entire subject is cloaked in secrecy, it is difficult to gauge the accuracy or importance of these findings. Only three states admit to possessing chemical weapons: the United States, Russia (following a Soviet declaration in 1987), and Iraq. Many of those identified as probable or possible possessors have issued denials. Furthermore, the phraseology used in such reports has not been helpful in ascertaining how many states actually possess chemical weapons or are simply engaged in a research and development (R&D) program aimed at possible future acquisition (something permissible under the international legal framework). Some reports have referred simply to "cw capable" states that might reasonably include many states with the industrial infrastructure, expertise, and access to materials necessary for the production of cw agents. Moreover, such reports indicate nothing about the military significance of the cw programs of the accused states. The military utility of toxic chemical agent is a direct function of the quantity and quality available, its mating with effective delivery systems, and the military capability to use—and exploit the use of—chemical weapons in war. The thresholds of quantity and quality vary with circumstance—what one state might find threatening another might dismiss as inconsequential. The U.S. government itself has been unclear on this point, with one official indicating in January 1989 that perhaps as few as five or six states might possess arsenals of chemical weapons of clear military significance.[16] The problem with the publicly available data is that they permit no study of these factors.[17]

---

16   Testimony of William F. Burns, then director of the U.S. Arms Control and Disarmament Agency, as reported in "Agency Gets Last Word on Poison Gas," *Washington Post*, December 13, 1989. The article discusses administration attempts to revise Burns's testimony after his departure from government on this specific point.

17   For a critical evaluation of the tendency to overstate the nature and character of chemical weapons proliferation, see Julian Perry Robinson, "Chemical Weapons Proliferation: The Problem in Perspective," in Trevor Findlay, ed., *Chemical Weapons and Missile Proliferation: With Implications for the Asia/Pacific Region* (Boulder, Colo.: Lynne Rienner Publishers, 1991), pp. 19–35.

The basic forces leading to the proliferation of chemical weapons are often misunderstood. Most commentators seem to attribute proliferation to one of two factors: greed within a business community willing to cut deals with unscrupulous leaders in the name of profits, or the desire of states to possess the equivalent of an atom bomb. Both views have some basis in fact. A few private firms in the developed countries have wittingly or unwittingly contributed to the buildup of chemical weapons production facilities in the developing world.[18] And some leaders such as Saddam Hussein of Iraq or Muammar Qaddafi of Libya have evidently valued their arsenals of chemical weapons as offering special strategic leverage. But these factors alone or in combination cannot account for the proliferation of chemical weapons of recent years.

Rather, such proliferation should be understood as the result of a lowering of barriers that previously had been significant. Some of these barriers were technical; but the globalization of industry has greatly eased access to the technology, expertise, and raw materials of chemical weapons. Other barriers were political; but the failure of the international community to respond forcefully to allegations of use by Iraq in the 1980s and to earlier charges of the use of chemical weapons by the USSR or its proxies (the so-called Yellow Rain episodes) undermined the expectation that a leader ordering the use of chemical weapons might expect to pay any significant international political costs. Perhaps the most important barriers were perceptual; but the view of chemical weapons as antiquated and unreliable was cast in doubt when Iraq used them against Iran. Iraq's chemical arsenal suggested that chemical weapons might have a usefulness in conflicts between or within states of the developing world that they were not understood to have for the advanced militaries of the developed world.

Moreover, concurrent with the easing of the barriers to the proliferation of chemical weapons was a number of incentives to proliferation grew in strength.

---

18   German firms have been singled out for international opprobrium but have not been the
      only ones engaged in this business. An early study prepared in 1990 of foreign suppliers to
      Iraq's unconventional weapons programs identified 207 firms in 21 countries. Simon
      Wiesenthal Center, *The Poison Gas Connection: Western suppliers of unconventional weapons and
      technologies to Iraq and Libya*, Special Report prepared by Kenneth R. Timmerman (Los
      Angeles, Calif.: Simon Wiesenthal Center, 1990). As of 1995 the UN Special Commission on
      Iraq continued to collect information on the foreign suppliers to Iraq's unconventional
      weapons programs, but had no plans to publicly identify those suppliers.

These included the general accumulation of advanced military capabilities by states of the developing world, a perceived need within some states to substitute chemical weapons for nuclear weapons beyond their reach (e.g., Syria) and, in Iraq at least, a view that chemical weapons might be useful in carving out new areas of influence as the bipolar structure of regional conflicts passed along with the Cold War.

Looking to the future, the distribution of chemical weapons around the world is likely to change substantially, and in patterns quite different from the nuclear area. The major chemically armed powers with the most sizable arsenals, namely Russia with approximately 50,000 tons of cw agents, and the United States with approximately 30,000 tons, are working to finalize and implement deep cuts in their arsenals, to 5,000 tons each. Moreover, each expects to completely eliminate its arsenal of chemical weapons in the context of the Chemical Weapons Convention (CWC), opened for signature in January 1993 and due to enter into force sometime in the mid-1990s. Under the CWC, all states party to the convention are to make declarations describing their arsenals of chemical weapons and related production capabilities and to implement their destruction within 10 years. Thus many of the chemical arsenals in both the developed and developing world appear slated for destruction, although some significant holdouts appear likely, especially in the Middle East.[19] If these bilateral and multilateral efforts collapse, however, the proliferation of chemical weapons may well accelerate.

Biological Weapons

Biological weapons may emerge as the principal unconventional weapons problem of the next decade. Reports indicate that 11 countries are pursuing offensive-oriented biological warfare programs, up from just 4 in the 1960s (of which 2 were the United States and the USSR).[20] Those publicly identified by U.S.

---

19 For more on the Chemical Weapons Convention see Brad Roberts, ed. *Chemical Disarmament and U.S. Security* (Boulder, Colo.: Westview Press for the Center for Strategic and International Studies, 1992); and Benoit Morel and Kyle Olson, eds., *The Chemical Weapons Convention: Shadow and Substance* (Boulder, Colo.: Westview Press, 1993).

20 Parts of this discussion are excerpted from the author's chapter, "New Challenges and New Policy Priorities for the 1990s," in Roberts, ed., *Biological Weapons: Weapons of the Future?*

government sources include Iraq, Iran, Syria, Libya, China, North Korea, and Taiwan.[21] The United States and the United Kingdom abandoned their biological warfare (bw) arsenals unilaterally in the 1960s, and neither has resumed work on offensive programs. The Soviet Union promised to abandon its offensive bw program in a bilateral agreement with the United States in 1970, and along with the United States and United Kingdom became an original signatory and depository state for the Biological and Toxin Weapons Convention (BTWC) of 1975, although President Boris Yeltsin of Russia subsequently confirmed suspicions long prevalent in Western intelligence circles that the USSR never actually abandoned such programs.[22] U.S. officials have also made a general statement that of those suspected of pursuing bw programs, some are in the Middle East, some are known sponsors of terrorism, and some are signatories of the BTWC.[23] The number of states engaged in bw programs with offensive applications could well be larger, because officials have underscored that evidence

---

(Washington, D.C.: Center for Strategic and International Studies, 1993), especially pp. 74–75. See also in that volume W. Seth Carus, "The Proliferation of Biological Weapons," and Graham Pearson, "Biological Weapons: The British View," as well as "Eleven Countries 'Defying Ban on Germ Weapons,'" *The Guardian*, November 5, 1991, p. 1.

21   For a review of these allegations by the U.S. government, see Elisa D. Harris, Statement to the Defense, Foreign Policy, and Space Task Force of the Budget Committee of the U.S. House of Representatives, May 22, 1991. A report of the Foreign Intelligence Service of Russia released in February 1993 provided a comprehensive assessment of the unconventional weapons capabilities, and an unprecedented level of detail about alleged biological weapons programs, in the developing world. See "A New Challenge After the Cold War: The Proliferation of Weapons of Mass Destruction," a report prepared by the Foreign Intelligence Service of the Russian Federation (Moscow, 1993), translated by Foreign Broadcast Information Service in February 1993. Summary and excerpts made available by U.S. Committee on Government Affairs, U.S. Senate, February 24, 1993, and subsequently published in *Proliferation Threats of the 1990's,* Hearing Before the Committee on Governmental Affairs, U.S. Senate, 103rd Cong., 1st Sess., February 24, 1993 (Washington, D.C.: GPO, 1993).

22   See Roberts, "New Challenges," pp. 78–81, on the Soviet/Russian biological warfare program.

23   See testimony by then director of central intelligence, William Webster, of February 9, 1989, in *Global Spread of Chemical and Biological Weapons,* Hearings Before the Committee on Governmental Affairs and Its Permanent Subcommittee on Investigations, U.S. Senate, February 9–10, May 2, 17, 1989 (Washington, D.C.: GPO, 1989).

of proscribed activities by these states has been uncovered virtually randomly and not as a result of a systematic survey.

Proliferation fears also stem from the collapse of the Soviet Union and the fear, parallel to that in the nuclear domain, that the biological weapons of the former Soviet military will trickle out to other states or that the expertise needed to produce biological weapons will be purchased from unemployed and hungry Soviet scientists. Reports of efforts to acquire such expertise and weapons have surfaced in the Russian press.[24]

The factors stimulating such proliferation probably closely parallel those in the chemical area. Declining barriers to acquisition have played a role, particularly with the steady diffusion of dual-use technologies. The revolution in bioengineering since the entry into force of the BTWC has raised concern about the ease with which bw agents can be produced, stockpiled, and used in war and about the new threats posed by novel, highly virulent agents. Regional conflict and strategic need may also have provided incentives as regional leaders have sought the means to deter well-armed neighbors or outside interveners, to coerce regional adversaries, or to seek victory in war. The difficulty of acquiring nuclear capabilities and the increasing political costs of chemical weapons, as well as their not inconsequential fiscal costs, may have stimulated specific interest in countries that pose a general proliferation risk. Mere curiosity may also explain some of the research work as some developing countries seek to understand the possible military applications of the new biological sciences increasingly within their reach.

Discovery of Iraq's bw program, which Iraqi officials have acknowledged was oriented toward developing offensive applications of warfare agents and not strictly for prophylactic defense purposes, helped to awaken the international community to the biological aspects of the proliferation problem.[25] But the continuing debate within the UN Special Commission on Iraq (UNSCOM) about the character and scale of Iraq's bw program echoes a similar debate in the

---

24 See "General Quizzed on Chemical Weapons Production," *Izvestiia*, in Foreign Broadcast Information Service—Soviet Union–92–082, April 28, 1992.

25 See Carus, "The Proliferation of Biological Weapons." See also "Iraqi CBW Armament and the UN Special Commission," *Chemical Weapons Convention Bulletin*, No. 13 (September 1991), pp. 21–22.

chemical area: What are the implications of simple statements about numbers of proliferators? Are all proliferators of equal significance?

The apparent basis of the proliferation charge against specific countries is the detection of quantities of infective materials for which no peaceful purposes are discernible. As in the nuclear and chemical areas, a certain type of proliferation ladder exists. Steps along the way to a full-blown military capability to use biological weapons for offensive purposes start with R&D and proceed to the proofing of weapon concepts, test production, scaling up of production capability, stockpiling of agent, weaponization, stockpiling of weapons, preparation of delivery systems, creation of the doctrine for use, and training. A significant bw program would probably also entail the acquisition of and training with protective measures; not every developing country will share the military and public safety concerns of the developed world, but many will find some protective measures prudent if only to preserve secrecy by preventing health problems that might be detected. In the R&D phase itself, there are important differences between programs that emphasize the relatively simple agents that were the focus of interest among the superpowers prior to their agreement to the BTWC and the novelties made possible by bioengineering. Of course, even a stockpile or capability deemed to be fairly rudimentary can be militarily significant in certain circumstances and thus is not to be dismissed lightly. Further analysis of these factors in terms of the biological weapons proliferation problem would help to bring the problem into sharper focus but cannot be performed so long as the necessary data remain classified.

Defining Military Significance

The widespread tendency in the research and policy communities to equate the military significance of different unconventional weapons can lead to a serious misunderstanding of the character and impact of different weapons programs in the developing world.[26]

---

26   For a review of the military utility of chemical weapons, see the appendix in Roberts, *Chemical Disarmament and International Security;* Stockholm International Peace Research Institute, *The Problem of Chemical and Biological Warfare,* Vol. 2, *CB Weapons Today* (Stockholm: Almqvist & Wiksell for Stockholm International Peace Research Institute, 1973); and Steve Fetter, "Ballistic Missiles and Weapons of Mass Destruction," *International*

Chemical and biological weapons are less certain in their effect than are nuclear weapons, given their vulnerability to meteorological conditions and protective measures and the need for near-perfect delivery on target. Moreover, there are also important differences between chemical and biological weapons, with the former requiring large quantities for decisive battlefield effect (in order to sustain lethal dosages) and the latter being ill-suited for battlefield use (given the delay arising from periods of incubation). Biological weapons in particular are potentially devastating against large population concentrations. But even in very low quantities, both operate quite effectively as weapons of terror.

The specific attributes of a country's capabilities are also relevant. Factors such as the quantity and quality of available weapons or stockpiles of cw or bw agent, the industrial capacity to surge production in time of war, types of delivery systems, and military doctrine and training will bear significantly on the character of the military threat posed by such systems. These factors are less relevant but still of consequence in the nuclear domain.

Military significance is also a function of circumstance. The cw and bw capabilities of states of the developing world may be strategic in conflict against similarly sized competitors in their region if they can be used to achieve massively destructive effects. The threat of their use will then operate powerfully on the perceived choices of the targeted nation's leaders. Not all of the cw or bw capabilities of the rumored proliferators are likely to meet this criterion. Moreover, against states of the developed world, the threat of such use would likely have only limited consequences. The military forces of such states, if capable of fighting in a chemically contaminated environment in a sound protective posture in the form of effective personal protective gear, detectors, and decontamination gear, should find limited chemical attack little more than a hindrance, except in circumstances when such attack can be massed or sustained for long periods. In the case of nuclear weapons, even small arsenals are likely to operate with profound effect on the choices of leaders of both small and powerful nations.

The purpose of this digression on military utility is to illustrate the important differences that exist among those weapons so often lumped into the general category of "unconventional weapons" or "weapons of mass destruction." Given

Security, Vol. 16, No. 1 (Summer 1991), pp. 5–42.

the unfamiliarity of many analysts with chemical and biological weapons, there is a tendency to equate these weapons with their nuclear counterparts in terms of their military and political weight. There is a similar tendency to equate R&D programs in terms of their strategic significance. But the differences among these weapons and programs are as important as their similarities.

The poor fit of these terms with the factors they describe has led to a debate about what other weapons might fit into this category or what other terms might be more accurate. Some have proposed, for example, that landmines be included in the description of weapons of mass destruction, given their indiscriminate effect, high long-term lethality, and extensive proliferation.[27] Others have proposed adopting the term "catastrophic weaponry" to signify those weapons, including missiles, that signify a state's commitment to total, as opposed to limited war.[28] For the moment, at least, existing terms are adequately descriptive so long as their limitations are kept in mind.

Missile Delivery Systems

Missile delivery systems are also proliferating. Two types of missiles are relevant to this discussion: ballistic and cruise.

Ballistic Missiles

Ballistic missiles have proliferated extensively in the last two decades. Writing in 1990, Seth Carus observed that:

> Twenty-two countries in the Third World currently possess ballistic missiles or are actively attempting to acquire them. Thirteen of these countries have programs to design and build ballistic missiles, and at least fifteen have operational missile forces. Six Third World countries have fired ballistic missiles at opponents....At least four

---

27 Arms Project of Human Rights Watch & Physicians for Human Rights, *Landmines: A Deadly Legacy* (New York, N.Y.: Human Rights Watch, 1993), pp. 3–5.

28 Barry Kellman, "Bridling the International Trade of Catastrophic Weaponry," *American University Law Review,* Vol. 43, No. 3 (Spring 1994), pp. 755–847.

Third World countries have deployed nuclear or chemical warheads for missiles.[29]

A senior U.S. official has estimated that by 2000 six of these forces will have intermediate-range capability (as distinct from the longer-range intercontinental ballistic missiles).[30]

Ballistic missiles add a new level of capability even in those arsenals equipped with advanced fighter-bombers because of their speed (and hence ability to deliver a surprise military blow) and relative insusceptibility to countermeasures (and hence certainty of impact). Yet because of the relative inaccuracy, limited payload, short range, and small number of these missiles, some forces in the developing world that are equipped with them have been of little more than nuisance value.[31] Few military systems better illustrate the fact that there are technological thresholds that determine the character of military threat presented by specific weapons at specific stages of their development.

As in the area of unconventional weapons, there is a growing possibility that military capabilities in the missile area will be created "instantaneously" as a result of transfers from one country to another, or that systems in the non-military sector, in this case space launch vehicles, will be reworked for military purposes.[32] Regarding the possibility of transfers, a trade in missiles has long been under way, building on the early transfers of Soviet-supplied short-range SCUDs. Looking to the future, a growing number of countries appear to be producing missiles, and some of them, such as China, desire to export them. A growing number are also marketing space launch services.[33] The

---

29   W. Seth Carus, *Ballistic Missiles in Modern Conflict* (New York, N.Y.: Praeger for the Center for Strategic and International Studies, 1991), pp. 1–2.

30   Testimony by William Webster, director of central intelligence, before the Senate Armed Services Committee, January 23, 1990.

31   Center for International Security and Arms Control, *Assessing Ballistic Missile Proliferation and Its Control*, Report (Stanford, Calif.: Stanford University, November 1991). See also John R. Harvey, "Regional Ballistic Missiles and Advanced Strike Aircraft: Comparing Military Effectiveness," *International Security*, Vol. 17, No. 2 (Fall 1992), pp. 41–83.

32   Woolsey statement.

33   Sidney Graybeal and Patricia McFate, *GPALs and Foreign Space Launch Vehicle Capabilities*, A report of the Science Applications International Corporation, McLean, Va., prepared for the

United States, USSR, and China all used ballistic missiles as space launchers.[34] The conversion of a space launcher to military purposes involves exchanging the payload for a reentry vehicle enclosing a warhead and modifying instructions in the guidance system.[35]

Looking to the next decade, it appears likely that many of these technological thresholds will be overcome by states such as India, Iran, North Korea, and possibly Iraq.[36] Accuracy is increasing, such that previously inaccurate missiles may in a decade or less have CEPs (circular error probable, which is the distance from target within which 50 percent of the fired missiles are likely to fall) of 100 meters or less. This will be made possible by, among other factors, the widespread commercial availability of Global Positioning System (GPS) receivers, which use satellite access to determine locations anywhere on the globe; reportedly, Pakistan and India are "at the threshold of being able to use GPS guidance on their missiles and some Middle East countries may soon follow."[37] Propulsion systems are improving with the fielding of multistage systems (which increase range) and a shift from liquid to solid fuels (making missiles easier to fire quickly). Production capabilities are improving such that better systems are produced in higher quantity, creating an ability to saturate targets and/or defenses. Warhead technology may shift from basically high explosive and limited chemical to advanced submunitions, fuel air explosives, or even in some cases nuclear warheads. The Persian Gulf War also drew attention to the importance of missile launcher mobility and its effect in terms of making it harder to target these missiles, requiring the redirection of forces from other missions in order to attempt to detect and destroy them.

Strategic Defense Initiative Organization, Washington, D.C., February 1992.

34   Proliferation Study Team, *The Emerging Ballistic Missile Threat to the United States,* Report (Washington, D.C., Proliferation Study Team, February 1993), p. 11.

35   Ibid., p. 12.

36   Carus, *Ballistic Missiles in Modern Conflict.*

37   David A. Fulghum, "Mideast Nations Seek to Counter Air Power," *Aviation Week & Space Technology,* June 7, 1993, p. 79.

Cruise Missiles

Cruise missile proliferation has received slight attention but is more advanced than ballistic missile proliferation, with over 70 countries possessing such missiles.[38] Anti-ship cruise missiles have been exported to virtually every navy in the world. Fielded as ground-, sea-, and air-launched systems, their significance will hinge primarily on their payload, flight path (well suited to delivery of chemical or biological agents), and low cost (meaning that they can be built in large numbers).

Technological thresholds currently limiting accuracy and quantity are likely to fall in the 1990s as more states acquire GPS systems and manufacturing capability. Russia and Ukraine are both marketing an advanced supersonic cruise missile, the SS–N–22, nicknamed the Sunburn, which at 1,900 miles per hour moves four times faster than the Exocets used by Argentina in the Falklands/Malvinas War, while traveling 15 feet above the ocean and executing evasive S-turns before slamming into its target.[39] Some countries are engaged in programs to convert anti-ship cruise missiles to land-attack capabilities, but have encountered difficulties in achieving necessary accuracies.[40]

Conventional Warfare Systems

Conventional warfare systems or subsystems for air, land, and naval operations have been exported to many countries of the developing world, in largely predictable flows from providers to clients.[41] When that trade began in the years

---

38   W. Seth Carus, *Cruise Missile Proliferation in the 1990s* (Washington, D.C.: Praeger for the Center for Strategic and International Studies, 1992). See also Joseph Lovece, "DIA: New Cruise Missile Threat to America Is Far Away," *Defense Week*, November 28, 1994, p. 7.

39   The U.S. Navy is negotiating the purchase of a large stock of such weapons. Iran also has purchased at least eight missiles and deployed them along the Persian Gulf. John Mintz, "Sweating Out the Sunburn," *Washington Post*, June 13, 1993, pp. H–1, 4–5; and Fulghum, "Mideast Nations Seek to Counter Air Power," p. 79. The missile is capable of carrying nuclear warheads. But a warhead is not required, given the devastating impact of the kinetic energy in a missile in supersonic flight.

40   Lovece, "DIA: New Cruise Missile Threat to America is Far Away."

41   Richard F. Grimmett, *Conventional Arms Transfers to the Third World, 1983–1990* (Washington, D.C.: Congressional Research Service, August 2, 1991).

after World War II, it consisted mainly of transfers of the victors' residual or outdated military hardware. As the Cold War sharpened, weapons were transferred in ever larger numbers to allies and clients. To cite one study, "the number of countries with significant arms imports more than doubled between 1951 and 1975 from 25 to 58. In 1989, 74 Third World countries imported arms."[42] The value of military hardware transferred to the Third World in the 1970s and 1980s was more than five times the value of transfers in the previous two decades ($398.4 billion vs. $77 billion).[43]

Over the last decade, patterns long prevalent in the arms trade have begun to break down. Wars in the South, such as the Iran–Iraq War, created substantial new markets while new suppliers emerged.[44] The end of the Cold War has also

---

42   R. Bates Gill, *Chinese Arms Transfers: Purposes, Patterns, and Prospects in the New World Order* (Westport, Conn.: Praeger, 1992), p. 30. The statistical base is of course influenced by the fact that the number of countries increased significantly during this period of decolonization.

43   "The average total value of weapons transferred each year in the 1980s is more than 10 times greater than the value of weapons sold in an average year during the 1950s, and nearly 5 times greater than in the 1960s. Another approach to measuring the quantity of arms transfers is to trace the number of transfers, rather than the cost....[F]or the 26-year period 1950 to 1975, a total of 5,019 actual arms transfers from industrialized states to 92 Third World states, or approximately 193 transfers a year [took place]. More recent research finds that for the 14-year period 1974 to 1987, there were over 8,000 transfers, including the transfer of licensed production rights, or an average of 571 deals per year. In 1990, arms transfer deals from the developed to the developing world, including licensed production rights, number 290; if one includes transfer deals from one developing country to another, the figure reaches 337. This marks a decline in the yearly total of arms transfers, and reflects the drawdown of conflicts in Afghanistan, between Iran and Iraq, in Angola, and in southeast Asia. However, the number of transfers per year in the 1980s continues to far outdistance the figures for the years 1950 to 1975....By the mid-1980s, more than 90 percent of the total volume of arms transferred to the Third World was new weapons." Ibid., pp. 27, 29.

44   A 1990 study by the North Atlantic Assembly identified the following principal effects of the Iran–Iraq War for the international arms trade. "First, it led to a substantial increase in the volume of sales at a time of slight overall decline in the arms trade....Second, the war enabled a number of countries new to the arms trade—such as China, Italy, Brazil and Spain—to develop lucrative arms export businesses....A third, related, effect of the war was to encourage suppliers—old and new—to assign more importance to the profit motive than to perceived geopolitical considerations. This tendency is well illustrated by the fact that of the 50 nations that sold weapons to Iran and Iraq, 28...supplied both countries....A fourth

disrupted traditional weapon flows; one indication of this was the drop in the number of countries in the South importing arms from 74 in 1989 to 68 in 1990.[45]

One noteworthy trend has been the tendency to export high technology products sooner: in the 1960s, arms transfer recipients received weapons a generation or two out of date, whereas by the late 1980s, many developing countries were receiving many of the most advanced weapons and technologies.[46] Figure 2–1 demonstrates the fact that many of the most advanced weapons have been exported by the United States, the former Soviet Union, and European nations. In the 1990s, Russia is seeking to export some of its most modern weapons, including even items still under development. Reportedly, these include their most advanced electronic countermeasures, high-powered jamming systems, tactical ballistic missiles, air-to-air missiles, and even directed energy laser weapons.[47]

A comprehensive review of the distribution of military assets in the international system is beyond the scope of this analysis. Rather the focus here is on the accretion of weapons and weapon systems that cross significant thresholds of range or lethality, particularly in the advanced technologies.

Naval Forces

Proliferation of advanced conventional warfare systems is particularly pronounced—but generally little noticed—in the area of naval systems. Forty-one navies (not including those of the United States or the former Soviet Union) together operate more than 400 conventional submarines,[48] with 23 of these

---

important legacy of the Iran–Iraq war was to encourage the growth of large 'black' and 'grey' markets for weapons." North Atlantic Assembly, Defence and Security Committee, *1990 Reports* (Brussels, November 1990), pp. 18–20.

45   Gill, *Chinese Arms Transfers*, p. 30.

46   See Grimmett, *Conventional Arms Transfers to the Third World*.

47   Tony Capaccio, "Ex-Soviets Eye Exports of Ship-Killing Missiles, Laser Weapons," *Defense Week*, December 7, 1992, p. 2.

48   John Benedict, "Third World Submarines & ASW [Anti-Submarine Warfare] Implications" (Unpublished research paper, Johns Hopkins University / Applied Physics Laboratory, Baltimore, Md.) cited in James A. Hazlett, "Low Intensity Conflict and Anti-Submarine Warfare" (Unpublished Research Paper, Center for Strategic and International Studies, June 1, 1992). See also "Navy Balances Sub Threats Against Budget Cuts," *Defense News*, June 24,

Figure 2–1
Selected Weapons Exported by the United States,
Soviet Union, and NATO Europe

Weapon System	United States	Soviet Union	NATO Europe
Main battle tanks	M1 Abrams	T-80, T-72	Leopard 2 (Germany)
	M1A1		Challenger (UK)
	M60	T-64	Leopard 1 (Germany)
			Chieftain (UK)
			AMX-30B2 (France)
			Vickers Mk 3 (UK)
			OTO Melara OF-40 (Italy
Figher/attack aircraft	F-16 Falcon	MiG-29 Fulcrum	Mirage F-1 (France)
	F-15 Eagle	Su-27 Flanker	Mirage 2000 (France)
	F/A-18 Hornet	Su-24 Fencer	Tornado (UK, Germany,
			Italy)
Missiles			
Air-to-air	AIM-9M Sidewinder	AA-8 Aphid	R550 Magic (France)
		AA-2 Atoll	
	AIM-7F Sparrow	AA-7 Apex	R530 (France)
			Aspide (Italy)
			Sky Flash (UK)
Antiship	RGM-84A Harpoon	SS-N-2 Styx	Exocet (France)
			Sea Eagle (UK)
			Sea Skua (UK)
			Penguin (Norway)
Antitank	BGM-71D TOW-2	AT-4 Spigot	Milan (France, Germany)
		AT-5 Spandrel	Eryx (France)
			HOT (France, Germany)
			Cobra (Germany)
			Swingfire (UK)

Source: Office of Technology Assessment, from data in Stockholm International Peace Research Institute, SIPRI Yearbooks, 1970 through 1990, *World Armaments and Disarmament.* Reprinted from *Global Arms Trade,* OTA–ISC–460 (Washington, D.C.: GPO, 1991).

outside of NATO and the erstwhile Warsaw Pact.[49] Figure 2–2 depicts the spread of submarines into the arsenals of the Third World. Note the increasing

---

1991, p. 6; and James Fitzgerald and John Benedict, "There Is a Sub Threat," *Proceedings* (U.S. Naval Institute) (August 1990), p. 57.

49 J. R. Hill, *Antisubmarine Warfare,* U.S. ed. (Annapolis, Md.: Naval Institute Press, 1985), p. 36, cited in Hazlett, "Low Intensity Conflict." By another count, more than 20 developing countries currently operate over 150 diesel attack submarines, including North Korea with 25, India with 18, Turkey with 15, Greece with 10, Egypt with 8, Libya with 6, and Pakistan with 6. From Daniel J. Revelle and Lora Lumpe, "Third World Submarines," *Scientific American,* August 1994, pp. 26-31.

Figure 2–2
Proliferation of Modern Submarines into Third World Arsenals

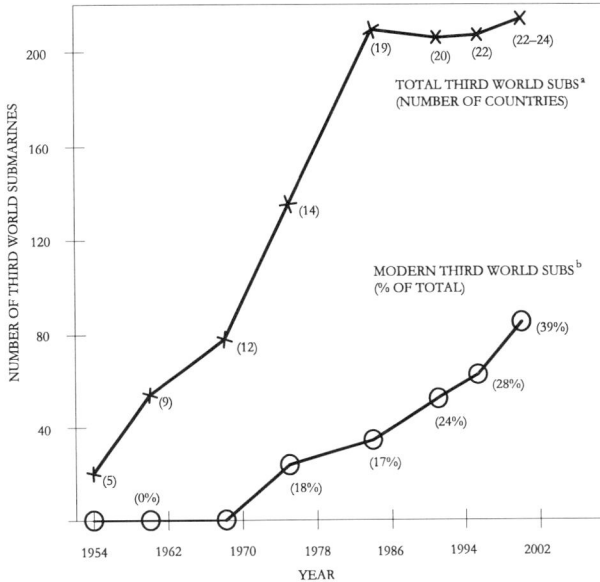

Notes: a. Mini-submarines/midgets excluded
      b. Western supplied and less than 20 years old; Soviet Kilos or follow-ons.

Source: John Benedict, "Third World Submarines and ASW Implications" (Johns Hopkins University Applied Physics Laboratory, Baltimore, Md., January 9, 1992). Reprinted from Henry D. Sokolski, "Nonapocalyptic Proliferation: A New Strategic Threat," *The Washington Quarterly*, vol. 17, no. 2 (Spring 1994), with permission from the Center for Strategic and International Studies and the Massachusetts Institute of Technology.

proportion of relatively modern submarines.[50] The submarine market includes a growing number of advanced conventional submarines with propulsion and weapons technologies that make them a significant threat to even the most modern navies[51] as well as difficult-to-detect mini-submarines.[52]

---

50   "Third World Offers New Threat," *Defense News*, June 24, 1991, p. 20, quoting John Benedict, a naval analyst at Johns Hopkins University's Applied Physics Laboratory.

51   "Propulsion Advances May Threaten Western Navies," *Defense News*, June 24, 1991, p. 10, reporting on developments in air-independent-propulsion being developed for Third World diesel submarines; David Silverberg, "Third World Sub Fleets Shrink, Still Pose Small Threat to West," *Defense Week*, June 8, 1992, pp. 14, 16; and Stan Zimmerman, "Modern

Forty-eight navies field cruise missiles. In 1990, more than 2,000 French-made Exocets and 10,000 Soviet-made Styx missiles were in developing country inventories.[53] The Harpoon missile has been exported to 21 nations.[54] A 1989 report indicated that the Styx had been sold to 19 nations and the Exocet to 14, with 8 more ordering an air-launched version.[55] A 1993 report indicated that Exocets were operational in 123 countries (presumably not all in naval roles).[56]

Ground Forces

A primary feature in the changing capabilities of land combat forces in the developing world is improved firepower, especially with the introduction of artillery-delivered high-precision munitions (ADHPM). Eighteen countries now have such munitions.[57] Another feature is improved maneuver and survivability through the deployment of advanced armored combat systems with passive and active protection systems, improved targeting capabilities, and advanced gunnery. The diffusion of fiber optically guided missiles is also under way, giving ground forces the ability to attack targets beyond their direct line of sight.[58]

The growing salience of ethnic conflict in the post–Cold War era has also drawn attention to the trade in small and light arms that reaches virtually every

---

Nonnuclear Subs Are Cheap and Deadly," *Armed Forces Journal International,* June 1991, p. 76. See also Brooks testimony of March 7, 1991.

52   In February 1992, Iran was reportedly negotiating the purchase of five mini-submarines. Robert Holzer and Neil Munro, "Iran Speeds Rearming Process: Government Seeks More Submarines to Control Straits," *Defense News,* February 17, 1992, p. 1.

53   "Antiship Missile Proliferation Stresses Ship Defenses," *Armed Forces Journal International,* September 1991, p. 48.

54   "Third World Offers New Threat," p. 20.

55   David Silverberg, "Third World Missiles Sales Will Keep Seas Hazardous," *Defense News,* December 11, 1989, pp. 8, 16.

56   Fulghum, "Mideast Nations Seek to Counter Air Power," p. 79.

57   This is a so-called smart munition that can be guided to its target after it has been fired. Citing informed sources, David Silverberg predicts that by 2005, more than 40 countries may field this type of munition. Silverberg, "Emerging Nations Hunger for Precision Weapons," *Defense News,* February 8–14, 1993, p. 9.

58   U.S. Department of Defense, *Technology Proliferation and U.S. Technological Superiority,* Joint Strategy Review Plan, Key Judgment Paper, Unclassified Final Draft (Washington, D.C.: U.S. Department of Defense, April 13, 1993).

conflict in the world. With an estimated value of $2.5 to $3.5 billion in recent years, annual expenditures by substate actors for such arms are a significant new feature of the proliferation problem with obvious importance for conflict, albeit one involving far from advanced technology.[59]

Air Forces

The existing fleets of advanced fighter/attack aircraft are undergoing a steady process of upgrading, with special emphasis on sensors and weapons. Air defense systems are undergoing steady modernization, especially after the successful use of aviation capabilities by Israel in the 1980s and by the United Nations UN coalition in the Persian Gulf War. By 2000, it is expected that the international market will include highly sophisticated anti-aircraft systems offering all-weather defense against ground attack aircraft and helicopters and systems of primarily European design utilizing active phased-array radar systems capable of three-dimensional search.[60] Quite a few countries with advanced combat aircraft also have programs for the development of weapons of mass destruction, as shown in figure 2–3.

Advanced anti-air systems are also proliferating. Russian-built AA–11s and AA–12s, operationally superior to advanced U.S. short- and medium-range air-to-air missiles, are moving rapidly into Third World inventories; by 1993, Russia had sold these missiles to China, North Korea, Iran, and at least 9 others.[61]

Command, Control, and Communications

Command, control, and communications systems depend upon advanced computer and communications technologies, many of which are being transferred to many developing countries for legitimate civilian applications,

---

59 Aaron Karp, *Arming Ethnic Conflict* (Lanham, Md.: United Nations University Press, 1995), Appendix II. As Karp notes, these figures are only the value of weapons used. They do not reflect actual prices paid, which are much harder to determine. Much of this equipment is captured, moreover, and, in a sense, costs nothing. See also Karp, "Trade in Small Arms," *The Washington Quarterly*, Vol. 17, No. 4 (Autumn 1994), pp. 65–77.

60 U.S. Department of Defense, *Technology Proliferation and U.S. Technological Superiority.*

61 David Fulghum, "Pentagon Pushes Air-to-Air Upgrades," *Aviation Week & Space Technology*, July 19, 1993, pp. 20–21.

Figure 2–3
Combat Aircraft and Mass-Destruction Weapon Programs in Non-NATO and Non-former Warsaw Pact Countries

Country a	FGA b	Fighter b	Bomber	Total b	WMD/M c	Example
China	600	4,600	630	5,830	(N)BCM	Q-5 (MiG-19)
North Korea	346	376-387	81?	814?	NBCM	MiG-29
India	400	327	9	736	NM	Mirage-2000
Israel	169	479	0	648	NBCM	F-15/16
Syria	170	302-463	0	633	BCM	MiG-29
Taiwan	512	0	0	512	BC	F-5
Japan	94-198	280	0	478	none	F-15
Egypt	113-149	295-323	0	472	CM	F-16
Sweden	97-237	214	0	451	none	JA-37
Yugoslavia d	213-283	126	0	409	none	MiG-29
South Korea	265	128	0	393	M?	F-16
Libya	128	238	5	371	BCM	Mirage F-1
Pakistan	126-150	214	0	364	NM	F-16
Iraq	130	180	6	316	[NBCM]	MiG-29
Saudi Arabia	97-152	102-132	0	284	M	F-15 C/D
Iran	130	132	0	262	NBCM	F-14
South Africa	116-245	14	0	259	[N]M?	Mirage F-1
Algeria	57	185	0	242	N?M?	MiG-23
Afghanistan	110	80-123	0	233	M	MiG-23
Switzerland	87	137	0	224	none	Mirage III
Brazil	200	18	0	218	[M]N	F-5
Singapore	107-149	38	0	187	none	F-16
Vietnam	60	125	0	185	C	Su-17
Cuba	20	140	0	160	none	MiG-29
Argentina	16-89	66	0	155	[NM]	Super Entendard

Key: FGA = fighter/ground-attack aircraft

Fighter = combat aircraft optimized for air-to-air mission

Bomber = aircraft optimized for carrying large payloads of bombs at relatively long range, possibly with internal bomb bay, and lacking air-combat capability

a Countries with less than 150 combat aircraft are not listed. The only such country that is frequently reported to have a mass-destruction weapon program is Myanmar (Burma), which is suspected of having chemical warfare capability and is reported to have 12 fighter aircraft.

b. Higher numbers include combat-capable trainer aircraft, which are also included in totals.

c. WMD/M = weapon of mass destruction or missile program:

N = frequently reported as having or trying to acquire nuclear weapons

B = frequently reported as having offensive biological warfare program

C = frequently reported as having offensive chemical warfare capability

M = suspected of having or developing ballistic missiles with range of at least 300 km, and not full member of MTCR as of March 1993

[ ] = program in reversal or no longer considered a proliferant threat

States are listed here as having nuclear, chemical, and biological weapon programs if they are commonly cited in the public literature as having such programs, as reviewed in chapter 2 of U.S. Congress, Office of Technology Assessment,

[Notes from Figure 2–3, continued from previous page.]

Proliferation of Weapons of Mass Destruction: Assessing the Risks, OTA–ISC–559 (Washington, D.C.: GPO, August 1993).
d. Federal Republic of Yugoslavia (Serbia-Montenegro)

Source: Office of Technology Assessment. Based on information drawn from International Institute for Strategic Studies, *The Military Balance 1992–1993* (London: International Institute for Strategic Studies, 1992). Reprinted from *Proliferation of Weapons of Mass Destruction: Assessing the Risks*, OTA–ISC–559 (Washington, D.C.: GPO, August 1993).

including digital networks, fusion centers, and broadband fiberoptics. One recent study observes that "global trends indicate that many nations are acquiring [these] precursor technologies."[62]

Access to Space

A related trend is the steadily growing number of states regularly gaining access to outer space or working with space-based systems. In 1993, there were 18 space launch centers around the globe, 13 of them outside the United States and Russia.[63] China, Israel, India, Brazil, and perhaps Pakistan are among those developing countries currently possessing or likely soon to possess independent access to space.[64] As of August 1994, 25 countries and 3 international organizations were operating some 2,168 payloads in space.[65] In 1992, 14 states operated communications satellites, with 5 more planning to do so.[66] By the year

---

62 U.S. Department of Defense, *Technology Proliferation and U.S. Technological Superiority.*

63 ANSER, *Decision Maker's Guide to International Space,* STDN 92–12 (Arlington, Va.: ANSER, August 1992), p. 180.

64 Michael Krepon et al., eds., *Commercial Observation Satellites and International Security* (New York, N.Y.: St. Martin's Press with the Carnegie Endowment for International Peace, 1990), p. 106.

65 *Air Force Magazine,* August 1994, p. 55. A chart on the preceding page summarizes total space activity, noting that between 1957 and 1993, 3,819 launches into space had occurred from 19 launch sites in 10 countries.

66 Thomas Mahnken, "Why Third World Space Systems Matter," *Orbis,* Vol. 35, No. 4 (Fall 1991), p. 566. For a comprehensive review of the space development activities of more than 40 countries see ANSER, *Decision Maker's Guide to International Space.* Mary Umberger depicts the issue as follows: "Landsat ground stations capable of receiving satellite data on a real-time basis are located in 16 countries—Argentina, Australia, Brazil, Canada, China, Ecuador, India, Italy, Japan, Pakistan, the Canary Islands, Saudi Arabia, South Africa, Sweden, Thailand, and the United States—and a station is currently under negotiation in

2000 the 6 nations that now deploy reconnaissance satellites could be joined by Canada, Germany, Israel, Italy, Pakistan, South Africa, South Korea, Spain, and Taiwan, with Argentina and Brazil following sometime thereafter.[67] Over 100 developing countries are involved in some aspect of space research.[68] All states now have access to commercially available satellite imagery.[69] For nations lacking

---

Indonesia. Currently operational SPOT receiving stations, often in the form of modified Landsat stations, are located in Brazil, Canada, the Canary Islands, France, India, Japan, Pakistan, Saudi Arabia, South Africa, Sweden, and Thailand. Plans for additional stations are under negotiation for Ecuador, Israel, China, Taiwan, Indonesia, and Australia. Many of these stations have been or are capable of being modified in the future to receive data from multiple satellites....Real-time data—i.e., data received directly from the satellite as it passes overhead—are received at a ground station over a specific range that is determined both by the satellite's capability to transmit data over distance and by agreement with the satellite owner/operator. Thailand's Landsat station operates within a 2,800 km radius of Bangkok, and its SPOT station has a range equivalent to a 2,500 km radius from the station. Japan's new SPOT station acquires imagery over all of Japan, Taiwan, North Korea, and South Korea, as well as over portions of the PRC and Soviet Union." Umberger, "Commercial Observation Satellite Capabilities," in Krepon *Commercial Observation Satellites*, pp. 11–13.

67   See Brooks testimony of March 7, 1991. K. Subrahmanyam reports that "among the more capable developing nations, there are important differences. Some—like China, India, Brazil and perhaps Pakistan—have or will soon have the capability of launching their own observation satellites. They will also be able to use internationally available commercial observation-satellite data. Other states, like Indonesia, have considerable expertise without having launch capabilities. There are perhaps a dozen developing nations in these categories; all are conscious of the advantages of satellite data and will continue efforts to obtain them. Another 20 to 25 large developing nations either do not face acute cross-border security threats, or cannot afford to use satellite data widely for national security purposes. Mexico, Chile, Argentina, and other large Latin American countries fit into this category." K. Subrahmanyam, "A View from the Developing Countries," in Krepon, *Commercial Observation Satellites*, p. 106. See also Michael Wines, "Third World Seeks Advanced Arms," *New York Times*, March 26, 1991, p. A–12.

68   Louis J. Levy and Susan B. Chodakawitz, "The Commercialization of Satellite Imagery," *Space Policy*, Vol. 6, No. 3 (August 1990), p. 211.

69   Krepon, *Commercial Observation Satellites*. In the early 1990s Russia began to sell high resolution (down to 2 meter) imagery. Reports have appeared suggesting that restrictions may be lifted in the United States that heretofore have prevented U.S. defense contractors from selling the most advanced satellite photos and spy systems to foreign governments, as well as U.S. businesses. "CIA May Let Firms Sell Spy-quality Satellites," *Baltimore Sun*, June 20, 1993, p. 21.

the expertise to operate satellite stations, professional services are available for hire; imagery enhancement and equipment repairs, for example, are available from over 150 vendors in 42 countries.[70]

Access to space does not necessarily have military purposes. On the other hand, it offers many military applications. Space launch vehicles can be modified to become surface-to-surface missiles for attack purposes. Anti-satellite systems can be developed and utilized. Targeting information can be derived from imagery. Moreover, the capacity to use space-based information assets for the command and control of military forces in time of war or near war can offer the state enjoying that capacity a significant advantage.

Subterranean Facilities

The Persian Gulf War highlighted the growing significance of underground facilities and their utility in hiding production or storage facilities and protecting them from air bombardment by technically superior forces. The war stimulated a surge in the construction of such facilities and today, according to one source,

> over 50 nations rely on underground facilities for strategic purposes and ten countries in the Middle East alone have such structures under construction. Current and intended uses include command and control, leadership protection, missile storage, nuclear and chemical weapons production, and storage of military supplies.[71]

Defense Industrial Base

This focus on weapons and weapon systems, however, obscures a parallel proliferation of equal and arguably more long-term significance—the proliferation of the defense industrial base.[72]

---

70 Krepon, *Commercial Observation Satellites,* p. 13.

71 From "Statement of Work for the Underground Facilities Signatures Program," Request For Proposal, Defense Nuclear Agency, U.S. Department of Defense, Washington, D.C., September 30, 1993.

72 Janne E. Nolan, *Trappings of Power: Ballistic Missiles in the Third World* (Washington, D.C.: Brookings Institution, 1991), especially chapter 1, "The Challenges of Technology

For Conventional Weapons

In 1945 only 4 countries outside the developed world—Argentina, Brazil, South Africa, and India—produced military equipment.[73] In 1986, the number had risen to 27.[74] By 1990, about 40 developing countries were producing some weaponry, with one-quarter of them possessing a significant military-industrial infrastructure.[75] The value of goods manufactured by defense industries in the developing world reflects this growth: in 1950, just $2 million worth of goods were produced; in 1984, the total was $1.1 billion.[76]

These defense industries have emerged as the result of a variety of factors. Some of them relate to a developing country's domestic priorities, and the belief that defense industrialization has broader benefits for economic development by fostering technology acquisition, high-skill employment, and export products. Others relate to the international market and the demand for weapons caused by war in the South and the globalization of the international trading system. Many developing countries began first by overhauling and repairing their own weapons and then those of their neighbors.[77] In the Pacific basin, many states have modernized previously existing capabilities to produce, maintain, and repair ships and to sustain an infrastructure for long-distance air travel.[78] Looking to the

---

Diffusion," pp. 1–31.

73   Robert M. Rosh, "Third World Arms Production and the Evolving Interstate System," *Journal of Conflict Resolution*, Vol. 34, No. 1 (March 1990), p. 57.

74   Stephanie Neuman, "The Arms Market: Who's On Top?" *Orbis*, Vol. 33, No. 4 (Fall 1989), p. 511.

75   Andrew L. Ross, "Do-It-Yourself Weaponry," *Bulletin of the Atomic Scientists*, Vol. 46, No. 4 (May 1990), p. 20. For an overview of defense industries in the developing world, see Ralph Sanders, *Arms Industries: New Suppliers and Regional Security* (Washington, D.C.: National Defense University, 1990); U.S. Congress, Office of Technology Assessment, *Global Arms Trade: Commerce in Advanced Military Technology and Weapons*, OTA–ISC–460 (Washington, D.C.: GPO, June 1991).

76   Ross, "Do-It-Yourself Weaponry," p. 20. Figures in constant 1975 dollars. See also Michael Brzoska and Thomas Ohlson, eds., *Arms Production in the Third World* (London: Taylor & Francis for the Stockholm International Peace Research Institute, 1986), p. 7.

77   Sanders, *Arms Industries*, p. 103.

78   Alex Gliksman, "Arms Production Spread: Implications for Pacific Rim Security," in Dora Alves, ed., *Evolving Pacific Basin Strategies* (Washington, D.C.: National Defense University Press, 1990), p. 66.

future, it appears likely that there will be a steadily growing demand for upgrading and retrofitting weapon systems exported by the erstwhile superpowers to their clients.[79]

A systemic analysis of the emergence of these defense industries emphasizes the changing nature of the global arms transfer and production system, in which vestiges of a hierarchical structure conflict with the beginnings of a globalization of such production. Keith Krause has elaborated the central characteristics of this system. First, it is driven by the development of new military technologies that create "gaps" in the capabilities of weapons possessed by states and the subsequent efforts to close these gaps. Second, dominant centers of military innovation have emerged in a small number of states in different historical periods, with a first tier of producers of potent arsenals, a second tier capable of some competitive armaments production, and a third tier that barely competes. Third, this system has an evolutionary dynamic, akin to a product cycle with different rates of technology innovation and diffusion.[80]

Within this global arms transfer and production system, much attention has been given to the role of the first tier, which for the last 40 years or so has in fact dominated the system. A continuing preoccupation with this tier in the post–Cold War era has focused attention largely on a downturn in production that has catapulted the United States into by far the dominant arms exporter position, albeit with reduced exports, trends clearly identified in figures 2–4 and 2–5.[81] But in this era of technological and industrial innovation, it is in the second

79 According to Paul Lewis and David Silverberg, "While the United States and the former Soviet Union provided the bulk of the world's equipment that now needs retrofits and upgrades, other countries with defense industries are actively competing in the world upgrade, retrofit, and maintenance market." The authors go on to cite Singapore, China, Israel, and South Africa as examples. Lewis and Silverberg, "Smaller Nations Emerge as Active Market Forces," *Defense News,* December 7–13, 1992, pp. 12–13.

80 See Keith Krause, *Arms and the State: Patterns of Military Production and Trade* (Cambridge: Cambridge University Press, 1992) and Krause and David Mutimer, "The Proliferation of Conventional Weapons: New Challenges for Control and Verification," in David Mutimer, ed., *Control But Verify: Verification and the New Non-Proliferation Agenda* (Toronto: Centre for International and Strategic Studies at York University, 1994), pp. 39–55. See also Edward J. Laurance, *The International Arms Trade* (Lexington, Mass.: Lexington Books, 1992).

81 Stockholm International Peace Research Institute, *SIPRI Yearbook 1993: World Armaments and Disarmament,* p. 477.

Figure 2–4
The Drop in Global Arms Deliveries
Major Exporters' Percent Change, 1986–93

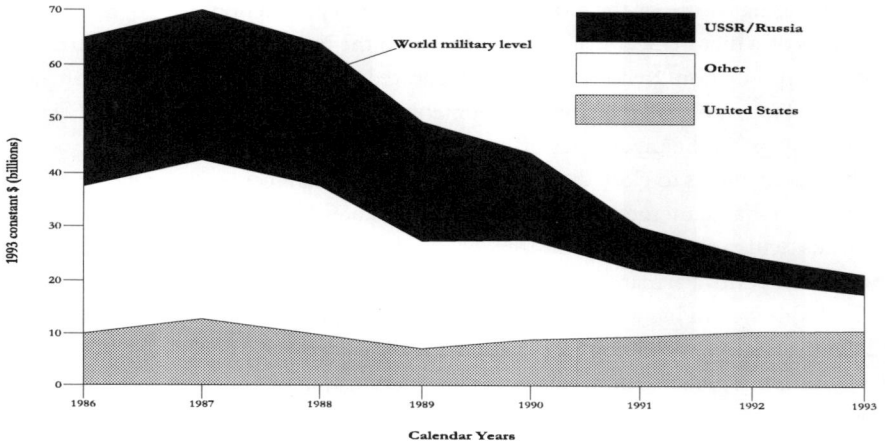

Sources: Richard F. Grimmett, "Conventional Arms Transfers to the Third World, 1986–93," Washington, D.C.: Congressional Research Service, July 29, 1994. Reprinted with permission from David Vadas, "World Defense Trade," *Aerospace Industries Association Newsletter*, November 1994.

and third tiers that evidence of a structural innovation can be found. As Richard Bitzinger has noted, increasing cost and declining markets have interacted to internationalize arms development and production, primarily among developed countries but also among the countries of the developing world and in cases where developed and developing countries work together.[82]

Some developing countries have been involved in the production of military systems for many years, as table 2–2 suggests. The military hardware produced in these second and third tiers is not as technologically advanced as the most advanced items produced in the developed world, nor are their national defense industries as diverse and sophisticated as those in the developed world. But today there is a noteworthy trend toward higher quality.

---

82   Richard A. Bitzinger, *The Globalization of Arms Production: Defense Markets in Transition* (Washington, D.C.: Defense Budget Project, December 1993).

Figure 2–5
Arms Exports: Percent Change by Supplier, 1987–93
(1993 constant $)

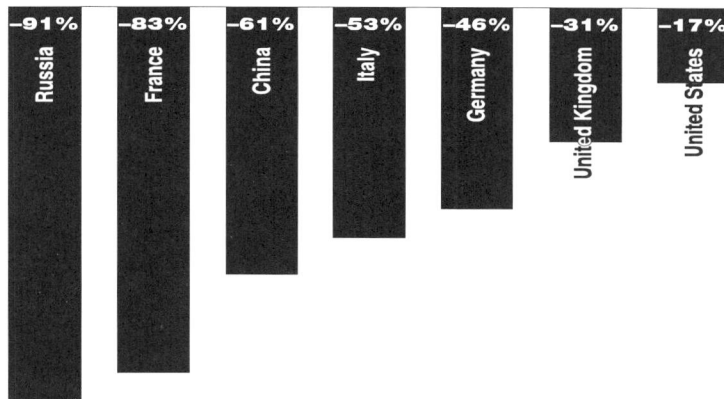

–91%	–83%	–61%	–53%	–46%	–31%	–17%
Russia	France	China	Italy	Germany	United Kingdom	United States

Source: Richard F. Grimmett, "Conventional Arms Transfers to the Third World, 1986–1993," Washington, D.C.: Congressional Research Service, July 29, 1994. Reprinted with permission from David Vadas, "World Defense Trade," *Aerospace Industries Association Newsletter*, November 1994.

A review of the defense industrial activities of the developing countries reveals a variety of types of activity, ranging from assembly of prefabricated parts, licensed production of components, licensed production of full systems, and modification of imported weapons, to production of domestically designed weapons.[83] Broken down by mission area and focusing only on advanced weapon systems, the military production of these countries includes the following.

In the case of major naval warfare systems, the number of developing countries producing domestically designed naval systems doubled from 9 to 18 between 1960 and 1980.[84] At least 19 developing countries build submarines.[85] Twenty-nine countries produce naval mines, of which 20 are attempting to export them.[86]

---

83   Ross, "Do-It-Yourself Weaponry."

84   Ibid.

85   "Third World Offers New Threat," p. 20.

86   Jason Glashow and Robert Holzer, "U.S. Confronts Non-Traditional Mine Threats," *Defense News*, November 14–20, 1994, p. 6.

Table 2–2
First Year of Indigenous Production
in Selected Weapon Categories

Country	Jet aircraft	Propellor driven aircraft	Heli-copters	Guided missiles	Main battle tanks	Other armored vehicles	Large-caliber artillery	Radar	Major surface warships	Sub-marines
Argentina	1987	1946	—	1978	—	1980	1978	—	1943	—
Brazil	1986	1944	—	1987	1985	1974	1969	—	1983	—
Chile	—	1990	—	—	—	1984	—	—	—	—
Egypt	—	—	—	1982	—	1966	1981	—	—	—
India *	1963	1953	*1995*	1994	*1995*	—	1980	1988	1978	—
Indonesia	—	1974	—	—	—	—	—	—	—	—
Israel	1971	1972	—	1970	1977	1975	1968	1977	—	—
Pakistan	—	—	—	—	—	—	1990	—	—	—
Singapore	—	—	—	—	—	—	1986	—	—	—
S. Africa	—	1961	1990	1975	1991	1973	1979	1991	—	—
S. Korea	—	—	—	—	1987	—	1976	—	1980	1983
Taiwan	1982	1976	—	1979	—	—	1976	—	—	—

* Years in italics indicate that some systems are not yet in full-scale production.

Reprinted, with permission and slight modifications, from Ian Anthony, "The Third Tier Counties: Production of Major Weapons," in Herbert Wulf, ed., *Arms Industry Limited* (Oxford: Oxford University Press for SIPRI, 1993).

In the case of combat systems for land warfare, the number of developing countries producing domestically designed armored systems increased from one to four between 1970 and 1980.[87] Cluster munition delivery systems are being produced by Brazil, Chile, Egypt, India, Iraq, Israel, South Africa, and South Korea.[88] There are 56 known production and development programs for ADHPMs in 22 countries.[89]

In the case of combat systems for air warfare, supersonic military aircraft are manufactured in at least six Third World countries—China, India, Israel, South Korea, South Africa, and Taiwan.[90] Some of these are coproduction

---

87 Ross, "Do-It-Yourself-Weaponry."

88 Carus, *Cruise Missile Proliferation*, p. 81.

89 U.S. Department of Defense, *Technology Proliferation and U.S. Technological Superiority,* appendix.

90 According to James G. Roche, "China produces the Soviet Mig–21, designated the F–7, under license at the Chengdu Aircraft Corporation, a Mig–19 derivative designated the Q–5 at the Nanchang Aircraft Manufacturing Company, a Chinese-designed fighter called the J–8 at the Shenyang Aircraft Corporation, and another Chinese designed fighter, the H–7 at the Xian Aircraft manufacturing company. India has assembled the Mig–21 and Mig–29 at

arrangements involving advanced systems with either the United States or Russia. Other countries currently manufacturing military aircraft or with plans to do so include: Argentina, Brazil, Egypt, Indonesia, and North Korea.[91] Still others, such as Chile and Singapore, have the ability to modernize combat aircraft.[92] In the Pacific basin, the Philippines and Thailand join their neighbors cited above among those involved in the production of light aircraft, either independently or under license, often in state-of-the-art facilities.[93] India, Israel, South Africa, and Taiwan currently have fighter engine manufacturing capabilities.[94] Remotely piloted vehicles (RPVs) are under production in at least 10 developing countries: Argentina, Brazil, India, Indonesia, Iran, Iraq, Israel, Saudi Arabia, South Africa, and South Korea.[95] The production of rotary wing aircraft is steadily diffusing, and by the end of the decade it is expected that global helicopter production will make extensive use of dual-use technologies in avionics, sensors, and fire control.[96] Air defense systems using advanced technologies are under development and production for export in China, South Africa, and South Korea.[97]

Hindustan Aeronautics Ltd and is now developing its own fighter, the Light Combat Aircraft. Israel designed extensive modifications to the French Mirage 5 fighter and manufactured it as the Kfir. They also designed and built prototypes of the Lavi fighter....South Korea has assembled U.S. F–5 fighters, and will co-produce U.S. F–16 fighters. South Africa has assembled French Mirage F–1 fighters, and has a program to produce the Atlas CAVA based on the Mirage III design. Taiwan is developing an Indigenous Defensive Fighter at its Aero Industry Development Center." Roche, "Proliferation of Tactical Aircraft and Ballistic and Cruise Missiles in the Developing World," in W. Thomas Wander, Eric H. Arnett, and Paul Bracken, eds., *The Diffusion of Advanced Weaponry: Technologies, Regional Implications, and Possible Responses* (Washington, D.C.: American Association for the Advancement of Science, 1994), pp. 64–65.

91 Carus, *Cruise Missile Proliferation*, p. 77.

92 Ibid., p. 77.

93 Alex Gliksman reports that these facilities are regarded in the region as important stepping stones to the production of complete military aircraft. Gliksman, "Arms Production Spread," p. 66.

94 Carus, *Cruise Missile Proliferation*, pp. 78–79.

95 Ibid., p. 77.

96 U.S. Department of Defense, *Technology Proliferation and U.S. Technological Superiority*.

97 Ibid.

In the case of ballistic missiles, countries believed to have development programs include Argentina, Brazil, Egypt, India, Indonesia, Iraq, Libya, North Korea, Pakistan, South Korea, and Taiwan. It is noteworthy that many of these are also countries reportedly possessing or actively developing unconventional weapons. As many as 15 countries in the Third World may be producing ballistic missiles by the year 2000.[98] The technology for reentry vehicles is widely available.[99]

In the case of cruise missiles, the number of developing countries capable of their production could increase to 15 during the 1990s.[100] Among those reported to be either manufacturing anti-ship cruise missiles or to have systems under development are Brazil, India, Israel, Iraq, North Korea, South Africa, and Taiwan.[101] Upgrades on cruise missiles are being produced in some countries; Taiwan, for example, is developing an improved version of the Harpoon missile sold to it by the United States.[102] Turbojet engines suitable for small, short-range cruise missiles are built in many countries.

Carus underscores the importance of looking beyond traditional ballistic and cruise missiles to understand the full extent of long-range land attack weaponry under development in the developing world, noting that there are programs in each of the following categories: long-range rocket artillery, ballistic missiles,

---

98   Carus, *Ballistic Missiles in Modern Conflict*, p. 20.

99   Some of this technology is commercially available, given the widespread availability of sounding rockets. See Proliferation Study Team, *Emerging Ballistic Missile Threat*, p. 12. Moreover, the open literature contains extensive information on the research that has been conducted on various materials in the search for effective, low-weight ablative materials for heat shields. See Graybeal and McFate, *GPALs and Foreign Space Launch Capabilities*, p. 7.

100 Carus, *Cruise Missile Proliferation*, p. 82. See also Lovece, "DIA: New Cruise Missile Threat to America Is Far Away," p. 7.

101 Seth Carus reports that "Israel, South Africa, and Taiwan produce cruise missiles relying on both turbojets and solid-fuel rocket motors, and Iraq and North Korea manufacture missiles with liquid-fuel rocket engines. In addition, Brazil and India have programs to develop rocket-powered anti-ship missiles." Carus, *Cruise Missile Proliferation*, pp. 34–35.

102 "Taiwan Confronts Chinese Threat," *Defense News*, March 30, 1992, p. 1. Taiwan may also coproduce the Patriot anti-missile system. See Barbara Opall and David Silverberg, "Taiwanese May Soon Coproduce Patriot," *Defense News*, February 22–28, 1993, pp. 1, 21. See also George Leopold and Vivek Raghuvanshi, "India Steps Up Cruise Missile Efforts," *Defense News*, August 2, 1993, pp. 3, 28.

ballistic missiles with guided reentry vehicles, semi-ballistic missiles, and cruise missiles.[103]

A variety of warheads for missiles are also under development in the developing world. These include the cluster munitions cited above as well as fuel air explosives that depend for their lethality on dispersion and subsequent ignition of a mist of highly combustible fuel. Argentina, Chile, India, Iraq, and Israel may have the technology for such warheads.[104] Presumably there are also unconventional warheads under development; the flight paths of cruise missiles make them far superior to ballistic missiles for the delivery of chemical and biological warfare agents. U.S. sources have expressed concern about the possibility that radiological materials might be carried in small cluster munitions atop missiles—perhaps as many as 1,000 5 to 10 pound cluster bombs of such material could reportedly be carried inside a SCUD shroud.[105]

A variety of guidance systems are also under development or in production in the developing world. Inertial navigation systems are in production.[106] The GPS satellite navigation system is under development in Israel (which has been shown to be willing to export such technology) as well as Chile, India, and South Africa; those who might acquire such technology include Brazil, Singapore, South Korea, and Taiwan.[107] India may be working on a radar area correlation system akin to the U.S.-developed terrain comparison (TERCOM) guidance system for its cruise missiles.[108]

The ability to design, produce, and field missile systems requires expertise in a variety of areas, including airframes, propulsion systems, flight controls, and warheads, as well as the ability to integrate them. Israel, South Africa, and Taiwan have designed indigenous anti-ship cruise missiles, and Brazil and India appear to be doing the same. Iraq and North Korea can assemble such missiles.[109]

---

103 Carus, *Cruise Missile Proliferation*, p. 5.

104 Ibid., p. 81.

105 David Fulghum, "Small Clustered Munitions May Carry Nuclear Waste," *Aviation Week & Space Technology*.

106 Ibid., p. 53.

107 Ibid., pp. 65–66.

108 Ibid., p. 55.

109 Ibid., p. 77.

The Production Base for Weapons of Mass Destruction

Proliferation of the means to produce weapons is not limited to the conventional area. The ability to produce unconventional weapons has proliferated much more widely than the weapons themselves.[110] In the nuclear area, for example, the Iklé–Wohlstetter commission projected that 40 nations would possess the technical ability to produce nuclear weapons by the year 2000.[111] The emergence in recent decades of a number of new suppliers of nuclear technology and other items suggests that this estimate may be correct. Such new suppliers include Argentina, Brazil, India, Iraq, Iran, Israel, Japan, Libya, North Korea, Pakistan, China, South Africa, South Korea, Spain, and Taiwan.[112]

The expertise to produce and work with nuclear technologies is also widely dispersing. Suggestive of this is the fact that more than 13,000 foreign nationals from non-Soviet bloc countries received nuclear training in the United States between 1954 and 1979; roughly one-quarter of them were from nations that declined to sign the 1968 NPT.[113] As Amy Sands, a U.S. nuclear expert argues, the improved scientific, technical, and engineering infrastructure and capabilities in

---

110 U.S. Congress, Office of Technology Assessment, *Proliferation of Weapons of Mass Destruction: Assessing the Risks*, OTA–ISC–559 (Washington, D.C.: GPO, August 1993), and *Technologies Underlying Weapons of Mass Destruction*, OTA–BP–ISA–115 (Washington, D.C.: GPO, December 1993).

111 Commission on Long-Range Integrated Strategy, *Discriminate Deterrence*, Report (Washington, D.C.: GPO, January 1988), p. 10.

112 In a review of this new tier of suppliers, William C. Potter concludes as follows: "The comparative case studies reveal no simple relationship between a technical capability to produce nuclear material, technology, and equipment, and the propensity to export those items. Nor do they reveal a relationship between formal nonproliferation commitments on the part of emerging nuclear supplier states and restraint in nuclear export behavior. Indeed, among the eleven countries in the initial survey, the one that possesses the most experienced and self-sufficient nuclear industry (and the one that also is the most consistent critic of existing nonproliferation structures)—India—has been largely inactive as a nuclear exporter, although there are some indications this may change. Among the other emerging supplier states, only the PRC has been a major exporter, although Argentina, Brazil, and Spain on occasion have exported materials and services that could be used in producing nuclear weapons. Japan also is likely to soon become a significant player." Potter, "The New Nuclear Suppliers," *Orbis*, Vol. 36, No. 2 (Spring 1992), pp. 199–200.

113 Frankel, *Opaque Nuclear Proliferation*, p. 3, especially footnote 8.

Figure 2–6
Number of Primitive Nuclear Bombs That Can
Be Made from Separated Plutonium

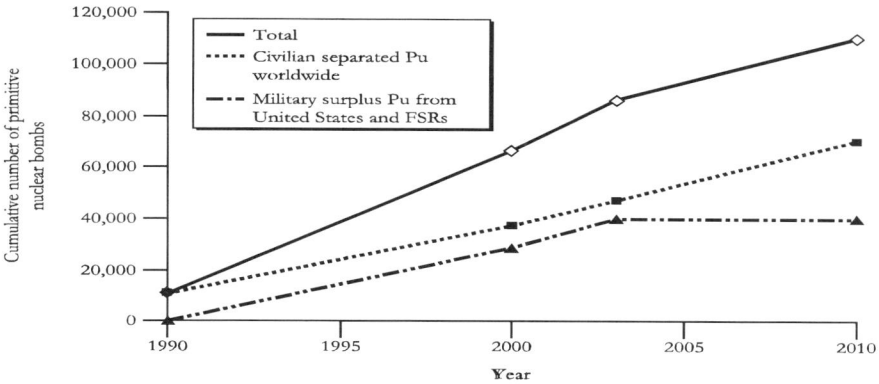

Reprinted with permission from Brian G. Chow and Kenneth A. Solomon, *Limiting the Spread of Weapon-Usable Fissile Materials*. RAND Report MR–346–USDP (Santa Monica, Calif.: RAND, 1993).

the developing world pose the "greatest technological threat" of nuclear proliferation.[114] Moreover, the technologies associated with nuclear weapons have grown less esoteric since the original devices in the 1940s.

The growing stockpiles of fissionable material in themselves are becoming a focus of proliferation concern. Twenty-two countries currently possess or control separated plutonium.[115] The dismantlement of large numbers of nuclear weapons by the United States and Russia will produce large quantities of weapon-usable plutonium. A RAND study concluded, however, that "Current plans for civilian nuclear development worldwide call for the separation of more weapon-usable plutonium from spent fuel by the year 2003 than from dismantled nuclear weapons,"[116] not least in Japan as its reprocessing program commences.

---

114 Amy Sands, "The Impact of New Technologies on Nuclear Weapons Proliferation," in Reiss and Litwak, *Nuclear Proliferation After the Cold War*, pp. 259–274.

115 George Perkovich, "The Plutonium Genie," *Foreign Affairs*, Vol. 72, No. 3 (Summer 1993), p. 154.

Figure 2–6 illustrates the extent of this problem. The possibility that such stockpiles might be diverted or rediverted to weapons purposes has generated efforts to formulate new forms of control.[117]

One of the implications of the existence of nuclear industries around the globe is the possibility that some states may opt to produce radiological rather than nuclear weapons. Such weapons depend for their effect not on the explosiveness of fissile materials but on the toxic effect of radioactivity. Such weapons have apparently been rejected by any nation capable of making the much more devastating atomic and thermonuclear devices, but they may become salient as the volume of nuclear fuels and wastes steadily increases.

In the chemical area perhaps as many as 100 countries possess the industrial infrastructure and expertise to produce chemical weapons.[118] In the biological area, estimates are not publicly available but more countries are capable in this area than in the nuclear area, because nuclear weapons technology is more esoteric than biological technology. Indeed, the number of biological-capable states may be as high or higher than the number of chemical-capable states.

In the chemical and biological areas, barriers to weapons production are falling with the global spread of the petrochemical, fertilizer, and pharmaceutical industries. Germany has identified 34 countries it considers to be of chemical and/or biological concern, and the United States 28, in preparing watch lists for export controls.[119]

Despite such watch lists, the technologies of unconventional warfare continue to flow in large volumes among states. One measure of that flow is the number of export licenses reviewed and approved by the United States for dual-use items in the nuclear, chemical, biological, and missile domains. In 1989, U.S. officials reviewed more than 120,000 license applications; following revisions to the export laws, the total in 1992 was 25,000; on average, only about 1 percent of such

---

116 Brian G. Chow and Kenneth A. Solomon, *Limiting the Spread of Weapon-Usable Fissile Materials*, RAND Report MR–346–USDP (Santa Monica, Calif., RAND, 1993), p. xi.

117 National Academy of Sciences, Committee on International Security and Arms Control, *Management and Disposition of Excess Weapons Plutonium*, Report (Washington, D.C.: National Academy Press, 1994).

118 Foreign Intelligence Service of the Russian Federation, "A New Challenge After the Cold War."

119 Information provided by Washington Resources International, Inc., March 23, 1992.

applications are denied.[120] For purposes of comparison, in 1988 the United Kingdom reviewed 90,000 such dual-use license applications.[121] One recent study of the supply of dual-use technologies to just three countries—Iran, Syria, and Libya—identified 300 suppliers in 38 countries.[122] Since the Persian Gulf War, items sold legitimately to the Middle East and South Asia include the precursors for chemical weapons, agent production reactors, computers, fermentation reactors, heavy water, and flash X-ray cameras.[123] Changing technological and market conditions will accelerate this process, particularly in the biological area, where biotechnology is having a revolutionary effect. In the United States alone, the market for biotechnology products is expected to grow by a factor of 30 during the 1990s, which portends the entrance of new technology suppliers.[124]

In a study of the diffusion of nuclear materials, technologies, and expertise, the RAND Corporation has postulated a number of asymptotic end-states in which the number of states possessing the essential capacities for weapons production eventually equals the number of states in the system.[125] This illustrates vividly the unique historical circumstance in which only a handful of

---

120 Information provided by Charles Duelfer, senior adviser for export controls, Bureau of Political-Military Affairs, U.S. Department of State, in June 1993. In 1992, 25,631 applications were received by the Department of Commerce, of which 21,060 were approved, 3,433 were returned without action, and 186 were denied. Information supplied by the Office of Export Licensing, U.S. Department of Commerce. This contrasts with approximately 50,000 export license applications for items on the munitions control lists (1992 figure).

121 John Thurlow, "Export Control Law Within a Regional Context: The European Experience" (Paper presented at a workshop of the Minsk Center for Nonproliferation and Export Controls, Minsk, Belarus, October 3–4, 1994).

122 Simon Wiesenthal Center, *Weapons of Mass Destruction: The Cases of Iran, Syria, and Libya* (Los Angeles, Calif.: Simon Wiesenthal Center, August 1992).

123 David A. Fulghum, "U.S. Developing Plan to Down Cruise Missiles," *Aviation Week & Space Technology,* March 22, 1993, p. 77.

124 D. Barnes, *New Life for Industry: Biotechnology, Industry and the Community in the 1990s and Beyond* (London: NEDC, 1991). Cited in Malcolm Dando, *Biological Warfare in the 21st Century: Biotechnology and the Proliferation of Biological Weapons* (London: Brassey's, 1994), p. 210.

125 Roger C. Molander and Peter A. Wilson, *The Nuclear Asymptote: On Containing Nuclear Proliferation* (Santa Monica, Ca.: RAND/UCLA Center for Soviet Studies, 1993) and idem, "On Dealing with the Prospect of Nuclear Chaos," *The Washington Quarterly,* Vol. 17, No. 3 (Summer 1994), pp. 19–39.

relatively wealthy industrialized powers established themselves as nuclear-weapon states. It also underscores that the present international system includes a number of virtual weapon states, which is to say states that in a relatively short period of time could establish themselves as new nuclear powers. James Keeley has described this as a process of latent proliferation.[126] This depiction of virtual weapon states comes close to capturing the reality that increasingly prevails in the unconventional weapons domain, where entirely peaceful processes of industrialization and development bring with them the competence to produce nuclear, chemical, and biological weapons—and the means of their delivery.

The Quality Issue

In the past, this military production base in the developing world has been judged of little or no consequence by many analysts in the developed world primarily for two reasons: the products of these industries were deemed of markedly inferior quality, and they had little significance in the larger global armaments trade. Each of these assessments merits reevaluation in the 1990s.

The challenges posed by the production of technologically sophisticated weapons in the developing world have indeed proven significant. Obstacles have sometimes emerged to block ambitious programs to produce globally competitive military hardware. One study by Rodney Jones and Steven Hildreth concluded in the early 1980s that there was little evidence anywhere in the Third World of truly indigenous technological innovation in the military sector.[127] A more recent study by Amit Gupta has pointed to some technological progress but continuing difficulties:

> By the start of the 1990s, the attempt by Third World countries to
> advance a technological level had met with mixed success. On the
> production side, most were able to expand their range of systems
> and to upgrade the quality of these systems. Thus the Israelis and

---

126 James F. Keeley, "Weapons of Mass Destruction as Mature Technologies," in Mutimer, *Control But Verify*, pp. 171–179.

127 Rodney W. Jones and Steven A. Hildreth, eds., *Emerging Powers: Defense and Security in the Third World* (New York, N.Y.: Praeger with the Center for Strategic and International Studies, 1986). See also Sanders, *Arms Industries*.

the Brazilians produced tanks, the Chileans and South Africans produced aircraft, and India began to build a new range of naval vessels. Further, in specific areas of weapons technology, particularly the development of a series of missiles, the research efforts of countries like India, Israel, and Iraq bore fruit. Certain Third World states were also able to make advances in the production of electronic subsystems—Israel and Singapore being the most prominent examples. But when it came to developing state-of-the-art conventional weapons, the track record was far less successful. A number of programs were either terminated or pushed to the point of becoming uneconomical because of high development costs, technology restrictions, and external pressures."[128]

The failure of India and China to produce fully indigenous high-performance fighter aircraft is symptomatic of the quality challenge. Yet, the increasing technological sophistication of weapons platforms and warheads in the developing world is symptomatic of the progress over the last decade or two.

There is considerable evidence to conclude, therefore, that the weaponry produced in the developing world will continue to improve in sophistication and quality.

R&D work in the developing world focuses on many of the very latest technologies: six developing countries are engaged in R&D projects on high temperature composite materials, five on fiber optics, three on microelectronic circuits, three on signature controls, two on computational fluid dynamics, and two on hypervelocity vehicles. Research can also be found on semiconductors, software productivity, sensitive radars, automated target recognition, high-power microwaves, and superconductivity.[129] A 1988 study by the U.S. Department of Defense reviewed 22 critical technologies and found that work on all but 2 of them was known to be under way in the Third World, often in more than just a

---

128 Amit Gupta, "Third World Militaries: New Suppliers, Deadlier Weapons," *Orbis,* Vol. 37, No. 1 (Winter 1993), pp. 60–62.

129 Ravinderpal Singh, "Advanced Weaponry for the Third World," in Eric Arnett, ed., *Science and International Security: Responding to a Changing World* (Washington, D.C.: American Association for the Advancement of Science, 1990), pp. 78–79.

Figure 2–7
Civil Programs and R&D Efforts

SPACE PROGRAMS / COUNTRY	Argentina	Australia	Austria *	Belgium *	Brazil	Bulgaria	Canada	Chile	China	Czechoslovakia	Denmark *	ESA	Finland *	France *	Germany *	Greece	Hungary	India	Indonesia	Iran	Iraq	Ireland *
1. Astrophysical		X	X	X		X	X		X	X	X	X		X	X		X	X				
2. Communications	X	X	X	X	X		X	X	X		X	X	X	X	X		X	X	X	X		X
3. Humans-in-Space			X	X		X	X					X		X	X		X					
4. Meteorological	X	X	X	X	X	X	X	X	X		X	X	X	X	X			X	X			
5. Microgravity			X	X		X	X		X			X		X	X		X					
6. Navigation							X		X			X		X	X			X				
7. Remote Sensing	X	X	X	X	X	X	X	X	X			X	X	X	X			X	X			
8. Space Environment	X	X	X		X	X	X		X	X	X	X	X	X	X	X	X	X				X
9. Space Stations							X					X			X							
10. Solar System Exploration (Robotic)												X										
11. Transportation (Launch)	X	X			X				X			X		X	X			X			X	
RESEARCH AND DEVELOPMENT EFFORTS																						
1. Aerobraking																						
2. Communications		X			X		X		X			X		X	X			X				
3. Electric Propulsion												X		X	X							
4. Electronics and Computers		X	X				X		X			X		X	X		X	X				X
5. Guidance, Navigation, and Control	X	X		X	X		X		X			X		X	X			X			X	
6. Life Sciences			X				X		X		X	X		X	X		X					
7. Liquid Propulsion									X			X		X	X			X			X	
8. Materials Research		X		X			X		X			X		X	X		X					
9. Optical Systems							X		X			X		X	X							
10. Recorders and Memories			X				X		X			X		X	X		X	X				
11. Robotics and Artificial Intelligence							X		X			X		X	X							
12. Scramjets												X		X	X							
13. Solar Electric Power		X		X	X		X		X			X		X	X			X				
14. Solid Fuel Propulsion	X				X		X		X			X		X	X			X			X	
15. Space Nuclear Power																						
16. Structures	X	X		X	X		X		X			X		X	X			X				
17. Tethers												X										
18. Thermal and Power Subsystems	X	X		X	X		X		X			X		X	X			X				

* Member of ESA

Figure 2–7
Civil Programs and R&D Efforts (continued)

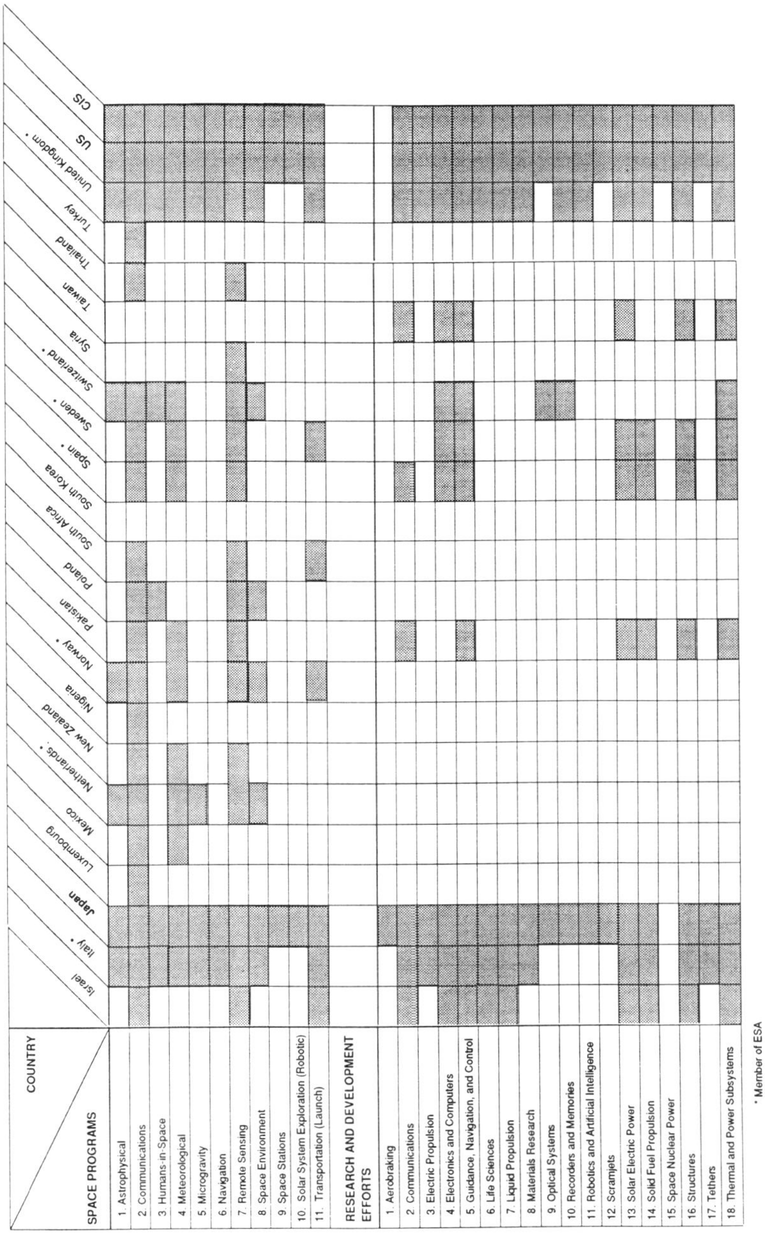

single state.[130] As figure 2–7 indicates, there is also extensive international collaboration on R&D programs in the area of civil space.

Perhaps as many as 17 countries are exploiting stealthy technologies; in India, Israel, South Africa, South Korea, and Taiwan there is evidence of work on composite materials to reduce radar observability.[131] The U.S. Department of Defense reportedly has predicted that cruise missiles with low observable characteristics, such as diffused and downward pointing exhausts with reduced radar cross-sections, and capable of flight at very low altitudes will be deployed by China, Iran, and Syria soon after the year 2000.[132]

Moreover, the technological and industrial base in the commercial sectors of some developing countries is steadily improving. The best example is in the area of data manipulation. The new availability of computing power could have a dramatic impact on many types of weapons programs. It has been estimated that a team of scientists using the calculators of the 1940s would take five years to solve what it takes a Cray computer one second to perform today. The implications for nuclear weapons design are considerable, not least in the suggestion that large-scale mobilization of vast sectors of society and huge financial investments of the kind made by the original atomic states "may be an historical relic."[133] In the 1950s, U.S. nuclear artillery shells and thermonuclear missile warheads were designed with computers operating with performance levels orders of magnitude below the power of today's personal computers. In the 1970s, small, lightweight warheads for submarine launched ballistic missiles

---

130 See "USA Lists Critical Technologies," *Jane's Defence Weekly*, Vol. 11, No. 13 (1989), p. 544.

131 Carus, *Cruise Missile Proliferation*, citing director of naval intelligence, p. 75. See also David Fulghum, "Cheap Cruise Missiles A Potent New Threat," *Aviation Week & Space Technology*, September 6, 1993, pp. 54–55. Fulghum identifies the following countries from which low observable technologies for missiles and aircraft could emerge: France, Japan, Israel, South Africa, China, North Korea, Taiwan, and Germany.

132 Fulghum, "U.S. Developing Plan to Down Cruise Missiles," p. 47. See also "Cruise Missiles Becoming Top Proliferation Threat," *Aviation Week & Space Technology*, February 1, 1993, p. 26.

133 Robert S. Norris, *British, French, and Chinese Nuclear Forces: Implications for Arms Control and Nonproliferation*, PRAC Paper No. 11 (College Park, Md.: Center for International and Security Studies at Maryland, Project on Rethinking Arms Control, September 1994), p. 15. Statistical reference is from U.S. Department of Energy, *The Need for Supercomputers in Nuclear Weapons Design* (Washington, D.C.: Department of Energy, January 1986), p. 11.

were designed with computers performing at the level of today's low-range PCs.[134] The diffusion of advanced computers is accompanied also by the growing sophistication of the interlinked computer networks, such as Internet, which offer the users of even minimally capable computers access to some of the most sophisticated computing power in the world.

But computers are not the only advanced commercial technologies of interest. The accumulation of advanced machine tools has also marked the development of sophisticated military industries in developing countries.[135] Items as diverse as compact disks and contact lenses are produced in the developing world, many of which involve a level of manufacturing precision akin to that used in production of the first generation of atomic weaponry.[136] In fact, many of the most sophisticated industrial production technologies have spread to developing countries, including computer-aided design, engineering, and manufacturing systems. One recent study surveyed six advanced industrial production technologies unevenly distributed among more than 40 developed and developing countries.[137]

---

134 John Harvey, "Common Sense About High-Technology Export Controls" (Unpublished research paper prepared for the Center for International Security and Arms Control, Stanford University, August 9, 1994), p. 7.

135 Machine tools accounted for 22 percent of all licensed exports to Iraq between 1981 and 1990, and for 30.6 percent of all licensed dual-use exports. Harald Müller et al., *From Black Sheep to White Angel? The New German Export Control Policy,* Report No. 32 (Frankfurt: Peace Research Institute, 1994). Many countries made deals with Iraq to supply technology and equipment for its nuclear and missile programs, ranging from construction of entire factories to the supply of machine tools or the training to operate them: Germany made 102 such deals, the United States 25, Switzerland 22, Britain 20, Brazil 14, Italy 13, Austria 9, France 6, Belgium 5, Japan 5, Saudi Arabia 3. Chile, Egypt, and Yugoslavia made 2 each and Argentina, China, Greece, Liechtenstein, Niger, Poland, Portugal, Soviet Union, Spain, Sweden made 1 each. Douglas Jehl, "Who Armed Iraq? Answers the West Didn't Want to Hear," *New York Times,* July 18, 1993, p. E–5, on findings of the Wisconsin Project on Nuclear Arms Control.

136 Tom Clancy and Russell Seitz, "Five Minutes Past Midnight—and Welcome to the Age of Proliferation," *National Interest,* No. 26 (Winter 1991/92), p. 10.

137 U.S. Department of Commerce, "Foreign Technology Assessment Summary," (Washington, D.C.: 1993). The specific technologies include: automation of industrial processes, metal working and industrial production, optical coatings, dimensional metrology, precision bearings, and micromechanical devices.

The growing trade in military technology (as distinct from whole military systems) will accelerate the process of military industrial innovation. In a bid to secure import income, Russia is marketing a host of advanced technologies, some of them still under development. For example, it has sold advanced missile manufacturing technology to China,[138] which China may be able to use to produce and export a new generation of missiles before the end of the decade.[139] But the international military technology market extends well beyond the Russian source. In the area of ballistic missile technology alone, since the Persian Gulf War the following have been sold in the Middle East and South Asia: fuel ingredients, machine tools for production, materials for missile skins, winding cases, carbon/carbon composites for nose cones, and guidance controls such as gyroscopes and accelerometers.[140]

The most significant flow of technology—and expertise—occurs as a result of cooperative manufacturing programs between states of the developed and developing worlds. In 1960, fewer than five major conventional weapon systems were licensed for production in the developing world; throughout the 1980s, the number of systems hovered above 90—which is equal to nearly half the total number of conventional weapon systems in production globally.[141] In 1988, India, Egypt, Indonesia, South Korea, Taiwan, and Brazil were producing 43 different major weapons under international licensing agreements.[142] Figure 2–8 depicts the licensed production of major conventional weapon systems by the country receiving the license. Figure 2–9 provides a cumulative summary of such licensed military production by developing nations, and figure 2–10 describes the total worldwide production of major conventional weapon systems, including those in the developed world. Figure 2–11 attests to the diversity of licensers and producers. India has produced 21 major conventional weapon systems under license; South Korea, 16; Taiwan, 13; Brazil and Indonesia, 12 each; Australia, 10, and Singapore, 6.[143]

---

138 Fulghum, "U.S. Developing Plan to Down Cruise Missiles," p. 77.

139 Ibid.

140 Ibid.

141 Office of Technology Assessment, *Global Arms Trade,* p. 1.

142 Ibid., p. 9.

143 Ibid., p. 25.

Figure 2–8

Worldwide Licensed Production of Major Conventional Weapon Systems, by Country Receiving License, 1960–89

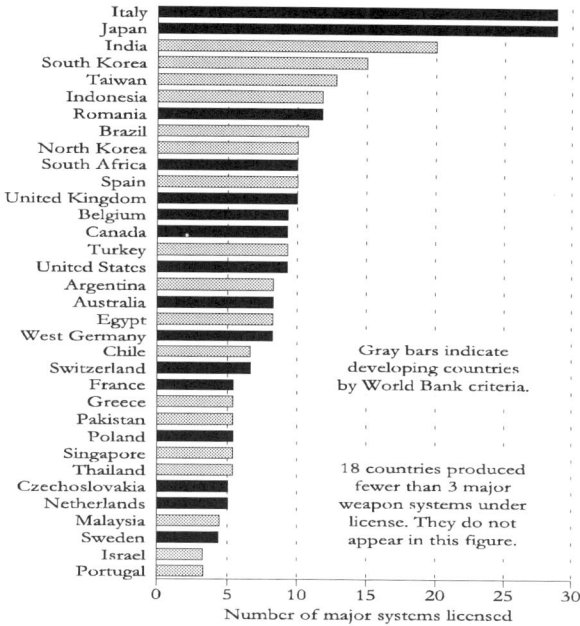

Gray bars indicate developing countries by World Bank criteria.

18 countries produced fewer than 3 major weapon systems under license. They do not appear in this figure.

Number of major systems licensed

Source: Office of Technology Assessment, from data in Stockholm International Peace Research Institute, SIPRI Yearbooks, 1970 through 1990, *World Armaments and Disarmament.* Reprinted from *Global Arms Trade*, OTA–ISC–460 (Washington, D.C.: GPO, 1991).

The level of dependence on such technology transfer is unequal in the developing world, with some countries, such as Brazil, China, and Israel, relatively less dependent today than other countries, and than they themselves were in decades past.[144] In individual weapon systems, the import content is only very rarely below 30 percent.[145] In the missile area, no Third World arms manufacturer is totally independent of foreign sources of supply; most are

---

144 C. Jesuran, ed., *Arms Production and Trade in South East Asia* (Singapore: Institute for Southeast Asian Studies, 1990), p. 161.

145 Rosh, "Third World Arms Production," p. 71.

Figure 2–9

Estimated Licensed Production of Major Conventional Weapon Systems by Developing Nations, 1960–88

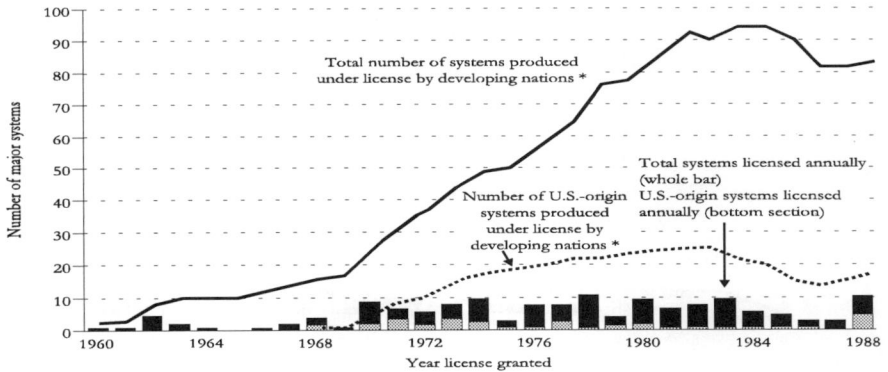

* Estimates based on the assumption that an average system is produced under license for 12 years.

Source: Office of Technology Assessment, from data in Stockholm International Peace Research Institute, SIPRI Yearbooks, 1970 through 1990, *World Armaments and Disarmament*. Reprinted from *Global Arms Trade*, OTA–ISC–460 (Washington, D.C.: GPO, 1991).

willing to rely on imported components or subsystems.[146] As Carus has pointed out, "Not all of these countries have the ability to develop all of the elements that go into the production of cruise missiles. But by relying on foreign assistance, even the countries with limited expertise might be able to build cruise missile systems."[147] Turkey and India are excellent examples of countries where the wish for greater independence in military acquisition conflicts with the reality of continued dependence in defense industries.[148]

---

146 Carus, *Cruise Missile Proliferation*, p. 34.

147 Ibid., p. 82.

148 Stockholm International Peace Research Institute, *SIPRI Yearbook 1993: World Armaments and Disarmament*, p. 532, and Eric Arnett, "Military Technology: The Case of India," in *SIPRI Yearbook 1994*, pp. 343–365.

Figure 2–10
Estimated Worldwide Licensed Production of Major Conventional Weapon Systems, 1960–88

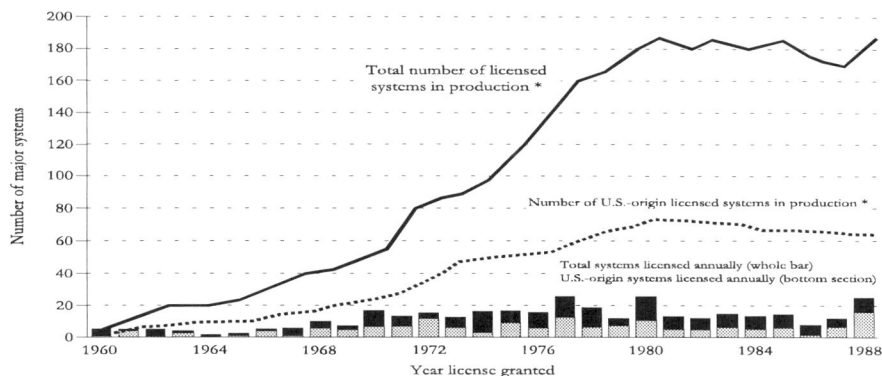

* Estimates based on the assumption that an average system is produced under license for 12 years.

Source: Office of Technology Assessment, from data in Stockholm International Peace Research Institute, SIPRI Yearbooks, 1970 through 1990, *World Armaments and Disarmament.* Reprinted from *Global Arms Trade*, OTA–ISC–460 (Washington, D.C.: GPO, 1991).

Technology dependence may well decline. With the slow diffusion of technology in the international system and the emergence of new suppliers of defense hardware, this is already happening.[149] Moreover, the technological competence of those developing countries with the most advanced capabilities is increasing as collaborative North–South endeavors focus increasingly on the earliest stages of R&D.[150] More generally, technology transfer agreements facilitate a diversification of a developing nation's defense industrial base. Figure

---

149 Carus, *Ballistic Missiles in Modern Conflict*, p. xvii.

150 "In the past 5 years, defense collaboration has moved into the early research and predevelopment stages with companies cooperating on design, fabrication, and application of advanced technologies. This approach, however, is restricted to relatively advanced arms producers." Office of Technology Assessment, *Global Arms Trade*, p. 125.

Figure 2–11

Licensed Production of European Major Conventional Weapon Systems by Developing Countries, 1960–88

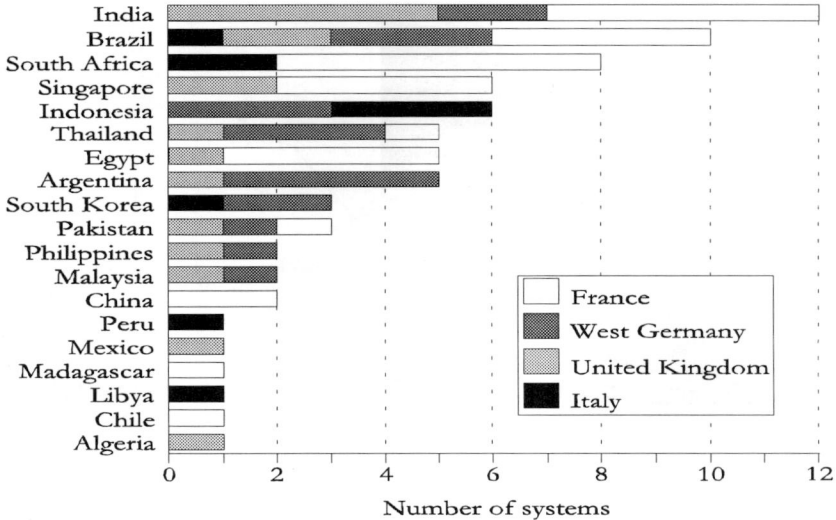

Source: Office of Technology Assessment, from data in Stockholm International Peace Research Institute, SIPRI Yearbooks, 1970 through 1990, *World Armaments and Disarmament.* Reprinted from *Global Arms Trade*, OTA–ISC–460 (Washington, D.C.: GPO, 1991).

2–12 demonstrates this point by defining 6 categories of weapons under licensed production in India.

One study assessing the arms production of 34 developing countries in the late 1970s identified 15 capable of diversified production, as opposed to simple assembly (10) or basic inability (9).[151] Eight countries—Argentina, Brazil, China, Egypt, India, Israel, South Africa, and Taiwan—have achieved the ability to produce each of the four basic types of weapon systems, air, naval, armor, and missiles.[152] In a study published in 1990, C. Jesuran stated:

---

151 Nicole Ball, *Security and Economy in the Third World* (Princeton, N.J.: Princeton University Press, 1988), p. 360.

152 Neuman, "The Arms Market," p. 511.

Figure 2–12

Indian Licensed Production of Major Conventional Weapons, by Type of Weapon, 1970–90

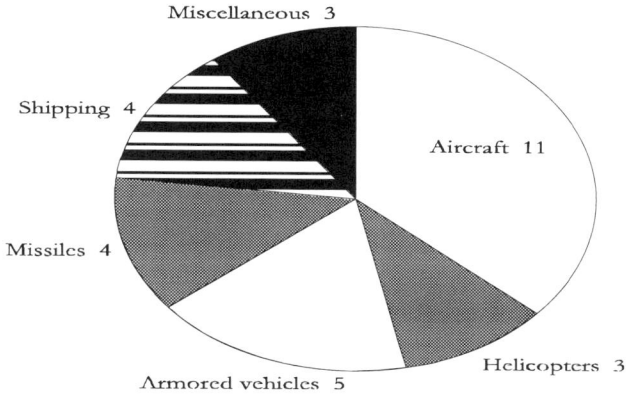

Source: Office of Technology Assessment, from data in Stockholm International Peace Research Institute, SIPRI Yearbooks, 1970 through 1990, *World Armaments and Disarmament.* Reprinted from *Global Arms Trade,* OTA–ISC–460 (Washington, D.C.: GPO, 1991).

In the early 1980s, about 15 developing countries had a reasonable volume of arms manufactures within their economies. This itself was a substantial rise from the situation about a decade back. By the late 1980s the number has risen to twenty-five countries which have progressed beyond the manufacture of small arms and have become capable of producing more sophisticated products.[153]

In this review of the quality of technology and weapons programs in the developing world, it is important to bear in mind the lessons born of Iraq's unconventional weapons programs—that second-best technology, or what Peter Zimmerman has called "bronze medal technology," may be enough to meet the demands of weapons production programs—after all, it sufficed at an earlier time in the history of the technologically advanced powers.[154]

---

153 Jesuran, *Arms Production and Trade in South East Asia,* p. 161.

154 Peter D. Zimmerman, "Proliferation: Bronze Medal Technology Is Enough," *Orbis,* Vol. 38, No. 1 (Winter 1994), pp. 67–82.

Figure 2–13
Arms Exported by Developing Nations, 1978–88

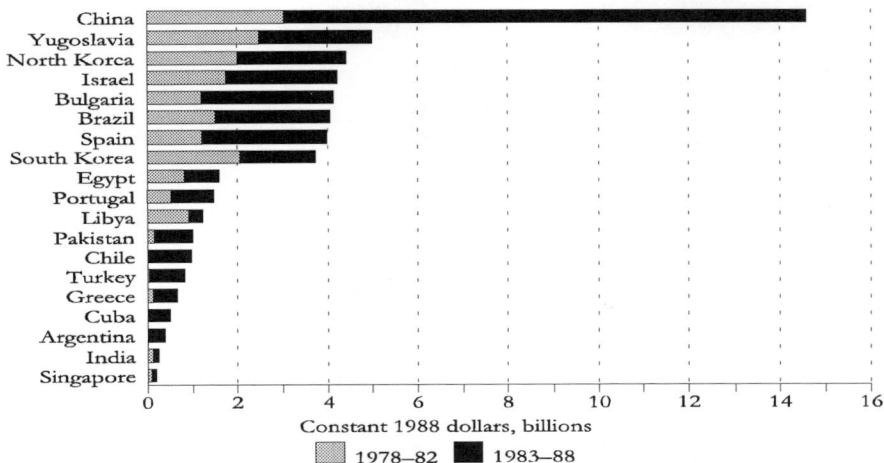

Constant 1988 dollars, billions

■ 1978–82 ■ 1983–88

Source: U.S. Arms Control and Disarmament Agency, *World Military Expenditures and Arms Transfers, 1989.* Reprinted from *Global Arms Trade,* OTA–ISC–460 (Washington, D.C.: GPO, 1991).

Developing Countries as Arms Exporters

The second basic reason for the dismissal of arms industries in the developing world as inconsequential relates to their relatively small size and minimal significance in the global arms market. This too merits a reassessment.

Over the last few decades the volume of arms exports from the developing world has grown steadily. In 1963, 8 developing countries (among the 32 states exporting arms) exported military goods worth $64 million, or a mere 0.4 percent of the total. In 1984, 14 developing countries (among 48 exporters) exported military goods worth $1.6 billion, or 4 percent of the total. Between 1978 and 1988, arms valued at nearly $50 billion were exported by developing country producers, as shown in figure 2–13.[155] In the first half of the 1980s, arms exports by developing countries grew rapidly at an average rate of 21 percent annually,

---

155 Neuman, "The Arms Market," p. 510; Michael T. Klare, "Growing Firepower in the Third World," *Bulletin of the Atomic Scientists,* May 1990, pp. 9–13; and Gupta, "Third World Militaries," pp. 57–68.

Table 2–3
Brazilian Arms Exports, 1977–88

Country	Number ordered *	Weapon system	Year ordered	Delivered *
Abu Dhabi	200	EE-9 Cascavel armored car	1977	
Algeria	2	EMB-111 marine patrol aircraft	1982	2
		EE-9 Cascave armored car	1985	
Angola	2	EMB-111 marine patrol aircraft	1988	2
Argentina	30	EMB-312 Tucano trainer	1987-88	30
Belgium	5	EMB-121 Xingu transport	1982	
Bolivia	3	HB-315B Gavalo helicopter	1984	3
		HB-315B Gavalo helicopter	1987-88	3
	40	Nelva T-25 Universal	1977	
Canada		EMB-312 Tucano trainer	1983	
Chile	2	EMB-120 Brasilia transport	1982	
	10	*Anchova*-class patrol craft	1980-81	10
	50	EE-11 Urutu armored personnel carrier	1981	50
	40	EE-17 Sucuri tank destroyer	1981	40
	6	EMB-126 Xavante transport/counterinsurgency	1978	
	20	Nelva T-25 Universal	1979	
	6	EMB-111 Bandelrante	1977	3
	10	Macharen fast patrol craft	1977	
Colombia	14	EMB-126 Xavante transport/counterinsurgency	1982	
Cyprus	120	EE-3 Jararaca scout car	1984-88	120
	120	EE-9 Cascave armored car	1984-88	120
	20	EE-9 Cascave armored car	1984	20
Ecuador	10	EMB-312 Tucano trainer	1983	
Egypt	110	EMB-312 Tucano trainer	1983	12
		(licensed production: 30 for Egypt, 80 for Iraq under a Saudi-financed, $180 million loan)	1986	48
France	41	EMB-121 Xingu transport	1981-84	8
	20	EMB-312 Tucano trainer	1988	
		(contingent order for up to 150 based on reciprocal helicopter purchase by Brazil)		
Gabon		EMB-111 marine patro aircraft	1981	1
		EE-9 Cascave armored car		6
	16	EE-11 Urutu armored personnel carrier		16
Guyana	1	EMB-110 Bandelrante transport		1
	1	Model-412 helicopter		1
	30	EE-11 Urutu armored personnel carrier		30
Honduras	12	EMB-312 Tucano trainer		12
Iraq	300	EE-3 Jararaca scout car	1984-85	300
	250	EE-9 Cascave armored car	1987-88	200
	80	EMB-312 Tucano trainer	1985	20
	200	EE-3 Jararaca scout car	1987	
	38	Astros II SS-30 multiple rocket launcher	1985-87	38
	20	Astros II SS-60 multiple rocket launcher	1981-88	20
	13	Astros II guidance and fire control system	1984-88	13
	640	SS-60 surface-to-surface missiles	1987-88	640
	150	EE-11 Urutu armored personnel carrier	1979-81	150
	150	EE-17 Sucuri tank destroyer	1979-81	250
	750	EE-9 Cascave armored car	1979-81	750
		MAS-1 Carcara air-to-surface missile	1981	
Iran	50	EMB-312 Tucano trainer	1988	
Libya	8	EMB-111 marine patro aircraft	1986	
	25	EMB-121 Xingu transport	1986	
	100	EMB-312 Tucano trainer	1986	
	100	X-2 180mm multiple rocket system	1987	50
		EE-11 Urutu armored personnel carrier	1986	
		EE-9 Cascave armored car	1986	
		EE-T1 Osorio main battle tank	1986	
	200	EE-9 Cascave armored car	1978	200
		Astros II SS-40 multiple rocket launcher	1986-88	30
		Astros II SS-60 multiple rocket launcher	1987	15
		EE-3 Jararaca scout car	1987	
	3	Astros II guidance and fire control system	1987-88	3
		(denied by Brazilian government)		
	450	SS-60 surface-to-surface missiles	1987-88	450
Madagascar		EMB-111 marine patro aircraft	1981	
Morocco	60	EE-11 Urutu armored personnel carrier	1986-87	60
		(17 on loan from Libya prior to delivery)		
Nigeria	50	EMB-312 Tucano trainer	1986	
	100	EE-9 Cascave armored car	1986	
	5	EMB-110 Bandelrante transport	1986	5

Table 2–3
Brazilian Arms Exports, 1977–88 (continued)

Country	Number ordered *	Weapon system	Year ordered	Delivered *
Paraguay	10	EMB-110 Bandelrante transport	1985	4
	2	HB-305M Esquilo helicopter (licensed from France)	1985	2
		EE-11 Urutu armored personnel carrier	1984	
		EE-9 Cascave armored car	1984	
	1	*Roranima*-class patrol craft	1985	1
	9	EMB-126 Xavante transport/counterinsurgency	1980	3
	12	Ulrapura	1979	
Portugal		EE-11 Urutu armored personnel carrier	1981	
		EE-9 Cascave armored car	1981	
Qatar	20	EE-9 Cascave armored car	1976-77	10
Saudi Arabia		EE-9 Cascave armored car	1984	
	30	EE-11 Urutu armored personnel carrier	1985	30
	[2,000]	EE-72 Osorio main battle tank	1985	(negotiating)
		Astros II SS-30 multiple rocket launcher	1988	10
		Astros II SS-40 multiple rocket launcher	1987-88	30
		Astros II guidance and fire control system	1987-88	4
Sudan	6	EMB-110 Bandelrante transport	1977	3
Suriname		EE-11 Urutu armored personnel carrier	1984	10
Thailand	56	EE-9 Cascave armored car	1981	56
Tunisia		EE-3 Jararaca scout car	1984	
United Arab Emirates		EE-11 Urutu armored personnel carrier	1985	30
United Kingdom	130	EMB-312 Tucano trainer	1985	(licensed production)
Upper Volta	1	EMB-110 Bandelrante transport	1981	1
Venezuela	30	EMB-312 Tucano trainer	1986-87	30
	30	EE-11 Urutu armored personnel carrier	1984	30
		EE-3 Jararaca scout car	1984	
	100	EE-11 Urutu armored personnel carrier	1988	
		EMB-312 Tucano trainer	1988	1
Zimbabwe	90	EE-9 Cascave armored car	1983	10

* Blanks indicate data not publicly available.

Source: Office of Technology Assessment, from data in Stockholm International Peace Research Institute, SIPRI Yearbooks, 1970 through 1990, *World Armaments and Disarmament.* Reprintedfrom *Global Arms Trade*, OTA–ISC–460 (Washington, D.C.: GPO, 1991).

reaching a peak of $7 billion in 1984. By 1985 these countries came to account for from 5 to 9 percent of the world's total arms exports.[156]

Of course, aggregate statistical data can mislead, by obscuring the role of sometimes dominant exporters. In the first half of the 1980s, Brazil and India accounted for about 80 percent of the Third World's exports of domestically produced major weapons.[157] Israel is also an important exporter. Tables 2–3 and 2–4 describe the arms exports of Brazil and Israel, respectively. Noteworthy in table 2–4 is the fact that Israel has licensed production of its own military systems by three other countries: the United States, South Africa, Taiwan. China has been particularly dominant over time. Between 1963 and 1986, the exports of developing countries other than China expanded by a factor of 13, while China's

---

156 Sanders, *Arms Industries*, p. 9.

157 Ibid., p. 10.

Table 2–4
Selected Arms Orders, Deliveries, and Licensed Production of Israeli Weapon Systems, 1986–88

Recipient	Number ordered*	Weapon name	Type	Year ordered	Year delivered	Number*
United States	37	Kfir-C1	Fighter	1984–86	1985–87	25
	12	Popeye	Antiship missile	1986	1987	6
	114	Have Nap	Antitank guided missile	1986–88	1987–88	14
Argentina	1	B-707-320C	Transport	1985	1987	1
	120	Shafir	Air-to-air missile	1986	1988	60
Chile	13	Kfir-C7	Fighter	1988		
	30	M-4 Sherman	Main battle tank	1987	1987	30
Colombia	14	Kfir-C2	Fighter	1981		
Ecuador	12	Kfir-C7	Fighter	1986	1986–87	12
	2	Barak launcher	Ship-to-air missile launcher	1984		
	16	Barak	Ship-to-air/surface-to-air point defense missile	1984		
	96	Shafir-2	Air-to-air missile	1986	1987	96
Paraguay		IAI-201 Arava	Transport	1985		
Lebanon	36	BTR-60P	Armored personnel carrier	1987	1987	18
	18	M-1944 100mm	Towed gun	1987	1987	18
	18	T-54	Main battle tank	1987	1987	18
Liberia	3	IAI-201 Arava	Transport	1984		
Cameroon	4	IAI-202 Arava	Transport	1985	1985	3
	10	Kfir-C7	Fighter	1985		
Sri Lanka	18	Dvora class	Fast attack craft	1985–87	1987–88	12
China		Mapats	Portable antitank missile	1986		
Thailand	12	Barlel-2	Ship-to-ship missile	1987	1988	12
Fiji	3	IAI-202 Arava	Transport	1986		1
Papua New Guinea	3	IAI-201 Arava	Transport		1985	2

Licensed production of Israeli weapon systems

Licensee	Number ordered	Weapon name	Type	Year ordered	Year delivered	Number
United States		EL/2106	Point defense radar	1983		
		Popeye	Antiship missile	1987		
South Africa	96	Gabriel-2	Ship-to-ship/surface-to-ship missile	1984	1986–88	36
	12	Reshef class	Fast attack craft	1974	1978–88	9
Taiwan		Gabriel	Ship-to-ship/surface-to-ship missile launcher	1978	1980–88	48
		Gabriel-2	Ship-to-ship/surface-to-ship missile	1978	1980–88	375

* Blanks indicate data not publicly available.

Source: Office of Technology Assessment, from data in Stockholm International Peace Research Institute, SIPRI Yearbooks, 1986 through 1989, *World Armaments and Disarmament.* Reprinted from *Global Arms Trade,* OTA–ISC–460 (Washington, D.C.: GPO, 1991).

increased by a factor of 60.[158] It became the fourth largest exporter of arms to the Third World in the 1980s. Among those receiving Chinese-manufactured weapons were Iran, Iraq, Pakistan, Saudi Arabia, Sri Lanka, Syria, Thailand, Myanmar, and Algeria.[159] From 1975 to its peak in 1988, Chinese arms exports to

---

158 Neuman, "The Arms Market," p. 511.

159 Gill, *Chinese Arms Transfers,* pp. 3-4. "Over the years since 1949, China has provided different forms of military transfers—training, advisers, military-related construction projects, small

Table 2–5

Values of Exports of Major Conventional Weapons by the 68 Exporting Countries, 1981–90 ★

Figures are SIPRI trend-indicator values, as expressed in U.S. $m., at constant (1985) prices

Rank	Exporter	1981	1982	1983	1984	1985	1986	1987	1988	1989	1990	Total
1	USSR	12,940	11,459	11,476	11,056	13,458	14,731	14,916	12,559	12,220	6,397	121,212
2	USA	12,265	12,523	12,174	10,722	8,943	10,304	12,596	10,503	11,749	9,528	111,307
3	France	4,319	3,808	3,685	3,724	3,970	4,096	3,011	2,300	2,577	1,821	33,311
4	UK	1,300	1,830	1,090	1,825	1,847	1,500	1,817	1,401	1,800	1,236	15,644
5	China	292	822	1,200	1,530	1,352	1,463	2,553	1,868	874	1,003	12,957
6	FRG	1,285	1,021	1,781	2,610	1,026	1,120	676	1,270	713	959	12,460
7	Italy	1,394	1,361	1,053	897	647	457	389	471	169	96	6,933
8	Czechoslovakia	583	664	644	634	497	497	570	548	437	355	5,429
9	Netherlands	533	518	87	98	88	240	265	532	637	152	3,151
10	Spain	97	360	589	475	139	172	139	199	506	74	2,750
11	Brazil	273	229	362	301	188	150	506	371	185	57	2,622
12	Israel	252	366	369	261	222	269	340	127	318	39	2,563
13	Sweden	130	95	30	114	163	324	489	575	311	115	2,346
14	Canada	95	215	209	107	132	317	265	106	54	60	1,560
15	Egypt	109	61	321	231	124	159	194	216	65	33	1,513
16	Poland	327	181	142	97	158	149	92	92	92	92	1,424
17	Switzerland	128	78	91	110	35	51	78	57	161	238	1,027
18	Austria	101	48	175	42	234	88	58	38	49	20	853
19	Libya	69	214	117	37	26	31	79	48	0	24	645
20	Romania	45	91	127	139	33	8	12	13	102	59	629
21	Norway	298	31	27	0	36	9	43	17	81	12	552
22	Korea, N.	10	34	57	36	95	48	103	128	11	11	531
23	Denmark	43	8	189	49	0	0	123	25	0	75	513
24	Korea, S.	94	47	52	96	80	79	0	40	14	0	501
25	Jordan	12	42	214	128	0	20	12	4	45	0	476
26	S. Africa	67	22	17	17	41	40	61	51	0	4	319
27	Australia	5	10	23	59	25	4	17	7	4	92	247
28	Iraq	0	0	66	0	0	0	2	128	22	0	218
29	Belgium	13	78	33	32	32	23	0	6	0	0	215
30	Yugoslavia	100	18	0	60	10	0	2	3	0	12	205
31	Saudi Arabia	18	0	0	2	0	43	125	0	0	0	188
32	Syria	0	92	17	1	16	18	0	8	8	0	159
33	Singapore	10	3	1	48	44	12	35	0	4	0	158
34	GDR	14	0	0	0	0	0	0	0	120	0	134
35	Vietnam	0	0	0	0	0	0	40	0	68	0	108
36	Peru	0	32	0	0	0	0	52	10	0	0	94
37	Turkey	8	42	42	0	0	0	0	0	0	0	92
38	Portugal	0	0	1	0	0	0	19	0	67	0	88
39	Pakistan	0	0	0	0	0	0	3	0	0	75	78
40	Indonesia	0	6	4	0	4	2	0	22	22	14	73
41	Iran	55	6	6	0	0	0	0	1	0	0	68
42	Japan	0	7	20	11	11	6	0	0	0	0	55
43	Bulgaria	0	0	4	8	8	8	8	8	8	0	55
44	Argentina	32	2	0	0	0	0	2	3	0	10	48
45	Chad	0	0	0	0	0	0	46	0	0	0	46

Table 2–5
Values of Exports of Major Conventional Weapons by the 68 Exporting Countries, 1981–90 (continued) *

Rank	Exporter	1981	1982	1983	1984	1985	1986	1987	1988	1989	1990	Total
46	Kuwait	0	0	0	36	0	6	0	0	0	0	42
47	Nigeria	0	0	0	5	24	0	0	0	7	4	40
48	Hungary	37	0	0	0	0	0	0	0	0	0	37
49	India	0	2	0	17	0	1	0	1	6	9	36
50	Ethiopia	0	0	0	22	0	0	6	2	0	0	31
51	Chile	1	0	1	0	2	3	2	17	1	0	28
52	Angola	0	0	0	0	0	0	12	5	0	0	17
53	UAE	0	0	14	0	0	0	0	0	0	2	16
54	New Zealand	1	2	0	7	5	0	0	0	0	0	14
55	Cuba	0	12	0	0	0	0	0	0	1	0	13
56	Iceland	0	0	0	12	0	0	0	0	0	0	12
57	Algeria	8	0	0	2	0	0	0	0	0	0	10
58	Malaysia	0	7	0	0	0	0	1	0	0	0	9
59	Greece	0	0	0	0	0	0	0	0	6	0	6
60	Finland	0	0	0	0	0	0	6	0	0	0	6
61	Afghanistan	0	0	0	0	0	0	5	0	0	0	5
62	Oman	0	0	0	0	0	4	0	0	0	0	4
63	Nicaragua	0	0	0	0	0	0	1	0	0	2	3
64	Ireland	3	0	0	0	0	0	0	0	0	0	3
65	Yemen, N.	0	0	0	0	0	2	0	0	0	0	2
66	Zambia	0	0	0	0	0	0	0	0	0	2	2
67	Philippines	0	0	0	0	0	1	0	0	0	0	1
68	Bolivia	0	0	0	0	0	0	1	0	0	0	1

* The figures for 1990 in this table may differ from those that appear in the SIPRI Yearbook 1991: *World Armaments and Disarmament* (Oxford: Oxford University Press, 1991), table 7.1, p. 198, since SIPRI regularly updates these data (see also SIPRI Yearbook 1992). Figures in the last column and last row may not add up to totals due to rounding.

Source: Reprinted by permission from Ian Anthony, ed., *Arms Export Regulations* (Oxford: Oxford University Press for SIPRI, 1991).

the Third World multiplied by 480 percent, a growth rate far outpacing that of any other major supplier.[160]

To date, the group of producers in the developing world has not emerged as a significant source of supply when measured against the traditional producers. Table 2–5 displays the values of exports of major conventional weapons by all 68 exporting countries in the decade of the 1980s.[161] Figure 2–13 displays the value

---

arms, licensed production agreements, and major conventional weapons exports—to no fewer than 29 armed movements and 40 countries....As for major conventional weapons exported by China between 1950 and 1990, 14 countries imported Chinese missiles, 25 countries received land armaments (artillery and armor) from the PRC, 23 countries imported Chinese naval vessels, and 20 countries took in PRC military aircraft" (pp. 40–41).

160 Ibid., p. 204.

161 Complementary data can be found in *SIPRI Yearbook 1993*, p. 477.

of exports by developing countries through 1992. Of course, not all producers of military hardware in the developing world have made exports a top priority. India, for example, has given primary emphasis to production for its own needs in a bid for self-reliance.[162]

But the market influence of developing country producers cannot be ignored. Its effects are being felt powerfully in two ways.

First, the new suppliers have been particularly important in niche markets, especially when they have been willing to export items and technologies to states denied access to such trade by the traditional suppliers of military products. China and North Korea have made significant inroads in the arms market of the Middle East, supplying missiles and unconventional weapons technologies.[163] China has supplied missiles and missile technology to nine countries and two insurgent groups, and nuclear-related technology to Algeria, Argentina, Brazil, India, Iran, Iraq, Pakistan, and South Korea.[164] It is now offering an advanced fuel air explosive to international buyers.[165] Iran's arms purchases since 1990 from just three suppliers—China, North Korea, and Russia—may total as much as $12 billion.[166] Israel reportedly has also sold weapons and technology to China.[167] More than 50 states supplied weapons, parts, or military technologies to both sides in the Iran–Iraq War.[168]

Second, trade among developing countries in arms has increased substantially, altering the traditional flow of military hardware from the developed to the developing world. "In 1963, South–South trade was a mere $4 million or 0.3

---

162 Jones and Hildreth, *Emerging Powers*, p. 414.

163 Joseph S. Bermudez, Jr., *Proliferation for Profit: North Korea in the Middle East*, Research Memorandum No. 27 (Washington, D.C.: The Washington Institute, July 1994).

164 Gill, *Chinese Arms Transfers*, pp. 3–4.

165 Richard A. Bitzinger, "Arms to Go: Chinese Arms Sales to the Third World," *International Security*, Vol. 17, No. 2 (Fall 1992), pp. 84–111. Lewis and Silverberg, "Smaller Nations Emerge as Active Market Forces," pp. 12, 16; and David Silverberg, "China Firm Takes Wraps Off New Fuel Air Bomb," *Defense News*, June 24, 1991.

166 Fulghum, "U.S. Developing Plan to Down Cruise Missiles," p. 79.

167 Michael R. Gordon, "Israel Sells Arms to China, U.S. Says," *New York Times*, October 13, 1993, p. 5.

168 Anthony Cordesman, *The Impact of Arms Transfers on the Iran/Iraq War* (London: Royal United Services Institute, 1987), p. 14.

percent of exports to the Third World; by 1986 it had risen to about $2.0 billion—or almost 8 percent."[169] In 1990, 33 states exported arms to the developing world, of which 14 were themselves in the developing world.[170] Some of these trade relationships developed even before the defense industrial bas: in the area of ballistic missiles, for example, a trade emerged has in the last couple of decades in Soviet-built and supplied SCUD missiles.[171] The role of new South–South trade patterns is especially pronounced in the cruise missile market. Israel, for example, has sold its Gabriel missile to Argentina, Malaysia, and Singapore.[172] According to Carus, "Although at least five countries in the Third World are known to have indigenous programs, many more rely on anti-ship cruise missiles acquired from other Third World countries."[173]

Arguably, there is a third market effect. By closing off ever larger portions of the international weapons market, defense industries in the developing world—especially those meeting the needs of large indigenous markets, as in China and India—deprive arms producers in the developed world of the economies of scale that might help them to survive the reductions in defense investment wrought by the end of the Cold War.

Defense industrial contacts between states of the developing world are not limited to exports between them. Collaboration on research, development, and production is also in evidence, as a way to reduce costs and to avoid restrictions on technology transfer or prohibitions on certain types of weapons.[174] In a related example, India and China may pool their talents in the commercial space domain.[175]

Looking to the future, defense industrial competence in the developing world a decade hence is difficult to predict. The end of the 1980s brought a downturn in some defense industries in the developing world, partly because of the end of the

---

169 Neuman, "The Arms Market," p. 511.

170 Gill, *Chinese Arms Transfers*, p. 29.

171 Carus, *Ballistic Missiles in Modern Conflict*, p. 17.

172 Silverberg, "Third World Missiles Sales Will Keep Seas Hazardous," pp. 8, 16.

173 Carus, *Cruise Missile Proliferation*, pp. 2–3.

174 Amit Gupta concludes that "such collaboration is likely to increase in the 1990s." Gupta, "Third World Militaries," p. 65. See also Office of Technology Assessment, *Global Arms Trade*, p. 26.

175 "New Cheapsat Source?" *Aviation Week & Space Technology*, January 4, 1993, p. 15.

Iran–Iraq War and partly because of the end of Cold War regional standoffs, although there is evidence to suggest at least a "partial rehabilitation" of production in those defense industries that rose and fell over the last decade.[176] The economic and societal underpinnings of these industries are discussed in greater detail in the following chapter. But it is fairly safe to predict that some of these industries will diversify and slowly increase their technical sophistication and that of their products, thanks to the ongoing diffusion of dual-use technologies in a global economy that, in its high-technology sectors at least, is undergoing a steady integration.

The Larger Picture

What does this technical survey reveal about the proliferation subject in the 1990s? It points to five conclusions.

First and most obviously, nuclear weapons can no longer be the sole focus of interest. In the 1980s chemical weapons emerged as weapons of concern within a number of regions and at the global level. Biological weapons are emerging as a new focal point in the 1990s. Medium- and long-range delivery systems are also spreading; although ballistic missile proliferation has attracted considerable attention, the spread of cruise missiles and advanced aircraft is more extensive. Advanced conventional warfare systems are widely traded on an international arms market that has been revolutionized over the last decade.

What are the implications of this first conclusion? At the very least, the multifaceted nature of proliferation raises questions about the wisdom of looking at it through just one dimension—the nuclear. New conceptual approaches are necessary. Distinctive new features of the proliferation problem require a familiarity with the concept of opaque proliferation, for example. Differences between military industrial modernization and arms racing require more study.

Second, the nuclear proliferation subject is itself changing. The problem of "instant proliferation" has gained dramatic new prominence with the breakup of the Soviet Union. The increasing prominence on the nuclear suspect list of states

---

176 Don Podesta, "Latin Weapons Industries Slip in Post-Cold War Chill," *Washington Post*, June 25, 1993, pp. A–27, 28.

with avowed hegemonic aspirations (e.g., Iran) and run by authoritarian if not also megalomaniacal leaders (e.g., North Korea) must change thinking about the potential consequences of nuclear proliferation. Perhaps the most striking change in the nuclear proliferation subject is the growing gap between the number of states capable of constructing a nuclear arsenal and those choosing to do so.

The changing nuclear problem illustrates the fragility of the current distribution of nuclear-weapon states in the international system. But it is also a direct challenge to the expectation of a broader proliferation of nuclear weapons in this uncertain era.

Third, the weapons themselves are in some sense merely the tip of a very large iceberg. The globalization of the industrial revolution and of the trading system has greatly accelerated the processes of technology diffusion, often in synergistic fashion. Dual-use technologies, that is, those with both civilian and military applications, are widely available today. So too are enabling technologies that facilitate the production, integration, and use of weaponry. The expertise to apply these technologies is spreading along with the technologies themselves. The defense industrial base to utilize this technology and expertise has begun to appear in many regions of the world in the last two decades. Indeed, the subsurface body of this iceberg barely existed two decades ago.

These new features of the proliferation problem require increasing attention to weapons capabilities in addition to the weapons themselves. They also require a new appreciation of the role of commercial firms as conduits of technology, in addition to states. They also illustrate movement toward an international system in which many states, whether great, middling, or small, must be considered "virtual weapon states" because of their ability to build weapons of strategic consequence by means of their own industrial infrastructure and by employing expertise and materials available either domestically or on an international market no longer dominated by a few suppliers. This strikes at the fundamental policy assumption that strategies of denial can prevent countries with the will to acquire advanced military capability from doing so. Such an international system will be marked by a steady accretion of military competence, but it will also be ripe for a burst of rapid proliferation in response to a catalytic event.

Fourth, this survey illustrates the risk of trivializing the proliferation problem by broadening its purview to cover everything of any potential military concern.[177] Few of the weapons and technologies surveyed here can be expected to have an impact on the international political system akin to that of the nuclear domain. Acknowledging this fact, the rest of the subject cannot be deemed inconsequential. This survey identifies many weapons and technologies that offer states military and political leverage. Leveraging technologies create military capabilities of strategic consequence, which is to say capabilities that operate fundamentally on the choices leaders of targeted nations perceive themselves to have by threatening those leaders with decisive defeat on the battlefield or with massively destructive attack on their population centers.

The inherited analytical distinction between unconventional and conventional weapons muddies this view of leveraging capabilities. Some unconventional weapons may not fall into this category—that is, chemical or biological weapons that have not been weaponized in ways that make them usable as weapons of mass destruction. Some conventional capabilities may have strategic consequences. This is obviously the case when they can be used to eliminate or defeat an adversary. But they also create significant leverage when one state enjoys a substantial improvement in its conventional warfare capabilities unmatched by its competitor(s) or when they can be exploited politically to compel or deter another state from pursuing its preferred course of action in war or diplomacy. Selective use of one or two advanced assets in an otherwise unsophisticated force structure can magnify capabilities, a fact well illustrated by the significant harassment of British naval forces by Argentina's one advanced submarine during the Falklands/Malvinas conflict.[178]

Many of these weapons and technologies offering high leverage are increasingly available indigenously or in markets outside the developed world. In regions of the developing world where conflict is sharp there is a noteworthy improvement in conventional capabilities brought about by the introduction of such high-leverage assets as unconventional weapons, advanced naval systems, cruise missiles, and air defenses. In only a few countries, such as China, India, and

---

177 Henry D. Sokolski, "Nonapocalyptic Proliferation: A New Strategic Threat?" *The Washington Quarterly*, Vol. 17, No. 2 (Spring 1994), pp. 115–128.

178 Max Hastings and Simon Jenkins, *The Battle for the Falklands* (New York, N.Y.: W. W. Norton and Co., 1983), p. 147. Noteworthy also was the concern within the U.S. security community caused by Iran's acquisition in 1992 of a single Russian-made conventional submarine, which underscored the U.S. Navy's vulnerability to shallow-water operations. See Nora Boustany, "Iran Getting Russian Submarine," *Washington Post*, October 2, 1992, p. A–40.

Israel, have these improvements been sought across the board. In most countries it is the addition of a few key capabilities that is influencing perceptions of power. Iran's acquisition of a Russian advanced conventional submarine, Pakistan's acquisition of F–16 aircraft, Libya's acquisition of sophisticated anti-aircraft missiles, and North Korea's production of intermediate-range ballistic missiles illustrate the selective use of one dominant conventional warfare system, perhaps synergistically with unconventional weaponry, to force opponents to rethink the consequences of confrontation.

The implications of this fourth conclusion are straightforward. An international system in which high leverage military assets have proliferated, only some of which offer the prospect of mass destruction, is an international system unlike any known heretofore. Nuclear weapons may remain the primary currency of hard power, but there are many new coins of the realm. Looked at in gross measures of military capability, the advanced powers continue to enjoy a measure of superiority in the form of large and diverse arsenals and a substantial production base, especially given the extent to which defense production today transcends borders among the developed world. But looked at in terms of trends, the existing military assets of the advanced powers are being pruned back substantially, in both the unconventional and conventional weapons domains, in contrast to the slow but steady accretion of military competence in the developing world.

Lastly, proliferation is best understood as a process rather than as an end state. Weapons and weapon systems emerge only as the result of development processes. There are many steps in the proliferation ladder, steps from one capability to another even within particular weapons areas. There are critical thresholds related to quality and quantity of weapons that determine the military and political utility of weapons. Proliferation occurs as a result of a confluence of economic, political, military, and international factors and is the result of a decision-making process usually involving a group of people seeking to bring together the necessary expertise, technology, military organization, and financing.

The fact that so many of the production and development programs of proliferation concern will reach significant thresholds over the next decade means that this same period will be one of critical policy importance. Many states with militarily relevant R&D programs are continuing their work with a wait-and-see posture, leaving evaluation of the merits of crossing key thresholds to a later date. If a decade or so hence a number of large-scale arms races in the conventional and unconventional domains in many regions in conflict emerge, the world is likely to witness a diffusion of military capability aptly characterized by the term proliferation—as in an abrupt, wildfire-like dispersal—rather than the more benign pattern of accretion to which, so far at least, the term has somewhat inaccurately been applied.

The larger picture, then, that emerges from this survey depicts the emergence of a tier of states technically empowered to build and use high-leverage military instruments, if they choose to do so. If the Iklé–Wohlstetter estimate is correct, this tier numbers about three dozen states beyond the established nuclear powers. The number is smaller if one factors in the ability to produce long-range delivery systems, such as missiles. But the number is considerably larger if one factors in the capability to produce militarily significant quantities of chemical and biological weapons. The emergence of a tier of states technically capable of producing high-leverage weapons is unprecedented in international affairs. Its emergence is coterminous with the end of the Cold War. The intersection of these two processes constitutes a moment in world affairs that is unique.

Chapter 3

The Politics and Economics of Proliferation

HOW THE NEW tier of technically empowered states responds to the new circumstances of the 1990s and beyond is a question of central importance for the future of the international system. Will they opt to exploit their weapons potential to buttress themselves in an uncertain world? Or will they eschew the weapons option and turn their technical talents to non-military purposes? Answers to these questions will help to reveal the essential political dynamics of proliferation and to predict the future rate and character of proliferation as well as lay the groundwork for the consideration in chapter 4 of proliferation's impact on the interstate system. If states in this tier can be kept firmly involved in the international effort to prevent the militarization of conflicts, to control armaments, and to promote the cooperative resolution of common problems, a durable world order appears likely. But if they drift away from these efforts, the consequences could be profound.

This chapter assesses the likely future orientation of this new tier of states toward their weapons capacity. It reviews multiple military, political, and economic factors that are having a significant impact on the actions of these states and the thinking of their leaders.

The Gloomy Prognosis

The case that technical capability will lead sooner or later to military prowess is not difficult to make. The argument has three constituent parts derived from state behavior in an anarchical system, the end of the Cold War, and the declining barriers to proliferation.

State Behavior in an Anarchical System

The history of the nineteenth and twentieth centuries is laden with examples of state power and especially military power that have developed along with industrial might. States with economic and geopolitical weight have usually deployed the most powerful military capabilities within their reach—the exceptions being contemporary Germany and Japan. Such behavior is predicted and explained by the realist school of international relations, as noted earlier, which emphasizes the anarchical nature of the international system and the principle of self-help that guides states in securing their own interests. This perspective establishes the expectation that states—especially aspiring great powers—will do what they can with all forms of power, hard and soft, to increase their influence and weight in an unstable international system.

In such a system, states are motivated to acquire high-leverage military capabilities for a variety of reasons. Six are discussed here and analyzed for their likely impact in the decade ahead: deterrence, aggression, coercion, status, regime survival, and self defense.

Deterrence serves as a central driving force in the decisions of states to acquire weapons. Weapons programs are intended to signal to a potential military competitor or competitors that any aggression will be met with a response that will deny the aggression any success and/or impose unacceptable punishment on the aggressor(s). The specific motives of states pursuing deterrence vary considerably.

Many states that import weapons in significant quantities or have made a major effort in recent decades to produce their own weapons have in recent times been at war.[1] K. Subrahmanyam has pointed out that nearly 160 of the 170

---

1   As Robert S. McNamara has noted, "Of the top 15 Third World arms importers, who together account for about three-quarters of the arms imported by the Third World, 13 have been party to conflicts of many years' duration. Iran and Iraq were at war from 1980 to 1988. Egypt, Syria, and Israel have all been involved in the Middle East conflict. Saudi Arabia has believed itself threatened by other regional powers, notably Iran and Iraq. Algeria has been involved in disputes with neighboring Morocco and Libya. Ethiopia, Afghanistan, and Angola have conducted civil wars, whereas Vietnam, Libya, Pakistan, and India are parties to long-standing regional disputes." McNamara, "Slowing Third World Militarization," *Issues in Science and Technology*, Vol. 9, No. 3 (Spring 1993), pp. 37–38. See Ralph Sanders, *Arms Industries: New Suppliers and Regional Security* (Washington, D.C.: National Defense

interstate wars that have occurred since 1945 have been in the developing world; he observes further that:

> It is difficult to maintain that arms acquisitions by these countries are for prestige purposes and are not directly related to the security threats they actually face...[they] have security problems arising out of either direct confrontation with the great powers of the world...or interaction with great-power interplay and the local conflict situations....In the Western strategic literature there is a trend to underestimate the sense of insecurity of developing nations which have been involved in wars in the recent period, while accepting the sense of insecurity among the rival blocs of industrialized nations which have not had a war for more than 40 years and the leaders of which have not fought a war in all of history except for a minor clash in 1918.[2]

Some of these countries face a tangible threat to their very existence; Israel and Pakistan are examples of states whose nuclear weapons programs are tied inextricably to the belief that their national survival requires them. For such states, a reliable source of supply of weapons may be of paramount concern to long-term deterrence strategies. The major weapons exporters have been fickle over the years, sometimes imposing embargoes (e.g., against Turkey after its invasion of Cyprus in 1973) or otherwise being unable for domestic political reasons to sustain supplies (as in the case of U.S. sales to Taiwan). The weakening of security commitments or guarantees by outside powers has been a stimulant as well. Israel and South Korea both embarked on weapons programs as a result of doubts about the reliability of the U.S. commitment; Australia, Singapore, Indonesia, and Taiwan have at different times pursued weapons development programs in response to British and later U.S. withdrawal from the region.[3]

University, 1990), p. 11.

2   K. Subrahmanyam, "Third World Arms Control in a Hegemonistic World," in Thomas Ohlson, ed., *Arms Transfer Limitations and Third World Security* (Oxford: Oxford University Press for the Stockholm International Peace Research Institute, 1988), p. 34.

3   U.S. Congress, Office of Technology Assessment, *Global Arms Trade: Commerce in Advanced Military Technology and Weapons*, OTA–ISC–460 (Washington, D.C.: GPO, June 1991), p. 126.

Some arsenals may be intended to provide extended deterrence, whether in the classic sense of extending a guarantee to a far-flung ally, or in the sense of seeking to prevent the projection of power into the region by the UN, United States, or another state by raising the cost of doing so if not actually defeating such use of force. Such arsenals may also have an intermediate deterrence role in instances short of all-out war. For example, they may be intended to deter preemptive strikes, such as those conducted by Israel on the nascent nuclear capabilities of Iraq at Osirak. Or they may be intended to deter escalation in time of war, even if they are unlikely to determine its final outcome (Egyptian military leaders, for example, may value their alleged chemical weapons as a way to make war more costly for Israel even if these weapons are not equal in deterrence or military value to Israel's alleged nuclear weapons).

This points to another type of deterrence—deterrence in kind, whereby chemical weapons are built to deter chemical attack by another state, or nuclear weapons to deter nuclear attack, and soon. For example, the alleged chemical arsenals of Israel, China, and Iran were probably acquired to deter chemical attack by a regional adversary. Alternatively, weapons of one kind may be intended to deter attack with other weapons of another that are deemed threatening or militarily significant. For example, the alleged biological weapons of Syria are probably intended in part to deter Israeli nuclear escalation, and the alleged chemical programs of North Korea, Vietnam, and Taiwan could be intended to deter the use of conventional capabilities by neighboring powers.[4]

Strategic purposes related to deterrence are not, of course, something that can be pursued in isolation—they are by definition a function of the intentions and capabilities of a potential military opponent. Thus decisions made about fashioning a military instrument of security policy must be made with the dictates of both defense and deterrence in mind. As one analyst has described it: "Deterrence refers to policies designed to discourage the enemy from taking military action by raising the cost so it outweighs the prospective gain. Defense policies are designed to reduce one's own costs and risks in the event deterrence fails."[5]

---

4   This discussion of strategic purposes draws heavily on Brad Roberts, *Chemical Disarmament and International Security*, Adelphi Paper No. 267 (London: Brassey's for the International Institute for Strategic Studies, 1992).

The interactions between and among states making choices about the most effective ingredients of deterrence produce a degree of decision-making and strategic complexity well beyond what the proponents of simple military strength generally anticipate. As the United States discovered in trying to maintain extended deterrence in Europe, those one seeks to deter sometimes respond to the military programs intended to deter them with military programs of their own that may negate the deterrence benefits of such defensive preparations while also deepening fears of war and aggression. (This is the classic security dilemma identified in scholarly literature.) Thus preserving a threat to use military force on behalf of the alliance that was also credible in the face of threats to the United States required not just more powerful weaponry but also force structure modifications and political action to sustain alliance cohesion. Striving for deterrence and achieving it are two different matters when the opponent is capable of technological and force structure advances of its own. The goal of recovering or sustaining a technological edge becomes a primary motive, sometimes imbuing the competitive acquisition of armaments with a momentum of its own.[6] These interactions may themselves create new risks and threats beyond those for which military power was being marshaled in the first place. Indeed, the perceived political or military value of weapons, especially unconventional ones, "may be offset by the costs of such a policy, including the risks of additional proliferation in the region, the escalated defense burden, the military disutility of such weapons under many conditions, and the reactions of the major powers."[7] This factor, explored in more detail in the following chapter,

---

5 Stephanie G. Neuman, "Defense Planning in Less Industrialized States: An Organizing Framework," in Neuman, ed., *Defense Planning in Less-Industrialized States: The Middle East and South Asia* (Lexington, Mass.: Lexington Books, 1984), p. 8. Neuman cites Glenn Snyder's formulation: "Deterrence works on the enemy's intentions; the deterrent value of military forces is their effect in reducing the likelihood of enemy military moves. Defense reduces the enemy's capability to damage or deprive us." Snyder, *Deterrence and Defense: Toward a Theory of National Security* (Princeton, N.J.: Princeton University Press, 1961), pp. 3–4.

6 W. Seth Carus has observed that missile proliferation has been driven in part by the desire of states to restore effectiveness of strike capabilities in the face of sophisticated air defenses. Carus, *Cruise Missile Proliferation in the 1990s* (New York, N.Y.: Praeger for the Center for Strategic and International Studies, 1992), p. 45.

7 Rodney W. Jones and Steven A. Hildreth, *Modern Weapons and Third World Powers*, Significant Issues Series, Vol. VI, No. 4 (Boulder, Colo.: Westview Press with the Center for

helps to account for why the near-nuclear powers have not opted for open deployment.

In the decade ahead these interactive factors may stimulate not just further weapons proliferation but a variety of destabilizing effects, making states seeking weapons even less secure, as discussed in chapter 4. This is the classic security dilemma identified in international relations theory. The prevalence of war in the international system suggests that the exigencies of deterrence will not soon disappear. The large number of ongoing civil wars suggests that such weakened states may also have to fend off neighbors seeking to exploit the situation to gain prized territories or to defeat hated enemies. Doubts about supplier predictability also appear to be growing: "Many Third World countries have come to believe that the West, and especially the United States, has not been a reliable and consistent arms supplier."[8] Even countries like Israel and Egypt, which are inclined to expect a stable defense supply relationship with the United States may well doubt the capacity of the U.S. defense industrial base to successfully weather the traumas induced by shrinking post–Cold War budgets. The collapse of the USSR has also created difficulties for its traditional arms recipients, despite Russia's continued, albeit haphazard, effort to export arms.[9] This may increase market opportunities for Third World exporters. Moreover, the challenges confronting states in the Middle East and South Asia in sustaining strategies of deterrence in a volatile technological environment appear to be magnifying.

Aggression is a second primary motive driving states to acquire high-leverage military capabilities. To grace such purposes with the academic term "compellence" is to obscure what is at work here: sheer rapacity. Such states may seek weapons and war in order to gain something of value, whether to advance territorial ambitions (e.g., Iraq vis-à-vis Kuwait) or annihilate a hated enemy. Or they may seek weapons and war in order to avert a loss by dealing with the consequences of a status quo circumstance that works increasingly against the

---

Strategic and International Studies, 1984), p. 9.

8   Sanders, *Arms Industries*, p. 13.

9   India is illustrative. The collapse of the Soviet military industrial structure has led India to ground as many as 50 percent of its fighter planes, consider mothballing up to one-third of its armored combat systems, shut down assembly lines for the T–72 tank, and cancel exercises to reduce wear—producing serious erosion in combat capability. Molly Moore, "India's Military Hit by Soviet Collapse," *Washington Post*, October 4, 1992. p. A–34.

perceived national interest (China's intervention in the Korean War being perhaps the best example).

Aggressive purposes may also flow from the instability of the regime in question. If it believes itself to be in a status quo moving against its interests or otherwise untenable, such a regime may be willing to take large risks. Such risk takers may not be aggressors in the classic sense that they seek territorial gain at the expense of another state. Rather, they may choose to make war in order to teach a lesson to a political adversary (as China sought to instruct the United States by its intervention in the Korean War) or to bolster claims to status (as the Soviet Union intended by invading Afghanistan in support of a Marxist-Leninist regime). A recent RAND study concludes that regime type is a critical determinant of the propensity to take the risks necessary to upset the status quo: illegitimate governments fall more readily into foreign crises than do legitimate ones because such crises tend to become inextricably linked with questions of regime survival.[10]

Predictions about the decade ahead are difficult to make. Saddam Hussein's attempt to annex Kuwait, defined by him explicitly as an opportunity if not an actual necessity created by the end of the Cold War and the demise of the Soviet Union, may be a harbinger of the future. But it is difficult to find many examples of leaders who profess a desire to conquer and annex a hated neighbor. The sources of conflict around the globe appear increasingly to be found in relations within states, or between states competing over disputed borders. This suggests that the number of states in this category will remain small.

Coercive purposes are those that go beyond mere influence and "a seat at the table" to coercion of others and the extension of regional hegemony.[11] States seeking weapons for coercive purposes may want to overcome a rival's power or to alter the terms on which a long-standing grievance can be settled. There may also be extra-regional coercive designs: weapons of mass destruction mated to long-range delivery systems may be seen as useful in engaging the interests and

---

10 Dean Wilkening and Kenneth Watman, *Deterring Nuclear Threats From Regional Adversaries*, DRR–544/2–A/AF (Santa Monica, Calif.: RAND, February 1994).

11 For an overview of compellence and national strategy, see Thomas C. Schelling, *The Strategy of Conflict* (New York, N.Y.: Oxford University Press, 1960).

manipulating the diplomacy of states beyond the region that are otherwise disinclined to become involved in the dispute.

This motive may explain in part the buildup of the Soviet arsenal of conventional and unconventional weapons. Iraq might also fit this category, if one accepts that its weapons acquisition and development programs in the 1980s fit with a strategy to exert more influence on the oil-pricing debate and on the dynamic of the Arab-Israeli dispute, short of actually using those forces to absorb neighboring territories. South Africa fits here as well, with a nuclear program apparently intended not to defeat an enemy on the battlefield but to engage outside powers in any large conflict that involved South Africa and threatened the regime.[12] This category also includes states such as Libya and Syria that may have acquired unconventional weapons for coercive purposes not in general strategies of hegemony but in key moments of confrontation with powers outside the region, just as terrorism has been exploited in recent decades in an attempt to manipulate Western governments to refrain from actions not desired by the states that sponsor the terrorism.

In the decade ahead the category of states pursuing weapons for purposes of coercion may not grow a great deal larger. At this moment in international affairs, states whose national strategies fit this coercive label are well identified. The coming decade may instead see a growth in the leverage of these states as their weapons capabilities expand and mature. Iraq's unconventional weapons programs suggest that such weapons in particular will come into increasing vogue among states that cannot compete with broad-based armaments modernization programs but desire to intimidate and direct their neighbors.

International status and national prestige provide a third set of motives. Westerners accustomed to defining concrete military threats and justifying weapons acquisition programs in terms of those threats tend to disparage this strategic motive, often without appreciating how prestige brings status, and how status can increase autonomy and influence while also helping a nation to feel more secure in its environs. The nuclear capabilities of India, France, Britain, and increasingly Russia and the United States are sometimes lumped into this category. Such states are seen to have security concerns relevant to their nuclear

---

12   R. Jeffrey Smith, "South Africa's 16-Year Secret: The Nuclear Bomb," *Washington Post*, May 12, 1993, p. A–1.

programs but that in and of themselves do not seem to outsiders to legitimize the level of investment in nuclear weapons. This motive thus lies elsewhere, such as in the desire to retain or acquire a "seat at the table" where major international decisions are made, such as the UN Security Council. Brazil is an example of a country that exports arms in part because of the status and influence it gains in its supplier role.[13] Status concerns figured in the 1960s in the motivations of newly decolonized nations to acquire conventional weapons to bolster their claims to sovereignty, such as Nigeria, and in the 1970s to stake claims to regional preeminence, as in the case of Iran.[14]

In the decade ahead considerations of prestige and status are likely to operate on separate types of weapons differently. Nuclear weapons are taken by many to be a fundamental symbol of state power and competence; the established nuclear powers seem as wedded as ever to their nuclear arsenals even though the strategic context that gave birth to them has now passed. Indeed, the erstwhile superpowers appear increasingly to think of their nuclear weapons in the way the historical great powers have done; like Britain and France, Russia and the United States attach an overwhelming political importance to the retention of nuclear competence even as the potential missions for such arsenals narrows substantially. On the other hand, prospective proliferators might also take note of the general loss of influence in the world of Russia, Britain, and France, and of the inability of China and India to exploit nuclear-weapon status to gain global influence, and conclude that the global political benefits of nuclearization have been overvalued.

Little or no status attaches to the possession of chemical and biological weapons in the larger international community, although it may be the case that

---

13 As Ralph Sanders has noted, "Export of arms is an effective way of enhancing their influence both within their region and beyond....The Brazilians have a mind-set that vigilant preparedness and military strength offer the key to stability, power, and prestige....However there is scant evidence to support the contention that Brazil actively seeks hegemony." Sanders, *Arms Industries,* pp. 17, 111.

14 Subrahmanyam, "Third World Arms Control in a Hegemonistic World," pp. 33–44. Again, Martin Wight contributes a useful perspective: "New powers will sometimes amass armaments and soldiers without having a coherent foreign policy. The intrinsic efficiency of weapons is attractive; they are useful to maintain internal power, or for prestige....The development of a foreign policy brings self-comparison with other powers, and especially with potential enemies." Wight, *Power Politics,* ed. Hedley Bull and Carsten Holbraad (London: Penguin Books and the Royal Institute of International Affairs, 1979), pp. 239–243.

the possession of such capabilities has regional import as a sign that a state's power and interests must be respected by others. But ballistic missiles especially have acquired a reputation as a source of prestige.[15]

In most of the regions of the world today, however, it appears to be the case that states that acquire weapons for the narrow national security benefits of enhanced prestige today increasingly confront the international consequences of their actions, which often are counterproductive to the intended goal. Rather than the unilateral benefits of prestige, they acquire competitors who feel threatened by those capabilities and compelled to match or overmatch them, thus precipitating arms races. If India intended its nuclear program largely for purposes of international prestige, it must account today for the fact that Pakistan has felt compelled to respond with a nuclear asset of its own.[16] Argentina, Chile, and Brazil offer a similar model of states that undertook national weapons programs for avowedly prestige purposes only to rethink those programs as a result of their international repercussions. This leads to speculation that this category of states may shrink in the years ahead.

Regime survival is also a factor in the orientation of some states toward their weapons capabilities. The prevalence of civil war in the 1990s underscores the vulnerability of many governments and regimes. Many more regimes remain unstable even if wars have not broken out. In both Iraq and Iran, for example, regimes are in place that have a tenuous hold on the country and for which well-equipped armies present paradoxically a potential threat to the regime itself

---

15   James G. Roche, "The Proliferation of Tactical Aircraft and Ballistic and Cruise Missiles in the Developing World," in W. Thomas Wander, Eric H. Arnett, and Paul Bracken, eds., *The Diffusion of Advanced Weaponry: Technologies, Regional Implications, and Possible Responses* (Washington, D.C.: American Association for the Advancement of Science, 1994), pp. 63–90. As W. Seth Carus has observed, "a country concerned about the perception of its military position may be tempted to acquire missiles even if it does not intend to use them....Saudi Arabia was less interested in obtaining a militarily effective arsenal than it was in acquiring a ballistic missile system." Carus, *Ballistic Missiles in Modern Conflict* (New York, N.Y.: Praeger with the Center for Strategic and International Studies, 1991), pp. 4–5.

16   "Strategic considerations—improved self-reliance, ensured security of supply, regional power aspirations, and local arms races—have often initiated the development of arms industries in the newly industrializing countries. India's extensive military build-up has been tied to its regional arms race with China and Pakistan." Office of Technology Assessment, *Global Arms Trade*, p. 123.

as well as a means to extend control. The use of chemical weapons by the Iraqi military against civilian opponents of the regime of Saddam Hussein points to the likelihood that many of the weapons development or acquisition programs in the developing world may be largely for domestic counterinsurgency purposes and for the direct suppression of subnational groups. Pariah states such as North Korea and South Africa during the apartheid years found solace in nuclear weapons as a way to cope with their isolation from the international community due to that community's overwhelming rejection of their sociopolitical systems. For North Korea, the nuclear program appears to have been pursued in part in support of a strategy of brinksmanship with the major powers involved in the region that was intended to extract political concessions that would enable the weak regime to escape its isolation as well as extort economic concessions that would reduce the hardships of its people.

In the decade ahead this category of states may well be smaller than in decades past. The military's declining role in governing developing societies associated with the movement toward democracy portends a circumstance in which the authority and legitimacy of regimes is derived from popular support and not the barrel of a gun. The outrage generated by Saddam Hussein's use of chemical weapons to exterminate Kurdish villagers as part of a depopulation campaign suggests that any developing country could not long brandish arsenals of unconventional weapons for domestic purposes. The Soviet Union and North Korea serve as glaring examples of states made strong by weapons alone and whose fixation on overwhelming military strength eviscerated the civilian economy and galvanized international opposition to the goals of the regime.

On the other hand, unstable state structures throughout Africa and Asia may portend a broader drift toward civil war in these regions, increasing the propensity of illegitimate leaders to seek authority by threatening violence against their opponents as well as the recourse of established governments to military operations to defeat armed challengers. Establishing the legitimacy of any government is not easy in many societies in the developing world, not just those in which corruption or repression are rampant. As Mohammed Ayoob has point out:

> State-making is a nasty business even in the best of circumstances
> and with unrestricted time to complete the task, as happened in the
> case of the earliest states in Europe. With time a scarce commodity
> and with the various phases of state- and nation-building

telescoped into one mammoth endeavor, the international
community's expectation that this endeavor be carried on
simultaneously with the attempt to achieve the multiple and
diverse goals of popular participation, economic redistribution, and
social justice makes state-making an extremely difficult and
complicated task. This overload on the political system leads
repeatedly to near-breakdowns and augments the sense of
insecurity from which Third World states and regimes suffer.[17]

Self-defense is perhaps the ultimate motivational force in the realist view of the
world: weapons acquisition for purposes of self-defense when war has broken out
in order to shape outcomes on the battlefield or to retaliate against aggression.
The Iraq of the 1980s is an example of one such state, because it first used
chemical weapons to prevent defeat at the hands of Iran (although in a war Iraq
had started). Another example is the Western allies in World War I; they rapidly
built up arsenals of chemical weapons after Germany initiated chemical attacks.
The desire of such countries for even conventional weapons is not automatically
embraced by foreign suppliers when their regimes are the object of broad
disapprobation. Their recourse to unconventional weapons in violation of
preexisting commitments would also meet with strong international reaction,
unless the case could credibly be made that their use was genuinely in last resort
and in the absence of a sufficient international effort to preserve their integrity.
Whether war will bring more states to this point in the decades ahead cannot, of
course, be known.

This discussion of strategic purpose is largely conjectural or inferential in
nature. As Nicole Ball has observed, "very few countries in any part of the world
and at any stage of development are generous with security-related
information."[18] Even in a country such as Iraq, whose weapons programs have
been exposed to wide-ranging international scrutiny after the Persian Gulf War,

---

17 Mohammed Ayoob, "State-Making and Third World Security," in Jasjit Singh and Thomas
Bernauer, eds., *Security of Third World Countries* (Geneva: United Nations Institute for
Disarmament Research, 1993), pp. 34–35.

18 Ball, *Security and Economy in the Third World* (Princeton, N.J.: Princeton University Press,
1988), p. xxv.

little definitive information has been uncovered clarifying the purposes for which the weapons development programs had been put in place.

This type of conjectural analysis about the strategic purposes and motives of states related to their armaments programs must, of course, be hedged with a number of caveats. Purposes are not fixed and unchanging. They can be redefined with the passage of time and as a result of alterations in the strategic environment. For example, the military buildup of Iran fostered by the United States in the 1970s under the shah has been put to altogether different purposes by the revolutionary government of the 1990s.

Furthermore, such categories suggest a tidiness to strategic orientation that does not always exist. Especially in regions where countries face multiple neighbors with changing ambitions and capabilities of their own, a given country may adopt a mixture of strategies embodying different purposes toward a mix of neighbors representing different threats at different times. Thus, for example, India's advanced weapons programs must be understood in the context of its desire for international status, for defense against aggression by China along their common border, for deterrence of Pakistan's nuclear capabilities, and for domestic economic and political benefits.[19] China's programs also reflect multiple purposes.[20] Moreover, this type of analysis suggests a false rationality;

19 The Office of Technology Assessment's study of the global arms trade echoes this conclusion that no single factor accounts for the emergence of new weapons producers: "Defense production in these countries stems from an amalgam of strategic, political, and economic motivations." Office of Technology Assessment, *Global Arms Trade*, p. 123. Also, "The security anxieties motivating India and Pakistan to contemplate nuclear arming are deeply rooted and complex, stemming both from an embittered bilateral relationship and from the involvement in the region of external powers, which are perceived by one or the other regional state as potentially hostile." Carnegie Task Force on Non-Proliferation and South Asian Security, *Nuclear Weapons and South Asian Security*, Report (Washington, D.C.: Carnegie Endowment for International Peace, 1988), p. 48.

20 As R. Bates Gill has noted, "Strategic motivations can be both 'positive' and 'negative' in character. That is, they may seek to actively enhance China's security in the face of threats from potentially or actually hostile parties (positive), or they may seek to deny the projection of hostility by others (negative). Political motivations are those that seek to enhance China's standing with its client, to draw the two countries closer together in their overall relationship or, through the client, to provide improved relations with third countries. Economic motivations are normally considered to be those that seek to gain foreign exchange earnings as a profit from the arms trade relationship." Gill, *Chinese Arms*

much of international conflict reflects deeply rooted historical impulses compounded by the ambitions, arrogance, stubbornness, or stupidity of political or military leaders. Nor does it encompass the dynamic element of strategic analysis and the possibility that in the very definition of potential threats states create enemies where none might have existed.[21]

If these caveats are kept in mind, however, this type of taxonomy is still useful in capturing the range of strategic orientations that exist in the states with weapons potential.

In sum, then, the expectation that the technically empowered new tier will, sooner or later, seek recourse to its nascent weapons capabilities is substantially supported by a strategic assessment of state behavior and historical motivations.

The End of the Cold War

The second element of the gloomy prognosis relates to the end of the Cold War and the possibility that this event may have unleashed forces that will accelerate the diffusion of weapons.

The end of the Cold War also brought to an end a bipolar order that to a substantial degree had structured the strategic orientations of the most technically competent states. In a more fluid and increasingly multipolar post–Cold War order, the exigencies that accompany an anarchical interstate system become of increasing importance. As traditional alliances weaken (as the transatlantic and U.S.–Japan alliances appear to be doing) or disappear (as in the case of the Warsaw Pact) states previously protected by these alliances may be compelled to bolster their capacities to act autonomously in defense of their own interests. This explains concerns in the nonproliferation community about a possible rearming of Japan and Germany with advanced high-leverage capabilities. Because the end of the Cold War also entailed the disintegration of

---

Transfers: Purposes, Patterns, and Prospects in the New World Order (Westport, Conn.: Praeger, 1992), p. 190.

21 "Small countries, like large ones, can be excessively preoccupied with threats to their security, and then not only deny themselves more of the many values that make life worth living and worth making secure but, by looking provocative and dangerous to others, they may also magnify their security problems." Klaus Knorr, *On the Uses of Military Power in the Nuclear Age* (Princeton, N.J.: Princeton University Press, 1966), p. 12.

the Soviet Union, there is a possibility that civil war within its former territory will precipitate a broader regional emphasis on military security.

The end of the Cold War also had the effect of removing the East-West overlay of regional conflicts, which may weaken the constraints against the escalation of those conflicts. During the Cold War the fear of both Washington and Moscow that any military confrontation in Korea and Berlin in the 1950s, Cuba and Vietnam in the 1960s, and the Middle East in the 1970s might escalate into nuclear war between them gave each strong incentive to keep conflicts localized and to prevent their allies, clients, and proxies from acquiring and/or using weapons of mass destruction. These strictures have weakened substantially with the end of the Cold War. Leaders of new nuclear powers may now calculate the consequences of nuclear-use against regional adversaries without primary reference to concerns in Washington or Moscow.

The end of the Cold War may also deepen the concerns of the non-nuclear-weapon states about the nuclear-weapon states. They may well interpret as threatening the fact that Cold-War-vintage nuclear capabilities are no longer targeted against Cold War adversaries but are being retained and justified for regional contingencies, among others. In the United States, some military planners are finding possible new roles for nuclear weapons that relate to the deterrence or defeat of nuclear-armed hegemons in the developing world (as discussed in chapter 5). In Russia, nuclear weapons remain important not just as a vestige of Moscow's great power status but also as part of the new strategic calculations among the states spawned of the Soviet empire, especially Ukraine and Kazakhstan. Moreover, the other nuclear-weapon states of the 1960s—Britain, France, and China—continue to modernize their forces rather than participate in the movement toward deep cuts. This may increase the interest of states like Iran and India in moving forward with nuclear weapons as a hedge against the ambitions of the nuclear-armed states and the possibility of great power intervention.

The end of the Cold War has also had wider-ranging implications for the functioning of the international system as a whole. To invoke Hedley Bull's terminology, this event has had repercussions for the effective functioning of basic institutions of world order, which he defined as being "not necessarily...an organization or administrative machinery, but rather a set of habits and practices shaped toward the realization of common goals."[22] Two such institutions have been influenced particularly by the end of the Cold War: the role of the great powers and the balance of power.

The role of the great powers has historically been a critical determinant of order in the modern interstate system. In a system marked by disparities of power and influence among autonomous units living together in a ubiquitous and essentially anarchic system, the most powerful and influential states have tended also to be those states with the largest stake in the effective functioning of the interstate system. As Bull has put it:

> Great powers are recognized by others to have, and conceived by their own leaders and peoples to have, certain special rights and duties. Great powers, for example, assert the right, and are accorded the right, to play a part in determining issues that affect the peace and security of the international system as a whole....Great powers contribute to international order in two main ways: by managing their relations with one another; and by exploiting their preponderance in such a way as to impart a degree of central direction to the affairs of society as a whole.[23]

They thus have assumed special responsibility for ensuring that the institutions of international society perform effectively. This effectiveness is a function of the degree to which their common interests are "sufficient to enable them to collaborate in relation to goals of minimum world order, and especially the avoidance of nuclear war."[24] The great power institution requires also some willingness among these nations to harness national power to collective purposes. Further, the great power institution in international affairs is not based on the denial to others of a responsibility to protect common interests and principles, although it has sometimes worked that way or at least created the impression of doing so. Their work in the UN Security Council is but one manifestation of the role of the great powers.

---

22   Hedley Bull, *The Anarchical Society: A Study of Order in World Politics* (New York, N.Y.: Columbia University Press, 1977), p. 74.

23   Ibid., pp. 202, 207.

24   Ibid., p. 315.

The great power system is clearly undergoing a period of substantial change. As noted above, the end of the Cold War has raised profound questions about the international roles of the two key great powers—the United States and Russia.

For the United States, the end of the Cold War has brought a "unipolar moment," in which it enjoys singular preeminence in global affairs.[25] But the United States at the same time has entered a period of drift and readjustment, because the end of the Cold War has robbed it of a guiding sense of purpose in international affairs. Indeed, the end of the Cold War has helped bring about a turn inward, because the country has elected a president committed to making the country's domestic agenda its first political priority, thereby raising questions about whether disengagement and isolationism might again come to dominate the country's orientation to the world, as they so often have at the conclusion of past international conflicts.[26]

Even an assertive U.S. policy would have to confront the fact of a decline in U.S. power. Seen in positive terms, that decline is only relative, and it reflects the success of international efforts to restore Europe and Japan to positions of global influence after World War II and to facilitate the economic and political development of countries elsewhere in the world. Seen in less positive terms, that decline reflects either an "imperial overstretch" by the United States, by which it has impoverished itself while maintaining an overextended quasi-imperial national strategy, or a squandering of political stature through the corrosive effects of social decay at home.[27] With this decline of U.S. power, the nation may find itself settling into a prominent but not preeminent position in world affairs, one commensurate with its weight and status in a "normal" international system, which is to say one in which U.S. power is not magnified beyond proportion by its emergence from World War II unscathed and its military buildup during the Cold War. In the future the United States may act more like a traditional great power

---

25 Charles Krauthammer, "The Unipolar Moment," *Foreign Affairs*, Vol. 70, No. 1 (America and the World, 1990/91), pp. 23–33.

26 Zbigniew Brzezinski has written of "the danger to American global preeminence generated by internal social and cultural dilemmas" and of the geopolitical vacuum emerging in global affairs. See Brzezinski, *Out of Control: Global Turmoil on the Eve of the 21st Century* (New York, N.Y.: Charles Scribner's Sons, 1993).

27 Paul Kennedy, *The Rise and Fall of the Great Powers: Economic Change and Military Conflict from 1500 to 2000* (New York, N.Y.: Random House, 1988).

than a superpower, that is, one using its power and influence selectively while competing with other powers in economic and political terms.

In either case, a diminished U.S. role in the world could have profound consequences. Writing in 1981, James Schlesinger argued that the decline of American preeminence would result in:

> instability for the balance of the century. The basic reason is also simple: the relative decline of American power, and associated with it, the reduced will of the American people to play a combined role as international guardian and self-appointed moral preceptor—in short, the end of *Pax Americana*....we are in a period of international transition...reflecting the slow unravelling of a framework of international security provided by the United States...for a period of 30 years after...World War II.[28]

An alternative to the diminished role is a chaotic, inconsistent one, in which the United States projects its political and military power on the international stage only episodically, without any reference to a coherent long-term strategy and largely unilaterally. Such fickle application of U.S. power would deepen the fears of allies and potential adversaries alike about the ability of the United States to use its power for larger shared purposes and to honor its national commitments. This, too, could contribute to the tendency toward anarchy.

The other superpower—the Soviet Union—has simply disappeared. Russia is today a relatively diminished power, engulfed in deep political and economic crisis. This combines with difficult civil-military relations and reservations about control over the nuclear arsenal of the defunct Union to cast doubt on Russia's ability to share the lead of the nuclear nonproliferation effort—or of any significant international endeavor.

Moreover, the great power system is under stress from other directions. Postcolonial Britain and France are now in the ranks of nuclear-armed middle powers, defined as states without the power or influence to significantly shape

---

28 James R. Schlesinger, "The International Implications of Third-World Conflict: An American Perspective," in Christoph Bertram, ed., *Third-World Conflict and International Security, Part I*, Adelphi Paper No. 166 (London: International Institute for Strategic Studies, Summer 1981), p. 5.

international affairs but whose voices must be taken into account in both regional and global affairs. Other middle powers in the developed world (such as Germany and Japan) and the developing one (such as India and Nigeria) aspire to join the club established at the end of World War II by joining the UN Security Council as permanent members. China stands out as a great power that eschews the principles of the European great power system and whose antipathy to the power of the Security Council may bear fruit in future efforts to impede its operation.

Furthermore, great power status is no longer clearly equated with military prowess. Economic giants Japan and Germany have emerged as large, non-military powers. Militarily robust but economically prostrate Russia is slipping from the global stage. Whether this new equation will long prevail is at the heart of the concern about a future nuclear-armed Germany and Japan.

One manifestation of this transformation of the role of the great powers in international affairs is a growing debate about the structure and role of the UN Security Council. This debate stands as witness to the deep global division about membership in the great power category and their specific rights and obligations internationally.

One of the primary impacts of a weakened great power system is being felt in the functioning of the NPT. Scholars have repeatedly underscored the importance of one country, or a small handful of them, taking special responsibility for the functioning of treaty regimes. As Benjamin Frankel has argued, "in the case of the nonproliferation regime, as in the case of any other regime, 'The choice may be...between the regime proposed by the strong and no regime at all.' If the strong are too weak or insecure or distracted to provide leadership, there will be no regime."[29] If the United States abandons its

---

29   Frankel is citing James F. Keeley, "Legitimacy, Capability, Effectiveness and the Future of the NPT," in David B. DeWitt, ed., *Nuclear Non-Proliferation and Global Security* (New York, N.Y.: St. Martin's Press, 1987), p. 29. He goes on to argue that "Any international regime's stability is fundamentally a product of how nations think about and organize their policy on that issue....Change is as inevitable in regimes as in all other facets of life, and what will be important in the stability of the non-proliferation regime is that the United States has an institutional commitment to non-proliferation which can bring to bear the resources and policy coordination necessary to deal with a changing environment." Frankel, ed., *Opaque Nuclear Proliferation: Methodological and Policy Implications* (London: Frank Cass, 1991), pp. 5–7, 112–113.

leadership of the nuclear nonproliferation regime, whether through increasing isolationism or simply neglect, no other state appears ready to assume the obligations of leadership or capable of bringing to bear the broad range of political, economic, and military power necessary to keep the disparate elements of the regime functioning.

The balance of power is the second main institution of world order whose world order role and impact on proliferation is much in doubt in the 1990s. Such a balance has operated historically to prevent major outbreaks of war by keeping in check the ambitions of challengers to the status quo.

During the Cold War, a certain balance prevailed between East and West, albeit a highly competitive balance and one in which war may have been prevented not so much by a balance of power as by a fear of mutual annihilation. With the demise of the Soviet Union, however, it is difficult to conceive of a global balance of power in a world in which one nation—the United States—possesses overwhelming military power. This has created a fear in the developing world of unbalanced U.S. power—of what might unfold in an era in which the interests and ambitions of the "sole remaining superpower" enjoying its "unipolar moment" go unchecked by a competing superpower. The history of unfettered great powers suggests that they tend to exert their influence beyond their borders, if not through military conquest then through political and economic means, and this has led some to fear the possibility that the United States will act as dominant powers in the past have often acted to exert their influence over others, whether through foreign military interventions or other means.[30] More specifically, some countries in the developing world fear that the United States will use its surfeit of power to control the institutions of international society. Because of the fear that uniquely U.S. predilections may prevent such institutions from acting in certain circumstances (e.g., where U.S. interests are not directly engaged) and, contrarily, because of the fear that the United States might intervene unilaterally as it takes up the role of world policeman, states such as India and Iran have come to talk increasingly of an

---

30   James O. C. Jonah, "Critical Commentary: A Third World View on the Implications of Superpower Collaboration," in Thomas G. Weiss and Meryl A. Kessler, eds., *Third World Security in the Post–Cold War Era* (Boulder, Colo.: Lynne Rienner Publishers, 1991), pp. 161–173.

independent national nuclear option as necessary to provide security when the international community will not act or to impose large costs on a United States seeking to act without the sanction of that community. The result may be a broader diffusion and legitimization of nuclear weapons in the decade ahead.

This imbalance of power may be counteracted by the fact that the United States finds itself impaired to act internationally by significant economic constraints and deep-seated political uncertainty about its international role and responsibilities. Moreover, the United States is also seen by many to be a benign great power whose unipolar moment can be exploited to common benefit by deepening the principles and institutions of a liberal international political and economic order.

The old balance of power has given way not simply to U.S. preeminence, however. In the 1990s an increasing diffusion and differentiation of power, in which regional power balances are becoming more salient, seems to be more prominent. U.S. preeminence may thus prove illusory. This new regionalism constitutes a fundamental reorientation of the international system, one without precedent in the modern interstate system and thus one about which the balance of power theorists of the Cold War period have done little thinking.

The possibility that the new regionalism will prove to be a source of disorder has been much discussed. Multipolar orders are generally believed to be more difficult to keep in balance than bipolar ones because of the diversity of interests that prevail in them. Regional tensions long suppressed by restraint imposed by the United States and Soviet Union may break out. As R. Bates Gill has observed, "While Washington and Moscow may see less reason to support clients, the clients nevertheless may still perceive very real security threats—threats which exist whether their former patrons continue to provide weapons or not."[31] Moreover, the passing of the East–West dyad in global affairs has not erased other lines of demarcation in global politics. According to Moyammed Ayoob:

> The end of the Cold War and the disintegration of the Soviet
> Union have lowered global tensions and temporarily reduced the
> intensity of great power competition for the Third World.
> However, these events by themselves can not alter the fundamental

---

31   Ibid., p. 34.

phenomenon of the division of the world between the industrial and strategic heartland, where violent interstate conflict is not permissible because it could escalate into nuclear holocaust, and the gray areas of the globe where interventions, wars by proxies, and the probing of global adversaries' political and military weaknesses are not ruled out.[32]

If regionalism helps to facilitate the emergence of a multipolar order in which the competing interests within and among regions are kept in some sort of balance, the bipolar order will have been succeeded by something valuable. One sign that this may be happening is the hopeful movement toward peace in the Middle East and the new diplomatic initiatives in Asia and elsewhere made either possible or necessary by the passing of the Cold War. These developments suggest that the new regionalism may work to promote order and the resolution of interstate conflicts. But a truly multipolar system is not yet in evidence, and instead regionalization mirrors a diffusion of power and influence in the international system and a competition over the nature and purposes of that power. An international system of unprecedented complexity appears in the offing, which raises doubts about the capacity of leaders and institutions to deal with the challenges it will entail.

It is, of course, too tidy to impute to the end of the Cold War all of the international factors of change bearing on the balance of power. In fact, the rigid Cold War confrontation and structures that emerged in the 1950s had already begun to attenuate in the 1960s. As Robert Tucker has observed, "the postwar order was itself breaking down during these years."[33] The diffusion of power in

---

32   Ayoob, "State-Making and Third World Security," p. 33.

33   Tucker went on to write, "Largely the creation of America, this order rested upon and reflected America's continued military, political, and economic supremacy. Even in the absence of Vietnam, the decline of the classic cold war was bound to challenge this supremacy by eroding the cohesiveness of the American-led alliance system." Robert W. Tucker, *The Inequality of Nations* (New York. N.Y.: Basic Books, 1977), p. 47. Other analysts framed the issues differently: "The reduced capacity of the United States to be a sole provider of international security in remote areas, and a search for alternative means of attending to those needs, was a major theme in the first years of the Nixon administration." Rodney W. Jones and Steven A. Hildreth, eds., *Emerging Powers: Defense and Security in the Third World* (New York, N.Y.: Praeger with the Center for Strategic and International

the international system was a major challenge for U.S. diplomacy in the late 1960s as it struggled with a war in Vietnam it would not or could not win and with the growing economic strength of allies in Europe and Asia.

Unfortunately, the preview of the broader transformation of the balance of power afforded by the experience of the 1960s is not particularly encouraging. The Nixon administration sought to accommodate an increasingly multipolar world by according regional powers greater responsibility in the management of regional security structures, for example, by bolstering South Vietnam and Japan in Asia and Iran in the Middle East. But this proved to be a strategy "fraught with pitfalls"—especially in the proliferation domain.[34] The decade that followed was marked by sharp proliferation concerns.[35] In the 1980s in contrast less concern was devoted to the proliferation subject, although weapons development programs put in place then may well bear fruit in the 1990s.

In sum, then, if disengagement by the heretofore great powers and the passing of the bipolar balance lead to or otherwise combine with a more chaotic international system, the consequences for proliferation could be substantial. With increasing uncertainty about the interests and behaviors of both major and minor powers, states may act with that self-help and narrow self-interest so well known in the international system. This would likely have the effect of increasing their reliance on military instruments of policy, with the concomitant difficulties of establishing and managing a balance of power system. Such an outcome would be given added impetus if this reliance on force weakens the credibility of guarantees or assurances extended by the UN or the great powers. As Frankel has argued,

> In a more fluid multipolar world, characterized by the flexibility of coalitions and the shifting of alliances, and in which capabilities among the major powers are more evenly distributed, the threatening effects of anarchy will be accentuated, not reduced. Unvarnished and uncompromising self-help as the principle of

---

Studies, 1986), p. 3.

34 Jones and Hildreth, *Emerging Powers*, p. 4.

35 Leonard S. Spector, "Nuclear Proliferation in the 1990s: The Storm after the Lull," in Aspen Strategy Group *New Threats: Responding to the Proliferation of Nuclear, Chemical, and Delivery Capabilities in the Third World* (Lanham, Md.: University Press of America, 1990).

action of states will once again, and more pronouncedly, come to characterize the international system....It is the political changes brought about by the demise of the bipolar structure that add the crucial, decisive ingredient of the nuclear proliferation drive and make it inexorable....Political conditions hospitable to nuclear proliferation combine with the spreading of growing technological capabilities to make the 1990s a grim, anxious decade on the nuclear proliferation front.[36]

Declining Barriers to Proliferation

The third constituent part in the gloomy prognosis about the future of weapons proliferation relates to the growing trivialization of barriers that heretofore have operated to prevent states from realizing their weapons potentials or ambitions. Chapter 1 described the ways in which technical barriers have diminished in recent decades. This analysis focuses on two other barriers that have been important historically: perceptions and economics.

This trivialization of barriers is well illustrated in perceptions about chemical weapons. In the past, the belief that these weapons were of little or no utility combined with the stigma that attached to them as particularly horrific weapons to limit their appeal. Until the 1980s, senior military officers in the developing world knew little about chemical weapons, other than their dismal reputation among the modern militaries of the West. That reputation—such weapons were unpredictable on the battlefield, ineffective against protected forces, and

---

36 Frankel, *Opaque Nuclear Proliferation,* pp. 2–7. See also Benjamin Frankel, "The Brooding Shadow: Systemic Incentives and Nuclear Weapons Proliferation," in Zachary S. Davis and Benjamin Frankel, eds., *The Proliferation Puzzle: Why Nuclear Weapons Spread (and What Results)* (London: Frank Cass, 1993), pp. 37–78, where he writes that "an examination of the differences between bipolar and multipolar orders shows that nuclear arms proliferation will likely intensify in the 1990s and beyond, and that the new owners of these newly acquired weapons will likely brandish them more openly to advance their political objectives" (page 39). See also the chapters by Zachary S. Davis ("The Realist Nuclear Regime," pp. 79–99) and Richard K. Betts ("Paranoids, Pygmies, Pariahs and Nonproliferation Revisited," pp. 100–124) in that volume as well as Lawrence Freedman, "Foreword," in Patrick Garrity and Steven A. Maaranen, eds., *Nuclear Weapons in the Changing World: Perspectives from Europe, Asia, and North America* (New York, N.Y.: Plenum Press, 1992).

dangerous to transport and use—probably was a more effective barrier than any other. But Iraq's use of chemical weapons with impunity in its war against Iran undermined a taboo that to many seemed as powerful as the taboo against the use of nuclear weapons. Further, the prolonged and inconclusive debate over the reported use of chemical agents and toxins—so-called Yellow Rain—suggested that international responses to allegations of such use would be delayed, if not derailed, over debates about ambiguous evidence.[37] Combined with the internationalization of the petrochemical, pesticide, and pharmaceutical industries, and the growth of a diversified trade in their production, these new developments mean that more states now have the means to produce chemical weapons and are less unwilling to do so.[38]

R. James Woolsey, then director of central intelligence, argued that perceptions about the utility of unconventional weapons in general are changing, with a growing number of states coming to believe that weapons of mass destruction can be useful for a variety of national purposes.[39]

The lethality of advanced conventional weapons has reinforced a perception that they are also effective. Ballistic missiles have come to be seen as possessing considerable deterrent value, especially in contrast to manned aircraft, not just because of certain advantages they enjoy in performance characteristics but also because of what they suggest about the general military prowess of the nation possessing them.[40] Anti-ship cruise missiles proliferated widely after the success

---

37 Skepticism about the credibility of the allegations by an ideologically charged Reagan administration was widespread, and a credible although inconclusive alternative explanation alleged that the matter in question actually was bee faeces has been offered. See Julian Robinson, Jeanne Guillemin, and Matthew Meselson, "Yellow Rain: The Story Collapses," *Foreign Policy*, No. 68 (Fall 1987), pp. 100–117.

38 This section is drawn from Roberts, *Chemical Disarmament and International Security*, pp. 16–17.

39 Statement by R. James Woolsey, director of central intelligence, Senate Committee on Governmental Affairs, February 24, 1993.

40 According to William H. Webster, director of central intelligence, in testimony on nuclear and missile proliferation before Senate Committee on Governmental Affairs, May 18, 1989, "the deterrent value of missiles is higher" than for manned aircraft because they cannot be destroyed by existing air defenses. In comparing aircraft and missiles, James G. Roche has concluded as follows: "To sum up the comparison between aircraft, ballistic and cruise missiles, it can generally be stated that aircraft tend to be superior in terms of range,

of Exocets in the war over the Falklands/Malvinas Islands, despite their high costs.[41] Advanced air defense systems, such as the Patriot missile defense system, and high-precision cruise missiles were given a boost by their use in the campaign to oust Iraq from Kuwait in 1991.

Thus, the reputation certain advanced conventional weapons have acquired in recent years—regardless of how well grounded or not that reputation is in actual performance—has increased the likelihood of proliferation by making these weapons seem more useful than was heretofore believed.

Another way in which barriers to proliferation are declining is in the economic domain. As Stephanie Neuman has observed, "Economic factors are often crucial and complicating factors in the defense-planning process. Concerns about local employment, the health of the industrial base, or balance-of-payments problems can determine acquisition policy more often than operational need and military preference."[42] Historically, poor states have been unable to afford the investments necessary to build or acquire the types of large and modern armed forces necessary to exert high leverage. But cost factors, like perceptions, are changing at the end of the twentieth century.

Despite the economic difficulties of the developing world, it *is* developing. With the notable exception of Africa and of individual countries in the Middle East, much of the developing world appears to be making headway economically. As Henry Rowen has commented, policymakers have succeeded in "breaking the code of economic development; the formula for any nation to become wealthy is now clear and is being increasingly applied."[43] Economies are slowly diversifying.

---

available warhead size and diversity, and weapon delivery accuracy, although the next generation cruise missiles will be comparable. On the other hand, missiles are superior in air defense penetration ability, ballistic missiles because of high speed and cruise missiles because of low altitude and circuitous approach. Overall, cruise missiles, as improved with GPS/inertial guidance, have distinct advantages over competing types of weapons. Experience in Desert Storm has shown that cruise missiles work. Although it is not expected that cruise missiles will entirely replace aircraft or ballistic missiles, they have come of age and will become more important in the future." Roche, "The Proliferation of Tactical Aircraft and Ballistic and Cruise Missiles in the Developing World."

41 Carus, *Cruise Missile Proliferation*, p. 47.

42 Neuman, *Defense Planning in Less-Industrialized States*, p. 14.

43 Henry S. Rowen, "The Prospect for Weapons of Mass Destruction in a Radically Changed World," in Joachim Krause, ed., *Kernwaffenverbreitung und internationaler Systemwandel*

The wave of privatization of the last decade has brought new sources of capital to an often volatile private sector. Wealth is being accumulated even if not always broadly distributed. In some of the more advanced developing countries, spending on R&D is steadily increasing. Figures 3-1 and 3-2 illustrate these factors.

Furthermore, military power tends to increase in the wake of economic progress.[44] World Bank research indicates that developing countries tend to spend a higher percentage of their gross domestic product (GDP) on the military than do developed countries,[45] a percentage that tends to increase as they grow more wealthy.[46] Combined with the passing, albeit slowly, of the debt crisis and the steady recovery of financial solvency in many developing countries, the capacity to invest in defense may expand in the 1990s, pointing to a slow but steady accumulation of military capability in countries successfully making the economic transition from underdevelopment to industrialization. The existence over recent decades of a cycle of growth and contraction in the global arms market reinforces the conclusion that the retrenchment evident since the mid- and late-1980s may give way in the coming years to resumed growth.[47]

In addition, it is not reasonable to assume that weapons development costs in the developing world will impose economic burdens there similar to those in the developed world. The cost to the United States of its program to develop, test, and deploy the first intercontinental ballistic missiles was almost $19 billion.[48]

(nuclear weapons proliferation and international systemic change) (Baden-Baden, Germany: Nomos Verlagsgesellschaft für die Stiftung Wissenschaft und Politik, 1994), p. 67.

44   A. F. Mullins, Jr., *Born Arming: Development and Military Power in New States* (Stanford, Calif.: Stanford University Press, 1987), p. 103.

45   Daniel Hewitt, "Controlling Military Expenditures: Military Expenditures in the Developing World," *Finance & Development*, Vol. 28, No. 3 (September 1991), p. 22. "Third World military expenditures now total nearly $200 billion per year—approximately 5 percent of gross domestic product (GDP), which is only slightly less than the total amount the developing countries spend on health and education." McNamara, "Slowing Third World Militarization," p. 37.

46   "The ratio of military expenditure to GDP is found to rise with GDP in low- and middle-income countries and remain constant for high income countries." Hewitt, "Controlling Military Expenditures," p. 22.

47   Saadet Deger, "The Economics of Disarmament: Prospects, Problems and Policies for the Disarmament Dividend," Innocenti Occasional Papers, Economic Policy Series, No. 30, UNICEF, International Child Development Centre, Florence, Italy (August 1992), p. 154.

Figure 3–1
Shares of World Output

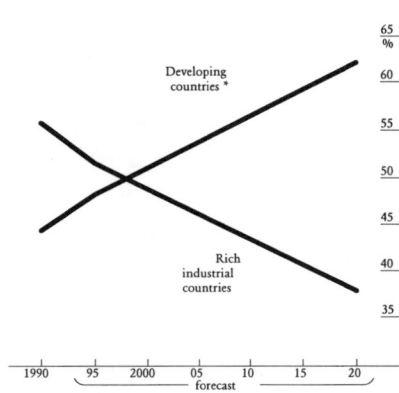

* Including Eastern Europe and the former Soviet Union

Source: World Bank.

India's Integrated Guided Missile Development Program, under which it is developing the Prithvi and Agni ballistic missiles, Akash and Trishul surface-to-air missiles, and Nag antitank missile, has cost $280 million.[49]

Cost calculations may also stimulate the proliferation of unconventional weapons. The costs associated with producing nuclear, chemical, and biological weapons all appear to be relatively low—and declining. The U.S. Manhattan Project that produced the first atomic bombs cost $1.88 billion through 1945;[50] in the 1960s, the UN calculated the cost of designing, building, and testing a

---

48 In 1965 dollars. Proliferation Study Team, Report *The Emerging Ballistic Missile Threat to the United States* (Washington, D.C.: Proliferation Study Team, February 1993), p. 7.

49 U.S. Congress, Congressional Research Service, *Iraq's Nuclear Achievements: Components, Sources, and Structure,* by Peter Zimmerman. (Washington, D.C.: Congressional Research Service, February 18, 1993), p. 8.

50 "Of the $1.88 billion total cost of the Manhattan Engineer District through December 31, 1945, $951 million, or just over half, went to Oak Ridge and the enrichment facilities there, an additional $390 million, 21 percent, was spent on the Hanford Engineer Works (plutonium production reactors), and only $74 million, or 3.9 percent of the entire project, went to research, design, and production of the weapons themselves at Los Alamos." Congressional Research Service, *Iraq's Nuclear Achievements,* p. 4.

Fig 3–2
R&D as % of GDP

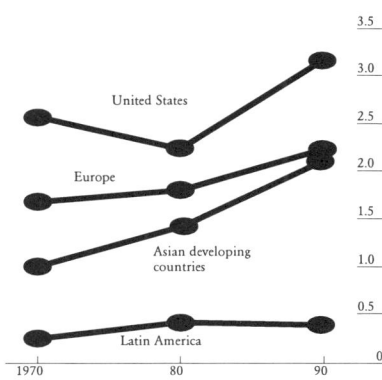

Source: United Nations Conference on Trade and Development.

plutonium-based nuclear device at $100 million, whereas subsequent studies by the U.S. Arms Control and Disarmament Agency cited a figure of $51 million for a country not already possessing fissile material and a mere $1 million if it did.[51] Chemical and biological warfare agents can easily be produced in basic facilities, even in those designed for legitimate commercial purposes. Indeed, there is evidence to suggest that Iraq, for example, set about creating its chemical weapons production facilities not just in order to acquire weapons but also to gain the commercial benefits of the sale of chemicals produced in those facilities.[52]

Of course, leaders do not evaluate costs merely in abstract terms but must weigh them in contrast to perceived benefits relative to national goals. Weapons are pursued not just if they are affordable on some narrow calculation of cost accountancy but also if they are efficient for national strategies. For example, indigenous missile production programs offering no prospect of long-term cost recovery may well be curtailed, but this is less likely if the nation in question also

---

51   Cited in Frankel, *Opaque Nuclear Proliferation*, p. 3.

52   Seth Carus, *The Genie Unleashed: Iraq's Chemical and Biological Weapons Production*, Policy Paper No. 14 (Washington, D.C.: Washington Institute for Near East Policy, 1989).

attaches high priority to development of a commercial space launch program.[53] For some states, any cost becomes bearable if the goal is important enough. Former Pakistani President Z. A. Bhutto is remembered for his statement that his compatriots would "eat grass" if that were the necessary cost of matching India's nuclear capability. Pakistan certainly suffered a complete cut-off of U.S. aid as the cost of achievement of a nuclear weapons capability. As one study has concluded, "money in many cases is not the overriding concern to a proliferant country."[54] Some of the poorest nations are among the most heavily armed.[55]

Thus, costly weapons and weapons development programs do not necessarily combine with economic difficulties in the developing countries to frustrate their ambitions to assemble the ingredients of a war-winning military employing some high-technology or other high-leverage systems.

In sum, then, there is a firm foundation for the gloomy prognosis that the new tier of technically empowered states will move to turn weapons potential into military prowess. The passing of the Cold War order combines with the classic security paradigm and the trivialization of past barriers to nourish the expectation of a future in which weapons proliferate broadly in the international system.

An Alternative Viewpoint

But if this were the whole picture, it seems likely that the international system would already have grown more chaotic and witnessed a more rapid and far-reaching diffusion of military capability in recent years. In fact, the realist model has failed to predict the most significant weapons-related activities of recent years—denuclearization by leading states and stronger nonproliferation concerns in the international community generally. Working in reverse order

---

53 Brian G. Chow, *Emerging National Space Launch Programs: Economics and Safeguards,* R–4179–USDP (Santa Monica, Calif., RAND, July 1993).

54 Proliferation Study Team, *The Emerging Ballistic Missile,* p. 5.

55 Some of the highest military spending per capita is in the poorest countries, where there is also a high ratio of military expenditures as a percent of combined education and health expenditure, with Syria topping the list in 1990–91 at 373 percent, followed by Iraq at 271 percent. See *Arms Trade News,* Council for Livable World Education Fund, June 1994.

through the three factors discussed in the first half of this chapter, what are the additional features of the issue that must be understood?

The Importance of Remaining Barriers

Although the barriers to proliferation are indeed growing more trivial, these barriers have not completely disappeared.

The *perceived utility* of some weapons may have changed, but by no means in decisive fashion. The perceived utility of nuclear, chemical, and biological weapons remains uncertain. No nuclear-armed state has found it necessary to use its nuclear weapons since the World War II bombings of Hiroshima and Nagasaki. For all of their destructiveness, nuclear weapons have become virtually unusable in the military operations of the advanced industrial states possessing them.[56] Potential proliferators in the developing world might well look at the records of the nuclear-armed United States in Vietnam, Soviet Union in Afghanistan, and Britain in the Falklands and conclude that nuclear weapons are not very useful in wars short of those for national survival. Chemical and biological weapons have reputations as of suspect utility and offering disputed military benefits, although this may be changing.[57] The sheer lethality of chemical and biological warfare agents does not translate easily into weapons offering decisive or even clear-cut military advantages, given the vulnerability of both to climate and an opponent's protective capabilities; today they are widely believed to be of little military consequence when the correct point is that they are less certain in their effect than nuclear weapons but can still be powerful instruments of terror against unprotected troops or cities and offer some important advantages, although only in specific tactical situations.

Some weapons also are believed to be especially risky to possess or use. Such risks may operate powerfully on the beliefs and perceptions of national leaders.

---

56 Godfried van Bentham van den Bergh, *Forced Restraint: The Nuclear Revolution and the End of the Cold War* (London: Macmillan, 1992); Bernard Brodie, ed., *The Absolute Weapon* (New York, N.Y.: Harcourt, Brace, 1946); and Edward N. Luttwak, "An Emerging Postnuclear Era?" *The Washington Quarterly*, Vol. 11, No. 1 (Winter 1988), pp. 5–15.

57 Roberts, *Chemical Disarmament and International Security,* and Brad Roberts, ed., *Biological Weapons: Weapons of the Future?* (Washington, D.C.: Center for Strategic and International Studies, 1993).

This is especially true if those arsenals possess a component that can be used on short notice and with massively destructive effect; it is less true if those arsenals are not vulnerable to surprise attack. These risks include the possibility of precipitating preemptive strikes or war, the likelihood that neighboring states will initiate countering military programs, the expectation of living closer to the brink of war in time of crisis because of the need to strike first, and isolation from the international community, thus weakening the claim to collective security responses. Many of the states that have refrained from constructing and deploying weapons of mass destruction during the twentieth century apparently concluded that such steps could lead to a significant long-term degradation of their security environment, of the political relations upon which their alliances were based, or of economic integration into a globalizing economy.

The reputations that attach to weapons are notoriously fickle, driven as they are by specific events. Moreover, the results of their use during such events may be perceived in many ways, given the substantial differences in orientation and experience of individual countries and their military and political leaders.[58] The Persian Gulf War of 1991, for example, reinforced contradictory impressions about the utility of nuclear weapons, strengthening the arguments of those who believe that nuclear weapons programs are destabilizing[59] while also strengthening the perception that nuclear weapons can be acquired surreptitiously even by states party to the NPT and may be necessary for a developing country contemplating the possibility of facing the advanced countries in combat. Some states will look at the failure of the Argentines in the Falklands and the Iraqis in Kuwait and conclude that developing countries cannot exploit modern armaments to maximum effect; others will look to these failures for lessons that will help them to avoid similar failures.[60]

---

58 Patrick J. Garrity, *Does the Gulf War Still Matter? Foreign Perspectives on the War and the Future of International Security*, CNSS Report No. 16 (Los Alamos, N.M.: Center for National Security Studies, Los Alamos National Laboratory, May 1993).

59 Garrity and Maaranen, *Nuclear Weapons in the Changing World*, p. 257. See also David Fischer et al., *A New Nuclear Triad: The Non-Proliferation of Nuclear Weapons, International Verification and the International Atomic Energy Agency* (Southampton, U.K.: Mountbatten Centre for International Studies, University of Southampton, September 1992), p. 27, summarizing Part 2 by Laurence Scheinman.

60 Paul Bracken, "The Military After Next," *The Washington Quarterly*, Vol. 16, No. 4 (Autumn

Economic barriers also remain important. Although the analysis of military expenditures by developing countries is clouded by unreliable data,[61] the data support the conclusion that defense expenditures are vulnerable to fiscal realities in developing countries. As a World Bank study has concluded, "Financial factors emerge as an important determinant of military expenditure. Thus, affordability appears to be a major consideration for government policymakers in the realm of military expenditures, as in other areas. Further, the observed pattern suggests that governments view the military as a luxury item instead of a necessity."[62] Especially for governments interested in creating a substantial, viable defense industrial base, the costs can be substantial.[63]

Financial hardship presses most of the countries with major armament acquisition and/or weapons development programs. In the Middle East, for example, the oil wealth of the 1970s and 1980s that fueled such a broad array of ambitious military modernization programs has given way in the 1990s to a period of economic decline and budgetary stringency. In South Asia, economic growth barely manages to keep pace with burgeoning populations. In Africa, sharp economic decline has decimated national budgets. Only in East Asia, and to a lesser extent in Latin America, does economic progress portend a growing capacity to invest in defense. Accordingly, levels of defense spending vary substantially among regions, and even within them; noteworthy, however, is the fact that gross regional differences in defense spending grew substantially narrower as a result of the debt crisis of the 1980s.[64] Thus, the increasing wealth of the developing world cited above is more significant in the aggregate than in

---

1993), p. 166.

61   Information about military expenditures in the developing world is fraught with inaccuracies and inconsistencies, and thus it is generally possible only to use such data illustratively to explore trends. Countries count different things when tabulating such expenses, and sometimes have motives for inflating or deflating statistics used in public discussion. Much defense spending remains hidden from public view. For a review of this methodological problem, see Ball, *Security and Economy in the Third World*, introduction.

62   Daniel Hewitt, "What Determines Military Expenditures?" *Finance & Development*, Vol. 28, No. 4 (December 1991), pp. 22–25.

63   "Massive investments are required to build manufacturing facilities, create R&D centers, and to pay for imports." Office of Technology Assessment, *Global Arms Trade*, p. 123.

64   Hewitt, "Controlling Military Expenditures," p. 22.

specific cases. Aggregate figures also mask a division between countries that are in fact developing and a growing number of countries whose economies are collapsing.[65]

Spending on military forces and infrastructure are significant not just as a drain on national wealth but also in their impact on macroeconomic effects of modernization. Those effects include changes in the structure of demand, supply, and income distribution patterns that promote the distribution of economic growth to ever larger segments of the population. Military spending can be a significant impediment to the modernization process. The UN has made the classic case:

> The continuing arms race will impede the world-wide prospects of economic growth and delay the developmental process with serious socio-economic consequences, particularly for the developing countries....Economic growth and developmental processes are closely interrelated as speedier economic growth can improve the developmental prospects. But in assessing the impact of the arms race on both it is helpful to maintain the distinction largely because, in simple terms, economic growth is described as increases in real income *per capita* and this implies more production, higher income and more consumption. Development, on the other hand, implies not only the existence of economic growth but also changes in the structure of demand, supply and income distribution patterns, changes in sociopolitical institutions and the improvement of material welfare. As some of our studies have shown, military expenditures have deleterious effects on these macroeconomic variables and, therefore, hinder, to say the least, the pace of economic growth and development.[66]

---

65 In 1971, the least developed countries numbered 24 (in terms of UN-defined criteria combining per capita GNP, literacy rates, and industrial development). In 1991, all 24 remain in that category while 17 more have been added. More than half of the 41 are retrogressing. United Nations, Institute for Disarmament Research, *Disarmament, Environment, and Development and Their Relevance to the Least Developed Countries*, UNIDIR Research Paper No. 10, UNIDIR/91/93 (Geneva, 1991).

66 United Nations, General Assembly, *Study on the Relationship between Disarmament and*

Stated differently, there are significant opportunity costs associated with spending on the military, whether lower overall economic growth or sustained domestic economic hardship.[67] Countries such as Iran, India, and Pakistan face increasingly difficult choices between their strategic and developmental priorities. Further illustration of the influence of financial concerns on defense spending is the fact that the debt crisis of many developing countries in the 1980s significantly reduced their capacity to invest in defense; Argentina's debt obligations certainly influenced its decision to abandon expensive strategic programs. In fact, defense spending was a major source of deficit spending and debt accumulation, accounting for as much as 40 percent of the debt incurred by developing countries during the 1980s.[68]

In fact, the economic troubles of the developing world have contributed to a steady decline over the last decade in the overall level of military spending there. As a SIPRI study has noted, "military expenditure in the developing world has been falling in aggregate from the early 1980s....Between 1985 and 1991 military spending in developing countries fell by over 10 percent."[69] A World Bank study has noted that, between 1983 and 1988, "the level of military expenditures in proportion to GDP among developing nations [fell] by over 25 percent from 6.3 to 4.7 percent."[70] Defense spending as a proportion of GDP was in any case

---

Development, Report of the Secretary-General, A/36/356, October 5, 1981, p. 78.

67 Hewitt, "Controlling Military Expenditures," p. 22. He states further, "Since the availability of funds is limited in the medium term, once a nation chooses to fund a given level of military expenditure, ways of financing must be located. Thus, there is always an opportunity cost to military spending. Although the transmission mechanisms are complicated and vary from country to country, the opportunity costs of military expenditures can be categorized into three basic options. A government can increase its overall budgetary expenditures, which in general will lead to lower levels of current private consumption. It can decrease social expenditures, which will lower the quality of social services. Or a government can cut expenditures designed to increase the productive capacity of the nation, such as public infrastructure and economic services, and thereby diminish economic growth" (pages 24–25).

68 Joseph F. Pilat and Robert E. Pendley, eds., *Beyond 1995: The Future of the NPT Regime* (New York, N.Y.: Plenum Press, 1990), p. 68.

69 Stockholm International Peace Research Institute, *SIPRI Yearbook, 1993, World Armaments and Disarmament* (Oxford: Oxford University Press for the Stockholm International Peace Research Institute, 1993), p. 392.

lower in the 1980s than in the 1970s.[71] Gill, writing in the early 1990s, observes that,

> Since 1984, there has been a steady decline in the overall level of military expenditures in the developing world, as well as in the ratio of military expenditures to GNP [gross national product] and to government expenditures in the developing world. From 1984 to 1988, military expenditures decreased by a total of 13 percent in the developing world; military spending as a percentage of GNP in the developing world dropped by nearly one-third; military spending as a percentage of government spending in the developing world also dropped over this period by nearly 12 percent. Should the worldwide recession of the early 1990s continue unabated, the decline in military budgets in the developing world should be expected to continue as well.[72]

The surge of the early and mid-1980s in defense acquisition and production in the developing world thus may have had as much to do with the oil wealth accumulated by a few states as with any enduring redistribution of economic power, or with the market created by the Iran-Iraq War, and thus may prove short-lived. Continued recession or stagnation in the global economy in the 1990s may well fatally weaken the armaments industries of the developing world.[73] As

---

70 Hewitt, "What Determines Military Expenditures?" p. 22.

71 Ibid., p. 25.

72 Gill, *Chinese Arms Transfers*, p. 32. As Stephanie Neuman has written, "To everyone's surprise the growth of the weapons trade ended in the mid-1980s—a by-product, not of arms restraint programs, but of worldwide economic and political developments.... [including] dwindling funds, rising costs and technological improvements, reduced assistance, the lessons of war, and fewer conflicts." Neuman, "The Arms Market: Who's On Top?" *Orbis*, Vol. 33, No. 4 (Fall 1989), pp. 512–514.

73 "The overall downturn in weapons procurement does not bode well for second- and third-tier arms producers who do not have a large home market and rely on exports to maintain the profitability of their defense industries ...(90 percent of Brazil's military production is exported)....Brazil's arms transfers have plummeted by 95 percent" [from 1987 to 1990]. Egypt's by 85 percent from 1988 to 1990, North Korea by 86 percent. Gill, *Chinese Arms Transfers*, pp. 32–34.

Ian Anthony has put it: "the party's over" for Third World defense industries that prospered during this period.[74]

The economics of defense production and acquisition in the developing world has been made even more difficult by the end of the Cold War. This has had two primary effects. First, arms producers in the developed world are competing more aggressively in export markets to compensate for shrinkage in their traditional market and are selling high-technology weapons that are in much demand. As one recent study concludes, "Third World arms production is running into a dilemma: what can be produced efficiently is not in demand, and products in demand cannot be produced."[75]

The second primary effect is the rapid shrinkage of security assistance funds from the major developed countries. Such funds often served to ease the costs associated with weapons purchases or development programs. Describing the 1980s, Robert McNamara has written that "over the past decade, 5 of the top 15 Third World arms importers (India, Cuba, Israel, Vietnam, and Egypt) have received many of their arms free of charge or at highly subsidized rates from their superpower patron."[76] The Clinton administration's decision to terminate the right of eight nations to use military assistance financing to buy defense equipment directly from U.S. companies is symptomatic of a general trend among the major weapon suppliers of recent decades that has compounded rather than eased the economic concerns of weapons buyers in the developing world. The disappearance of the Soviet Union from the international arms market has meant the end of no-cost or low-cost concessionary weapons development programs for its traditional clients; India, for example, is finding it difficult to replace not just its weapons purchases from the USSR but the defense industrial structures created for final assembly of Soviet-supplied subassemblies.[77]

---

74   Ian Anthony, "The 'Third Tier' Countries: Production of Major Weapons," in Herbert Wulf, ed., *Arms Industry Limited* (Oxford: Oxford University Press for the Stockholm International Peace Research Institute, 1993), p. 365. Anthony notes that much of the arms industry in Latin America is idle and predicts that new capacities are unlikely to be added.

75   Michael Brzoska and Thomas Ohlson, eds., *Arms Production in the Third World* (London: Taylor & Francis for the Stockholm International Peace Research Institute, 1986), p. 288.

76   McNamara, "Slowing Third World Militarization," p. 38.

77   Moore, "India's Military Hit by Soviet Collapse."

On the other hand, Soviet collapse has also brought a short-term glut of advanced equipment at bargain basement prices.

Even in the domain of unconventional weapons, cost factors may continue to shape weapons programs. Significant incremental cost increases are incurred when weapons programs move from the development phase to the creation of a nascent capability to first deployment and then the building up of an arsenal and the creation of the necessary appurtenances of command, control, and survivability. States capable of constructing a single nuclear explosive device must expect significantly increased costs if they seek to design and build sophisticated devices small enough to be carried on missiles. The cost of competing with the United States and the Soviet Union in terms of building up significant arsenals, modern delivery systems, and survivable basing and command and control figured in the decisions of states like Sweden and Canada not to pursue the nuclear option.[78] In the case of chemical and biological weapons, the costs of accurate delivery systems and the necessary associated costs of self-protection equipment may tally to significantly more than the costs of the agents and weapons themselves.

In assessing the prospects for future defense expenditures in the developing world, the key is to anticipate the way states will adjust defense spending priorities within a changing macroeconomic context. There are four evident responses among countries with indigenous weapons production programs.

First, in the short term, priorities seem to be shifting away from the acquisition of major new systems. Instead, emphasis is being given to the integration of advanced technology subsystems. Economic factors are combining with technical ones to

> dictate a change in the nature of procurement, rather than a real reduction in the level of arms imports. That is, the import of major and complete weapons platforms such as tanks, aircraft, and naval vessels will decrease, only to be replaced by the import of smaller, technologically advanced upgrade and retrofit packages. Such

---

78   For a discussion of the factors that have led a number of near-nuclear states to abandon their weapons programs, see Leonard S. Spector, "Repentant Nuclear Proliferants," *Foreign Policy*, No. 88 (Fall 1992), pp. 3–20.

procurement policies have the attraction of being cheaper and easing the transition to new and more sophisticated technologies, while at the same time increasing the effectiveness of existing weapons systems.[79]

New Zealand's upgrade to its A–4 Skyhawks, giving them capabilities nearly equal to advanced airframes currently in production, suggests what is possible in this domain; Israel's technology insertion program for the Mig–21 is another example.[80] Toward this end, there has also been a shifting of funds away from procurement priorities into R&D programs—which have long-term payoffs.

Second, high cost is also influencing choices among specific types of weapons. The high cost of modern fighter/attack aircraft has increased interest in missiles, for example.[81] The purchase of advanced tanks in the Middle East has slowed in part because of the approximately $1 million unit cost for service and upkeep on top of the $1 million purchase price.[82]

Third, high cost has reinforced the priority given exports, as a way to recoup high development costs, cope with the overcapacity frequent in many Third World defense industries, and generate income while also avoiding spending scant foreign exchange on imported arms.[83] This points to the possibility of heightened competition among defense producers in the developing world and greater aggressiveness in their marketing.[84] To date, Third World defense industries dependent on exports have demonstrated a capacity to adjust to severe economic constraints without altogether abandoning the business.[85]

---

79 Gill, *Chinese Arms Transfers*, p. 36.

80 Martyn Gosling, "'Paddy's Axe' Gets a New Blade: And Our Skyhawks Outclass Both Thai F–16s and British Harriers," *New Zealand Defence Quarterly*, Vol. 1, No. 1 (Winter 1993), pp. 27–30.

81 "While the costs of weapons systems are very dependent on specific purchase conditions, the disparity in rough costs between U.S. aircraft at $20–30 million and U.S. cruise missiles at $1–2 million does serve to illustrate the cost difference." Roche, "The Proliferation of Tactical Aircraft and Ballistic and Cruise Missiles to the Developing World."

82 Anthony Cordesman, "Current Trends in Arms Sales and Proliferation in the Middle East," released by the office of Senator John McCain (Washington, D.C., January 1992).

83 Sanders, *Arms Industries*, pp. 97–100. See also Ball, *Security and Economy in the Third World*, p. 385. And Office of Technology Assessment, *Global Arms Trade*, p. 26.

84 Gill, *Chinese Arms Transfers*, p. 35.

Finally, economic constraints are forcing trade-offs among competing military priorities, for example, between weapons procurement and force readiness.[86] The relative fiscal costs of national deterrence strategies based on conventional versus unconventional weapons are also relevant to the choices made by some states. For Pakistan and Israel, for example, deterrence relying on a preponderance of conventional forces alone appears prohibitively expensive in the face of overwhelming neighboring firepower, whereas nuclear deterrence gives at least the appearance of being more cost effective. This echoes the experience of the United States and indeed of the Western alliance as a whole in the 1950s and 1960s. The costs associated with arming large forces with advanced weapons are also stimulating greater interest in selective acquisition of weapons offering particularly high leverage, especially in those countries contemplating a future war against a foe armed with far superior conventional weapons—hence the new interest in advanced cruise missiles for attack against the command and control forces (e.g., AWACs aircraft) of an advanced country.

Herbert Wulf has summarized the mixed experiences of developing countries in assembling an arms industrial base.

> Five types of experience can be distinguished. 1. Countries that have developed ambitious arms development and production facilities and have encountered serious difficulties in keeping abreast of modern technology and fully utilizing existing capabilities (Argentina, Brazil, and to some extent South Africa). 2. Countries that have developed substantial arms development and production facilities at a very high cost and are prepared for political and security reasons to continue to pay the price for these programmes (India, Israel, and Pakistan). 3. Countries that have started late to develop arms industrial bases which are still in the

---

85   "[Brazil's] Avibras has gotten considerably smaller. It operated with 5,000 employees in the early 1980s but dropped to about 300. After reorganizing, the company's staff is up to about 700. Avibras, which had sales of about $350 million a year in the late 1980s, is now doing about $40 million worth of business a year—enough to turn a profit once again after losses in 1989 and 1990." Don Podesta, "Latin Weapons Industries Slip in Post–Cold War Chill," *Washington Post*, June 25, 1993, pp. A–27, 28.

86   Jones and Hildreth, *Emerging Powers*, p. 416.

process of expansion despite the negative experience of other countries (Egypt, South Korea, Taiwan and to a lesser degree Indonesia). 4. Countries that have specialized in certain sectors of arms production and try to co-operate internationally, with some commercial success (Singapore and to some extent also Israel). Other countries are also moving towards privatization and commercialization of arms production, particularly South Africa, South Korea, Singapore, and Taiwan. 5. Countries that are known to have or are claimed to have important arms-production capacities, but for which knowledge about their facilities is limited and information about it is highly speculative (North Korea, Iran and Iraq).[87]

Looking to the decade ahead, those developing country defense industries most likely to weather the economic downturn are those that are integrated into a relatively diversified economy, offering infrastructural resilience and technological depth, and that enjoy export markets for their products. This suggests that defense production will continue and grow most rapidly in the large and growing economies of East Asia, less rapidly in Latin America, and least rapidly if at all in the Arab world.[88] Even in those countries where investments might be sustainable, decision makers must cope with the fact that "it is extremely difficult for developing countries to attain the two main economic objectives of domestic arms production: the promotion of industrialization and the reduction of foreign exchange outlays in the defense sector." Ibid., p. 383.

Barriers related to military competence play a little-studied role in determining the orientation of states toward their weapons capacities. These barriers are increasingly salient as the proliferation subject changes from its traditional nuclear focus to include a much broader range of military capabilities.

The historical record suggests that Western analysts have done a relatively poor job of assessing the military capabilities of developing countries. As Neuman has written,

---

87   Herbert Wulf, "Arms Industry Unlimited: The Turning-Point in the 1990s" in Wulf, *Arms Industry Limited*, pp. 11–12.

88   See Ball, *Security and Economy in the Third World*, p. 358.

the divergence between the nominal military capabilities of many
LDC countries (their weapons inventories and force structures) and
their abilities to wage war is only dimly understood....It is little
wonder, then that both Western and Soviet defense circles have
often grossly exaggerated or underestimated LDC military
capabilities (particularly power projection beyond their own
borders), made erroneous assumptions about the relative balance
of power in various regions of the Third World, and sometimes
seriously miscalculated the effectiveness of security assistance in
local conflicts.[89]

Ample evidence supports skepticism about the ability of developing countries
to use advanced technologies in militarily effective ways. The examples are
numerous of developing countries that possess military assets but do not operate
them at or near their potential. Only half of China's submarines, for example, are
considered to be operable;[90] and only one or two of Libya's six Soviet-supplied
Foxtrot submarines are potentially operable.[91] As one study conducted in the
early 1980s concluded, "their overall [military] performance has been far from
impressive."[92] On the other hand, Eliot Cohen has cautioned that "Western
analysts seem consistently to have underestimated the ability of Third World
states to handle advanced technology."[93] How should this problem be properly
understood?

The ability of states to use technically complex military systems is a function
of their basic military competence. Evaluated in generic terms, such competence
has a number of elements, found to varying degrees in various quantities in the
developing (and developed) world.

---

89   Neuman, *Defense Planning in Less-Industrialized States,* p. 2.

90   James Fitzgerald and John Benedict, "There is a Sub Threat," *Proceedings* (U.S. Naval
     Institute) (August 1990), p. 58.

91   "Third World Offers New Threat," *Defense News,* June 24, 1991, p. 20.

92   "The important exceptions are Brazil, South Korea, the PRC, and India," especially as
     regards defense industrial capacity. Jones and Hildreth, *Emerging Powers,* p. 413.

93   Eliot A. Cohen, "Distant Battles: Modern War in the Third World," *International Security,*
     Vol. 10, No. 4 (Spring 1986), p. 159.

At its most basic level, such competence is a function of the abilities of individual soldiers and thus of whether they are sufficiently educated and trained to operate the weapon systems in their charge. A related question is whether they have the ability to maintain their equipment and to repair it in both peace and war (the latter posing far more demanding circumstances).[94] These demands require a broad range of skills, which grow in number and sophistication with the inclusion of more advanced weaponry. Whether soldiers are adequately trained can be a function of funding, because training with high-technology systems such as aircraft, naval forces, and armored combat systems, especially in combined arms exercises, can be quite expensive, as is the acquisition of advanced simulators (although the relative cost is of course much lower). The disrepair of the submarine forces cited above suggests that these skills are in short supply.

As Jasjit Singh has reported:

> The abilities to absorb, assimilate, and "indigenize" high-tech weaponry can, to an extent, be understood by developing criteria or social indicators, for example, literacy levels; availability of technically trained manpower and engineering skills; levels of mechanization, national productivity, and development; automation of public communications and information systems; and per capita utilization of mechanized transport. The limitations imposed on a large number of Third World countries in maintaining and effectively utilizing advanced technologies are more complex than those observed.[95]

---

94 "Maintenance and training will determine if these submarines are force multipliers or drains on their navy's capabilities....limited maintenance experience with high-tech systems and reliance on foreign spare parts and technical personnel will limit the utility and readiness." James A. Hazlett, "Low Intensity Conflict and Anti-Submarine Warfare" (Unpublished research paper prepared for the Center for Strategic and International Studies, Washington, D.C.: June 1, 1992), p. 7.

95 Singh, "Trends in Military Expenditures," in Singh, ed., *Asian Strategic Review, 1991–92* (New Delhi: Institute for Defence Studies and Analyses, 1992), pp. 72–73.

Competent foot soldiers will make an ineffective fighting force in the absence of competence at the command level. This is a function of the training command personnel receive in military institutions as well as the character of the military institution itself. The key criterion of relevance to exploiting the tactical benefits of advanced military technologies is whether the command structure is capable of waging offensive warfare on an ever more complex battlefield. Stephen Biddle warns of the difficulties here:

> New technology imposes systematically higher levels of complexity on unit commanders, operators, and maintainers. The ability to cope with this increasing complexity is thus a powerful influence on a state's ability to exploit the potential advantages of the new technologies. Even where a state can afford the financial costs of acquiring the new systems, to obtain their military payoff demands the capacity to tolerate complexity—and to do so under the demanding environment of combat.[96]

Mere technical competence is not the sole issue, however. Officers must be skilled in command, themselves well motivated, and capable of generating loyalty among the soldiers they lead. Of course, the more professional an officer corps is, the more likely it is to compete effectively for national resources for coveted weapons programs.

Militaries of a largely agrarian, revolutionary, or praetorian character remain in most parts of the developing world, although the introduction of advanced weapons is having the effect in some of stimulating changes within the military in the direction of greater professionalization.[97] Low social and economic indicators generally point to military forces that lack the skills to operate complex, high-technology systems at or even near their potential. Pakistan's conscript-based military for example has been hurt by relatively low literacy rates and a weak education system, although its officer corps excels on this score. The militaries of the Central Asian states of the former Soviet Union, for example,

---

96   Stephen Biddle, "Recent Trends in Armor, Infantry and Artillery Technology: Developments and Implications," in Wander, Arnett, and Bracken, *The Diffusion of Advanced Weaponry*, pp. 91–125.

97   Ibid.

many of which have inherited advanced weaponry, have had their officer corps decimated by the collapse of old military structures; in the case of Kazakhstan, for example, only three Kazakhs had attained officer rank in 74 years of Soviet rule.[98] At the other end of the spectrum, Turkey has shown itself able to build on rising economic and social indicators to create military forces capable of operating advanced-technology conventional weapons. Moreover, in many developing countries there are well-educated elites that enjoy high standards of living and hence educational standards and that enrich the pool of talent available to the officer corps.

A third element of military competence is the existence of the doctrine necessary to reap the benefits of advancing technology. This is in part a function of organization—the creation of entities within the military command to provide innovation in the operational concepts governing the use of weaponry. Without such concepts, the operational benefits of many new technologies and weapons incorporating those technologies will be lost to states possessing them.[99]

Relatively little attention has been given to the defense doctrines of the developing world.[100] Evidence suggests that most developing countries have been less successful than the advanced countries at conceptual innovation in the military. The problem stems in part from the fact that much of their military hardware is imported: "Tactical employment concepts for imported advanced systems invariably are modeled on those of the country supplying and, consequently, are dissonant with the recipient's operational doctrine, planning, and even organizations."[101] Doctrinal innovation may also be limited by political

---

98 [Citation from research paper prepared for project on Global Technology Diffusion, Center for Strategic and International Studies, Washington, D.C., July 1993; publication forthcoming.]

99 Michael J. Mazarr, *The Military Technical Revolution,* Final Report of the CSIS Study Group on the MTR (Washington, D.C.: Center for Strategic and International Studies, March 1993). See also Dan Gouré, "Is There a Military-Technical Revolution in America's Future?" *The Washington Quarterly,* Vol. 16, No. 4 (Autumn 1993), pp. 175–192.

100 "While much has been written in recent years about the flow of arms to these states, there has been little systematic research on their defense doctrines. In most cases, little is known about how these decisions are made, which factors influence them, or what constraints limit the options of LDC defense planners." Neuman, *Defense Planning in Less-Industrialized States,* p. 2.

101 Singh, "Trends in Military Expenditures," p. 73.

considerations.[102] Moreover, doctrinal sophistication is not generally a top priority among developing countries.[103] So far at least, the United States appears to be the only country working in a concerted fashion to exploit the benefits of technological change to create a military-technical revolution in its operational capabilities, but there is evidence that some developing countries, such as China, India, and Iran, have been struggling with some of the same questions in anticipation of a possible armed confrontation with the United States.[104]

Some countries have done better than others. The doctrinal adaptations and growing tactical sophistication of Iraq's ground combat forces during its war with Iran, and especially its growing skill in conducting combined arms operations, suggested that developing country militaries are capable of doctrinal innovation.[105] Iranian military leaders appear to have concluded that their inability to conduct modern combined arms operations contributed significantly to Iran's poor performance, for reasons having to do with poor force organization, ineffective leadership, and equipment shortages.[106]

A fourth element of military competence is the existence of the military infrastructure to support advanced weaponry. In the case of advanced naval systems, for example, infrastructural inadequacies have proven to be a major obstacle.[107] Turkey and India stand out as examples of countries that have put in

---

102 "Assuming that crews are competent (which demands training and exercises, which in turn boost running costs) submarines still find it difficult to find, follow, target and attack surface ships which can defend themselves. Other kinds of submarine campaigns—against merchant shipping for example—have been prevented by political rather than military considerations." Ian Anthony, *Arms Export Regulations* (Oxford: Oxford University Press with the Stockholm International Peace Research Institute, 1991), p. 51.

103 Jones and Hildreth, *Modern Weapons and Third World Powers*, p. 53.

104 [Citation forthcoming from CSIS research project on Global Technology Diffusion.]

105 Stephen C. Pelletiere, Douglas V. Johnson II, and Leif R. Rosenberger, *Iraqi Power and U.S. Security in the Middle East* (Carlisle Barracks, Pa.: Strategic Studies Institute, U.S. Army War College, 1990).

106 [Citation forthcoming from CSIS research project on Global Technology Diffusion.]

107 "The obstacles to operating a submarine fleet are considerable for a country which does not possess a relatively well-developed naval infrastructure. The operating and repair facilities needed for a submarine force are more complex than those required for a surface fleet. In addition to the normal shipyard equipment it is necessary to have equipment for battery recharging and supplying oxygen to the on-board life support systems. Another complicated

place indigenous infrastructure to sustain military capabilities. Pakistan and Iran are examples of countries that rely more heavily on internationally based infrastructures, meaning supply and support relations with other countries. The growing number of suppliers of technologies and weapons may alleviate some of these concerns for some states, although they will have to worry about the availability of sources of supply both in time of peace and in time of war. Managerial ineffectiveness has proven to be a problem in the military programs of China, India, and Iraq.[108]

Moreover, the increasing sophistication of advanced weaponry, as measured here in terms of its reliability and ease of operation, may relax some of the constraints that some developing countries experience in operating some systems, encouraging them to select a handful of weapons or weapon systems that offer significant leverage and that are also increasingly simple to utilize. This may explain the decision by states such as Iran and Pakistan to acquire the latest-technology submarines, which can be operated with far smaller crews than those of the past. This may also help to account for the appeal of missile systems, which generally place relatively minimal demands on the ability of a military force to maintain and operate them.

But technical improvements do not eliminate issues of military competence here. Aviation and ground combat systems appear to be increasingly simple to operate and maintain, but only in relative terms, because the demands in terms of the diversity and sophistication of skills remain considerable. Moreover, continued technological change will only magnify the challenges of operating these systems in greater concert.

---

area is communications with other naval vessels or with land bases....For these reasons, the countries which find it easiest to develop submarine forces are those which are building on an existing naval infrastructure." Ian Anthony, *The Naval Arms Trade* (Oxford: Oxford University Press with the Stockholm International Peace Research Institute, 1990), p. 49.

108 See Michael D. Swaine, *The Modernization of the Chinese People's Liberation Army: Prospects and Implications for Northeast Asia*, Vol. 5, No. 3 (Seattle, Wash.: National Bureau of Asian Research, October 1994); Chris Smith, *India's Ad Hoc Arsenal: Direction or Drift in Defence Policy?* (Oxford: Oxford University Press for the Stockholm International Peace Research Institute, 1994); and Browne & Shaw Research Corporation, *The Diffusion of Combat Aircraft, Missiles, and Their Supporting Technologies*, Report Prepared for the Office of the Assistant Secretary of Defense for International Security Affairs (Washington, D.C.: October 1966).

A related element of military competence is in the acquisition process. Frequently, weapon systems are purchased that are difficult for the military to assimilate and integrate into battlefield operations despite the availability of other technologies that might offer more military payoff even if less sophisticated. As Jasjit Singh has observed, "not all advanced technologies may be appropriate."[109] The acquisition of inappropriate technologies is a problem in part of the absence of technically skilled analytical staffs in Third World military institutions. It is also a problem of politics, whether the desire to satisfy local political demands[110] or the wish to acquire weapons at least as modern as those of a neighbor so as to reap the deterrence advantages of being seen to be of equal sophistication.[111] The ability of the military to react to changes in technology that increase the attractiveness of land attack cruise missiles will be a key determinant of their future proliferation.[112]

This set of criteria of military competence focuses largely on conventional weapons. But what about unconventional weapons? Here too, questions of

---

109 Singh, "Trends in Military Expenditures," pp. 79–80.

110 "National political constraints (for example, the expected procurement of components from domestic suppliers, and social and cultural differences in management practices and production standards) may increase difficulties in equipment integration and standardization." Jones and Hildreth, *Emerging Powers*, p. 416.

111 As Jones and Hildreth noted, "There is a common propensity to acquire as first-line equipment very sophisticated systems and technology, however expensive. This occurs despite well-known problems of absorption (for example, lack of skilled manpower, poor logistics and support or maintenance, and inadequate integration for combined arms employment) and the availability of less expensive military technology or serviceable secondhand equipment on the international arms market. The rationale behind this is generally similar among the cases. It is a combination of two factors. One is the superficial level of knowledge of specific weapon systems and military technology (in terms of their operational applicability to local conflicts and security threats or the readiness of indigenous forces to sustain and use them). The other is a more political than a military consideration, but nonetheless keyed to judgments about what best serves a country's defense against local aggression. It is the desire to deploy systems that are as advanced or modern as those of a neighbor on the grounds that this would be the most effective deterrent, even if the equipment itself is not the most operationally useful combat match." Ibid., p. 415. See also Jones and Hildreth, *Modern Weapons and Third World Powers*, p. 60.

112 Carus, *Cruise Missile Proliferation*, p. 42.

military competence are important, although not quite as important as in the conventional case.

The skills necessary to use weapons of mass destruction are in general less demanding than those necessary for conventional weapons, especially when they are used in attacks against an opponent's cities or major military formations. But barriers remain, especially when chemical and biological weapons are used for tactical purposes on the battlefield. The attributes of able foot soldiers, command competence, doctrinal sophistication, and logistics remain salient here. Chemical and biological weapons are difficult to use in tactical situations if the state using them hopes to reap the maximum benefits of their use while minimizing the considerable risks to its own forces and population. They require up-to-date meteorological information, precise targeting and weapons delivery, and skill with detection, protection, and decontamination equipment. Logistics obstacles are also relevant to a state's ability to build up a stockpile of unconventional weapons, including availability of precursor elements and production technologies. Iraq and Pakistan, for example, encountered delays in their weapons programs because of the need to acquire certain critical pieces of technology surreptitiously.[113]

The ability of a state to use its unconventional weapons effectively is a function not just of its ability to use them in war but also of its ability to exploit them for purposes of deterrence or coercion in time of peace. This invokes concerns about maintaining effective command and control and ensuring the weapons' survivability so that they will remain available for use in the event of an attempted preemptive strike against them.

The features of military competence discussed here are not so much barriers to the utilization of advanced or unconventional weapons as they are conditioning factors. To be sure, developing countries encounter a great deal of difficulty in exploiting deployed high-technology weapons to good effect in time of war, for reasons described above. But few states are wholly devoid of the ability to exploit high-technology weapons. Most have genuine strengths in some areas. In time of war, military outcomes will be determined by which state can do a better job of

---

113 Michael J. Witt, "Flow of Nuclear Arms Slows, Logistics Prevent Proliferation, U.K. Group Says," *Defense News*, October 12–18, 1992, citing release of IISS, *The Military Balance 1992–1993* (London: Brassey's for the International Institute for Strategic Studies, 1993).

maximizing its advantages and minimizing its weaknesses while also exploiting an opponent's weaknesses and avoiding his strengths.

To state this point somewhat differently, a state's individual mix of strengths and weaknesses is relevant only in comparative terms. It is less important that a state be perfect on each criterion than that it be better than its likely adversary on the most significant or the majority of them. Pakistan, for example, cannot hope to achieve an equilibrium of conventional military forces with India but it does appear to have succeeded in putting in place strategies for land, air, and naval conflict that exploit one or two high-technology systems in each domain and that significantly diminish India's ability to exploit its advantages for prompt and decisive wartime gains.[114]

Looking to the future, it appears likely that states making a concerted effort to broaden and deepen their areas of military competence will enjoy some successes. The following factors appear especially relevant to the speed and success with which states of the developing world will overcome these obstacles to military competence.

One is the expansion of literacy and the accumulation of high-technology skills in the developing world. From the perspective of military competence, the key issue is whether and how educational improvements translate into growing scientific and engineering competence. A critical mass of expertise is necessary if states are to successfully develop major weapon systems, and especially to achieve the systems integration skills necessary to assemble sophisticated weapons.[115] That critical mass exists today in a few places. Scientific and engineering expertise is available in abundance in India (with more than 2 million scientists and engineers), but far less so in Iran (where technical expertise was gutted by the revolution) and to the five Central Asian states of the former USSR (which together inherited less than 5 percent of Soviet defense industrial facilities and an

---

114 [Citation forthcoming from CSIS research project on Global Technology Diffusion.]

115 That critical mass may not be especially large. "One analysis conducted by the U.S. Air Force concluded that a 10-year program to develop a 1,000-km ballistic missile would initially require a cadre of perhaps 25 engineers, expanding to approximately 2,000 in 3 years. India's IGMDP program employs 400 scientists working in 15 laboratories and 60 other work centers." Proliferation Study Team, *The Emerging Ballistic Missile Threat*, p. 8. Regarding systems integration, see especially Carus's discussion of the skills necessary to build advanced cruise missiles in his *Cruise Missile Proliferation*, p. 43.

even smaller percentage of workers in those facilities, given the former preponderance of ethnic Russians in them). In some other countries, such as Pakistan and Egypt, that critical mass exists only where it is supplemented by foreign assets.

Of course, there is the important question, critical mass for what? The scientific and engineering requirements of different types of weapons vary considerably. Indigenous programs to produce nuclear weapons, advanced fighter aircraft, or modern electronic warfare systems place more demands on a nation's intellectual resources than do those to produce chemical weapons, cruise missiles, or ammunition. This helps to explain the success in many of these countries of those less-demanding production programs despite low social standards.

A parallel question should be asked with regard to military competence: What critical mass of military expertise is necessary to successfully exploit the high-technology advantages of complex weapon systems in war? Again, the demands of different systems differ. But as noted earlier, the performance of soldiers and officers alike with high-technology systems has not so far been distinguished in the developing world.

The trends in this regard are ambiguous. In Asia, developmental indicators point to substantial improvement in the years ahead. In the Middle East, Africa, and Central Asia, however, nations appear to be growing more rather than less impoverished. Generic figures such as these are misleading, however. India, for example, is a country with dire economic problems and a population immersed in poverty, yet it possesses a wealthy and educated middle class that numbers well above 200 million. In some regions, arms industries themselves "have provided the impetus for the creation of institutions for scientific and applied technology. However, the majority of the developing countries do not possess advanced R&D programs or institutions for educating technicians and scientists."[116] It is noteworthy that "the percentage of the world's scientists and engineers resident in the developing world rose from 7.6 percent to 10.2 percent between 1970 and 1980 and today exceeds 13 percent."[117]

---

116 Office of Technology Assessment, *Global Arms Trade*, pp. 123–124.

117 Tom Clancy and Russell Seitz, "Five Minutes Past Midnight—and Welcome to the Age of Proliferation," *National Interest*, Winter 1991/92, pp. 91–92.

A second factor will contribute to greater future success in utilizing or creating advanced military systems—industrialization and the economic diversification attendant on it. Without an industrial base of some sophistication, the manufacture of sophisticated armaments is ruled out or is likely to fail for technical or economic reasons (although this is much less true in the area of chemical and biological weapons).[118] As one study concluded, "defense production...is one of the most complex manufacturing activities, and requires extensive industrial inputs from such sectors as steel, metallurgy, machinery, and electronics. The recent increase in arms production among such defense industrializing countries as Singapore and Indonesia is explained in large part by their growing manufacturing capabilities."[119]

An important related factor is the independence of these industries from foreign sources of supply and technology, which remains as yet limited, even among those with modern industrial facilities.[120] As yet, there are few examples of complete independence from external sources among the defense industries of the developing world, although the dependence of China appears particularly low. But foreign dependence has a different political context in the post–Cold War era from that of years past, when military industrial relations flowed from a small group of advanced countries to clients in the developing world; today, military industries in developing countries can find many suppliers of technologies and components for weapon systems and their vulnerability to a cutoff of supplies is probably lower than in the past.

Unfortunately, little research attention has been given to the diffusion of the industrial foundation upon which advanced military capabilities rest: for example,

---

118 "With so much of today's military systems rooted in civilian industry, arms production spread is likely to be a natural by-product of economic development." Alex Gliksman, "Arms Production Spread: Implications for Pacific Rim Security," in Dora Alves, ed., *Evolving Pacific Basin Strategies* (Washington, D.C.: National Defense University Press, 1990), p. 69.

119 Office of Technology Assessment, *Global Arms Trade*, p. 124.

120 "India provides a paradoxical example of a country that possesses the largest military-industrial research complex of the developing nations, and at the same time depends disproportionately on transfers of foreign defense technology. Its failed policy of self-sufficiency (because of overly ambitious attempts to produce sophisticated weapon systems) has necessitated substantial imports from and licensing agreements with the Soviet Union and more recently with West European states." Ibid., p. 126.

expertise in computer-aided design and manufacturing techniques, microelectronics, aeronautics, advanced materials development, and precision engineering. The flow of supercomputers and advanced machine tools to the developing world has been slowed by the efforts of the major supplier states, but systems that a decade or two ago designed today's sophisticated weapons are generally available on the international market.[121]

How might countries eager to pursue the acquisition of advanced weapons seek to manage or circumvent these considerations of cost and competence in order to accelerate their achievement of significant strategic leverage? Some countries have begun to put in place strategies to do just that. These so-called hedging strategies take a variety of forms.

Some hedging strategies emphasize competence within the military to conduct complex operations. In Iraq, for example, the Republican Guard was built up in part to provide a core of expertise for sophisticated combat operations.[122] The conversion of a core of soldiers to advanced combat is likely to prove far easier than converting an entire standing army of uneven education and command excellence.

Some of these strategies emphasize the interface of military systems with the domestic infrastructure. India, China, Israel, and Brazil, for example, have put in place special strategies to generate technical military excellence within a domestic industrial context that is less robust. This recalls the examples of the superpowers, which did not rely simply on the effervescence of technically sophisticated military hardware from out of the civilian economy; the Soviet Union found limited technical excellence amid profound backwardness, whereas the United States has constantly pursued qualitative superiority through its national laboratories and defense industries.

Some of these strategies emphasize compensations in military tactics and strategy for continued technical inferiority. The proliferation of chemical and biological weapons of recent decades suggests that some states may be abandoning a strategy of territorial defense for one of strategic deterrence. The

---

121 John Markoff, "U.S. Seeks Broad Ban on Computers," *New York Times,* March 11, 1991, p. D–1; Stuart Auerbach, "Cray Deal a Casualty of Atomic Weapons Fears," *Washington Post,* March 19, 1993, pp. C–1, 3.

122 Pelletiere, Johnson, and Rosenberger, *Iraqi Power and U.S. Security.*

huge buildup of ammunition and spare parts in some countries, for example, suggests a belief that long wars cannot be sustained and thus they must be ready to prevail in relatively short wars.[123] States unable to counter advanced precision targeting systems by electronic means are responding with a mix of lesser technological countermeasures and new operational concepts.[124] Where an across-the-board improvement in conventional warfare capabilities is impossible or prohibitively expensive, states are increasingly looking for those key elements where leverage can be gained and used successfully in asymmetric strategies against more powerful enemies.[125] The proliferation of chemical and biological weapons to states with substantial conventional arsenals suggests the belief that they might be valuable in a circumstance in which conventional defense and deterrence cannot be sustained.

In sum, then, the fact that barriers to proliferation are declining, as described in the first half of this chapter, does not also mean that those barriers have completely disappeared. Important perceptual, economic, and military barriers remain. The general drift of events is certainly in the direction of an easing of constraints, and a few states have adopted strategies to accelerate that process. But for the next decade or two, if not longer, the factors described here will have an important conditioning role that will act as a brake on the programs of all but the most ambitious of technically empowered states.

The "New World Order"

If the gloomy prognosis is too pessimistic in its view of declining barriers, it is also one-sided in its view of the significance for proliferation of the end of the Cold War.

---

123 Klaus Knorr, "Constraints on the Defense of a Small Country," in Center for Strategic Studies, Tel Aviv University, *The Defense of Small and Medium-Sized Countries*, Paper No. 17 (August 1982).

124 Thomas G. Mahnken, *Shiva's Trident: Prospects for India's Acquisition of Advanced Military Technologies* (Unpublished research paper, Washington, D.C., July 19, 1993).

125 Garrity, *Does the Gulf War Still Matter?*; Patrick J. Gartity, "Implications of the Persian Gulf War for Regional Powers," *The Washington Quarterly*, Vol. 16, No. 3 (Summer 1993), pp. 153–170; and Thomas G. Mahnken, "America's Next War," *The Washington Quarterly*, Vol. 16, No. 3 (Summer 1993).

The end of the Cold War has had positive repercussions for the proliferation subject in addition to the negative ones cited above. It may not have eliminated the place of nuclear weapons in great power politics, but it has certainly and significantly diminished the reliance of the nuclear-weapon states on their nuclear arsenals. Over the last decade the United States and the Soviet Union, now Russia, have made substantial arms control progress, with a string of arms control measures providing for the elimination of certain types of weapons (e.g., the treaty on Intermediate-range Nuclear Forces in Europe) and deep cuts in others (e.g., the Strategic Arms Reduction Treaties I and II). This factor may prove a significant boon to the NPT, which established not only a division between the nuclear-weapon states and the non-weapon states but also the goal of diminishing the preponderance of the nuclear powers by working toward eventual nuclear disarmament (although the treaty does not actually embody a commitment by the nuclear-weapon states to that final step).

Moreover, with the end of the Cold War, the United States and Russia no longer must choose between Cold-War-vintage interests and weapons proliferation concerns. This has helped them to expand their cooperation in the area, increase the salience of proliferation concerns in their overall policy priorities, and work to broaden the international coalition against proliferation. Proxy warfare is now a relic of history. During the Cold War, regional conflicts were viewed in Washington and Moscow primarily for their relevance to the East-West conflict. Their weight was measured in global terms—for their potential to advance the cause of one side or the other or to erupt in a conflagration between the two—and the local sources of conflict or means of accommodation were generally given scant attention. Accustomed to looking at regional affairs in these universalist terms, Western policymakers readily added the proliferation concern to their set of filters, and it became easy to fault any acquisition of nuclear weapons as destabilizing in global terms without giving much consideration to the exigencies operating in the region and on the perceptions of local decision makers. The passing of this Cold War overlay thus creates new possibilities for both peacemaking and nonproliferation.

Another positive result of the end of the Cold War is reflected in the decisions of France and China to join the NPT. Hitherto both states have remained outside the regime largely in order to preserve their independence in an era of superpower dominance, but in the post–Cold War world their stake in preventing the further proliferation of nuclear weapons has apparently come to outweigh their desire for complete legal independence in the nuclear area.

These political factors have translated into a more active nuclear nonproliferation regime in response to the major challenges in Iraq and North Korea. The International Atomic Energy Agency (IAEA) has benefited from the increased commitment of the major powers and especially their willingness to share intelligence about possible proliferators with the organization. The organization has been empowered to act with more independence to pursue malefactors, and in the case of the two of most immediate concern, Iraq and North Korea, the greater convergence of views in Washington and Moscow has provided the foundation for more aggressive diplomatic efforts to halt or reverse proliferation than were heretofore possible.

Both of these crises in nuclear diplomacy have also, however, revealed the limits on the ability of the great powers to cooperate for nonproliferation purposes. In the case of Iraq, the economic interests of France and Russia have come into increasing conflict with the mandate of the UN Special Commission on Iraq to oversee the cessation and destruction of Iraq's strategic weapons programs. In the case of North Korea, China's unwillingness to support a sanctions strategy has forced recourse to an unpopular political deal.

Furthermore, the end of the Cold War did not end the U.S. alliances established at its height, alliances of direct relevance to the future of particularly nuclear proliferation in the developed world. The transatlantic alliance remains intact, albeit battered by the civil war in Yugoslavia and debates about when and how far to extend eastwards. The U.S. nuclear umbrella remains over Europe, meaning that Germany and other nuclear-capable but non-nuclear states in Europe need not contemplate early acquisition of nuclear weapons. And the U.S.-Japan bilateral alliance also remains and helps to insulate Japan from regional pressures for nuclearization. Thus the keen interest in both Europe and Asia in the durability of the U.S. security guarantee and the depth of the U.S. isolationist impulse.

Lastly, it is possible to overstate the reach of the bipolar order that prevailed during the Cold War. In the 1960s, theoreticians in the academic world had already begun to distinguish patterns of international interaction beyond the strictly bipolar. Thus the passing of a bipolar order may have a salience for the two poles out of proportion to its significance for other parts of the international system.[126]

Thus, assessed in geopolitical terms, the end of the Cold War cannot be seen at this early stage as having a decisively positive or negative impact on the proliferation problem.[127] The short-term impact appears on balance positive, but doubts about the longer term grow the farther into the future one looks.

The end of the Cold War is a kind of shorthand for the larger transition in world order evident at the end of the twentieth century. The collapse of the Soviet Union and the end of bipolarity are but two parts of a more far-reaching process: the transition away from a certain type of world order to an unknown future.

What type of transition do we confront? The close of the twentieth century is marked not just by the end of the East–West confrontation and the breakup of the Soviet Union but also by a rekindling of hope in the UN, the reunification of Germany, significant steps in Europe toward integration, the growth of Japan as an economic giant and of East Asia as an engine of global growth, a widespread embrace of liberal political and economic ideals that transcends boundaries of geography and culture, the birth of a trading system covering most of the world, and the emergence of a host of issues of a genuinely global character requiring collective responses, ranging from the environment to organized crime. This acceleration of international change in recent years represents a watershed of historic proportions.

The international community has begun to grapple with the new issues of world order, if only haltingly. UN Secretary General Boutros Boutros-Ghali's vision of a more effective UN dealing more successfully with problems of peacekeeping and peacemaking represents one such effort.[128] Another was the

---

126 As J. Martin Rochester has noted, "Mortan Kaplan distinguished between loose and tight bipolarity, Richard Rosecrance discerned bimultipolarity, Oran Young and others pointed out discontinuities and subsystems in the global polity, and Stanley Hoffmann found polycentrism and multiple game boards." Rochester, *Waiting for the Millennium: The United Nations and the Future of World Order* (Columbia, S.C.: University of South Carolina Press, 1993), p. 235, especially footnote 2.

127 See John Lewis Gaddis, "Nuclear Weapons, the End of the Cold War, and the Future of the International System," in Garrity and Maaranen, *Nuclear Weapons in the Changing World*, pp. 15–32.

128 Boutros Boutros-Ghali, *An Agenda for Peace: Preventive Diplomacy, Peacemaking and Peace-keeping* (New York, N.Y.: United Nations, 1992).

ill-fated beginning made by U.S. President George Bush, with his "new world order" theme. Bush defined the new agenda as follows:

> It is in our hands...to press forward to cap a historic movement toward a new world order, and a long era of peace. We have a vision of a new partnership of nations that transcends the cold war; a partnership based on consultation, cooperation, and collective action, especially through international and regional organizations; a partnership united by principle and the rule of law and supported by an equitable sharing of both costs and commitment; a partnership whose goals are to increase democracy, increase prosperity, increase the peace and reduce arms.[129]

Bush's rhetoric has receded into American political history but the world order task remains. The profound changes in the global community of the last decade make it unlikely that a new world order will be quickly achieved. Such a delay is even more likely if one assumes that such an order must be built on some degree of international consensus on questions of purpose, principle, and power in the international system. Such a consensus might evolve quickly among the wealthy and secure countries, but is likely to be slower to emerge among countries less satisfied with the status quo. Because a broad global consensus will be slow to evolve—if it ever does—it is reasonable to expect a period of transition and flux

---

129 George Bush, "Aggression in the Gulf: A Partnership of Nations," *Vital Speeches of the Day* (October 15, 1990), p. 3. See also statements by President George Bush, September 11, 1990; January 29, 1991; and April 13, 1991 reprinted respectively in *Public Papers of the Presidents of the United States: George Bush, 1990*, Book II (Washington, D.C.: GPO, 1991), p. 1219 and *Public Papers of the Presidents of the United States: George Bush, 1991*, Book I (Washington, D.C.: GPO, 1992), pp. 79 and 366. In Bush's last public statement on the theme, he argues that the term "refers to ways of working with other nations to deter aggression and to achieve stability, to achieve prosperity, and above all, to achieve peace. It springs from hopes for a world based on a shared commitment among nations large and small to a set of principles that undergird our relations. Peaceful settlement of disputes, solidarity against aggression, reduced and controlled arsenals, and just treatment of all peoples." "The Possibility of a New World Order: Unlocking the Promise of Freedom," *Vital Speeches of the Day* (October 15, 1991), p. 4.

in the political life of the international community, one that parallels that period of technological transition defined in the last chapter.

Having made a fetish first of Bush's new world order, pundits have now made a fetish of the new world disorder. But how accurate a view of contemporary international affairs is this disorderly impression? Is the post–Cold War international system one in which realpolitik rules of the jungle apply, in which states act as they often have in the past to maximize power at all times? Chapter 1 provided a partial answer to these questions by emphasizing the bifurcated nature of the world in which one part is relatively secure and prosperous and the other part is neither, and thus where different expectations prevail about the use of force. The declining problem of interstate war noted there also raises a question about whether the problem of future war may be overemphasized today in the same way that it was underemphasized in the thinking of students of world politics a century ago. It is noteworthy, for example, that more than half of all states never participated in a war between 1816 and 1980 and of the 91 states that became members of the international system between 1946 and 1991, 80 percent have never participated in wars.[130]

In a survey of the foundations of the post–Cold War world order, Paul Schroeder describes a level of orderliness in global affairs an order of magnitude more substantial than what has been known previously—at the economic, political, and military levels. In his view, this order is far more durable than the pundits of the new world disorder assert. Furthermore, he defines the primary political dynamic within this world order as associational, because states are choosing to behave in ways that will allow them to derive the benefits of inclusion in global economic and political life, rather than punitive or deterrent. Efforts to construct world order around these latter principles, he argues, may prove counterproductive by generating the very problems of international security such strategies are intended to prevent. Schroeder's analysis is a powerful critique of prevailing thinking within the realist and neorealist schools and one that goes to the core of expectations about the future orderliness of the international system.[131]

---

130 Steve Chan, "Mirror, Mirror on the Wall...Are Freer Countries More Pacific?" *Journal of Conflict Resolution*, Vol. 28, No. 4 (December 1984), pp. 617–648.

131 Paul W. Schroeder, "The New World Order: A Historical Perspective," *The Washington*

Schroeder's critique is an important corrective to those who assess the likelihood of a new world order with reference only to the effectiveness of the UN. The hopes of many that the UN might emerge from its Cold War paralysis as the leader of a consensus-based, multilaterally managed new world order have fallen on hard times as the UN has found itself increasingly overextended and as the post–Cold War great power consensus has reached its limits. The UN now struggles with a broad array of new challenges and with disaffection among some members of the developing world who fear the new activism of the Security Council and the loss of a system of "checks and balances" inherent in the Cold War stand-off.[132] But whatever troubles befall the UN in future years, its shortcomings should not distract attention from the patterns of cooperation and habits of multilateralism that reach far beyond that one institution.

One place where cooperative interests intersect with inherited, Cold War–vintage institutions is of central relevance to the proliferation subject—the multilateral treaties for the control of nuclear, chemical, and biological weapons. As discussed in chapter 5, these institutions are gaining new prominence in the post–Cold War system, even as their future efficacy is in growing doubt.

In sum, then, the negative implications of the end of the Cold War must be weighed against the positive if balanced predictions of its systemic effects are to be made. Moreover, it is important to look beyond the end of the Cold War and to broader systemic factors, many of which point to a quite orderly world, if negative and positive factors are to be seen in proper balance.

Quarterly, Vol. 17, No. 2 (Spring 1994), pp. 25–43.

132 In summarizing the chapters in an edited volume, two authors have described the key point in the paper by James O. C. Jonah, under secretary general of the Department of Special Political Questions at the United Nations, as follows: "The central question of Jonah's essay emerges from the juxtaposition of two possible descriptions for the emerging world order—'community' versus 'emerging directorate.' While he denies that Third World countries have a nostalgia for the Cold War, he carefully delineates the growing concern that the new solidarity among the permanent members of the UN Security Council may have removed the 'checks and balances' that have characterized international deliberations since the end of World War II." Weiss and Kessler, *Third World Security in the Post–Cold War Era*, p. 11.

State Behavior and the Democratic Revolution

The final problem with the gloomy prognosis is that it fails to encompass the full range of state behavior in evidence today. The list of six motives discussed in the opening section of this chapter is hardly exhaustive. In fact, there are at least three other categories of states, as defined in terms of their orientation to their weapons potential.

One category consists of states that pursue weapons production programs for primarily economic, developmental purposes. This is especially the case with conventional weapons programs, although it might also apply to states that pursue nuclear, chemical, or biological developmental programs for their potential commercial or public health spin-offs. As one recent study has concluded:

> Increasingly, economic incentives play an important role in motivating the newly industrialized nations to undertake extensive arms production. These countries argue that indigenous production can lead to cost reductions and potential foreign exchange earnings through exports. Additionally, defense programs are believed to contribute to the civilian economy indirectly by providing spin-offs to other industrial sectors, and by upgrading the skills and productivity of the industrial labor force.[133]

India, Indonesia, and Turkey are examples of countries that have pursued weapons development and production programs in significant measure because these programs have had a broader impact on national development by generating jobs, especially high-skill jobs, and reducing foreign exchange costs. Brazil and China are examples of countries that have combined these purposes with the goal of generating national income through exports of military hardware.[134]

---

133 Office of Technology Assessment, *Global Arms Trade*, p. 123.

134 "A number of scholars see Chinese arms exports during the 1980s as being largely devoid of political and strategic motives, and suggest they are driven rather by economic considerations of profit and the acquisition of hard currency." Gill, *Chinese Arms Transfers*, p. 13.

In the decade ahead it would appear that fewer states will pursue weapons development programs for these purposes. Although the evidence is uneven, doubt has been cast on the validity of the theory underlying the "military-as-modernizer" viewpoint because military-led industrialization has failed to generate sustainable economic development just as military-led political institutions have failed to provide sustainable governance. States have found it difficult to reap the benefits of expenditures in weapons development and production programs. As one recent comprehensive study has concluded, "expenditure in the security sector is more likely to hinder than to promote economic growth and development in the Third World."[135]

A second category consists of those states that have weapons or weapons development programs in place but that lack specific strategic purposes. Western analysts, inured to years of seeking to divine the purposes behind Soviet weapons modernization programs, are accustomed to imputing purpose to programs where none may in fact exist. This phenomenon is well illustrated in the chemical weapons domain, where some states may be engaged in limited R&D programs simply to preserve a rudimentary capability acquired in an earlier era; to understand the military implications of technology imported for civilian purposes; to respond to military interest generated by the Iran–Iraq War of the 1980s; or as a hedge against the possible future emergence of a regional competitor armed with unconventional weapons. Similar factors operate in the nuclear and biological domains and also with regard to conventional armaments, where the military ambition to have the latest, best, and most sophisticated—and

---

135 Ball, *Security and Economy in the Third World,* p. 388. In her introduction, Ball describes the study in greater detail. "Chapter 1 describes two main schools of thought concerning the developmental role of the security sector—the military-as-modernizer and the military-as-promoter-of-underdevelopment—and identifies their strengths and weaknesses. It shows that both sets of theories fail to evaluate the role that the security sector plays in promoting or hindering development in a satisfactory manner....Chapter 9 critically appraises the contention that the creation of military industries stimulates the industrialization process in Third World countries through purchases from domestic industry, the transfer of technology, foreign exchange savings generated by reduced weapons procurement from abroad, and manpower training" (pages xxv–xxvi). She observes further that "although the disadvantages of allocating human, financial, and material resources to the security sector tend to outweigh the advantages, it is important to recognize both positive and negative outcomes" (p. 388).

the political desire to satisfy the military—can produce weapons programs almost without specific combat or strategic purposes. Shahram Chubin depicts Iran in this category, concluding that "Its embryonic nuclear program appears to be designed as a general hedge, an option, rather than a crash program with a particular enemy in mind."[136]

In the decade ahead, it is possible and perhaps even likely that this category of states will increase in number. The increasing availability of more sophisticated technologies, especially of a dual-use variety, may stimulate more interest without also specific strategic justification for developmental programs.

The third category is by far the largest among states capable of making weapons of high leverage: for such states weapons, especially those designed for high leverage over other states, are irrelevant to national strategy. To be sure, rare is the country that has forsworn the military instrument entirely, although they exist (Costa Rica, for example). But the vast majority of the nearly 180 states in the interstate system attach little or no importance to accumulating large arsenals of conventional and unconventional weapons. For all of the concern about the proliferation problem, it is important to bear in mind that only a very few countries present proliferation threats with weapons of mass destruction, meaning that they are actively engaged in efforts to develop, produce, or deploy weapons of mass destruction. Most states do not possess weapons of mass destruction, have no desire to do so, and evidently have decided that their security is better served by keeping such weapons out of the local military environment · than by arming themselves with them. The abandonment of nuclear capabilities by South Africa and former republics of the Soviet Union underscores the point that not all states value such capabilities.[137] Many more, although not all, possess military forces equipped with conventional armaments but appear to maintain those forces largely as symbols of the state or for domestic purposes and thus are not engaged in competitive relations with their neighbors. This category of states includes modern industrialized powers like Germany and Japan, other developed

---

136 Shahram Chubin, *Iran's National Security Policy: Capabilities, Intentions, and Impact* (Washington, D.C.: Carnegie Endowment for International Peace, 1994), p. 75.

137 For a discussion of the motives leading the nuclear armed republics of the former Soviet Union to relinquish their arsenals, see Lewis A. Dunn, *Containing Nuclear Proliferation*, Adelphi Paper No. 263 (London: Brassey's for International Institute for Strategic Studies, 1991), pp. 22–24.

countries in Europe and East Asia, as well as the bulk of states in Latin America and Africa, as well as some in Central Asia. The problem of weapons imports and developing armaments industries is noteworthy for its concentration in the Middle East and South and East Asia.

In the decade ahead, this category of states does not appear likely to grow appreciably larger or smaller. The continued credibility of alliances involving Germany and Japan will be a critical determinant of the future orientation of these countries toward their weapons potential. In the developing world, there has been a subtle but important change in thinking about the military instrument. In the early post-colonial years, many new countries in Africa and Asia sought to build up the military as an essential part of national identity, strength, and statecraft. Today, throughout much of the developing world the military has lost its luster as a source of authority and legitimacy or as an institution that could be used to further development goals. As it tries to find a role more consistent with the exigencies of civilian rule and social development, the military's power to dominate the state's definition of its self-interest has dissipated and shows little sign of being quickly restored. In places like Indonesia and Thailand, for example, the military remains an essential factor in national politics, but in a more fractious and open domestic political context. At the margins, this may work to broaden the number of states in the first of these categories discussed here.

These three motives not arming have been little studied in the strategic literature. In contrast to the quantity of analysis devoted to the question of why states arm, much less has focused on why states do not arm, even when they face an uncertain international environment. The gap between the number of states capable of producing nuclear, biological, chemical, and other weapons of high leverage and the actual numbers doing so is a striking feature of the international system of the late twentieth century, and one that underscores the deficiencies in much of the traditional thinking about how states behave.

In speculating about the future orientation of states toward their weapons potential, it is important also to attempt to factor in ongoing changes within those states themselves. A striking feature of the international system of the last two decades is the the movement toward more democratic forms of governance that has touched every region of the world. This broad movement includes not just the collapse of totalitarianism in the Soviet Union and the Communist orbit but also the rejection of authoritarianism in Latin Europe in the 1970s and throughout Latin America in the 1980s, as well as the recent strengthening of democratic institutions and pluralism in many parts of Asia and Africa.[138] There are a number of reasons to believe that this trend has had and will continue to have a significant impact on the proliferation trend.

The debate about whether and how a state's internal structure influences its international behavior is one of the oldest in the study of international relations, with a division between those who see state behavior largely in terms of geography, national power, and realpolitik competition for influence and those who emphasize the aggressive tendencies of authoritarian states and the more pacific nature of democracies, which is tied to their internal diffusion of power, their emphasis on public welfare, or their propensity to trust and trade with states of like constitutional character. As Immanuel Kant once wrote,

> The republican constitution...gives a favorable prospect for the desired consequence, for example, perpetual peace. The reason is this: if the consent of the citizens is required in order to decide that war should be declared (and in this constitution it cannot but be the case), nothing is more natural than that they would be very cautious in commencing such a poor game, decreeing for themselves all the calamities of war....[O]n the other hand, in a constitution which is not republican, and under which the subjects are not citizens, a declaration of war is the easiest thing in the world to decide upon, because war does not require of the ruler, who is the propriety and not a member of the state, the least of the pleasures of his table.[139]

---

138 Larry Diamond and Marc F. Plattner, eds., *The Global Resurgence of Democracy* (Baltimore, Md.: Johns Hopkins University Press, 1993). See also Carl Gershman, "The United States and the World Democratic Revolution," in Brad Roberts, ed., *The New Democracies: Global Change and U.S. Policy* (Cambridge, Mass.: MIT Press, 1990), pp. 3–15.

139 Immanuel Kant, *Perpetual Peace*, trans. Lewis White Beck (New York, N.Y.: Library of Liberal Arts/Bobbs–Merrill, 1957), pp. 12–13. As Michael Howard has explained, "By the end of the eighteenth century a complete [classical] liberal theory of international relations, of war and peace, had...developed....Peace was...fundamentally a question of the establishment of democratic institutions throughout the world." Howard, *War and Liberal Consciousness* (New Brunswick, N.J.: Rutgers University Press, 1978, p. 31.

In more recent times, Quincy Wright has suggested that "it appears that absolutist states with geographically and functionally centralized governments under autocratic leadership are likely to be most belligerent, while constitutional states with geographically and functionally federalized governments under democratic leadership are likely to be the most peaceful."[140]

Quantitative analysis suggests a strong link between democracy and more peaceful international relations in the modern system. The record suggests that democracies do not make war, at least on one another. "With only very marginal exceptions, democratic states have not fought one another in the modern era. This is one of the strongest nontrivial or nontautological generalizations that can be made about international relations."[141] A noteworthy caveat refers to the fact that there is no discernible difference in types of state with regard to their foreign military interventions.[142] Moreover, a debate has emerged about whether statistical correlations might be falsely perceived, such that either random chance or alternative explanations account for the supposed peacefulness of democracies.[143]

Contemporary political scientists have added to the thinking of the eighteenth-century philosophers by emphasizing a number of additional factors.[144] Some take note of the fact that democracies tend to spend less on

---

140 Quincy Wright, *A Study of War*, 2d ed. (Chicago: University of Chicago Press, 1965), pp. 847–848.

141 Bruce Russett, *Controlling the Sword: The Democratic Governance of National Security* (Cambridge, Mass.: Harvard University Press, 1990), p. 123.

142 "[F]oreign military interventions have not been uniquely characteristic of any particular type of state. The Kantian link between democracy and war proneness does not hold for foreign military interventions....Rather foreign military intervention is one of those phenomena endemic in the quasi-anarchic nature of the international system." Ariel E. Levite, Bruce W. Jentleson, and Larry Berman, eds., *Foreign Military Intervention: The Dynamics of Protracted Conflict* (New York, N.Y.: Columbia University Press, 1992), p. 14.

143 For the random chance argument, see David E. Spiro, "The Insignificance of the Liberal Peace," *International Security*, Vol. 19, No. 2 (Fall 1994), pp. 50–86; For the argument that the democratic peace theory is founded on wishful thinking, see Christopher Layne, "Kant or Cant: The Myth of the Democratic Peace," *International Security*, Vol. 19, No. 2 (Fall 1994), pp. 5–49. For an argument that both institutional and normative explanations are necessary, see John M. Owen, "How Liberalism Produces Democratic Peace," *International Security*, Vol. 19, No. 2 (Fall 1994), pp. 87–125.

military preparations than other types of government, relative to national wealth.[145] Others emphasize the salience of shared democratic principles in creating the basis for cooperation on questions of international security, citing both Europe and Latin America as examples.[146] Yet others identify liberal democracy as a sufficient condition for arriving at a cooperative national role conception.[147] It also appears to be the case that democracy and democratization tend to influence national debates about the strategic purposes to which the military instrument is put. A converse argument, drawn from the record of nondemocratic states falling into civil war and international conflict, is simply that democratic systems are more stable, less violent, and thus a greater source of international security than the alternative.[148]

---

144 See especially Michael W. Doyle, "An International Liberal Community," in Graham Allison and Gregory F. Treverton, eds., *Rethinking America's Security: Beyond Cold War to New World Order* (New York, N.Y.: W. W. Norton & Company for the American Assembly, 1992), pp. 307–333, and Doyle, "Kant, Liberal Legacies, and Foreign Affairs," *Philosophy and Public Affairs*, Vol. 12, No. 3 (June 1983), pp. 205–235 (part 1) and No. 4 (October 1983), pp. 323–353 (part 2). For a recent review of the empirical evidence, see Randall L. Schweller, "Domestic Structure and Preventive War: Are Democracies More Pacific?" *World Politics*, Vol. 44, No. 2 (January 1992), pp. 235–269, and David A. Lake, "Powerful Pacifists: Democratic States and War," *American Political Science Review*, Vol. 86, No. 1 (March 1992), pp. 24–37. For a general review of the connection between democratization and international security in the 1990s, see Brad Roberts, "Democracy and World Order," *Fletcher Forum of World Affairs*, Vol. 15, No. 2 (Summer 1991), pp. 9–25.

145 "Countries engaged in international war spend the most and those engaged in civil war are second highest, as expected. Among the other variables, the ranking from highest to lowest expenditures on the military was monarchy, military government, socialist government, and others. By inference, multiparty democracies are found to spend the least on the military....the direct effect of the form of government on military spending dominates the indirect in each case. Therefore, monarchies and military governments allocate a larger share of GDP to the military than socialist governments when both direct and indirect effects are combined." Hewitt, "Controlling Military Expenditures," p. 23.

146 Ivo H. Daalder, *Cooperative Arms Control: A New Agenda for the Post–Cold War Era*, Paper No. 1 (College Park, Md.: Center for International Security Studies at Maryland School of Public Affairs, University of Maryland at College Park, October 1991), pp. 40–45.

147 Glenn Chafetz, "The End of the Cold War and the Future of Nuclear Proliferation," *Security Studies*, Vol. 2, Nos. 3–4 (Spring/Summer 1993), pp. 127–158.

148 R. J. Rummel, *Death by Government* (New Brunswick, N.J.: Transaction Publishers, 1994), p. 20.

As Frankel has argued in writing about the way nuclear weapons issues have been dealt with by democracies,

> Raising an issue's priority on the public agenda may not guarantee a sound policy; it would, however, help to bring new actors and information into the policy process and to mobilize new intellectual and political resources to address the problem....new concepts may end up affecting the practices of governments, not only because they offer a superior or even a new understanding of the situation but also because they carry political clout as a collective interpretation of the national interest and of international stability.[149]

This is not to argue that democracy works inexorably to dampen the tendency to build armaments or to exploit domestic industrial competence for power accumulation purposes. Clearly, domestic political decision-making processes combine in individual countries with complex historical and political forces, the personal predispositions of leaders, perceptions of the utility of global intstitutions for nations interests, and myriad geopolitical factors to shape national strategies. But the global movement toward democracy suggests the possible emergence of an international environment in which resort to war will become less credible or frequent, thus dampening proliferation. Among the great powers, Kant's vision does in fact seem to prevail; whether it lasts and for how long is a primary question of international security for the century ahead.[150] Democratization may also broaden the basis for cooperation to limit proliferation, as appears already to be the case in the domain of export controls.[151]

---

149 Frankel, *Opaque Nuclear Proliferation*, pp. 143, 193.

150 Glenn Chafetz, "The End of the Cold War and the Future of Nuclear Proliferation: An Alternative to the Neorealist Perspective," in Davis and Frankel, *The Proliferation Puzzle*, pp. 127–158.

151 Gary K. Bertsch and Richard T. Cupitt, "Nonproliferation in the 1990s: Enhancing International Cooperation on Export Controls," *The Washington Quarterly*, Vol. 16, No. 4 (Autumn 1993), pp. 53–70.

The movement toward democracy may have a specific and positive impact on one issue of governance directly relevant to the proliferation subject: civil-military relations. The decisions of Argentina and Brazil to step back from nuclear confrontation had much to do with the shifting balance between civil and military power in those countries—and with the quality of dialogue within and between those countries about their national interests that became possible with abandonment of military government. As each moved toward more open government, the perceived threat of each to the other declined, and unconventional weapons programs were set aside. Military leaders were brought into broad national debates about national goals, leading ultimately to a reorientation away from the military instrument and especially weapons of mass destruction and in the direction of addressing pressing national economic priorities as well as military professionalization.[152] Such an opening up of debate has the effect of opening up to examination by diverse constituencies the myths that prevail in key influential sectors about the exigencies of national strategy. In the nuclear area, for example, weapons programs have often been lobbied for by an elite group of scientifically trained and well-positioned individuals— mythmakers—whose strategic beliefs and political activities have been the catalyst for national weapons programs that have not survived broader national scrutiny.[153] South Africa is an excellent case in point. If in democracies nuclear

---

152 Lars Schoultz, William C. Smith, and Augusto Varas, eds., *Security, Democracy, and Development in U.S.–Latin American Relations* (Miami, Fla.: North–South Center of the University of Miami, distributed by Transaction Publishers, 1994), especially chapters 9–11. For a discussion of the way in which democratization allows new constituencies to become players in defining nuclear postures, see Etel Solingen, *The Domestic Sources of Nuclear Postures: Influencing "Fence-sitters" in the Post–Cold War Era*, Policy Paper No. 8 (La Jolla, Calif.: Institute on Global Conflict and Cooperation, University of California, October 1994).

153 As Peter Lavoy explains, "A government is likely to go nuclear' when proficient and well-positioned individuals, who want their country to build nuclear bombs, exaggerate security threats to make a 'myth of nuclear security' more compelling. In contrast to familiar accounts of nuclear proliferation which emphasize the security, technology, or prestige determinants of nuclear arms acquisition, I stress the importance of nuclear myths and myth makers. The strategic beliefs and political activities of highly motivated and resourceful individuals are where the sources of nuclear proliferation can be found." Peter R. Lavoy, "Nuclear Myths and the Causes of Nuclear Proliferation," *Security Studies*, Vol. 2, No. 3/4 (Spring/Summer 1993), p. 192.

postures are increasingly reflective of the thinking of a key domestic political coalition, it is possible also that economic interests within that coalition might provide a point of leverage for those seeking to prevent nuclearization.[154]

Improvements in the relationship between civil and military authorities will have an additional, unanticipated impact on proliferation—evidence suggests that such improvements also contribute to improved military competence. This relationship has been a critical but little noticed determinant of the ability of military forces in the developing world to make good use of advanced, complex technologies.

Bruce Russett has pointed to the interesting statistical correlation that democracies more often win their wars than do authoritarian states. He posits that this may have to do with the fact that "they are more effective in marshaling their resources or are more accurate and efficient information processors."[155] Another explanation may be that among civilians fear of the military leads the former to impose political constraints on the latter that sustain control and reward loyalty at the expense of initiative, creativity, and excellence. Stephen Biddle and Robert Zirkle have expanded usefully on this point:

> In states such as Iraq...the threat of political violence by the military creates powerful incentives for civilian interventions that reduce the military's ability to cope with advanced technology. Such interventions can include frequent rotation of commanders and purges of the officer corps; suppression of horizontal communications within the military hierarchy; divided lines of command; isolation from foreign sources of expertise or training; exploitation of ethnic divisions in officer selection or combat unit organization; surveillance of military personnel; promotion based on political loyalty rather than military ability; or execution of suspected dissident officers....These draconian measures can enable

---

154 Solingen, *Domestic Sources of Nuclear Postures*, p. 3. See also Etel Solingen, "The Political Economy of Nuclear Restraint," *International Security*, Vol. 19, No. 2 (Fall 1994), pp. 126–169.

155 Bruce Russett, *Grasping the Democratic Peace: Principles for a Post–Cold War World* (Princeton, N.J.: Princeton University Press, 1993), p. 137, citing research by Lake ("Powerful Pacifists: Democratic States and War") and Karl W. Deutsch, *The Nerves of Government: Models of Political Communication and Control* (New York, N.Y.: Free Press, 1963).

an autocrat like Saddam Hussein to control the threat of coup to an impressive degree. But they also systematically interfere with the military's ability to develop the expertise and the skills necessary to cope with advanced weapons; to coordinate the activities of mutually supporting systems for maximum effect in time of war; or to motivate officers and troops to follow exacting procedures for the operation of complex equipment.[156]

Later in their study, Biddle and Zirkle argue that

less conflictual civil-military relations alone cannot be a sufficient condition for effective use of technology: poor morale in the ranks, hide-boundness or obstinacy in the officer corps, or any of a variety of other pathologies unrelated to civil-military relations per se could certainly prevent effective technology use. But while civil-military relations alone cannot be considered *sufficient* to explain the PAVN's [People's Army of Vietnam] success, it does constitute an important enabling condition.[157]

The quality of relations between civil and military officials most likely to generate technical innovation and excellence is most commonly found in the democracies of the world. Because of their agreed procedures for the delegation and transfer of power and authority in society, democracies tend to define a specific and fixed political role for the military. A similar commonality of interests may also be found in revolutionary movements, where political and military leaders are virtually identical. The authoritarian regimes common in the Middle East and Asia are thus likely to confront difficulties in keeping the military effectively focused on reaping the benefits of technical advance. The movement toward more democratic forms of government in many countries points to the possibility that civil-military relations will improve in the years ahead, as evident in Argentina, Turkey, and Kazakhstan, for example. On the other hand, continued competition between these two sources of power may, of course, continue in

---

156 Stephen Biddle and Robert Zirkle, "Technology, Civil-Military Relations, and Warfare in the Developing World" (Institute for Defense Analyses, Arlington, Va., January 28, 1993), p. 3.

157 Ibid., p. 42. See also Jones and Hildreth, *Modern Weapons and Third World Powers*, p. 4.

many societies, as it seems to have in Pakistan, Iran, and parts of Latin America, with detrimental effects to their military modernization programs.

Moreover, the susceptibility of democratic governments in the developing world to political opinion may directly affect choices among types of weapons. As Jasjit Singh has observed:

> It is important to reconcile systems that are militarily desirable and cost effective with political aspirations and constraints, both domestic and international. Although technologies for nuclear, chemical, or biological weapons may offer countervalue deterrence, they will be opposed by international nonproliferation lobbies and sizeable segments of domestic opinion in some of the Third World democracies. Although technologies exploiting firepower and maneuverability may offer economical and effective defensive capabilities, yielding national territory for operational advantage may not be politically acceptable, particularly in the politically fragile peripheries of developing countries. Consequently, Third World countries are likely to seek politically desirable and powerful—yet cheaper—capabilities. Such a force design may place less emphasis on armor than on precision-guided munitions, smart mines, antitank helicopters, real-time surveillance, and information processing.[158]

Nuclear weapons have presented a special dilemma to democratic states. These weapons are of such paramount importance to national security and standing that leaders have sometimes deemed it necessary to narrowly limit debate about the development or deployment of such weapons. In the United States, Britain, and France, broader debate about the purposes of nuclear weapons and their attendant costs and risks has occurred not when these weapons were first built or arsenals accumulated but only in subsequent decades when questions arose about the appropriate pace of modernization or optimal force structure. Countries like Israel, India, Pakistan, and South Africa have pursued nuclear weapons without open parliamentary debate. Arguably, this has weakened their democratic

---

158 Singh, "Trends in Military Expenditures," p. 81.

institutions[159] and significantly narrowed their latitude for major departures in national strategy by leaving rumored programs wrapped in myth and ideology. It has given their neighbors some political room for maneuver, but has also contributed to international uncertainty and fear about the purposes of such weapons and programs.

If the movement toward democracy is essentially positive in terms of its impact on the proliferation problem, contrary effects may also be anticipated. Democracies after all are not well known for their preparedness for international crisis.[160] They are sometimes much less willing or able to absorb or inflict violence.[161] The public temper sometimes is more inflamed than the thinking of elected officials.[162] Especially in countries where long periods of military rule are coming to an end, stable civil-military relations appear unlikely and civilian leaders are generally left with little room to maneuver either domestically or internationally on questions of international security—witness the circumstance of weak democratic governments in Russia and Latin America.[163] In such countries, political reform may lay the ground for a stronger military, as economic reform provides more wealth and domestic production capacity.

The potential negative implications of the movement toward democracy may be especially pressing in the short-term.[164] A flood into the international system

---

159 As Frankel has written, "The scope of commitment involved makes the absence of public debate of nuclear issues in opaque proliferation societies even more glaring....What we see here is that the most fateful decision a nation can make is made by a tiny coterie of people who act in isolation from the public and its representatives....Opacity thus depends on a continuous voluntary subversion of democratic institutions." Frankel, *Opaque Nuclear Proliferation*, p. 33. He emphasizes further that this puts a premium on "strong leadership in the face of domestic enthusiasms" (page 89).

160 Josef Joffe, "Tocqueville Revisited: Are Good Democracies Bad Players in the Game of Nations?" in Roberts, *New Democracies*, pp. 123–134.

161 This is a point made frequently by Israelis, noting the incapacity of their small country to absorb casualties in contrast to Arab states whose leaders sometimes appear to feel no compunction about sacrificing the lives of their compatriots in large numbers.

162 A point made by Alexis de Tocqueville in *Democracy in America*, ed. J. P. Mayer and trans. George Lawrence (New York, N.Y.: Doubleday, Anchor Books, 1969).

163 Ball, *Security and Economy in the Third World*, p. xxiii.

164 John Mearsheimer, "Back to the Future: Instability in Europe After the Cold War," *International Security*, Vol. 15, No. 1 (Summer 1990), pp. 184–197.

of new states with a weak sense of nationhood and fragile structures of government, festering civil conflicts, and elites new to democracy and thus poorly anchored in the liberal values of the West may not contribute greatly, if at all in the short term, to more pacific international relations.[165]

Although it is important to understand the impact of democratization on proliferation, so too it is important not to overstate the connections. Rare is the region or country where the impact of democracy on security calculations can be isolated from other significant factors, such as the end of the Cold War or the existence of regional adversaries apparently bent on aggression. It is important also to recognize that democracy offers no guarantees—it offers only the possibility of stable governance that is not predatory in nature. Given the weakness of many of the new democratic or newly more democratic countries today, there is also a real possibility that disillusionment with democracy will lead to its rejection and a restoration of the ancien regime or other political forces intent on building national or messianic power through weapons. Moreover, the liberal paradigm is hardly uncontested in the world.[166] And lastly, as many developing countries accurately point out, most of the major acknowledged nuclear powers are democracies.

In sum, then, many of the markers set out in the gloomy prognosis of state behavior are insufficient for capturing the full range of behavior evident today. There are substantial sources of order in the international system and a variety of political trends that point toward continued amelioration of the pressures to proliferate.

Conclusion

The forces that will act on the new tier of technically empowered states are numerous, making predictions about the future risky. A strong case can be made

---

165 Robert L. Rothstein notes that the democracies of the developing world are weak and unstable and thus that the character of the interaction among them may not soon mirror that of the relations between the developed democracies. See Rothstein, "Democracy, Conflict, and Development in the Third World," *The Washington Quarterly*, Vol. 14, No. 2 (Spring 1991), pp. 43–63.

166 Thomas G. Weiss, ed., *Collective Security in a Changing World* (Boulder, Colo.: Lynne Rienner Publishers, 1993), p. 169.

that weapons potential will turn in to weapons prowess. But there is little basis for predicting that high-leverage weapons will spread like wildfire through the international system in the near term, meaning the next 5 or 10 years. There is a more solid basis for anticipating broader diffusion in subsequent decades, given trends related to the easing of barriers and the declining influence of traditional institutions of world order. On the other hand, there are countervailing political and economic trends that may, in the long run, prevail over those tendencies.

From a political science point of view, the realist view that states will act when they can to maximize their power has done a poor job of predicting the absence of strategic weapons production in the post–Cold War era. The neorealist perspective may yet be proven right, if a weakening of traditional structures of economic, political, and military cooperation in this decade precipitates broader weapons proliferation. But new structures may supplant those old ones, or new patterns of state behavior may prevail.

This chapter reveals the great variety of strategic orientations among the new tier of technically empowered states. The range of ambitions and perceptions is striking, as are the differences in levels of economic and political development. This tier is hardly the unified South imagined by those who predict a future North–South divide in world politics; but its component countries share the challenges with which an uncertain world confronts them.

This chapter has also illuminated the prominence of perceptions and beliefs about the utility and viability of international institutions, formal and informal, in the strategic orientations of states. This points to the fundamental role of policy—of the actions of governments to sustain those institutions and to shape those perceptions—in determining the future shape and character of proliferation. It points also to the impact of proliferation itself on those institutions and perceptions. The following chapter will discuss this subject in more detail.

Chapter 4

Proliferation's Implications for Geopolitics in the Post–Cold War Era

WILL THE WORLD be more or less secure in an era of the proliferation of high-leverage weapons and the diffusion of military industrial competence? Will proliferation's impact be felt as a marginal influence in the world system or will it influence core institutions and processes? Will it prove to be a spiraling process, in which each new proliferation step begets more proliferation, or will new incentives come into being to break the process? How useful is Cold War–vintage thinking for evaluating the implications of proliferation in the post–Cold War era?

In an effort to answer these questions, this chapter proceeds as follows. It begins with a review of the debate about the implications of proliferation as it has developed over recent decades. It then surveys the impact of proliferation in different regions of the world in order to explore similarities and differences in those experiences. Lastly, it turns to the implications of proliferation for the international system generally.

The Cold War–Vintage Debate about Proliferation

The explosion of the atomic bomb in 1945 inspired an awe that led to a widespread conviction that something wholly new had been brought into being, something that would revolutionize relations among nations by making war genuinely total.[1] Fear of the huge power that would accrue to any state enjoying a monopoly on such weapons led to early efforts to internationalize their control, as under the Baruch Plan, but these were effectively scuttled with the deepening of the Cold War.

As the superpower nuclear confrontation began to take shape, maintaining some sort of balance became a major preoccupation, with the attendant fears that the nuclearization of additional states would upset the nuclear balance. Early concern focused on the defeated Axis powers: as the eventual reconstruction of Germany and Japan came into focus, preventing their future nuclearization became a justification for strong security commitments by the United States. As the threat of war in Europe appeared to recede in the 1960s, the risks of war involving allies or clients in other regions became a preoccupation, with the fear that nuclear proliferation in the Middle East could reach out to engage and engulf the superpowers in a nuclear confrontation neither desired. By the 1980s concerns had come to focus on the difficulties for regional stability associated with the transition from non-nuclear to openly nuclear military balances, difficulties that arose from the increasing incentive for vulnerable states to strike first in time of near war, so as to lower the likelihood of nuclear annihilation at the hands of an adversary. There remained, however, a grudging acceptance in some quarters that in certain rare instances some nuclear proliferation might increase regional stability by providing the ultimate means of a nation's self-defense, as in Israel. There also remained a recognition that nuclear proliferation might reduce the risk of nuclear war by decreasing superpower interventions in local conflicts.[2] In the 1990s, the fears inspired by the prospect of nuclear-armed renegades, willing to use their weapons for purposes of aggression and terror and in ways otherwise inconsistent with agreed norms of international behavior, have been brought into sharper focus by nuclear programs in Iraq, Iran, and North Korea.

Thus proliferation came to be understood as threatening to the relations between established nuclear states and as a generator of instability. Instability

---

1   For a general discussion of technology and conflict, see Martin van Creveld, *Technology and War: From 2000 BC to the Present* (New York, N.Y.: Free Press, 1989).

2   Fred C. Iklé, "Nth Countries and Disarmament," *Bulletin of Atomic Scientists* (December 1966).

would be measured by some combination of increased arms competition, an increase in the tendency to resort to war, an increase in the potential intensity or destructiveness of war, an increase in uncertainty about international alignments (and the corresponding distribution of power), and, as a net effect, an increase in the general level of international tension.[3] As Albert Wohlstetter concluded in a landmark study of nuclear proliferation, "Our analysis of what it would be like to live in a crowd of nuclear nations leaves very little doubt that the potential spread would introduce new and very threatening dangers to the world."[4]

This way of thinking about the effects of nuclear proliferation has been much debated. Three alternative critiques have been offered. One comes from the advocates of various national nuclear weapons programs, who tend to praise the virtues of proliferation in terms of its potential for strengthening stability in regions in conflict by creating relationships of mutual deterrence among adversaries and by inducing more prudent behavior by governments to avoid war or even conflicts that might erupt into war.[5] Some also assert that proliferation of this kind helps to create the conditions necessary to build peaceful relations among heretofore warring adversaries, as in the Middle East. Some such advocates have dismissed the anxious advocacy of nonproliferation by the established nuclear powers as nothing but a mask for an effort to preserve and enhance their own power while seeking to deny other states their own instruments of security.

The belief that weapons and weapon development programs bring security is deeply ingrained in the strategic communities of all countries, whether military officers working within the traditions of their institution or diplomats and statesmen who have inherited a nineteenth-century-based understanding of an anarchic international system in which self-defense is the primary right and task

---

3   Rodney W. Jones, *Small Nuclear Forces* (New York, N.Y.: Praeger with the Center for Strategic and International Studies, 1984), p. 52.

4   Albert Wohlstetter, *The Spread of Nuclear Bombs: Predictions, Premises, and Policies* (Los Angeles, Calif.: Pan Heuristics, 1977), p. 7.

5   Shireen Mazari, "The Case of South Asia: A Pakistani Perspective," in W. Thomas Wander, Eric H. Arnett, and Paul Bracken, eds., *The Diffusion of Advanced Weaponry: Technologies, Regional Implications, and Possible Responses* (Washington, D.C.: American Association for the Advancement of Science, 1994); and Shai Feldman, *Israeli Nuclear Deterrence: A Strategy for the 1980s* (New York, N.Y.: Columbia University Press, 1982).

of states. Such advocates also tend to equate national security with international stability and thus peace, out of a belief that any individual nation's efforts to make itself more secure will also translate into a broader systemic effect that reduces the likelihood of war.[6]

Anecdotal evidence suggests that strategists in the developing world rigidly equate security and stability and believe that stable deterrence is achieved through military strength. Indian strategists cite the absence of major war with China as evidence of the success of such policies. Both Indians and Pakistanis cite the fact that the Kashmir dispute of summer 1990 did not erupt into war as proof that deterrence under the nuclear shadow works. Israelis cite the benefits of the undeclared "bomb in the basement" for securing Arab recognition of Israel's right to exist (or at least the futility of trying to drive the Israelis back into the sea). Iranians praise unconventional weapons as necessary to prevent the United States from capriciously using its power to again foment revolution in Iran. These strategists from the developing world tend to dismiss doubts in the developed world about the stability of deterrence in their regions as born of hubris among the technologically advanced or the racism of white societies.

A countercritique of this way of thinking about proliferation has developed, and it focuses on this ready equation of the security of one state with the stability of the larger international system. The attributes of stability differ from those of security. Crisis stability is a quality reflecting the capacity of a system to remain in balance even as states move separately and competitively to strengthen their military capabilities. Arms race stability is a reflection of the capacity of a system to safely weather the demands of uneven armaments acquisitions that might otherwise aggravate the situation or accelerate the drift to violent resolution. Stable deterrence must encompass both notions of stability. This means that once states embark on programs to promote their security through the acquisition of ever more powerful weapons capable of inflicting mass destruction on an opponent, reaping those security benefits is possible only if unsettling crises or

---

6   Kenneth N. Waltz has warned against conflating peace and stability. "The occurrence of major wars is often identified with a system's instability. Yet systems that survive major wars thereby demonstrate their stability. The multipolar world was highly stable, but all too war-prone. The bipolar world has been highly peaceful, but unfortunately less stable than its predecessor." Waltz, "The Emerging Structure of International Politics," *International Security*, Vol. 18, No. 2 (Fall 1993), p. 45.

uncontrollable arms races do not intervene or cannot be dealt with effectively. But this becomes ever more difficult as a result of the interaction of responses and counterresponses among adversaries. Another way to state the problem is that the international security context can generate unintended consequences beyond the benefits of unilateral possession, which leaders may or may not recognize or respond to.

A second critique of the view of proliferation as destabilizing is offered by those who have studied the pacifying effect of nuclearization on the behavior of the great powers. Pierre Gallois, for example, wrote that "when two nations are armed with nuclear weapons, even if they are unequally armed, the status quo is inevitable....Under certain conditions, a new form of equality can be established among nations. In questions of security and defense, there can no longer be strong nations and weak nations—at least in facing certain dangers."[7] Kenneth Waltz has offered his provocative thesis that "more may be better" in the area of nuclear proliferation because "new nuclear states will confront the possibilities and feel the constraints that present nuclear states have experienced" and thus their combative behavior will be moderated.[8] And Godfried van Benthem van den Bergh has described the pattern of "common deterrence" (deterrence by shared danger rather than each other) that emerges among states capable of inflicting assured destruction on their adversaries and that transforms unstable, competitive relations into more stable, cooperative ones as these states, whatever their official war planning strategies, seek to avoid the unacceptable consequences of nuclear escalation and therefore to avoid serious crises such as the Cuban missile crisis.[9] The basis of this critique of proliferation as destabilizing is that any state undergoing a nuclearization of its security relations with others must inevitably confront the dilemmas of that process, whatever its history, cultural attributes, or security orientation. Moreover, the process of coping with these dilemmas is likely to contribute to great caution in the use of

---

7   Pierre Gallois, *The Balance of Terror, Strategy for the Nuclear Age* (Boston: Houghton Mifflin, 1961), pp. 7–9.

8   Kenneth Waltz, *The Spread of Nuclear Weapons: More May Be Better*, Adelphi Paper No. 171 (London: International Institute for Strategic Studies, 1981), p. 30.

9   Godfried van Benthem van den Bergh, *Forced Restraint: The Nuclear Revolution and the End of the Cold War* (London: Macmillan, 1992).

such weapons and to the evolution of political relations among adversaries that make such use less likely.[10]

In support of this way of thinking analysts cite the fact that the Cold War never became hot, despite a number of ostensibly destabilizing crises such as those in Cuba and Berlin, as well as the pattern of stable cooperation that prevails among the nuclear-armed Western powers. If superpower experience is any guide, the introduction of nuclear weapons goes far beyond the existing dissuasive effect of even large, non-nuclear wars in deterring conflict escalation. In both East and West, the initial inclination to think of nuclear weapons as simply bigger, better bombs steadily gave way to an understanding of the unintended consequences of having them. Such consequences include the race to build forces capable of sustaining a surprise attack and remaining to fight and prevail in subsequent volleys of weapons; the need to create high-confidence command and control procedures to prevent unauthorized or accidental use; and the need to maintain the kind of conventional forces that made recourse to nuclear weapons an option of truly last resort. As Robert Tucker and John Weltman have argued:

> For a short period the assimilation of nuclear weapons could be undertaken in a straightforward manner. The weapons were conceived as means of strategic bombardment of the opponent's industrial structure in much the same way as such bombardment had been carried out during the Second World War....It was not until the prospect of Soviet acquisition of nuclear weapons loomed that a change of focus involving some degree of novelty was to be introduced. That novelty, of course, lay with the importance of the notion of deterrence as the central organizing concept.[11]

---

10 See also Martin van Creveld, *Nuclear Proliferation and the Future of Conflict* (New York, N.Y.: Free Press, 1993), who "views nuclear proliferation as more of a threat to traditional military strategy than to bitter adversaries."

11 Robert W. Tucker and John J. Weltman, "The Nuclear Future," in Patrick J. Garrity and Steven A. Maaranen, eds., *Nuclear Weapons in the Changing World: Perspectives from Europe, Asia, and North America* (New York, N.Y.: Plenum Press, 1992), p. 242.

The emergence of a nuclear deterrence relationship between East and West lends credibility to the argument that stable relationships of mutual deterrence can or will emerge in other parts of the world as a result of the efforts of individual states to create deterrent forces. The existence of the danger of mutual assured destruction in the event of all-out nuclear war constituted a historic departure in relations among great powers. This danger made the situation "radically different from a past in which governments could, often correctly, anticipate wars that would bring them considerable political benefits while exacting very little in the way of costs."[12]

Three countercritiques to this way of thinking have been offered. One disputes the relevance of nuclear weapons to the pacification effect being studied. John Mueller argues that nuclear weapons have been "essentially irrelevant" in bringing about stability because the risks of nuclear escalation have been less important in war avoidance than the accumulating wealth and interaction of developed countries, which have led the advanced industrial societies to regard the costs of war as sufficiently high to make them want to prevent conflict, even at less than massively destructive levels.[13] This viewpoint has been echoed by John Lewis Gaddis, who writes that "Because the atomic bomb preceded the onset of the Cold War, it has been too easy for us simply to assume that nuclear weapons are what transformed that conflict over time into a long peace."[14] As

---

12   Bernard Brodie, Michael D. Intriligator, and Roman Kolkowicz, eds., *National Security and International Stability* (Cambridge, Mass.: Oelgeschlager, Gunn & Hain for the Center for International and Strategic Studies, 1983), p. 6.

13   See John Mueller, *Retreat from Doomsday: The Obsolescence of Major War* (New York, N.Y.: Basic Books, 1989) and his "The Essential Irrelevance of Nuclear Weapons: Stability in the Postwar World," *International Security*, Vol. 13, No. 2 (Fall 1988), pp. 55–79. For a critique of this thesis as ahistorical, see van Bentham van den Bergh, *Forced Restraint*, p. 278, footnote 2; Carl Kaysen, "Is War Obsolete? A Review Essay," *International Security*, Vol. 14, No. 4 (Spring 1990); and Robert Jervis, "The Political Effects of Nuclear Weapons," in Sean M. Lynn-Jones, Steven E. Miller, and Stephen van Evera, eds., *Nuclear Diplomacy and Crisis Management* (Cambridge, Mass.: MIT Press, 1990), pp. 28–38.

14   John Lewis Gaddis offers three propositions about the nuclear revolution: that nuclear weapons have reinforced an already declining propensity on the part of great powers to fight one another; that the possession of nuclear weapons diminishes, more than it encourages, the tendency of nations to take risks; although nuclear weapons did not create the bipolar character of international relations of the Cold War, they did prolong it; and that nuclear

Edward Kolodziej and Patrick Morgan have argued, the stabilizing effect of nuclear weapons may have been overrated—their impact on the great powers may have been neither good nor bad, and may have done little more than reinforce existing patterns of international conduct.[15]

The second countercritique holds that the lessons of the superpower experience are of limited utility for the kinds of states likely to acquire nuclear weapons in the future. Some who take this point of view use a psychological explanation to argue that the relatively rational behavior that prevailed in the East–West competition—which is to say that leaders on both sides clearly understood the costs and risks of war and communicated one to another about their intentions—may not prevail in countries with different levels of political development, where political leaders may lack the cognitive predilections, training, or even emotional stability to make deterrence work.[16] Others of this opinion use an organizational model to explain why pacification effects evident in the superpower relationship that derived from institutional factors within those countries have not been replicated in the developing world. Scott Sagan, for example, has written that:

> professional military organizations...display strong proclivities
> toward organizational behaviors that lead to deterrence failures.
> Unlike the widespread psychological critique of rational deterrence
> theory...this organizational critique argues that professional military
> organizations, if left on their own, are unlikely to fulfill the
> operational requirements for rational nuclear deterrence...such
> organizational proclivities can be effectively countered only by tight

---

weapons perpetuated the Cold War by making its costs bearable on both sides. Gaddis, "Nuclear Weapons, the End of the Cold War, and the Future of the International System," in Garrity and Maaranen, *Nuclear Weapons in the Changing World*, p. 16.

15 Edward A. Kolodziej and Patrick M. Morgan, eds., *Security and Arms Control*, Vol. 2: *A Guide to International Policymaking* (New York, N.Y.: Greenwood Press, 1989), p. 321, citing A.F.K. Organski, *World Politics*, 2d ed. (New York, N.Y.: Alfred A. Knopf, 1968), pp. 334–337.

16 For a general discussion of the connection between cognition and deterrence, see Robert Jervis, *Perception and Misperception in International Politics* (Princeton, N.J.: Princeton University Press, 1976), especially chapter 3, "Deterrence, the Spiral Model, and Intentions of the Adversary."

and sustained civilian control of the military. Unfortunately, there are strong reasons to believe that future nuclear-armed states will lack such positive mechanisms of civilian control.[17]

The third countercritique derives from an assessment that the stability in East–West relations was more perceived than real. This is a view of the superpower nuclear experience that is highly cautionary and one based in the burgeoning post–Cold War debate about what types of crises actually transpired that also entailed nuclear risks. Part of the argument is that the revolutionary effect of nuclear weapons on the military equation does not appear to have been well understood in the 1940s and 1950s.[18] It is unclear, for example, whether Soviet military doctrine in this period (and into the 1960s and 1970s) ever moved as far as that of the United States in centralizing deterrence as the primary function of its strategic forces (although this may not have precluded a strongly based deterrent relationship in fact).[19] The command and control structures of both East and West may have been far more brittle and unreliable than imagined.[20]

---

17 Scott D. Sagan, "The Perils of Proliferation: Organization Theory, Deterrence Theory, and the Spread of Nuclear Weapons," *International Security*, Vol. 18, No. 4 (Spring 1994), pp. 66–107. An updated version was published in Scott D. Sagan, ed., *Civil-Military Relations and Nuclear Weapons* (Stanford, Calif.: Center for International Security and Arms Control, Stanford University, 1994), pp. 3–34.

18 James Digby and J. J. Martin, "On Not Confusing Ourselves: Contributions of the Wohlstetters to U.S. Strategy and Strategic Thought," in Andrew W. Marshall, J. J. Martin, and Henry S. Rowen, eds., *On Not Confusing Ourselves: Essays on National Security Strategy in Honor of Albert and Roberta Wohlstetter* (Boulder, Colo.: Westview Press, 1991), pp. 3–16.

19 The new U.S. way of thinking was nicely summarized in 1946: "Thus far the chief purpose of our military establishment has been to win wars. From now its chief purpose must be to avert them. It can have almost no other useful purpose." Bernard Brodie, Frederick S. Dunn, Arnold Wolfers, Percey E. Corbett, and William T. R. Fox writing in Brodie, ed., *The Absolute Weapon* (New York, N.Y.: Harcourt, Brace, 1946), p. 76. In contrast, the Soviets "appear persuaded that in the nuclear age no less than before, the most reliable way to prevent war is to maintain the appropriate wherewithal to fight and win should it occur." Benjamin S. Lambeth, "The Political Potential of Soviet Equivalence," *International Security*, Fall 1979, p. 27. This is a dispute of historical substance awaiting new research with the opening of Soviet/Russian archives.

20 According to Bruce G. Blair, "The risk of nuclear inadvertence was much greater than has

A final critique of proliferation as destabilizing has been offered by those who recognize that it has certain destabilizing consequences but view them as essentially manageable. Michael Intriligator and Dagobert Brito have observed that "where there are adverse effects on world stability from an additional nuclear nation, these effects may be partly offset by policies and programs which have the effect of reducing the probability of accidental or irrational war."[21]

This school identifies both stabilizing and destabilizing influences of nuclearization in the superpower relationship, concluding that nuclear weapons contributed to a devaluation of force in the superpower relationship for any purpose short of survival once mutual assured destruction was achieved, although force was not devalued in relations with other adversaries incapable of inflicting assured destruction.[22] It prescribes a mix of measures, including alliances, technical assistance, conventional arms sales, arms control, and collective security responses, for addressing the instabilities associated with nuclear proliferation.

At the core of these different attitudes about the implications of proliferation is a set of ideas about stability. What is stability? For whom? For most analysts in the developed world, the Cold War provided a set of ready answers to such questions. Stability was measured in terms of the character of the relationships between the superpowers and their allies and clients. The stability that mattered most was the stability of the superpower relationship, because anything that destabilized it might have led to globally catastrophic nuclear war. With the passing of the Cold War, these questions are more difficult to answer or, more precisely, global answers that address general stability needs of the larger

---

generally been recognized. The danger lurked in the command and control systems governing the forces....The distinct possibility existed that a nuclear war could begin through unauthorized use, by accident, or, more likely, because of erroneous information about the other side's nuclear intentions or actions." Blair, *The Logic of Accidental Nuclear War* (Washington, D.C.: Brookings Institution, 1993), p. 1.

21 Michael Intriligator and Dagobert L. Brito, "Nuclear Proliferation and the Probability of Nuclear War," in Brodie, Intriligator, and Kolkowicz, *National Security and International Stability*, pp. 257–271.

22 For the argument that second-strike capability is a per se balancer, see John Mearsheimer, "Back to the Future: Instability in Europe After the Cold War," *International Security*, Vol. 15, No. 1 (Summer 1990).

community are less easy to formulate than answers with a national or regional focus.

The end of the Cold War has not brought a resolution among these competing schools of thought. What is the legacy of this history to those assessing the proliferation challenges of the post–Cold War era?

First, this body of debate looks little beyond the nuclear experience of the superpowers to derive theories and lessons. To be sure, there is much to be mined from that experience, but nuclear history is already broader. Other nuclear powers exist, some in alliance with one another and others in proximity but not alliance or conflict. The heavy emphasis in the theory on the effect of nuclearization on adversarial dyadic relationships misses the effects of nuclearization on nonadversarial relationships and on complex relations involving multiple players. Godfried van Benthem van den Bergh's, with its focus on systemic effects of mutual assured destruction, comes closest to a general theory of nuclearization by opening up the subject to other means of inflicting assured destruction in any geostrategic context.

Moreover, the body of experience gained in the East-West conflict may not equip analysts with a sufficiently broad base for understanding the issues of deterrence, stability, arms competition, and crisis management in the developing world. For example, a great deal of the thinking in the United States about deterrence is rooted in the unique circumstances of the effort to ensure credible extended deterrence in Europe. Central deterrence may prove a simpler—or more even more complicated—proposition in regions not sharply defined by bloc politics.

Second, this body of debate looks little beyond the nuclear experience at all. It says little if anything about the consequences of the proliferation of other types of weapons. Chemical and biological weapons were treated as taboo and the consequences of their proliferation thus were subjected to little or no systematic thinking. To the extent there was any thought about the diffusion of nuclear technology, fuels, and expertise for civilian purposes such as energy production, it actively encouraged such diffusion for many years, originally under the aegis of the Atoms for Peace program. Indeed, the IAEA has a mandate to provide monitoring support to the NPT while also promoting the peaceful applications of nuclear technology. It was deemed conducive to more peaceful relations among states to share the peaceful virtues of this new technology and help developing states to meet their energy needs. A growing chorus of critics has, however, faulted the promotion of nuclear technology as foolish for security reasons and harmful to the environment.

To the extent that there was any thinking on the non-nuclear dimensions of this subject during the Cold War, such diffusion, especially in the conventional weapons domain, was apparently understood on balance to be more helpful than not to international security, because it strengthened the self-defense capacities of nations, thereby lowering the prospects of war. Weapon sales were accepted as legitimate in an international system that provides the right to self-defense. They were deemed necessary to maintain the capacity for self-defense and local balances of power in places like the Middle East and as sometimes useful for weakening the perceived need for nuclear weapons, as in Pakistan. The absence of a global norm against such diffusion has been evident in the competition among the suppliers of such hardware over the decades. These suppliers also advertised the supposed political leverage they gained over recipients of arms transfers—a leverage useful presumably for preventing states from using these weapons for purposes of aggression.

To the extent much concern focused during the Cold War years on the potential negative effects of such proliferation on peace and stability, it emphasized the possibility that the arms trade would nourish arms races among competitors, especially in advanced weaponry. But most of the research on conventional arms races in the decade has disputed the conventional wisdom that they are destabilizing. As Frederic S. Pearson and Michael Brzoska have written,

> The starting point has been the hypothesis that "arms-tension"
> spirals increase the probability of war. A number of empirical tests
> have failed to produce a statistically conclusive relationship
> between arms build-ups, or more specifically, arms races and war.
> Many studies have found weak correlations, but no major author
> has found a strong contribution of armaments to war.[23]

---

23 Frederic S. Pearson and Michael Brzoska, "The Register as an Early Warning System: Case Studies and Empirical Evidence of the Role of Conventional Arms in Conflict," in Malcolm Chalmers et al., *Developing the UN Register of Conventional Arms* (Bradford, U.K.: Department of Peace Studies, University of Bradford, 1994), p. 245. Grant T. Hammond has argued that "Arms races are both a means of communicating intent and capability and a means of attempting to change or maintain the balance of power, politically and militarily, without

There is also a noteworthy contrast between the voluminous literature on nuclear deterrence and the relative paucity of work on conventional deterrence.[24]

Proliferation and Stability After the Cold War

A fresh assessment of the consequences of proliferation is thus necessary in the post–Cold War era. Using the taxonomy developed in chapter 2, this section surveys first nuclear proliferation and then turns to other unconventional weapons, missile delivery systems, conventional weapons, and the defense industrial base.

Nuclear Proliferation

Surveying the global scene of the 1990s, it appears that nuclear proliferation is having a broad set of effects, positive and negative. In some regions, nuclear

---

resort to the use of force. They are gambles....as conducive to peace as they are to war. Just as policies of other sorts—alliances, collective security arrangements, isolation—may succeed or fail, so may arms races." Hammond, *Plowshares into Swords: Arms Races in International Politics, 1840–1991* (Columbia, S.C.: University of South Carolina Press, 1993), pp. 244, 263. See also Martin Wight, *Power Politics*, ed. Hedley Bull and Carsten Holbraad (London: Penguin Books and the Royal Institute of International Affairs, 1979), pp. 251, 254.

24 For a literature review on deterrence, see Barry Buzan, *Introduction to Strategic Studies* (London: Macmillan, 1989), part 3, who underscores the complexity of the subject relative to nuclear deterrence and the heavy reliance in the existing literature on experience drawn narrowly from large army confrontations in Europe. See also John J. Mearsheimer, *Conventional Deterrence* (Ithaca, N.Y.: Cornell University Press, 1983). See also Efraim Inbar and Shmuel Sandler, "Israel's Deterrence Strategy Revisited," *Security Studies*, Vol. 3, No. 2 (Winter 1993/94), pp. 330–358. For more the consequences of proliferation generally, see John J. Weltman, "Nuclear Devolution and World Order," *World Politics*, Vol. 32 (January 1980), pp. 169–93; idem, "Managing Nuclear Multipolarity," *International Security*, Vol. 6, No. 3 (Winter 1981–82); Shai Feldman, "Managing Nuclear Proliferation," in Jed C. Snyder and Samuel F. Wells, eds., *Limiting Nuclear Proliferation* (Cambridge, Mass.: Ballinger, 1985); Bruce D. Berkowitz, "Proliferation and the Likelihood of War," *Journal of Conflict Resolution* (March 1985), pp. 57–82; Joseph S. Nye, Jr., "Maintaining the Non-Proliferation Regime," *International Organization*, Vol. 35, No. 1 (Winter 1981); Dagobert L. Brito and Michael D. Intriligator, "Proliferation and the Probability of War: Global and Regional Issues," in Brito et al., *Strategies for Managing Nuclear Proliferation* (Lexington, Mass.: Lexington Books, 1983), pp. 135–144; and Garrity and Maaranen, *Nuclear Weapons in the Changing World*.

proliferation seems to be working as Waltz and others of like mind have predicted, which is to say to induce a level of stability within regions prone to armed conflict. The Middle East is one example. Here, a region marked by the competitive acquisition of conventional and unconventional weapons and by Israeli nuclear preponderance has been torn by many wars, but the state system has been stable enough to survive those wars. The changing military equation in the region has been one of many political, economic, and military factors that have nurtured a peace process that has borne partial fruit. As Geoffrey Kemp has put it:

> [E]very country in the Middle East has great reason for concerns about the current trend in proliferation. While economic and political constraints may hold down the speed with which weapons of mass destruction can be obtained, a highly armed Middle East with unresolved conflicts is likely to be infinitely more dangerous ten years from now than at any time in the recent past. This dilemma affects each country in different ways, yet all have an interest in achieving some semblance of stability.[25]

Further nuclearization is especially intolerable from the point of view of the only nuclear power in the region—Israel—whose leaders adhere to the view that "nuclear weapons are a radically distinct type of weapon, the only single weapon with the potential to destroy the whole Zionist experiment."[26] Of course, mutual deterrence has been purchased by Israel and Syria, among others, at a cost of shorter warning times, greater pressures to strike first in time of near war, and greater devastation by war should it occur. Moreover, the arsenals that have been created for deterrence purposes may also be used for compellence in the event of regime change.

---

25 Geoffrey Kemp, "Middle East Proliferation Scenarios," in Joachim Krause, ed., *Kernwaffenverbreitung und internationaler Systemwandel* (nuclear weapons proliferation and a changing international system) (Baden-Baden, Germany: Nomos Verlagsgesellschaft für die Stiftung Wissenschaft und Politik, 1994), p. 190.

26 Avner Cohen, "Nuclear Weapons, Opacity, and Democracy: Understanding the Israeli Case" (Unpublished paper, March 1992), p. 21.

South Asia provides another example of a region in which the stabilizing influences of nuclearization appear to be increasingly prominent. The apparent achievement of assured destruction capabilities by both India and Pakistan has induced a new measure of prudence in their relations. The new nuclear overlay to war on the subcontinent has begun to change the ways leaders think about war and has induced them to seek new ways to limit the likelihood of conflict and the risks of escalation.[27]

Other regions demonstrate more clearly the destabilizing consequences of nuclear proliferation. In East Asia, nuclear acquisition by North Korea has emerged as a major challenge to regional order because it has heightened the perceived risk of war on the peninsula and has extended the threat of war to Japan and others beyond the peninsula. In the Persian Gulf, potential nuclear acquisition by Iraq remains a subject of intense international concern as the UN undertakes long-term monitoring of Iraq's strategic weapons potential. Iran's ambitions in the nuclear area are also a subject of intense interest, given its uncertain role within the region and its outspoken advocacy of an anti-Western agenda. In Central Asia and Eastern Europe, possible nuclear weapons retention by successor states of the Soviet Union other than Russia has raised questions about the possibility of future civil wars within or among those territories, wars that might spill over into other regions. Within each of these regions, the destabilizing aspects of nuclearization tend not to be related to an increased propensity for war but rather to an increased ability to exploit weapons for coercive purposes within and beyond the region.

Yet other regions demonstrate proliferation's potential impact in revolutionizing state relations. In South America, for example, the risks associated

---

27   George K. Tanham, *Indian Strategic Thought: An Interpretive Essay,* R–4207–USDP (Santa Monica, Calif.: RAND, 1992); Raju C. G. Thomas, *South Asian Security in the 1990s,* Adelphi Paper No. 278 (London: Brassey's for the International Institute for Strategic Studies, 1993), p. 69; Neil Joeck, "Tacit Bargaining and Stable Proliferation in South Asia," in Benjamin Frankel, ed., *Opaque Nuclear Proliferation: Methodological and Policy Implications* (London: Frank Cass, 1991), p. 89; C. Raja Mohan, "Crisis Management and Confidence-Building in South Asia" (Research paper prepared for the United States Institute of Peace, Washington, D.C., 1993); and George H. Quester, *Nuclear Pakistan and Nuclear India: Stable Deterrent or Proliferation Challenge?* (Carlisle, Pa.: Strategic Studies Institute, U.S. Army War College, 1992).

with the incipient nuclear competition between Argentina and Brazil led not to a stabilization of military competition at higher levels of potential destructiveness but an abandonment of that competition altogether and adoption of a regional nuclear cooperation mechanism. Similarly, in Africa and the South Pacific the specter of nuclear proliferation has led to major new diplomatic efforts to construct nuclear-weapons-free zones.

In those regions where proliferation has occurred, how likely is it that states will be able to reap the stabilizing benefits predicted by some and so far observable to a limited extent in a few regions? The inherited debate on proliferation suggests two points of vulnerability: crisis instability and arms race instability.

As noted earlier, crisis stability reflects the capacity of a system of states in confrontation to avoid recourse to war in the face of major disruptions to their political, economic, or military relationships or status. As crises between states unfold, human and organizational factors can contribute to a loss of control.[28] One recent study of international crisis management has concluded that, "the basic politics of crisis escalation between nation-states have changed very little from the time of the ancient Greeks; they operate, at least in the early stages, largely independent of the costs of war. And once a crisis is deeply engaged, the mechanics of preemption take account mainly of the likelihood of war, not the costs of war."[29] This echoes Clausewitz's dictum that the presence of the reasons for a conflict does not limit its violence. As crises grow more intense and fast-paced, the pressure to strike preemptively grows considerably.[30] Cold War thinking suggests that leaders engaged in near-nuclear confrontations are pressured to use conventional military force in decisive ways in the hope that this will prevent nuclear use by demonstrating their resolve and commitment—and thus presumably establishing the credibility of the threat to retaliate with nuclear weapons if attacked first.[31] And as Lawrence Freedman has written, "The

---

28   Gilbert R. Winham, *New Issues in International Crisis Management* (Boulder, Colo.: Westview Press, 1988), p. 232.

29   Ibid., p. 227. Winham goes on to conclude that "Once a crisis is underway, the outcome is as dependent on the process of crisis management as on the substance of dispute" (page 229).

30   Blair, *Logic of Accidental Nuclear War*, p. 9.

31   See the analysis of Thomas Schelling's arguments on this point by Stanley Hoffmann, "The Problem of Intervention," in Hedley Bull, ed., *Intervention in World Politics* (Oxford:

capacity of states to cope with nuclear responsibility must vary. This is more than just a question of command-and-control arrangements."[32]

Crisis stability thus depends on perceptions of the likelihood of unacceptable harm resulting from the decision to initiate war. The East-West experience has come to be seen, correctly or not, as one in which responsible political leaders on both sides were capable of calculating the costs and benefits of decisions to acquire and use weapons.[33] But Robert Jervis has argued that overconfidence, a refusal to see value trade-offs, and difficulties in assimilating new information to preexisting beliefs impair the ability to perceive the risks and costs of war clearly.[34] Perfect rationality is hardly an attribute of national leaders acting under the pressures of a crisis circumstance, whether because of shortcomings in the institutions that support them (e.g., intelligence organizations), the blinders of ideology, or the decision-making distortions caused by the bureaucratization of governance or the stresses of crisis.

The success of the superpowers in navigating their various crises and surviving the problems identified by Jervis has created a belief that their high standards of organizational control, managerial acumen, and technical sophistication are the sine qua non of successful nuclear crisis management. But few of the political,

---

Clarendon Press, 1984). See also Ariel E. Levite, Bruce W. Jentleson, and Larry Berman, eds., *Foreign Military Intervention: The Dynamics of Protracted Conflict* (New York, N.Y.: Columbia University Press, 1992), p. 12.

32 Lawrence Freedman, "Great Powers, Vital Interests, and Nuclear Weapons," *Survival*, Vol. 34, No. 4 (Winter 1994/95), p. 36.

33 This question of rationality has been subject to much debate, especially because it was asserted that nuclear deterrence required that leaders contemplate global suicide by threatening to retaliate with a massively destructive attack once deterrence had broken down and their own society lay in ruins. Such retaliation would be virtually without military purpose. As Bruce Blair has commented, "This internal contradiction, accorded the status of a genuine paradox, undermined the theory [of deterrence]. But by invoking 'the threat that leaves something to chance' (which presumes the existence of an inherent, irreducible risk of inadvertence), arguing that a potential aggressor could not count on pure reason to dictate its victim's response, the theory disposed of the conundrum....The party that acts with reckless abandon may get its way by playing on a more cautious opponent's fear of inadvertent escalation." Blair, *Logic of Accidental Nuclear War*, pp. 5–6.

34 Robert Jervis, "Deterrence and Perception," in Brodie, Intriligator, and Kolkowicz, *National Security and International Stability*, pp. 131–156.

social, and technical factors that helped to promote crisis stability in the superpower era appear to be operative among the new nuclear-weapon states. Especially in the early phases of a nuclear program, when it may be relatively vulnerable to preemptive attack, such stability may be much in doubt; enhanced survivability through technical sophistication is likely to ease this concern. These weak foundations of crisis stability raise doubts about whether the nuclear states of the developing world can muster the essential qualities in their military institutions, national leaders, and societies necessary to control rather than be consumed by their nuclear arsenals. This concern has been dismissed as racist by commentators in the developing world, but they have done little in the public literature to address the underlying substantive concern.

Crises between nuclear-armed adversaries in the developing world appear likely. Such adversaries may live side by side for extended periods without having to confront the fact of their neighbor's nuclear power, but most of these states have long-standing border disputes, insecure political regimes, and/or deep historical enmities, suggesting that crises between them are inevitable. Moreover, their nuclear arsenals exist precisely because force is an established and legitimate instrument of diplomacy within these regions. By contrast, the developed world may well have been—and may remain—insulated from these crisis instabilities by the political and economic context that made strategic conflict unacceptable, as Mueller has argued. Moreover, the risks of crisis instability may have been much lower than perceived, if in fact leaders in both West and East believed that any nuclear use was suicidal, as van Benthem van den Bergh has argued. Might these or other factors also insulate nuclear rivals in the developing world from crisis instabilities?

The factors cited by Mueller appear less operative in the countries of the developing world than the developed, given their political and technical underdevelopment and the domestic instabilities that plague many such countries arising from fragile political structures and cleavages along ethnic or other lines. In regions such as Latin America, Southeast Asia, and Central Europe, however, the orientation of the new political leadership groups toward democratization, economic liberalization, and integration with regional trading partners and global regimes suggests that the Mueller hypothesis may be borne out ceteris paribus in those regions as well. But it is difficult to conceive of these factors operating on the nuclear crisis behavior of the leaders of North Korea or Iraq, for whom national survival may be relatively less important than regime or personal survival.

The key question, then, is whether leaders of states in near nuclear crisis will believe nuclear use to be suicidal; if not, the common deterrence described by van Benthem van den Bergh might not work. Such a belief requires first and foremost an understanding of the costs and risks of war. Unfortunately, the isolated dictators in charge of some of the most significant regional military powers are notorious for their isolation from informed debate and for their willingness to accept or inflict huge numbers of casualties in the pursuit of some larger purpose. Isolated dictators will not be alone in having a difficult time balancing the concerns of heightened risk against a background of unresolved political disputes and a history of active military conflict.[35] Especially in those states where ideology is a prime feature of political fealty and where leaders are sheltered from reality by their own propaganda and minions, the risks are substantial that the cost/benefit calculus may not operate as a brake on war plans as it did in Moscow and Washington. Moreover, in states lacking the just war traditions of the West or unsusceptible to public opinion that opposes massively destructive warfare, it is uncertain that leaders will think of nuclear and other high-leverage weapons as usable only in last resort. A recent study by the United States Institute of Peace concludes that cultural factors play a significant role in shaping strategic culture and deterrence.[36]

On the other hand, the very threat of annihilation is likely to have the effect of concentrating a debate among senior leaders on why and how such weapons might be used and on the risks of miscalculation. This was experience of the first nuclear-armed states and it seems reasonable to believe that new nuclear states will face the same pressures. Experience in the Middle East and South Asia suggests that it is reasonable to expect a process of analysis and learning by states facing nuclear proliferation. The overriding destructiveness of nuclear weapons compels attention as well as recognition that as the risks of miscalculation go up with the advent of new and unstable circumstances, so too do the costs of

---

35   See Yezid Sayigh, "Middle East Stability and the Proliferation of Weapons of Mass Destruction," in Efraim Karsh, Martin S. Navias, and Philip Sabin, eds., *Non-Conventional Weapons Proliferation in the Middle East* (Oxford: Clarendon Press, 1993), pp. 179–203.

36   United States Institute of Peace, "The Cultural Determinants of Deterrence" (Washington, D.C.: United States Institute of Peace, forthcoming).

miscalculation, meaning that proliferation over time may increase the emphasis on crisis avoidance.

In other words, so long as the core understanding of nuclear use as suicidal remains intact, the analytical community's concerns about perceptions and risks may be exaggerated. The frailties of perception and misperception may not matter all that much to nuclear crisis stability in the developing world so long as two conditions are met. First, both parties to a conflict must possess the means to inflict mass destruction—or at least the party that may be subjected to aggression by another. Second, both parties must also believe that the other side has a capacity to survive a first strike and issue a retaliatory strike of assured destruction. This may help to explain why previous military crises in the Middle East have not degenerated into nuclear use. It also accounts, however, for the continued concern about whether India and Pakistan can safely weather future crises, given doubts about the security of their retaliatory capabilities. Furthermore, in circumstances in which possession is one-sided and only in the hands of the aggressor, or where mutual destruction is much in doubt, crisis instability will be more pronounced.

In interstate relations in which nuclear weapons are an open and accepted fact, perceptions of the opponent are likely to be relatively clear, which will contribute to stability in times of crisis. But in relations dominated by opaque patterns of nuclearization, perceptions will be less clear, which may well aggravate instability in times of crisis. The very opacity of the proliferation process complicates the task of clearly understanding stakes, risks, and consequences.[37] The salience of the risks associated with uncertainties in opaque circumstances will depend significantly on the propensity of leaders to run those risks; as discussed in chapter 3, risk-taking is a marked propensity among regimes that find the status quo untenable. In the case of Israel, for example, opacity operates not so much to create doubts about the existence of an Israeli nuclear option but about the stage in a military crisis when it might be threatened or used, with a result that leaders of opposing states might miscalculate that threshold. In the case of South Asia, opacity leaves doubts about the degree to which either Pakistan or India might

---

37 Yair Evron, "Opaque Proliferation: The Israeli Case," in Frankel, *Opaque Nuclear Proliferation*, p. 59.

have secure retaliatory capabilities, and thus it may contribute to a decision to strike first in time of near war in order to avoid a devastating first strike.

The requirement that strategic force be invulnerable to a first strike becomes of paramount concern once violent confrontation becomes possible and brings us to the second vulnerability mentioned above: arms race instability, as measured in the ability of the prevailing military balance—in this case, mutual assured destruction—to withstand competitive armaments acquisition. The U.S.–Soviet strategic relationship suffered few such instabilities, although the so-called window of vulnerability of U.S. land-based missiles to Soviet missiles tipped with multiple independently targetable reentry vehicles (MIRVs) occasioned major readjustments in the strategic competition and the perceived balance of power. Today, little is known about the degree to which new arms deployments might diminish or increase a belief in the security of retaliatory capabilities among the new nuclear states. Israel and India appear less vulnerable on this score than states such as Pakistan and North Korea that are reputed to have smaller numbers of weapons. In both the Middle East and South Asia, arms race instabilities derive more from the competition for military advantage in the conventional domain.[38] Conventional weapons proliferation, particularly of cruise missiles, might change part of this calculus by promising precise and undetected attack against nuclear weapon storage depots.

In sum, there are reasons for both optimism and pessimism in speculating about the future impact of proliferation on regional stability.

On the positive side are a number of important factors. Among erstwhile nuclear adversaries in South America and potential nuclear adversaries in Southeast Asia economic development is proceeding, along with patterns of economic and political interaction, to the point that major armed confrontation with weapons of any kind may be, as Mueller predicts, a source of stability well beyond that which might have been wrought with nuclear weapons. In the Middle East and South Asia, the dilemmas of nuclearization described by Waltz and others are also well in focus and encouraging key states to move in more

---

38 Center for Strategic and International Studies, *Dynamic Net Military Assessment of the Middle East* (Washington, D.C.: Center for Strategic and International Studies, 1992), and Edward B. Atkeson, "The Middle East: A Dynamic Military Net Assessment for the 1990s," *The Washington Quarterly*, Vol. 16, No. 2 (Spring 1993), pp. 115–133.

cooperative directions. The movement toward democracy discussed in chapter 3 and its largely positive impact both on civil-military relations and on the quality of domestic political dialogue about the national interest thus plays an important role in clarifying the risks and costs of nuclear use. These factors are tenuous but cannot be dismissed. In each of these regions, the political, social, and institutional capacities that served in the Cold War to moderate East-West confrontation are not of a caliber equal to those of the erstwhile superpowers, but they appear for the time being to be adequate to the task.

Many factors also appear, however, on the negative side. The military and political institutions in some new or potential nuclear powers, such as Iraq, Iran, and North Korea, exhibit many of the shortcomings identified by Jervis and Sagan, and key questions remain about the degree to which the dilemmas of assured destruction will influence their thinking. This again underscores the relevance of the democratic movement in world politics. Bruce Blair's concern that nuclear forces may be neither controllable nor survivable is also germane. There are reasons to be skeptical that the nuclear forces of the developing world are subjected to the type of rigorous technical control common among the major nuclear-weapon states, raising the possibility that accidental use or wars resulting from such incidents are more likely than in the past.[39] This underscores the relevance of the diffusion of technical competence described in chapter 2 for the long-term impact of proliferation. The advocates of nuclearization in most of these countries have not clearly articulated the characteristics of a mutual deterrence relationship that can survive periods of crisis. Nor have they delineated the means by which stable deterrence will emerge during the period of one-sided advantage or one-sided vulnerability during the transition phase, although they have rightly denounced as ethnocentric the Western belief that stable deterrence cannot possibly emerge.

Moreover, in no region where nuclear weapons proliferation is an issue do the conflictual relationships share the tightly bilateral character of the Cold War.[40] It may be that the stabilizing benefits of nuclear weapons in the Cold War context

---

39 See Sagan, "The Perils of Proliferation," and Freedman, "Great Powers, Vital Interests, and Nuclear Weapons."

40 For a discussion of the ways in which structural attributes in regional systems vary and their implications for stability, see Yair Evron, *Israel's Nuclear Dilemma* (Ithaca, N.Y.: Cornell University Press, 1994), p. 87.

will be more difficult to derive in more diffuse regional relations in which some or many different states with markedly different military capabilities, political ambitions, and societal competencies are acquiring nuclear arsenals. The larger number of potential conflict pairs certainly increases the statistical risks of accidents and escalation. On the other hand, the risks associated with nuclear attack from whatever direction cannot be ignored.

It is not surprising then, that many experts who have surveyed the possible stabilizing and destabilizing consequences of proliferation for regional security conclude that, on balance, the latter are likely to outweigh the former in the long run.[41]

Much of the debate about proliferation's impact seems to assume an evolutionary change of the military relationship between states as they take incremental steps up the nuclear ladder—but what about a more revolutionary pattern of change, in which, for whatever reason, there is both a rapid horizontal and/or vertical proliferation of nuclear weapons?

It would appear that such an outcome is highly unlikely at this time. To understand this point, it is useful to recall the varieties of strategic motives discussed in chapter 3, and to amalgamate them in three basic categories: those states that impute little or no importance to weaponry; those states whose commitment to their weapons or weapons development programs must be understood as less than absolute; and those states that for reasons of self-defense or deterrence are determined proliferators.

For the first category of states, those not interested in weapons, proliferation is relevant to their national interests as a long-term regional threat, if at all. Significant proliferation events or slow erosion of the regimes created to prevent such proliferation bring into focus their shared interests with the states interested in preventing proliferation.

For the second category, proliferation has largely negative implications. For those states engaged in armaments production or acquisition programs without any immediate strategic purpose, proliferation may serve as a justification—or an

---

41   Lewis A. Dunn, *Containing Nuclear Proliferation,* Adelphi Paper No. 263 (London: Brassey's for International Institute for Strategic Studies, 1991), and Barry R. Schneider, "Nuclear Proliferation and Counter-Proliferation: Policy Issues and Debates," *Mershon International Studies Review* (supplement to the *International Studies Quarterly*), Vol. 38, Supplement 2 (October 1994), pp. 209–234.

excuse—to bring weapons development programs to a high level of commitment or visibility or to define strategic purposes for them where none have previously existed. But it also brings into focus for national leaders the costs associated with such programs and the possibilities for meeting security needs without sole reliance on armaments. For those motivated largely by economic and developmental purposes, proliferation may have the effect of narrowing their opportunities to derive economic advantage by increasing the militarization of the economy or by depriving them of access to international markets or finance because of broader international opposition to proliferation. For those states acquiring high-leverage and high-visibility weapons largely for purposes of national prestige and international status, further proliferation is a cause for concern because it diminishes the status they enjoy as sole local possessor while also increasing the risks of war and the costs of war should it occur. Thus their prestige benefits may be short-lived or not substantial.

For the third category of states, proliferation is either unimportant or marginally beneficial. For states acquiring weapons for purposes of regime survival, what happens in the larger regional or global system may be of little or no relevance to their national security interests as perceived by the regime in power. On the other hand, they may be anxious to forestall broader weapons proliferation in case it strengthens the desire of the international community to clamp down on armaments programs or to increase the political or economic price that states pay for breaking with nonproliferation treaties and norms.

For those motivated by aspirations to hegemony or conquest, proliferation works to their advantage, in the short term at least, by easing the challenges they face in acquiring technology, materials, or expertise. But in the long term, proliferation may be seen as less consistent with national interests, because it may strengthen opponents or reinforce the will of the international community to prevent aggression or manage regional crises so as to minimize broader instabilities. Leaders of such states can expect to preserve unilateral advantages in an era of proliferation only by "racing" with regional adversaries to create arsenals offering ever more leverage, whether through raw quantitative measures of the number of weapons or through qualitative ones, such as the sophistication or lethality of specific weapons.

For those states in this third category motivated primarily by the desire to deter a potential opponent, proliferation is a second-order concern, one that steadily complicates the challenge of deterring a prospective aggressor but that is also a lesser priority than deterrence in the first place. For these states, affordable deterrence in a context in which their opponent has ready access to military capability may prove difficult to achieve. Large and ambitious programs to manufacture or even purchase advanced weaponry in pursuit of a balance of conventional forces may prove prohibitively expensive or beyond a nation's technical capacity. Similarly, combined arms operations exploiting the benefits of electronic warfare may prove beyond the skills of many militaries of the developing world (as in the Arab armies confronting an Israeli military more adept at doing so), or beyond the limits of what the political leadership can tolerate if it is also concerned about maintaining reliable control over its armed forces (as in Iraq). This reinforces the tendency to develop or increase reliance on unconventional weapons that appear to offer greater leverage for lower investment.

The striking conclusion from this short review is that few states in the developing world have an interest in fostering an unbridled competition for more and significantly more destructive weapons in the arsenals of an ever larger number of states. Even those acquiring weapons for purposes of aggression must see such proliferation as ultimately narrowing their room for maneuver. A little proliferation may work to their advantage; a lot of proliferation could work against the interests of even the most aggressive states.

Nonetheless, the breakup of the Soviet Union has raised the prospect of a sudden burst of horizontal proliferation in which more states acquire weapons and thus become nuclear-weapon states virtually overnight. The risk that Russia too might splinter keeps this issue alive. Such suddenness would truncate the process of dialogue and learning described above and thus could sow deep doubts about either the intention of the acquiring state to use its nuclear weapons for aggressive or coercive purposes and its belief in the risks of nuclear suicide. This concern shapes thinking about possible opportunistic nuclear acquisition by Iran. A belief that such suddenness would have major implications for both local and global politics and thus might generate a crisis atmosphere akin to that occasioned by nuclear missile deployments to Cuba in 1963 may act as a brake on the ambition of states to acquire weapons in this way—or at least to brandish them openly if acquisition is successful.

A future of more rapid vertical proliferation, in which new nuclear states take steps up the proliferation ladder by building larger arsenals of more powerful weapons, can also not be ruled out. The large nuclear buildups of the superpowers suggest that nuclear weapons programs acquire an momentum of their own, although the behavior of the other established nuclear powers, marked by only periodic modernization and enlargement, poses a different set of expectations. Rapid vertical proliferation could have the effect of sowing fears about the intentions of states to go beyond deterrence to compellence by seeking to deny an opponent a second-strike capability. On the other hand, as Freedman has suggested, "the size of a nation's nuclear arsenal is still an inadequate guide to political impact. The first few items in a new nuclear arsenal will have a disproportionate influence, while a vast arsenal may be irrelevant if it no longer performs any strategic function."[42]

Biological and Chemical Weapons

The expansion of the proliferation problem beyond the nuclear domain requires some testing of these conclusions in different areas. If Wohlstetter is correct that "it is the character of weapons as much as their quantity, probably more than their quantity, that makes the military environment stable or unstable,"[43] then the proliferation of other types of weapons or capabilities is unlikely to work in precisely the same way on the relations among states and the propensity for war between them. This section reviews the consequences of the proliferation of chemical and biological weapons, and following sections examine the implications of the proliferation of advanced conventional weapons and military production capabilities.

Chemical and biological weapons are generally characterized as weapons of mass destruction and thus one might anticipate some political effects similar to those offered by nuclear weapons. Biological weapons are capable of causing the same levels of casualties as nuclear weapons. Targeted against population centers, agricultural or livestock resources, or water supplies, these weapons are capable

---

42 Freedman, "Great Powers, Vital Interests, and Nuclear Weapons," p. 36.

43 To quote further: "Arms and military organizations can hardly be considered the exclusively determining factors in international conflict, but neither can they be considered neutral....the *likelihood* of war is determined by how great a reward attaches to jumping the gun, how strong the incentive to hedge against war itself by starting it, how great the penalty on giving the peace the benefit of the doubt in a crisis." Albert Wohlstetter, "The Delicate Balance of Terror," *Foreign Affairs*, Vol. 37, No. 2 (January 1959), pp. 234–235, 244.

of decimating a society. Because they are so lethal, such weapons might be seen as contributing to a nation's well-being by deterring opponents or extending influence over others.

Yet biological weapons are far less certain in their effects than nuclear weapons, given their vulnerability to meteorological conditions and susceptibility to medical countermeasures such as vaccines or to other protective responses, such as filtration masks. Moreover, they have not been steeped in the politics of intense Cold War confrontation, and their threatened use may not operate as fundamentally on the perceptions of leaders as do nuclear arsenals.

Chemical weapons can also be used to achieve massive civilian casualties or to defeat an armored enemy not equipped with protective gear. But their effect is even less certain than that of biological weapons and more difficult to achieve given the quantities of chemical agent that must be applied and, usually, reapplied to sustain lethal dosages. They, too, are susceptible to protective or prophylactic countermeasures. The benefits of their use against a well-protected enemy on the battlefield are few, unless they can be delivered steadily on target in large numbers. If their use is threatened by a state against a militarily far superior power equipped with chemical protective gear, their tactical utility will be limited, perhaps even nonexistent. In battlefield conflicts between roughly equivalent military powers, their effect may be more important because they can force a degradation in the military performance of troops required to don protective gear. Like biological weapons, chemical weapons offer their most decisive effects in attacks on unprotected civilian populations, and the very threat of such attack can terrorize cities and generate intense political pressures.

Thus it is conceivable that the use or threatened use of chemical and biological weapons will influence decision makers in the same way that nuclear weapons might. But that impact will depend on specific context, including the availability of protective or prophylactic measures and of delivery systems sufficient to deliver such weapons and to sustain dosage levels for extended periods. Moreover, substantial disapprobation continues to attach internationally to chemical and biological weapons, leading states pursuing such programs to keep them secret. It is far easier to reap the deterrence or coercive benefits of a threatened military action with visible or well-understood programs than to do so with something that formally does not exist. Such programs may thus be valued in countries pursuing them not so much for deterrent or coercive purposes but as weapons of last resort.[44] This points to the conclusion that the consequences of chemical and biological weapons proliferation are not today as significant as the consequences of nuclear proliferation.[45]

This simple conclusion is complicated by the fact that in places like the Middle East, there are clear synergies among the different weapons types. For those states desirous of a strategic counterweight to Israeli nuclear weapons, chemical and biological weapons have apparently proven to be useful. Syria, for example, is widely rumored to possess biological warheads for its missiles that can strike Israeli cities. Egypt and others cling to their right to possess chemical weapons not exactly as a counterweight to Israeli nuclear weaponry but as a means to exact a significant toll from Israel so that it cannot use force with impunity in the region to advance territorial ambitions or strike at hated enemies living in neighboring population centers. As Said Aly has argued:

> For too long, the Arab military establishments have looked for the same weapons that Israel possessed whether they were long-range aircraft, nuclear weapons, and/or space technology. Although these strategies reflect the general tendency of states to achieve "strategic parity" with their adversaries, they have been very expensive when applied to the specific Middle East context....Consequently what is needed for the Arab world is not the follow up of Israel in every technological step forward, but the better use of suitable and low cost technologies that make the Arab quantity more effectively deterring. The Arab world, according to this view, does not need nuclear weapons to match those of Israel. In fact, possessing nuclear weapons has no strategic value because Arab countries cannot use them against Israel where the Palestinian Arabs are living and many Arab countries will be affected by the nuclear fall out. What Arab states need, however, is an "above conventional" weapon—such as chemical weapons—to achieve deterrence capability.[46]

---

44 Philip Sabin, "Restraints on Chemical, Biological, and Nuclear Use: Some Lessons from History," in Karsh, Navias, and Sabin, *Non-Conventional Weapons Proliferation in the Middle East,* pp. 9–30.

45 Lewis Dunn comes to the same conclusion in *Containing Nuclear Proliferation,* p. 3.

46 Said Aly, [....], in Shelley A. Stahl and Geoffrey Kemp, eds., *Arms Control and Weapons*

Conventional Weapons and Missiles

The proliferation of advanced conventional weaponry has generally been defended by both the providers and recipients of such weapons transfers as contributing to the national security of recipient states and thus to regional stability. Such transfers have sometimes been defended as a way to forestall or prevent the proliferation of more dangerous and destabilizing weapons of mass destruction, as in the case of the fleet of F-16s provided to Pakistan in a bid by the United States to discourage its pursuit of nuclear weapons. The accumulation of sophisticated conventional military capabilities, however, has frequently been more noteworthy for the responses it induces in competitors to keep even than for its contributions to the emergence of stable relations among states in conflict.[47]

These generalities do not do full justice to the subject because, by and large, the stabilizing or destabilizing aspects of conventional weapons are highly contextual and are dependent on the national strategies of the acquiring states, on geography, and on the competence of the acquiring military to exploit the technical characteristics of new weapons. They are also a function of the political context,[48] and of the attributes of specific technologies. The attributes of specific weapon systems that determine the amount of time available to decision makers in time of crisis and the vulnerability of those weapons and associated command and control systems to preemptive attack are the features most salient to crisis stability.[49]

The proliferation of ballistic missile delivery systems, especially where unconventional warheads are mated to them, can significantly alter the dynamics

---

Proliferation in the Middle East and South Asia (New York, N.Y.: St. Martin's Press for the Carnegie Endowment for International Peace, 1992), [pp. 28–29 of conference paper.]

47 For a review of this subject from the perspective of a strategic analyst of the developing world, see Jasjit Singh, "Arms Control and the Proliferation of High-Technology Weapons in South Asia and the Middle East: A View from India," in Stahl and Kemp, *Arms Control and Weapons Proliferation in the Middle East and South Asia*, pp. 123–134.

48 James Fergusson, "Conventional Weapons Proliferation: A Unique and Dubious Proposition," in Steven Mataija and Lyne C. Bourque, eds., *Proliferation and International Security: Converging Roles of Verification, Confidence Building and Peacekeeping* (Toronto: Centre for International and Strategic Studies at York University, 1993), pp. 41–53.

49 Winham, *New Issues in International Crisis Management*, p. 230.

of conflict. Until such time as states begin to deploy effective defenses against missile attack, these systems will enjoy a reputation for assured delivery on target. Ballistic missiles are ideal weapons of surprise attack given their short flight time and high accuracy.[50] This makes them important use-or-lose weapons. Their deployment in time of crisis is more provocative than an increase in aircraft sorties because they cannot be recalled in the way aircraft can. Both of these factors aggravate crisis instability. By threatening to carry war over the heads of clashing armies and directly to the heart of a nation's population, governmental center, or societal identity, missiles can be nearly as important as the warheads they carry in acting upon the perceptions and decisions of national leaders. In this sense it is not their range so much as their political effect that gives them their strategic character.

Cruise missiles, though slower than ballistic missiles in reaching long-distance targets, offer many of the same attributes. They are difficult to detect and thus likely to reach their targets. The proliferation of anti-ship cruise missiles has been especially significant to date by enabling otherwise marginally capable navies in the developing world to field standoff strike systems capable of delivering decisive punches against even advanced naval vessels.[51]

Missile proliferation can also generate arms race instability in regions where states compete to field more and better missiles—and defensive counter-missiles—as a way to match or deter such use. As Ruchita Beri has commented:

> [P]roliferation of missiles in Asia has a negative impact on India's security. In such an environment and in the absence of credible means of defence, deterrence appears to be the only credible means of restoring stability in the short run. Therefore, India needs to go ahead with its development of ballistic missiles....Missiles are a serious source of instability at the global and regional levels and

---

50 Thomas G. Mahnken and Timothy D. Hoyt, "Missile Proliferation and American Interests," *SAIS Review*, Vol. 10, No. 1 (Winter–Spring 1990), pp. 102–103.

51 W. Seth Carus, *Cruise Missile Proliferation in the 1990s* (New York, N.Y.: Praeger for the Center for Strategic and International Studies, 1992), pp. 15–18.

serious efforts are needed to check proliferation and increase strategic stability."[52]

In a general sense, missile proliferation is also having the effect of eroding the boundaries that in the past helped to keep local wars local.[53] The increased range of weapons may make it possible for states to compel the involvement of extra-regional players in their disputes. The increasing operational range of air forces and missiles in the Middle East has had the effect of creating a connection between the conflicts of the Persian Gulf and those of Israel and the Arabs further to the West. A similar interconnection wrought by the proliferation of long-range delivery systems is evident in Central Asia, where a strategic nexus is emerging among states that no longer discount the nuclear missile capabilities of their neighbors. In southern Europe states are beginning to come within reach of missiles deployed by their neighbors across the Mediterranean. In each case a political context marked by friction and conflict suggests that the new strategic interconnections may prove inflammatory.

Put differently, missiles have the ability to change the scale of conflict as their range increases. If North Korea succeeds in fielding its long-range No-dong missile with a range of 1,000 km, not only all of Japan but major portions of Russia and China, as well as U.S. bases in Japan and in the South Pacific will then be within striking distance. If Iran purchases some such missiles, or builds ones of its own, it will have a new ability to threaten military strikes against Israel, India, and Turkey (and U.S. bases there).

This process will accelerate as the range of missiles in the developing world improves. This illustrates the importance of geography in determining the implications of different types of proliferation. Of the countries of the developing world that have or are developing ballistic missiles, almost all have had missiles with ranges under 200 km for years, fewer have extended-range missiles with ranges between 200 and 900 km, and fewer yet have missiles with a range of more than 900 km, these being far more expensive and sophisticated.[54] For those

---

52   Ruchita Beri, "Ballistic Missile Proliferation," in Jasjit Singh, ed., *Asian Strategic Review, 1991–92* (New Delhi: Institute for Defence Studies and Analyses, 1992), pp. 198–199.

53   W. Seth Carus, *Ballistic Missiles in Modern Conflict* (New York, N.Y.: Praeger for the Center for Strategic and International Studies, 1991), p. viii.

54   North Atlantic Assembly, Defence and Security Committee, *1990 Reports* (Brussels,

whose adversaries have national capitals within 200 km, the strategic effects of missile proliferation need not await longer range; for those whose adversaries have capitals a continent away even extended-range missiles may not offer decisive strategic effect.

In sum, the impact of missile proliferation on regions in conflict will be determined by the degree to which it undermines crisis stability, upsets military balances, leads to arms races, and aggravates political tensions in and among regions.[55] In both East Asia and the Middle East, missiles have in recent years had a more significant impact on regional conflict dynamics than unconventional weapons. Such proliferation is increasing the risks of war and its destructiveness if it occurs. But it is also increasing the incentive for regional adversaries to find new ways to avoid war. As Israel's Foreign Minister Shimon Peres has observed, "[W]e have to face the new technologies and processes in the world. We cannot run away from them. The range of a missile forces us to have regional security."[56] In regions not in conflict, where peaceful relations prevail, missile proliferation may provide some basis for increased transparency in military programs and crisis warning in the event of unauthorized or accidental launch.

The increasing access to space operations and resources enjoyed by states of the developing world also promises to complicate existing military relations. The increased availability of satellite imagery may improve warning time, make an adversary's capabilities and intent more transparent, and increase confidence in verification efforts. On the other hand, it may also improve weapons targeting and serve as a tool of deception. It will deter the massing of forces for surprise attack, or encourage them to mass knowing that a political signal will be sent. At the very least, it is changing the military geography of regions by altering or removing the significance of basic geographic features.[57]

November 1990), pp. 22–23.

55   Center for International Security and Arms Control, *Assessing Ballistic Missile Proliferation and Its Control* (Stanford, Calif.: Stanford University, November 1991), pp. 105–115.

56   Shimon Peres, Remarks on the MacNeil–Lehrer Newshour on September 23, 1992, as cited in "For the Record," *Washington Post,* September 25, 1992.

57   Robert L. Butterworth, *Space Systems and the Military Geography of Future Regional Conflicts,* Report No. 14 (Los Alamos, N. Mex.: Center for National Security Studies, Los Alamos National Laboratory, January 1992). See also Michael Krepon et al., eds., *Commercial Observation Satellites and International Security* (New York, N.Y.: St. Martin's Press with the

The implications of wider access to this technology are well summarized by Bobby Inman:

> The advent of new and better commercial observation satellites complicates matters greatly in a world of asymmetries between countries, their systems of government, and their basic approaches to issues of information availability and information flow....the reduction of uncertainty regarding military capabilities and the removal of the element of surprise will generally improve global stability.[58]

With regard to other types of advanced conventional weaponry, the impact is similarly diverse. The diffusion of advanced air combat systems such as sophisticated fighter-attack aircraft, aerial refueling systems, and air-to-air missiles strengthens the capacity of individual air forces to prevail against lesser opponents. The diffusion of advanced naval combat systems such as anti-ship cruise missiles, advanced torpedoes, and quiet submarines is significantly increasing the lethal punch of coastal navies of heretofore negligible importance. The diffusion of advanced land combat systems such as anti-armor weapons, smart submunitions, and long-range artillery is increasing the intensity of combat and the premium on both mobile, dispersed forces and the ability to conduct around-the-clock operations that inflict the highest possible attrition ratios so as to outlast opponents.[59]

More generally, the destabilizing effects of such proliferation are more noticeable for arms race than crisis stability. States race not only to best one another with the most modern systems but also to modernize in ways that minimize key vulnerabilities while exploiting those of the opponent. This puts a premium on technically astute military planning organizations and on military organizations capable of reaping the benefits of high-technology systems. As Stephen Rosen has observed:

Carnegie Endowment for International Peace, 1990).

58 Bobby Inman, "Introduction," in Krepon et al., *Commercial Observation Satellites and International Security*, pp. 4, 8.

59 Interview with Maj. Gen. Amraam Mitzne, director, strategic plans and policy, Israeli Defense Force, *Defense News*, January 18–24, 1993, p. 38.

> The overall effect of the technological revolution will probably be to increase the demands on a core of highly trained personnel and to increase the advantage of an officer corps that can adapt and improvise....A larger degree of authority will have to be delegated to lower command levels....the net effect of the new technologies will be to enhance rather than reduce the importance of the human qualitative factor. On the higher level of strategy and war planning, the very speed of technological change and innovation may reward the side that is able to modify its organization and force posturing more rapidly and to absorb and integrate new equipment on shorter lead times.[60]

As argued in the previous chapter, these attributes are not equally available in the developing world.

As before, the synergies among weapons types and the different strategic environments of states color expectations about the impact of conventional weaponry proliferation. The increasing accuracy of missiles available to the more sophisticated developing countries may diminish their incentive to rely on unconventional warheads, if increasing accuracy decreases reliance on mass destruction. The availability of pieces of technology on the global market helps countries to circumvent the full development process. The increased availability of conventional warfare capabilities combined with a continued nuclear taboo may stimulate the proliferation of conventional assets capable of strategic missions, further blurring the Cold War–vintage distinctions between conventional/tactical weapons and unconventional/strategic weapons.[61] A failure to adapt conventional assets to strategic missions could, however, create new incentives for the proliferation of nuclear weapons.[62]

---

60 Steven J. Rosen, "The Proliferation of New Land-Based Technologies: Implications for Local Military Balances," in Stephanie G. Neuman and Robert E. Harkavy, eds., *Arms Transfers in the Modern World* (New York, N.Y.: Praeger, 1979), p. 126.

61 Thomas J. Welch, "Weapons of Disutility" (Uunpublished and undated paper). See also Richard Burt, *Nuclear Proliferation and Conventional Arms Transfers: The Missing Link*, Discussion Paper No. 76 (California Seminar on Arms Control and Policy, September 1977).

62 Carl H. Builder, *The Prospects and Implications of Non-nuclear Means for Strategic Conflict*, Adelphi Paper No. 200 (London: International Institute for Strategic Studies, 1985).

Gauging the significance of the proliferation of specific weapons or technologies in the conventional domain is particularly difficult because each piece generally makes only an incremental difference to the overall balance of power among nations. These balances (or imbalances) are inherently dynamic, responding not just to changes in military arsenals but also to the larger strategic environment. Yohanan Cohen supports this view:

"Balance of forces," for example, is a rather complex concept expressed not only in the number of divisions, tanks and aircraft, but also in the small nation's cohesion, its leadership's wisdom and determination, its army's combative morale, preparedness and technological standard, which reflects the caliber of the entire national society and the international constellation.[63]

The synergies among these factors as much as the synergies among specific weapons contribute to stability or instability among states. For Western analysts accustomed to conceiving of stability in relatively static terms related to orders of battle in the European theater or tabulations of deployed or stockpiled weapons, appreciating the full range of factors bearing on stability in other regions of the world may prove challenging.[64]

Thus in speculating about the possible future implications of such proliferation, it is important not to overstate the general impact of the proliferation of advanced air, sea, or land combat systems on countries of the developing world. It is the existence of capable military establishments, and not the specific weapons that they utilize, that has the greater impact. No clear connection can be demonstrated between the volumes of arms flowing into a region and the occurrence of war, nor between technical sophistication and wars with the highest civilian and military casualties.[65] Rarely in confrontations between states have single pieces of hardware been decisive, either because they have lacked the capacity to deliver knockout punches or because other social, organizational, or political factors are paramount.[66] Despite the spread of

---

63 Yohanan Cohen, *Small Nations in Times of Crisis and Confrontation* (New York, N.Y.: State University of New York Press, 1989), p. 332.

64 Geoffrey Kemp, "Arms Transfers and the "Back-End" Problem in Developing Countries," in Neuman and Harkavy, *Arms Transfers in the Modern World*, p. 264.

65 Anthony H. Cordesman, "Current Trends in Arms Sales and Proliferation in the Middle East" (Paper released by the office of Senator John McCain, Washington, D.C., January 1992).

modern aircraft and missiles, the number of air forces capable of conducting strategic bombardment remains small, and these limits on the ability to strike deep and often into an enemy's territory have, in Seth Carus's words, "helped to keep local wars local and regional confrontations regional."[67]

But it is equally important not to understate the impact. If asymmetrical, the diffusion of advanced conventional capabilities can reinforce threat perceptions in regions, or at least the desire to stay competitive with neighboring powers. This encourages arms races among states that at the very least draw resources away from the management of other problems and thus may cause domestic insecurity and instability. This cost of competing to field and use advanced conventional weapons increases with the sophistication of the weaponry and becomes an additional incentive to seek alternatives to such costly preparations.[68] The availability of high-technology conventional weapons on the global market has also intensified regional conflicts. It is increasing the strategic reach of combatants, enabling them to broaden the range of conflict. It is also putting modern weapons at the disposal of terrorist organizations, over whom suppliers have little influence. It is strengthening the hands of states that might wish to use weapons for purposes of aggression, while also strengthening the capacity of states to defend against intervention by larger powers.[69]

In sum, the proliferation of conventional weapons has implications and consequences considerably more complicated than those understood or expected during the Cold War. New patterns of diffusion, new technologies, and new concerns about both crisis and arms race instability complicate the old notion that this type of proliferation is in the constructive service of the right to self-defense.

---

66   Rodney W. Jones and Steven A. Hildreth, *Modern Weapons and Third World Powers* (Boulder, Colo.: Westview Press with the Center for Strategic and International Studies, 1984), pp. 7, 12, 64–68.

67   Carus, *Ballistic Missiles in Modern Conflict*, p. viii.

68   Chris Smith, "Third World Arms Control, Military Technology and Alternative Security," in Thomas Ohlson, ed., *Arms Transfer Limitations and Third World Security* (Oxford: Oxford University Press for the Stockholm International Peace Research Institute, 1988), p. 68.

69   Jed C. Snyder, "Weapons Proliferation and the New Security Agenda," in Marshall, Martin, and Rowen, *On Not Confusing Ourselves*, pp. 274–275.

The Defense Industrial Base and Technology

The proliferation of the ability to produce conventional weapons is having a number of effects. The emergence of defense industries strengthens the technological infrastructure of semi-industrialized nations thus diminishing the dependence of countries of the developing world on arms sales or transfers from their traditional suppliers in both the short and long term.[70] Only rarely, however, as in the case of China, does indigenous production today suffice for domestic needs—and especially not in advanced-technology weapons. Moreover, in no instance has a protracted, high-intensity conflict in the developing world gone on for any extended period of time without arms supplies from the developed world.[71] Local arms industries might increase threat perceptions among regional adversaries and reinforce the confidence of local hegemons, but these effects should not be overstated. Local arms production is only one element of national power, and nowhere today is it the dominant one.[72] As Ralph Sanders has concluded, "greater self-sufficiency in arms production has not yet given, and in the foreseeable future is unlikely to give, any nation the opportunity to gain hegemony in its region. The spread of arms production might alter power relationships, but up to now it has failed to elevate one state to true dominance in any part of the Third World."[73]

Increasing reliance on local arms industries might also have the effect of changing military operations themselves. Cost factors make it unlikely that states will field such weapons in large numbers, which will put new constraints on the intensity, duration, and scale of conflicts in the developing world. Military institutions may respond by implementing new operational concepts emphasizing, for example, preemptive attacks, with the attendant risks.[74]

---

70 Ralph Sanders, *Arms Industries: New Suppliers and Regional Security* (Washington, D.C.: National Defense University, 1990), p. 112. See also José O. Maldifassi and Pier A. Abetti, *Defense Industries in Latin American Countries: Argentina, Brazil, and Chile* (Westport, Conn.: Praeger, 1994), p. 230.

71 Kemp, "Arms Transfers and the 'Back-End' Problem," p. 270.

72 Michael Moodie, "Defense Industries in the Third World: Problems and Promise," in Neuman and Harkavy, *Arms Transfers in the Modern World*, p. 306.

73 Sanders, *Arms Industries*, p. 114.

74 Ravinderpal Singh, "Advanced Weaponry for the Third World," in Eric A. Arnett, Elizabeth J. Kirk, and W. Thomas Wander, eds., *Critical Choices: Setting Priorities in the Changing Security*

The diffusion of the ability to produce weapons of mass destruction may be having a number of implications for stability. It can increase the incentive to strike preemptively against weapons production sites in time of near war, thus making war more likely. Crisis instability is further aggravated by the short lead times necessary to move from nascent capability to militarily effective weapons in the chemical and biological domains, meaning that states will live closer than ever before to the brink of major competition in these areas.

Technology diffusion more generally must also be understood to have a number of important implications. Its primary implication was noted earlier in the conclusion to chapter 2: a growing tier of technically empowered states with a latent capacity to develop high-leverage military systems, among which is a significant core of virtual weapon states, capable of emerging as major military powers with the most advanced weaponry in a very short period. RAND's recent work on nuclear proliferation posits a range of different end-states, with different characteristics of stability and instability, resulting from the transition of an interstate system in which only a few great powers have nuclear weapons to a system in which many if not most countries have such recourse. The RAND study concludes that the balance between stabilizing and destabilizing consequences depends ultimately on the policies of a few leading governments at this time, and not solely on technical diffusion itself (as discussed further in chapter 5).[75]

The competitive pursuit of technological advantage in the military domain also deserves attention, given that it may become a source of instability in regions with high investments in R&D, as in East Asia. As Michael Klare has argued, "A full-blown Asian arms competition could...replace the now defunct U.S.–Soviet rivalry as the driving force in the worldwide evolution of military technology."[76] Technological change will be easiest to manage and exploit for the most modernized of the developing countries, a situation that is likely over the long term to tilt power balances in their favor, so long as unconventional

---

Environment (Washington, D.C.: American Association for the Advancement of Science, 1991), p. 84.

75   Roger C. Molander and Peter A. Wilson, *The Nuclear Asymptote: On Containing Nuclear Proliferation* (Santa Monica, Calif.: RAND/UCLA Center for Soviet Studies, 1993).

76   See Michael T. Klare, "The Next Great Arms Race," *Foreign Affairs*, Vol. 72, No. 3 (Summer 1993), pp. 136–154.

weapons are not the dominant factor in their regional security situations. Uneven technical competence will reinforce imbalances in other ways, as Sanders has argued:

> The weapons containing the highest technology relate to air warfare while the ground forces seem to do more often with middle and low technology weapons. In some cases the air war could become relatively unimportant to the conflict on the ground. Consequently, a nation producing effective middle level military technologies for ground warfare could achieve military objectives even if the enemy had available high technology air weapons. The inability of Third World countries to produce indigenous high technology air warfare items might not appear to be worrisome—as long as a fighting force has sound ground weapons—including an anti-aircraft system.[77]

This picture of technological change and diffusion implies that such change will necessarily have negative consequences for the ability to control proliferation and limit its destabilizing consequences. It is risky to ignore new technological developments or to underestimate the potential impact of technology diffusion.[78] But the focus of this picture is too narrow. Technological change and diffusion have also had positive benefits, especially those that increase transparency in military affairs. These technologies are improving information collection abilities as well as data integration and response capabilities, thereby increasing confidence in the ability to detect illicit programs and hopefully thereby help to deter them.[79]

In sum, this review suggests that definitive answers to questions about whether proliferation of specific weapons is stabilizing or destabilizing for states in the

---

77 Sanders, *Arms Industries*, pp. 19–20.

78 Adam Roberts, "The Future of Medium Armies in the Face of Military Technological Developments," in Center for Strategic Studies, Tel Aviv University, *The Defense of Small and Medium-Sized Countries*, Paper No. 17 (Tel Aviv, August 1982), p. 13.

79 Amy Sands, "The Impact of New Technologies on Nuclear Weapons Proliferation," in Mitchell Reiss and Robert S. Litwak, eds., *Nuclear Proliferation After the Cold War* (Washington, D.C.: Woodrow Wilson Center Press, 1994), pp. 259–274.

developing world are often impossible to answer without specific reference to political and geographical context and to specific weapons technologies. It is difficult to deny the argument that weapons, even unconventional ones, can contribute to the security of individual nations when they are acquired for purposes of deterrence or when they help to create a system of common deterrence. But such security is purchased at the price of numerous unintended consequences. These could include an increased incentive to strike preemptively in time of near war as well as more difficult challenges in the management of competitive regional relations as each side acquires new and more lethal armaments.[80] Thus, if there is any point of consensus between those emphasizing positive and others emphasizing negative aspects of proliferation, it must be simply that the fewer the number of proliferants and the longer the delay in proliferation, the better.[81]

Implications for the Developed World

Proliferation's implications are not limited solely to its stability consequences for states of the developing world where such proliferation is occurring. Proliferation also has a wide range of implications for the states of the developed world. This review identifies both military and political implications.

Military Implications

The ability of states of the developing world to threaten direct attack on the territories of states of the developed world is increasing. Long-range delivery systems are putting the territories and population centers of North America, Western Europe, and East Asia within the military reach of an increasing number of states outside those regions. This is not an entirely new threat, given the

---

80   The common tendency to decry proliferation as increasing the lethality of war has been challenged by Eliot A. Cohen. Noting that most casualties in conflicts in the Third World occur as a result of small arms or artillery, Cohen argues that high-technology systems may actually decrease the numbers of people killed in war. See Cohen, "Distant Battles: Modern War in the Third World," *International Security*, Vol. 10, No. 4 (Spring 1986), pp. 158–159.

81   William Potter, "On Nuclear Proliferation," in Kolodziej and Morgan, eds., *Security and Arms Control*, Vol. 2, p. 321. He echoes conclusions of Wohlstetter, *Spread of Nuclear Bombs*.

decades-long struggle to prevent attack on these places by small military units or politically backed terrorists. But the proliferation of ballistic and cruise missiles creates a new problem, on an order of magnitude more challenging than the terrorist threat, given the increasing number of weapons—and the types of weapons—that these forces can deliver to their targets. The noteworthy coincidence of programs to produce weapons of mass destruction among many of the states also pursuing ballistic missile programs sharpens concern about the strategic leverage these states will derive over the advanced countries from these new systems. Although ballistic missiles tipped with nuclear weapons and capable of striking developed countries in North America, Western Europe, and East Asia remain in the hands of only a few other advanced states, a much larger number of states will soon have within their means ballistic or cruise missiles tipped with biological or chemical weapons which, although less certain in their effects, could still inflict huge numbers of civilian casualties if targeted on population centers.

The vulnerabilities of the states of the developed world to this direct threat are conspicuously uneven. European capitals are today within range of ballistic missiles in the Middle East; as those missile forces grow more modern and numerous, European vulnerability will increase. Japan is falling within range of missiles being developed in North Korea. Russia finds itself with many states around its periphery able to fire missiles into its territory. The United States is the least vulnerable of all, given its relative isolation from regional ballistic missile forces. Its current vulnerability to cruise missile attack may be underestimated, however.[82]

Moreover, as more developing countries acquire the ability to launch missiles into space and master (or acquire) the technologies and expertise of precise space vehicle reentry, locations all over the globe will become equally vulnerable to long-range missile attack. Whether this happens over 5, 25, or 50 years, some such outcome is inevitable. Timing is, however, critical, in evaluating the nature of the military and political threat and the urgency of responses. The U.S. Central Intelligence Agency (CIA) has recently concluded that of the countries with possible political motivation to attack the United States (identified as North Korea, Iran, Iraq, and Libya), none shows evidence of developing missiles for purposes of such attack and, although all but Libya are deemed capable of

---

82   Carus, *Cruise Missile Proliferation*, p. 87.

building such missiles in 15 years, the probability is low that any of these four will complete development in that time."[83] But even existing missile launch capabilities may accentuate what one former CIA analyst has described as a marked new vulnerability of U.S. satellites to attack by developing countries, whether with sounding rockets, lasers, or electronic warfare.[84]

This is not to argue that the threat to the United States or its allies posed by the proliferation of military capabilities matches or replaces the erstwhile Soviet threat. In today's world, it is difficult to envisage scenarios in which a state of the developing world would attempt to make all-out war against a developed state in an attempt to occupy and dominate it. The proliferation that appears possible or reasonably likely over the next decade or two has not empowered small states to mount significant geopolitical threats against the great powers.[85] With the passing of the Cold War and the implementation of strategic arms reductions, the developed world is more secure than at any time in recent decades. But these states have gained an unprecedented capacity to engage the strategic interests of the more powerful states and thus a new capacity to coerce, compel, or deter them, as discussed in the previous chapter. Looking to the longer term, however, it may well be that nuclear technology, if backed with survivable, long-range delivery systems will enable small states to threaten total war against large ones, whatever their level of development or industrialization. In the medium term, biological warfare capabilities mated to long-range delivery systems may provide similar capability. In the short term, the salient capabilities may be those that exploit vulnerabilities created by sheer negligence or oversight by the advanced

---

83 Thomas W. Lippman, "ICBM Threat to U.S. Is Called Slight," *Washington Post*, December 24, 1993, p. A–9. Joseph Lovece, "CIA: North Korea Won't Build ICBMs for at Least 15 Years," *Defense Week*, November 29, 1993, pp. 1, 7, 12.

84 Unpublished paper by former CIA analyst Allen Thomson, entitled "Satellite Vulnerability: A Post Cold War Issue?" as described in Vincent Kiernan, "Analyst: U.S. Spy Satellites Are Open to Attack," *Defense News*, August 29–September 4, 1994, pp. 4, 50.

85 As Robert W. Tucker and John J. Weltman have argued, "Significant geopolitical threats cannot be mounted against great powers by small powers, and particularly by developing smaller powers. Only great powers can seriously threaten great powers." Tucker and Weltman, "The Nuclear Future," in Garrity and Maaranen, *Nuclear Weapons in the Changing World*, p. 252.

countries. The vulnerability of the U.S. Navy to modern mines and of the U.S. Army to attack by SCUDs are cases in point.[86]

The more tangible and immediate way in which proliferation affects the interests and security of states of the developed world is the threat to their power projection forces. Currently, such forces are used overseas in three different ways: (1) to "show the flag" and demonstrate presence; (2) to honor alliance relations with regional partners; and (3) to intervene, whether collectively in support of a UN Security Council resolution or unilaterally in defense of local interests. Each such usage faces new challenges because of the proliferation of advanced weaponry, especially if clear superiority has disappeared.

The presence function is usually accomplished with naval forces, whether locally offshore or on the sea lanes of communication of the high seas. Offshore operations are increasingly at risk with the proliferation of anti-ship cruise missiles and other advanced coastal policing assets.[87] They are also at risk of attack with biological warfare agent distributed upwind from airborne or fixed point generators. This is, of course, a function of the geography of specific regions as it is of the attributes of specific weapons. In the Persian Gulf, for example, Iranian anti-ship missiles increased the risks of the commercial vessel reflagging exercise of the late 1980s, and the Iranian naval buildup of the 1990s has greatly increased the risks to foreign naval vessels operating there. As Ian Anthony has argued:

---

86   Henry D. Sokolski, "Nonapocalyptic Proliferation: A New Strategic Threat?" *The Washington Quarterly*, Vol. 17, No. 2 (Spring 1994), pp. 115–128. See also Edward J. Walsh, "Navy and Marines Focus on Achilles' Heel: Shallow-Water Mines," *Armed Forces Journal International*, August 1993, pp. 35–38.

87   James A. Hazlett has described this as follows: "Low Intensity Conflict ASW [anti-submarine warfare] could be potentially quite humbling for the world's premier ASW navy. As the Secretary of the Navy has stated, 'The proliferation of submarine technology in the Third World adds a new challenge. We will have to counter quiet, modern non-nuclear submarines in shallow and littoral waters to support power projection operations. It will be one of our toughest problems in the future.'" Hazlett, "Low Intensity Conflict and Anti-Submarine Warfare" (Unpublished research paper prepared for the Center for Strategic and International Studies, Washington, D.C., June 1, 1992), pp. 19–20, citing the Posture Statement of the Secretary of the Navy, February 1991. See also Center for Naval Analyses, *Weapons Proliferation and U.S. National Security*, Symposia Series (Alexandria, Va.: Center for Naval Analyses, 1990).

> The possession of anti-ship missiles is not sufficient in itself to threaten the naval forces of major powers except in some specific circumstances—such as those pertaining in the closed waters of the Persian Gulf....This is not to imply that this kind of missile proliferation is unimportant, but simply to point out that its importance does not stem from specific technical characteristics of the weapons themselves. Rather, it is derived from the specific context of the Persian Gulf.[88]

Proliferation also increases the likelihood of increased interference with the right to safe and unfettered trade on the seas. The extension of national economic zones out to 200 miles offshore has resulted in a scramble to acquire the means to assert and defend such sovereignty that, especially in archipelagic regions, presages intensified naval confrontation at sea. One possible response for advanced navies to the heightened missile threat is to depend increasingly on submarines for power projection, but by their very invisibility they are less well suited to the presence function of naval forces in "show the flag" operations.

The alliance function is usually accomplished with a mix of locally deployed forces and political commitments to extend protection in case of war or threatened war. At the very least, proliferation increases the risks to locally deployed forces while also increasing the difficulty of deploying reinforcements in time of war or near war. Moreover, regional instabilities wrought by the competitive acquisition of armaments and by their increasing reach and destructiveness threaten to alter the dynamics of such force projection for alliance purposes. Surveying the military dynamic in the Middle East and East Asia, where the United States has alliance relations with Israel and South Korea and Japan, respectively, U.S. analysts underscore that proliferation heightens the likelihood of war in these regions in a number of ways. It nourishes the ambitions of regional hegemons, increases regional frictions and thus the number of military crises, decreases the ability to coerce states away from the brink of war, heightens the risk of unauthorized or accidental use of weapons of mass destruction thus compelling states to shoot first in time of near war, increases the

---

88   Ian Anthony, *The Naval Arms Trade* (Oxford: Oxford University Press with the Stockholm International Peace Research Institute, 1990), p. 55.

destructiveness of war when it occurs, and improves the ability of regional actors to threaten military conflict outside the region.

Nuclear proliferation especially impinges on the credibility of extended deterrence. More than any other aspect of proliferation, it increases the potential costs of exercising military functions in support of alliance commitments. As Ted Galen Carpenter has argued, the United States could find itself "in the position of having to shield an assortment of non-nuclear allies from a rogues' gallery of nuclear-armed adversaries. That would be a more difficult, and ultimately more dangerous, mission than shielding those allies from Soviet aggression during the Cold War."[89] Such proliferation aggravates an old fact of history: the stronger guarantor state is often reluctant to involve itself deeply in high-risk military confrontations.[90] Eric Arnett has argued that nuclear proliferation will increasingly make a difference to U.S. regional commitments, forcing the United States to reevaluate its interests and to set priorities for only the most important.[91]

The intervention function is usually accomplished with the insertion of military forces into hostile settings, where they must fight to control the situation on the ground. As Fred Iklé and Albert Wohlstetter have observed,

> The arsenals of the lesser powers will make it riskier and more difficult for the superpowers to intervene in regional wars. The U.S. ability to support its allies around the world will increasingly be called into question. Where American intervention seems necessary, it will generally require far more cooperation with Third World countries than has been required in the past.[92]

---

89 Ted Galen Carpenter, "A New Proliferation Policy," *National Interest*, No. 28 (Summer 1992), pp. 66.

90 "The historical examples in this book prove that at the moment of trial, when the friendly superpower is supposed to meet its commitment—not only to warn and deter, but to come to the small nation's aid—reluctance often outweighs commitment." Yohanan Cohen, *Small Nations in Times of Crisis and Confrontation*, pp. 338–339.

91 Eric H. Arnett, *Gunboat Diplomacy and the Bomb: Nuclear Proliferation and the U.S. Navy* (New York, N.Y.: Praeger, 1989), p. xvi.

92 Commission on Integrated Long-Term Strategy, *Discriminate Deterrence* (Washington, D.C.: GPO, January 1988), p. 10.

Accustomed to thinking of conflict with regional adversaries in "low-intensity" terms, the intervening powers must begin to anticipate mid- and high-intensity operations, as the British learned in the Falklands/Malvinas conflict and as the international coalition learned in expelling Iraq from Kuwait. The proliferation of specific types of technologies is having specific effects: the proliferation of surveillance and imaging systems, for example, is reducing the ability to achieve tactical or strategic surprise either locally or at staging sites outside a region. Regional ballistic missiles—today largely nuisance-value political weapons—will become more effective weapons against military assets. One potential long-term impact of such missiles will be to bring the battlefield intelligence satellites of the more technologically advanced countries within range of anti-satellite weapons. Ironically, it is increasingly common to find weapons transferred to the developing world used against those who sold them, as illustrated in the Persian Gulf War of 1991 and the Falklands/Malvinas War a decade earlier.[93]

In some states of the developing world open discussion of the need to create a deterrent to intervention by developed states can be found. The former Indian Army chief of staff, General K. Sundarji, has endorsed a "minimum deterrent" meant to discourage "U.S. bullying" and "possible racist aggression from the West."[94] Two other Indian analysts have pointed out that: "Sophisticated weapons can come in handy for inflicting punishing damage by a technologically superior nation on a less capable one. They also may be useful for developing nations to raise the cost of intervention and to help in defense, as detailed in *Discriminate Deterrence*."[95] Muammar Qaddafi has called for "a deterrent—missiles that could reach New York....We should build this force so that they and others will no longer think about an attack."[96]

---

93 U.S. Congress, Office of Technology Assessment, *Global Arms Trade: Commerce in Advanced Military Technology and Weapons*, OTA–ISC–460 (Washington, D.C.: GPO, June 1991), p. 17.

94 Foreign Broadcast Information Service, *Daily Report: Near East and South Asia* (FBIS–NES–92–199), October 14, 1992, p. 46.

95 C. Raja Mohan and K. Subrahmanyam, "High-Technology Weapons in the Developing World," in Eric Arnett, ed., *Science and Security: Technology Advances and the Arms Control Agenda* (Washington, D.C.: American Association for the Advancement of Science, 1989), p. 236.

96 Speech by Muammar Qaddafi at a meeting of students of the Higher Institute for Applied Social Studies at the Great al-Fatih University, April 18, 1990, translated in

Thus the proliferation of advanced military capabilities has made the projection of power more difficult and costly, and the proliferation of weapons of mass destruction in particular has increased the likelihood that the costs in human terms will be large. This has accelerated the passing of an era in which the advanced powers of the developed world could intervene militarily in the developing one without serious fear of the military consequences. As Les Aspin has argued, in the past nuclear weapons "were the great equalizer that enabled Western capitals to deal with numerically larger Eastern bloc forces....Nuclear weapons still serve the same purpose—as a great equalizer. But it is the United States that is now the potential equalizee."[97] Such equalization occurs as a result not of comparably scaled nuclear capabilities but of comparably credible threats to impose unacceptable costs on others.

The new vulnerabilities of developed countries described here will have a domestic political impact as well that is relevant to the intervention question. As publics come to understand the heightened risks associated with the projection of power abroad, or as those risks are magnified through relentless television coverage, their reluctance to support such deployments will increase. This may also precipitate political crises in the intervening state as a backlash develops that ultimately compels disengagement, a process that is usually also attended by a change of political power in the intervening state.[98]

Generally speaking, in facing the new military capabilities of the developing world, the states of the developed world rely complacently on the huge gap that remains between their military acumen (both existing forces and R&D programs) and that of developing states. This gap should provide an element of reassurance—there is no reason currently to believe that states in the developing world—even the oil-rich ones—have the resources to compete with the military development programs of the advanced industrial nations.[99]

But this complacency is foolish. "Second-best" works just fine for many military applications. The inability of the United States to secure a military

FBIS–NES–90–078, April 23, 1990, p. 8.

97 Les Aspin, *From Deterring to Denuking: Dealing with Proliferation in the 1990s* (Washington, D.C.: House Committee on Armed Services, 1992), p. 4.

98 Levite, Jentleson, and Berman, p. 313.

99 Sanders, *Arms Industries*, p. 18.

victory over a technically inferior North Vietnam serves as a reminder of this basic point. Outdated technologies are perfectly functional in the unconventional area; inspections of Iraq's nuclear programs have revealed just how close it came to a nuclear weapon using 1950s technology. But it is also true in the conventional domain, where certain types of outdated technologies, such as slow and non-stealthy cruise missiles, could have a significant impact if deployed in sufficient numbers against more sophisticated militaries. Moreover, superiority may not be locally applicable in a timely fashion in specific conflicts. Circumstances may unfold with a speed that deprives the militarily superior state of the ability to employ its power in decisive fashion at the early phase of a conflict. A state opposing intervention could exploit its local superiority to delay, disrupt, or defeat an effort to insert military forces. Chemical and biological weapons might be especially attractive for this purpose because of their usefulness in contaminating airfields, ports, or staging areas. Or the full application of military power may be inhibited by a fear of nuclear escalation or by political factors, as during the Vietnam War.

Moreover, potential adversaries contemplating the possibility of war against a state in the developed world may find reason to think that they will at least survive if not actually prevail. Leaders of such states may not find the substantial military superiority of the United States or of an international coalition to be an overriding deterrent. Surveying history they will find many instances in which the weak have not been deterred from making war on the strong. Iraq's failure to avoid confrontation with the UN coalition provides one such example.[100] Barry Wolf has surveyed such failures of deterrence and concluded that the credibility of the stronger state's threatened response is often in doubt, or it is irrelevant to some leaders who act without reference to possible responses by others. He notes further that:

> An examination of historical materials reveals three primary factors associated with threats against, or attacks on, substantially stronger states: the weaker state was highly motivated...the weaker state misperceived some facet of the situation...the stronger state was

---

100 Alexander L. George, *Bridging the Gap: Theory and Practice in Foreign Policy* (Washington, D.C.: United States Institute of Peace, 1993), chapters 5 and 6, pp. 71–88.

vulnerable....Aggression by states against substantially stronger states, though not common, is far from unprecedented.[101]

This may be especially true in the nuclear era, when a military challenger to a regional interest of a remote nuclear-armed power may well doubt that the remote power will find that interest sufficiently compelling to pay the political price associated with nuclear use. In any subsequent game of nuclear brinksmanship, the regional adversary may well have an advantage.[102]

Potential adversaries surveying history will also find examples of conflicts between strong and weak in which the weak deterred the strong or actually prevailed in conflict. Israel's success in this regard provides one example. As Yohanan Cohen has written:

> [A] small nation does stand a chance of surviving a clash with a mighty neighbor, in times of both crisis and confrontation (and this is so insofar as the confrontation is military, not only political, and as long as it is waged with "conventional" tools of war, assuming that the small nation has them in reasonable quantities). All this, if—and this "if" is an integral part of the problem—it knows how to implement its strengths and maneuverability resolutely, wisely, and competently. "A chance of surviving a clash" does not mean the small nation can register a "victory," let alone a sure victory. It suffices for a small nation to frustrate and disrupt the enemy's intent, to repel his demands and pressures.....A small nation's army cannot dictate terms to the enemy and ensure a protracted period of stable peace and security thereby. A small nation's army can further, but not replace, policy....It needs diplomacy to surmount crises in its foreign relations, to prevent potential confrontation with a mighty neighbor, and to bring the confrontation, once begun, to an end. Its diplomacy must be more active and competent than that of a large, strong nation.[103]

---

101 Barry Wolf, "When the Weak Attack the Strong: Failures of Deterrence," RAND Note N–3261–A (Santa Monica, Calif.: RAND, 1991), pp. 1, 5, 15.

102 Kenneth Watman and Dean Wilkening, *U.S. Regional Deterrence Strategy*, DRR–544/1–A/AF (Santa Monica, Calif.: RAND, February 1994), pp. ix and xii.

Facing the possibility of armed conflict against a better-armed and stronger power, these leaders will pursue the age-old art of pitting their strengths against an opponent's weaknesses, perhaps taking a lesson from the Persian Gulf War that time plays to the advantages of the stronger power.[104] Such strategies have been termed asymmetric strategies to convey the gaps in power between the contending parties, gaps that the weaker party seeks to negate. As Garrity has described these strategies,

> The essential goal of an asymmetrical strategy would be regime survival, not military victory over the United States or an international coalition. A hostile power's asymmetrical strategy would thus depend first and foremost on avoiding the decapitation of the political and military leadership by [an] air campaign, especially at the outset of a conflict. Second, a hostile state would try to prevent or dissuade the United States from "taking Baghdad" on the ground in later stages of the war. The hostile state may be unable to do this by military means, as Iraq could not; it must therefore provide the United States with incentives not to occupy the entire country.[105]

And as Max Jakobson has observed, "In a conflict between a great power with wide and varied interests and commitments and a small nation with a single

---

103 Yohanan Cohen, *Small Nations in Times of Crisis and Confrontation*, pp. 334–335. See also A. Hamish Ion and E. J. Errington, eds., *Great Powers and Little Wars: The Limits of Power* (Westport, Conn.: Praeger, 1993); Andrew Mack, "Why Big Nations Lose Small Wars: The Politics of Asymmetric Conflict," in Klaus Knorr, ed., *Power, Strategy, and Security* (Princeton, N.J.: Princeton University Press, 1983); and Frank C. Zagare and D. Marc Kilgour, "Asymmetric Deterrence," *International Studies Quarterly*, Vol. 37, No. 1 (March 1993), pp. 1–28.

104 Wolf, "When the Weak Attack the Strong," and Patrick Garrity, "Implications of the Persian Gulf War for Regional Powers," *The Washington Quarterly*, Vol. 16, No. 3 (Summer 1993), pp. 153–170.

105 Patrick J. Garrity, *Does the Gulf War Still Matter? Foreign Perspectives on the War and the Future of International Security*, CNSS Report No. 16 (Los Alamos, N.Mex.: Center for National Security Studies, Los Alamos National Laboratory, May 1993), p. 10.

objective of survival, the balance of forces cannot always be calculated by simple arithmetic."[106]

Given the perception that the political commitment of democracies to high-cost overseas campaigns is weak and vulnerable to disruption by media-fed fear, terrorism may be given prominence in such asymmetric strategies.[107] This brings us full circle to the subject of homeland vulnerability. In pursuit of asymmetric strategies, military opponents in the developing world may strike blows against cities or military installations in the developed one in the hope of crippling the will of policymakers there to sustain a confrontation. Unconventional weapons—especially the chemical or biological, whose pernicious effects may be slow to develop or difficult to trace back to the initiating party—may prove particularly desirable to the proponents of such strategies.

The United States stands out as a particularly likely target on this score. Because the United States is the primary defender of the international status quo, and because its power and influence will be critical to virtually any major collective use of force, whether under the auspices of the UN, NATO, or regional organizations such as the Organization of American States, the question of U.S. political will and commitment is paramount. U.S. allies might also be vulnerable to asymmetric strategies, not least because of the weight that their vulnerability would inevitably carry in the political debate in Washington. Attacks on allies with unconventional weapons that generate low casualties but seem to promise more, as with selective strikes with biological weapons, might be deemed particularly advantageous in asymmetric strategies that seek to break public will without prompting public outrage. For these reasons, the actual risks of attack on the West with unconventional weapons may have increased with the passing of the Cold War, although not of the kind of massively destructive attack with huge numbers of weapons intended to cripple entire societies.

---

106 Max Jakobson, "Finland: Substance and Appearance," *Foreign Affairs,* Vol. 58, No. 5 (Summer 1980), p. 1037.

107 For a general review of the terrorist threat in an era of proliferation of unconventional weapons, see James Adams, *Engines of War: Merchants of Death and the New Arms Race* (New York, N.Y.: Atlantic Monthly Press, 1990). See also Thomas G. Mahnken, "America's Next War," *The Washington Quarterly,* Vol. 16, No. 3 (Summer 1993), pp. 171–184.

Writing in 1984, Rodney Jones and Steven Hildreth concluded that the military capabilities of states of the developing world "are not now, nor for the foreseeable future, sufficient to threaten major military powers significantly. These military capabilities are relevant essentially to internal and localized threats."[108] A decade later, these conclusions can no longer be stated with such confidence. To be sure, a significant element of truth remains—Desert Storm revealed the very different competencies of advanced and developing countries.

But as Jones and Hildreth went on to observe, "Third World military acquisitions may increase local capabilities to engage in low-intensity conflict, but the systems that are procured usually do not appear to have defense against low-intensity threats primarily in mind."[109] Today these countries plan increasingly in the high-intensity context. A decade hence, the latitude of the developed world to project military power into the developing one is likely to be more constrained than today, even if the former retains the ability to inflict decisive defeat on the battlefield, because the cost of victory may be too high.

Moreover, the surfeit of military power and competence enjoyed by the United States is not widely shared by other developed countries. Britain is a mid-ranked military power that, if the Falklands/Malvinas War is any indication, already in the 1980s faced significant doubts about its ability to fight and prevail in regional contingencies outside of a collective framework. France's military establishment has not been similarly tested in recent times, but is of a scale similar to that of the United Kingdom. Germany and Japan are large powers equipped with modest self-defense capabilities. Russia retains a substantial military establishment capable of projecting force outside its territory, but that capability has been severely hampered by the travails of reform and democratization and its future competence at generating, maintaining, and using effectively high-technology weaponry is in considerable doubt today. Hence the United States should be cautious in characterizing its own thinking about the military aspects of regional crises as universally shared among the other developed countries.

---

108 Jones and Hildreth, *Modern Weapons and Third World Powers*, p. 5.
109 Ibid., p. 5.

Political Implications

Beyond these various military implications, how should the political implications of proliferation for the developed world be evaluated?

First, proliferation diminishes the influence of the developed world on events in the developing one by bringing power resources into closer symmetry. Indeed, Iklé and Wohlstetter have argued that proliferation will change the very nature of the relationship between heretofore major and minor powers by the early twenty-first century.[110] Minor powers enjoy new freedom of maneuver in regional and global affairs as a result of the diversification of the arms market, their increasing strategic reach, and the withering of regional strategic exigencies wrought by the Cold War. Such freedom may be used to formulate new types of relations or alignments or to push conflicts where desired.[111] Conversely, the states of the developed world, marginalized strategically by the end of the Cold War and, with the exception of the United States so far, selling fewer armaments, suffer declining influence on and leverage over events.[112] This is not to argue that the major arms exporters have been eclipsed by new producers or that leverage has been reliably exploitable in the past; rather, it is to point to trends in the changing relationships between states of the developed and developing world in this particular respect.

Second, proliferation raises the costs of the use of force by the developed world in pursuit of foreign policy goals in the developing one. Both unconventional and conventional weapons have the effect of creating military

---

110 Commission on Integrated Long-Term Strategy, *Discriminate Deterrence.*

111 See Sanders, *Arms Industries,* where in the first 10 pages he reviews the different perspectives on this question. Arguing that it is important not to overstate or understate the implications of the proliferation of defense production, he summarizes conclusions of his study of defense industries in the newly industrializing countries as follows. "This study agrees with [Andrew] Pierre's contention that the emergence of new arms sources cannot soon challenge the preeminent position of the United States, Great Britain, France, West Germany, and the Soviet Union in the global arms market. It departs from Pierre's argument by contending that the production and export of arms and military equipment are having and will continue to have significant consequences globally and regionally" (pp. 3–8).

112 See Alex Gliksman, "Arms Production Spread: Implications for Pacific Rim Security," in Dora Alves, ed., *Evolving Pacific Basin Strategies* (Washington, D.C.: National Defense University Press, 1990), p. 70.

challenges in the developing world that cannot be dismissed, as in the past, as insignificant or militarily not taxing. Some in the developing world will cheer this result, having actively worked to create it, accustomed as they are to a history of interference by the more advanced countries in the affairs of the less advanced. But a developed world that is militarily and politically crippled in its ability to use force is a world unable to deliver on security guarantees or to implement collective security undertakings. Such a world might also be targeted by messianic leaders seeking to wage wars of righteousness against what they perceive to be a corrupt, secular world, in the name of Islam or any other ideology or grievance that might suffice. Less apocalyptically, proliferation may put high-leverage systems in the hands of leaders who see a confrontation with the United States or the UN as necessary to some national goal.

As Amit Gupta has argued, "The real threat is not that Third World military industrialization is going to hurt the West's defensive capability, but it will blunt the offensive capability of the West."[113] But as argued earlier, this is a continuing theme. Whereas a century ago the advanced countries could use military power with impunity to conquer and occupy others in imperial fashion, those countries have grown ever less capable of using force to control others for extended periods. The costs of occupation are usually high and wars have tended to degenerate into prolonged stalemate. Thus, proliferation accentuates this existing trend in global politics.

Third, proliferation raises major questions about the global role of the United States. Proliferation is sharpening the U.S. debate about vital versus peripheral national interests. It undermines political support for military intervention or even long-term engagement, increases perceived vulnerability to coercive diplomacy by regional actors, and narrows the room for maneuver in a more fluid international environment. At a time when isolationist impulses are resurgent in U.S. politics, the effect of proliferation will be to cast new doubt on U.S. credibility among allies and friends and on American self-confidence.[114] In an era relatively more secure than the Cold War, Americans ask more and more

---

113 Amit Gupta, "Third World Militaries: New Suppliers, Deadlier Weapons," *Orbis*, Vol. 37, No. 1 (Winter 1993), p. 68.

114 Commission on Integrated Long-Term Strategy, *Discriminate Deterrence*, p. 13.

frequently why they should bear the risks of engagement, especially if U.S. cities might be held hostage to attack with weapons of mass destruction.

Thus the proliferation problem casts a revealing light on the debate begun by Paul Kennedy about a United States in decline because of imperial overstretch. Charles Wolf takes the argument a step further:

> [T]he important point is not so much decline or incline, but rather that the emerging world environment is likely to be one of greater instability and a probably considerably lessened capacity of the United States to control events. The source of this loss of control is not, however, the relative position of the United States compared, say, to that of Japan or the other large powers. Instead, it is more directly attributable to the emergence and increasing capabilities of middle-level powers and independent actors in the Third World itself.[115]

These political factors make likely a more modest role for the United States and reinforce the historic U.S. tendency toward isolationism.[116] To be sure, countervailing factors remain. The United States cannot quickly or painlessly extricate itself from the global entanglements of the international trading system, huge energy markets, and transnational problems such as the environment—even if it could somehow prevent its emerging vulnerability to attack with ballistic missiles.

If uncertainty deepens about U.S. constancy and engagement, other developed countries may seek to strengthen themselves militarily. Japan and Germany, for example, might opt in the long term to acquire nuclear weapons to compensate for a more isolated United States. Or conversely, such uncertainty may weaken their resolve to play leadership roles of any kind on the world stage, thus contributing to an erosion of international cooperation.

---

115 Charles Wolf, Jr., "The Third World in U.S.–Soviet Competition: From Playing Field to Player," in Marshall, Martin, and Rowen, *On Not Confusing Ourselves*, pp. 258–259. See also Paul Kennedy, *The Rise and Fall of the Great Powers: Economic Change and Military Conflict from 1500 to 2000* (New York, N.Y.: Random House, 1987).

116 Tucker and Weltman, "Nuclear Future," p. 258.

Finally, proliferation reinforces the stake of the developed world in the achievement and maintenance of stability and security in the developing one. Because states of the developing world increasingly have the ability to menace the interests of states of the developed one with long-range delivery systems and weapons of mass destruction, or to threaten significant regional interests such as energy supplies or local allies, the developed world should expect to pay an increasing price for trying to sit idly by, as it has in Bosnia, while instability and chaos engulf other parts of the globe. Europe's security is tied increasingly to the achievement of stability in the Middle East. Japan's security is tied increasingly to preservation of a peaceful balance of power in East Asia. U.S. security is less directly tied to any one region, but as the principal global power widely perceived as the defender of the global status quo, it will be seen by others to have a stake in their affairs even when it might not share that view. If policymakers in the developed world are not able to work cooperatively with states of the developing world to achieve stable relations, they will also be frustrated in attempting the larger cooperative projects of the post–Cold War era, such as protecting the global commons and advancing economic integration.

A World Order Issue

This review so far has focused on the impact of proliferation on the interests of different types of states, those of the developed and developing worlds. It is necessary also to look beyond these parochial perspectives and interests to assess the impact of proliferation on the functioning of the interstate system itself. More specifically, what impact will proliferation have on the basic institutions of world order? To invoke Hedley Bull again, five institutions have served historically as the basis of order: the great power system, the balance of power, war, international law, and diplomacy.

Proliferation and the Great Power System

The great power system, as noted in chapter 3, is in a period of substantial flux. The great powers today are a changing cast of players, with the claims of France and Britain in growing dispute, Russia playing a much diminished role, China's credentials tarnished, new contenders in the developing world such as India and Iran on the brink of stepping forward, and a United States stuck halfway between superpower status and status as a mere great power. The willingness of these various powers to tie their aspirations to common purposes and to fulfill special duties while being accorded special rights is in doubt. Moreover, the very nature of state power is in debate as the "soft" power of economics and politics plays an increasingly prominent role internationally, and new powers great in economic but not military prowess have emerged (Germany and Japan). These great powers jockey for advantage over one another on various commercial and diplomatic fronts, but the possibility of hegemonic competition and war among them—long a major obstacle to orderly relations in the state system generally—has been effectively eliminated by the capacity that each has to inflict assured destruction on the other.

This period of flux need not necessarily portend the end of the great power system. A new cast of great powers may emerge and act in concert to fulfill those special duties. Indeed, the passing of ideological conflict in the developed world raises the possibility of a future great power system composed of the democratic and developed states of the world, which who might well act with greater coherence and effectiveness than in the past. As Stephen van Evera has argued, with the major causes of war "tamed...possibilities for wider great power cooperation to prevent war worldwide would be opened."[117]

For the next decade or two, proliferation is likely to have the effect of accentuating and reinforcing the negative perturbations in the great power system. At the most basic level, the redistribution of military capabilities inherent in the proliferation process portends a redistribution of power in the international system. The great powers are becoming less dominant insofar as their ability to project power in defense of individual or collective interests is diminishing with the diffusion of power. Those interests are more easily challenged by others, some of whom may seek to blackmail the advanced powers into not using that military power. Moreover, nuclear proliferation in particular is having different implications for different great powers, encouraging some like the United States and Russia to make cuts in their nuclear arsenals as a way, in part, to limit proliferation, while encouraging France, Britain, and China to keep or even modernize their weapons as testaments of their great power status in an uncertain world.[118]

---

117 Stephen van Evera, "Preserving Peace in the New Era," *Boston Review*, Vol. 17, No. 6 (November/December 1992), p. 4.

The proliferation of unconventional weapons especially portends the end of an era of human history when military strength represented the culmination of the resources and competencies of an industrializing society. Today, any state possessing even a few badly made or stolen nuclear weapons or a batch of biological weapons has the capacity to inflict devastation well beyond the great armies of history. The proliferation of technical competence generally will weaken the technological stratification upon which Western power has depended. As Janne Nolan has observed:

> If current trends continue, the pace of diffusion may eventually vitiate the reliance of industrial countries on technological superiority to influence international events. The rapid transformation of technology from state-of-the-art to obsolescence may make the quest for advantage ever more elusive....there may be a point of exhaustion in which an increment in technological superiority yields diminishing military returns.[119]

This is readily demonstrated in relation to space launch capabilities, the proliferation of which

> will contribute to a decline in the hegemony of the foremost powers and the loss of influence of second-ranked powers in a more multi-polar world. These developments might cause some concern to those nations that wish to maintain the present international status quo, but will not in any way affect the slow and progressive transformation of the international order to a less dominated system of nations.[120]

---

118 John C. Hopkins and Weixing Hu, eds., *Strategic Views from the Second Tier: The Nuclear Weapons Policies of France, Britain, and China* (La Jolla, Calif.: University of California Institute on Global Conflict and Cooperation, 1994).

119 Janne E. Nolan, *Trappings of Power: Ballistic Missiles in the Third World* (Washington, D.C.: Brookings Institution, 1991), p. 7.

120 K. Subrahmanyam, "A View from the Developing World," in Krepon et al., *Commercial Observation Satellites and International Security*, p. 108.

Freedman has summarized the impact of nuclear proliferation, particularly on the great power system:

> As nuclear arsenals spread, despite the non-proliferation regime,
> more parts of the world move beyond the effective influence of the
> former great powers....The spread of nuclear weapons, in terms of
> political control as much as absolute numbers, encourages strategic
> disengagement and thus a loss of influence in regions where
> important, if not quite vital, interests are involved....Proliferation
> feeds on and then reinforces an existing tendency to reduce the
> security links between the declared nuclear powers and those parts
> of their "far abroads" that are not covered by a well-established
> alliance.[121]

Freedman goes on to note, however, that proliferation has a contrary effect in the sense that for any state a nuclear explosion, or the threat of one, creates a vital interest, in the sense that all major states will exert maximum power to avoid the radiological and political consequences of the outbreak of nuclear war. He notes also that "actively obstructing a capacity for nuclear self-defence creates an obligation to provide a security guarantee."[122] Thus the great powers may indeed have vital interests in the developing world, but not quite as before—interests related to conflict prevention rather than power competition.[123]

Proliferation also has a primary effect on one of the basic manifestations of the great power system—the principle of collective security and its embodiment in the special obligations for international peace and security of the UN Security Council. Proliferation has the effect of making collective security operations more risky and costly for their underwriters. It increases the premium on war-prevention rather than war-fighting. But it also provides one of the strongest arguments for constructing and sustaining a functioning collective security system.[124]

---

121 Freedman, "Great Powers, Vital Interests, and Nuclear Weapons," pp. 37, 48.

122 Ibid., p. 40.

123 Ibid., p. 39.

124 Thomas G. Weiss, ed., *Collective Security in a Changing World* (Boulder, Colo.: Lynne Rienner Publishers, 1993), p. 160.

The weakening of the great power system is not in and of itself a negative circumstance, so long as other institutions of order compensate. A rudderless state system in which no one state or group of states takes a special interest in the global institutions of order would not likely long remain peaceful as challengers to the distribution of power, such as ambitious industrializing nations, or to the nature of power and order itself, such as revolutionary non-secular movements operating under the guise of state power, as in Iran, press their cases.

Proliferation and the Balance of Power

The balance of power is also in great flux. A general balance that prevailed during the Cold War to structure major features of the international system and to align the major powers so as to hold the most aggressive ambitions in check has given way to a much more fluid world, characterized by competing strains of unipolarity, multipolarity, and regionalism. The differentiation of power into the hard and soft kinds referred to above combines with the emergence of a global trading system, a globalization of liberal political values, and an unprecedented wave of intrastate war to confound previous understanding of how a balance of power among states might provide order. Bipolar systems are reputed to be more likely to sustain orderly international relations than the alternatives.[125]

Might a new balance emerge to take the place of the now defunct Cold War balance? Waltz argues that "over time, unbalanced power will be checked by the responses of the weaker who will, rightly or not, feel put upon."[126] One prominent Third World scholar, Rajni Kothari, writing in the 1970s, looked to the proliferation of nuclear technology among other factors to help redistribute power and influence in favor of the Third World.[127]

Proliferation may well be laying the seeds of a future clash between states of the North and South, which is to say between the established, status quo powers

---

125 The greater ease derives from the benefits of fewer actors, simpler communications, and reduced dangers of misperception. See Kenneth N. Waltz, *Theory of International Politics* (Reading, Mass.: Addison Wesley, 1979).

126 Kenneth N. Waltz, "The Emerging Structure of International Politics," *International Security*, Vol. 18, No. 2 (Fall 1993), p. 79.

127 Rajni Kothari, *Footsteps Into the Future: Diagnosis of the Present World and a Design for an Alternative* (New Delhi: Orient Longman, 1974).

and those members of the new tier discontented with their status or wealth. Another possibility is that proliferation will accelerate the competitive tendencies of a more multipolar system and generate new conflict among regions as well as rivalries within them for preeminence.[128]

In fact, proliferation seems to be moving the world in rather a different direction, because the capacity to exploit high-leverage military capabilities acts as a great equalizer, enabling middle-range states to achieve minimal deterrence against the great powers. Morton Kaplan has described this as a unit-veto-based international system, by which a large number of nuclear-armed states would participate in a system of minimal deterrence that would essentially preclude any form of great power intervention.[129] But minimum nuclear deterrence—defined as the lowest level of forces necessary to inflict unacceptable damage—has been little studied for its impact on international politics.[130]

But whether such a system is either likely or would promise stability and order is disputed by both Wohlstetter and Bull. Wohlstetter cautions that:

> The dispersion of nuclear weapons will affect the world distribution of power. It will do so because something real will have changed. On the other hand, world power relationships will probably not be wholly transformed. For instance, it is difficult to find evidence that the British, French and Chinese nuclear programs have radically added to the effective power of these countries and, as we have seen, even greater constraints will be faced by smaller nuclear forces than these....[A] highly decentralized system...seems unlikely to emerge despite the "leveling" tendency of nuclear weapons, a tendency which is modest. One can only conjecture as to whether the existence of a highly dispersed power system would provide a stable international system. Equilibriating alliances might be formed. But alliances

---

128 Thomas Ohlson, "Introduction," in Ohlson, ed., *Arms Transfer Limitations and Third World Security*, p. 8.

129 Morton Kaplan, *System and Process in International Politics* (New York, N.Y.: John Wiley, 1975).

130 Peter Gizewski makes this point in his chapter, "The Logic of Minimum Deterrence: Retrospect and Prospect," in Gizewski, ed., *Minimum Nuclear Deterrence in a New World Order*, Aurora Papers No. 23 (Ottawa: Canadian Centre for Global Security, 1994), p. 1.

among small nations possessing nuclear weapons might also seem dangerous and be avoided by countries geographically or in other ways able to do so.[131]

Bull argues that significant gradations of power would continue to exist even in a world of broad-based mutual nuclear deterrence and that order might well not be likely because of the limits of nuclear deterrence, "which can be overthrown by political or technical change, and which even while it lasts does not make nuclear war impossible but simply renders it 'irrational.'"[132]

Proliferation and War

The institution of war is being buffeted by many forces in the late twentieth century, among them a dramatic increase in intrastate war along with a decline in interstate war and a decline in the perceived legitimacy of war among the advanced countries. The threat of war among the great powers is so widely discounted as to be irrelevant to relations among them. Wars of outright aggression and of long-term occupation are also noteworthy mostly for their absence from the interstate system. Proliferation itself is having something to do with these changes.

Proliferation is, quite simply, changing conflict. The competitive accumulation of military capabilities within regions in conflict appears to be having the effect

---

131 Albert Wohlstetter et al., *Moving Toward Life in a Nuclear Armed Crowd?* (Report prepared for the U.S. Arms Control and Disarmament Agency by Pan Heuristics, ACDA/PAB–263, Los Angeles, Calif., April 22, 1976), pp. 153–154.

132 Hedley Bull, *The Anarchical Society: A Study of Order in World Politics* (New York, N.Y.: Columbia University Press, 1977). Thomas G. Weiss echoes these concerns in a commentary on John Mearsheimer. "Proliferation thus becomes, in his view, a potential antidote to the comparative instability of a multipolar compared with a bipolar structure of power. To mine that potential, however, proliferation must be managed in order to avoid (1) nuclear weapons acquisition by states without the will, resources, and orderly command and control required to safely deploy a credible second-strike force and (2) preemptive attacks on a state as it is transiting to privileged nuclear status. While professing to believe that these risks are manageable, Mearsheimer fails to explain how the management system would function....By themselves, weapons of mass destruction offer one of the strongest arguments for attempting, in the face of realist skepticism, to constructive collective security systems." In Weiss, *Collective Security in a Changing World*, p. 160.

of revolutionizing military balances much as nuclear weapons and later high-technology systems revolutionized thinking about war in Europe. For example, the greater availability of long-range delivery systems changes the value to security of territory and distance. One effect of this, as seen in the Persian Gulf War, is the increasing temptation of states at war to expand the conflict to non-belligerent third parties. Another effect is to greatly magnify the complexities of military confrontations in the developing world, thereby also clouding the costs and benefits of using military force.

Thus even where nuclear weapons may not yet have proliferated, the character of military confrontation between states is increasingly strategic. By this is meant the diffusion of high-leverage military systems that operate fundamentally on the perceptions of national decision makers, usually by threatening to carry war to population centers, but sometimes by so severely constraining options for conventional warfare that leaders can no longer expect to rely on the military instrument for intended purposes, whether of deterrence or compellence. The diffusion of high-leverage capabilities increases the options available to leaders in regions of conflict to compel and coerce others—to see their instruments of war as those of suasion rather than dissuasion. Transitory advantages created by the introduction of new capabilities create incentives for some leaders to exploit those advantages and thus to seek war; they also provide incentives to competitors to strike preemptively, thus bringing about war. But such capabilities also appear to be strengthening deterrence among these states, in the sense that they deprive leaders of the confidence that the objectives of their warfare can be obtained.

New technologies have increased the risks of escalation, thereby constraining the room for maneuver of states. Yezid Sayigh depicts a developing world increasingly confronting the classic elements of the security dilemma discussed in chapter 1:

> Accumulation of military strength risks being either too successful or not successful enough; in the first case, exaggerated power can lead to aggression; in the second case an arms build-up may alarm neighbors and provoke them into a counter-build-up, eventually threatening the first state and leaving it less secure than it started....The imperatives of national security may lead to domestic and foreign policies that are actually disruptive of regional relations

and that run counter to the demands of integration into the
international order.[133]

Moreover, the last major interstate war between states of the developing
world—the Iran–Iraq War—illustrated vividly the general impact of
industrialization on war, as described by Russell Weigley:

> To expect from war any positive gains at less than a
> disproportionate cost is to ignore the whole tendency of war to
> degenerate into stalemate, a tendency evident from at least the
> American Civil War, through the World Wars, and on to the
> Iran–Iraq War. Such stalemates have been resolved only by the
> exhaustion of one side purchased with the near-exhaustion of the
> other.[134]

This is leading to a circumstance of increasing stalemate among traditional
regional competitors, to what William Zartman has called "hurting stalemates,"
in which the risks of catastrophic confrontation create new perceptions about the
means to secure national interests and promote national security. These
heightened instabilities and changing perceptions may combine to lead states
away from the attempt to maintain autonomous security postures.

The Middle East provides perhaps the best example of a strategic landscape
rewritten by the diffusion of military capability, conventional and
unconventional. As Avi Kober has observed, the Persian Gulf War compelled
Israel to confront these new strategic realities:

> The advantages that Israel had until then enjoyed—both in the
> military aspect of the national security equation and in the military
> balance—were shown to be eroding, so that a previously

---

133 Yezid Sayigh, *Confronting the 1990s: Security in the Developing Countries*, Adelphi Paper No. 251
(London: Brassey's for the International Institute for Strategic Studies, 1990), pp. 52, 70. He
cites Abdul-Monem Al-Mashat, *National Security in the Third World* (Boulder, Colo.:
Westview Press, 1985), p. 13.

134 Russell F. Weigley, "War and the Paradox of Technology," *International Security*, Vol. 14,
No. 2 (Fall 1989), p. 201.

non-existent military symmetry was establishing itself between
Israel and the Arabs. The Gulf War indicated that Israel could no
longer regard itself as immune against active deterrence operated
against it, or against decisions taken by its enemies to cross
thresholds of self-restraint. The war also indicated that early
warning time was becoming shorter and that certain
processes...were extending the size of the confrontation area to
cover the entire distance from the battlefield itself to the civilian
rear.[135]

The stalemated conflict between India and Pakistan provides another example.
Analysts of countries facing these stalemates describe a shift in the thinking of
leaders in these countries about the best ways to achieve security and stability in
the future. Saadet Deger concluded in 1993 that:

There is no doubt that broader international security
considerations are gaining ground against the narrower older
doctrines which emphasized territorial national defence. Concern
for global security is now far greater than it was in the recent
past.[136]

Jasjit Singh of India, in a survey of Asian security written in 1992, concluded that:

In the post–Cold War period, especially as states move to cope with
unpredictable multidirectional challenges to security, it will be
increasingly difficult for states to maintain autonomous—at times
unilateral—security postures....States are being forced by
economic, technological, and strategic parameters to seek the

---

135 Avi Kober, "Deterrence, Early Warning and Strategic Decision: The Israeli Security
Conception in the Wake of the Gulf War" (Unpublished and undated paper), p. 30. For more
on the way in which changing perceptions of military security have influenced Israeli
thinking about the peace process, see Efraim Inbar, "Israel and Arms Control," *Arms Control*,
Vol. 13, No. 2 (September 1992), pp. 214–221.

136 Saadet Deger, "World Military Expenditure," in Stockholm International Peace Research
Institute, *SIPRI Yearbook, 1993, World Armaments and Disarmament* (Oxford: Oxford University
Press for the Stockholm International Peace Research Institute, 1993), p. 396.

cooperation of the adversary. This holds out the promise of a new
security paradigm being established....There is a noticeable shift
away from the autonomous competitive security framework. The
challenge of international security now is the formulation and
establishment of cooperative security paradigms at the
international and regional levels.[137]

Evidence of such a departure from traditional dependence on military
buildups can be found in both South Asia and the Middle East, where leaders are
beginning to explore formally or informally the means to limit conflict and
escalation.[138] As Chris Smith has stated, "The mounting evidence regarding the
adverse cost and utility of advanced military technology for Third World
countries is a persuasive argument for radical changes in defence policy."[139] In
Southeast Asia, the nascent competition in conventional armaments is beginning
to generate concern about preventing a larger arms race, although here, too, the
incentives to create new forms of international relations are not yet dominant.[140]

Thus rather than reinforcing the prevalence of war in the international system,
proliferation appears to be increasing the interest of leaders in finding means
other than war and military preparations to resolve or at least manage conflicts.
As Zartman has written, changing perceptions may create "ripe moments" in
which breakthroughs can be achieved on the basis of changed national ambitions
and strengthened security at lower levels of armaments.[141] But if not captured,
such moments may rapidly pass, as the dynamic of arms race and crisis instability,
reinforced by a souring of political relations and hardening of opinions around

---

137 Singh, "Security in a Period of Strategic Uncertainty," in *Asian Strategic Review*, pp. 13, 25.

138 See for example Neil Joeck, "Tacit Bargaining and Stable Proliferation in South Asia," p. 89;
Anthony Cordesman, [CHECK], in Stahl and Kemp, *Arms Control and Weapons Proliferation in
the Middle East and South Asia;* and Avner Cohen, "Nuclear Weapons, Opacity, and
Democracy: Understanding the Israeli Case," p. 21.

139 Smith, "Third World Arms Control, Military Technology and Alternative Security," p. 68.

140 Gerald Segal, "Managing New Arms Races in the Asia/Pacific," *The Washington Quarterly*,
Vol. 15, No. 3 (Summer 1992), pp. 83–101; and Muthiah Alagappa and Noordin Sopiee,
"Problems and Prospects for Arms Control in South-East Asia," in Ohlson, *Arms Transfer
Limitations and Third World Security*, p. 196.

141 [William Zartman book]

extreme positions, leads to catastrophe. Such choices are hardly new to small states that have long lived in the shadows of aggressive or otherwise hegemonic neighbors.[142] But they may become increasingly prevalent in the thinking of larger states.

The dilemma that many of these countries now confront is that they have been caught intellectually unprepared, much like their Cold War counterparts in the developed world, for these new circumstances. Strategic analysis has been slower to emerge in these regions than the weapons themselves and the realities they have created. This was also true in the experience of the superpowers. In the United States, an open political environment encouraged civilians working independently of the military to put together the pieces of a strategic concept suited to the post–World War II nuclear era, including not just the essentials of nuclear strategy such as nuclear deterrence, strategic war, limited war, and the escalation process, but also the elements of arms control.[143] Some of these ideas certainly can be, and have been, imported into the strategic concepts of the states of the developing world. But to an outsider at least the work appears to be going slowly, and is sharply constrained by the legacy of confrontational rhetoric, state secrecy, and an unfamiliarity with basic weapons effects. The trend toward more democratic governance discussed in chapter 3, and the promise it holds out to replace authoritarian demagogues with pragmatic leaders focused on solving national problems, may contribute significantly to the emergence of new strategic concepts in the developing world better suited to the task of assuring national security through international means.

---

142 Yohanan Cohen, *Small Nations in Times of Crisis and Confrontation*, p. 1.

143 "Virtually all of the basic ideas and philosophies about nuclear weapons and their use have been generated by civilians working independently of the military." Bernard Brodie, "The Development of Nuclear Strategy," in Brodie, Intriligator, and Kolkowicz, *National Security and International Stability*, p. 7. "Nuclear arms control, both as a concept and as a blueprint for action, resulted from expectations of Americans who, becoming aware of their nuclear weapons vulnerability and concerned about the reciprocal fear of surprise attack, started to think about the future (indeed, anticipating the future) in terms of strategic stability." Emanuel Adler, "'Opaque Nuclear Proliferation' and the Political Selection of Arms Control Concepts," in Frankel, *Opaque Nuclear Proliferation*, p. 196.

Proliferation and International Law

International law enjoys a widening purview in the international system of the late twentieth century. Proliferation serves as a stimulus to the deepening of a law-governed state system, given the pressure to have legal frameworks sufficiently robust to deal with the problems of malefactors armed with great power. But it also undermines that system, as disputes deepen about the legitimacy of those laws and as doubts grow about their effectiveness in dealing with proliferation-related problems.

The best demonstration of this dilemma is the global treaty regime. The legal instrumentalities designed to control the proliferation and use of nuclear, biological, and chemical weapons enjoy a new prominence in the post–Cold War era as multilateral negotiations to strengthen and broaden the regime have moved forward. But the political engagement of leading states has been episodic and the evidence of proliferation in each area has undermined a belief in the utility of these regimes. Moreover, the power of international law to punish malefactors and its blindness to the special interests of the great powers have not been well demonstrated in the 1990s. Many of the actions of the UN Security Council in undertaking new peacemaking roles have gone beyond the legal boundaries established in the charter and raised doubts about whether the laws being enforced are anything other than laws of convenience for the permanent members of the Security Council.[144]

A law-governed interstate system requires also some degree of shared interests, values, and perceptions. In the 1990s, there is evidence that these are growing both weaker and stronger. The evidence that they are growing weaker includes the growing distance between the erstwhile great powers and their critics, who contest the distribution of power and authority within these institutions and resist the injunctions of the developed world to adhere to norms and legal obligations associated with global treaties. The spread of democratic principles and forms of governance, a steadily expanding international economy based on the exchange of goods and services by private sector enterprises, the rejuvenation of multilateral institutions with the passing of the Cold War, and the emergence

---

144 Jose E. Alvarez, "The Once and Future Security Council," *The Washington Quarterly*, Vol. 18, No. 2 (Spring 1995), pp. 5–22.

of a transnational agenda related to the environment all point to a more global consciousness and sense of shared interests.

Proliferation is having an ambiguous impact on these perceptions and values. It underscores that most global institutions and rules have their roots firmly in an era when the world was dominated by the European system of states as reinforced by a United States that emerged virtually unscathed from World War II. This is most in evidence in the debate about the norms embodied in international legal structures, such as the principles in the UN Charter and the global arms control treaties, which one now hears dismissed as imperialist vestiges of a corrupt world order by diplomats not just from Iran or North Korea but from Singapore, Mexico, Egypt, Russia, and China. Rejuvenation of those norms, by giving them firmer political roots in non-Western societies, is an urgent requirement if international society is to be sustained in an era of technology diffusion.

But proliferation is also stimulating the emergence of a common intellectual culture about problems of war and peace in a nuclear era. Emanuel Adler describes this as a process of "evolutionary epistemology" by which "nations diffuse their concepts and understandings to each other" about security, arms control, and national strategy "not only because they offer a superior or even a new understanding of the situation but also because they carry political clout as a collective interpretation of the national interest and of international stability."[145]

Proliferation and Diplomacy

The last of Bull's five institutions is diplomacy. This, too, is undergoing significant changes at a time when advanced communications and broad-based international contacts are marginalizing the influence of traditional diplomacy. A primary challenge to the institution of diplomacy is the increasing prominence of non-state actors internationally, especially firms and enterprises managing huge trade and investment flows.

Once again, proliferation aggravates the challenges confronting this institution. Proliferation puts new demands on multilateral diplomacy in the search for stronger legal mechanisms; especially among the great powers, multilateralism

---

145 Adler, "'Opaque Nuclear Proliferation' and the Political Selection of Arms Control Concepts," pp. 192–193.

has not been a strong point. Proliferation has marginalized the great powers and particularly the United States, as noted above, just when management of the proliferation problem takes on an increasingly political dimension. Proliferation puts new demands on the capacity of diplomats to exert leverage over the most egregious violators of agreed norms and laws, demands that include integrating economic, political, and military factors in an international system of diffuse influence.[146]

Weapons Proliferation and World Order

Bull's taxonomy provides a useful way of thinking about the elements of world order. It is important to recall that it is a heuristic device, not a coda reflecting a consensus of the community of states.

As a heuristic device, it enables the analyst to pose questions about whether it includes all of the essential ingredients of order. It is, for example, unclear that Bull's list sufficiently encompasses the sources of order in the globalizing economy and the transnational agenda, as well as the sources of disorder in the changing role of the state in organizing political life. Developing countries, for example, face an increasingly complex challenge of achieving security as they struggle with technological advance, the information revolution, problems of adjustment in the domestic and global economy, and a rise of local discontent; an orderly state system as conceived by Bull may not provide much order for such states. The tension between complex interdependence, the imbalance of power, and weak states provides a new set of challenges for international order.[147]

---

146 To illustrate this point, consider the arms embargo. This standard tool of diplomacy promises a short-term effect in cutting off or at least curtailing a state's access to weapons. But in today's world, its long-term impact appears to be to strengthen the drive toward purchaser independence and a diversification of arms producers. "By threatening and/or implementing an arms embargo, several developed states (the United States in particular) have attempted to use their position as major arms suppliers as mechanisms to control the policies of their clients. In so doing, they have inadvertently sowed the seeds for Third World indigenous arms production; in addition, such policies have helped provide the impetus for Third World countries, which do not have the economic resources to engage in arms production, to diversify their suppliers, and consequently increase their arms imports from other Third World states." Robert M. Rosh, "Third World Arms Production and the Evolving Interstate System," *Journal of Conflict Resolution*, Vol. 34, No. 1 (March 1990), p. 58.

Furthermore, Bull's taxonomy enables the analyst to speculate about the changing utility of specific elements and about the balance among them. The diffusion of Westernized and secular society throughout the international system may, for example, compensate for a weakening of the great power system by helping to sustain public perceptions of shared transnational interests.

Lastly, it helps to underscore that not all states share an equal investment in any particular order, and some actively promote disorder as a way to upset perceived injustices and outdated values. China at the peak of its revolutionary fervor stands out as one of the most passionate critics of orderly international affairs. In the words of Chou En-Lai in 1973: "Such great disorder is a good thing for the people, thus helping the international situation develop further in the direction favourable to the people, and unfavourable to imperialism, and modern revisionism, and all reaction."[148]

Bull himself is careful to note that even the effective functioning of these institutions might provide a type of order inappropriate or dysfunctional for the international community:

> Order is defined as an actual or possible situation or state of affairs, not as a value, goal, or objective. Thus it is not to be assumed that order...is a desirable goal, still less that it is an overriding one. To say that such and such an institution or course of action helps to sustain order in world politics is not to recommend that that institution should be preserved or that course of action followed....World order is wider than international order because to give an account of it we have to deal not only with order among states but also with order on a domestic or municipal scale, provided within particular states, and with order within the wider

---

147 These issues are particular evident in Asia. See Desmond Ball, "Arms and Affluence: Military Acquisitions in the Asia–Pacific Region," *International Security*, Vol. 18, No. 3 (Winter 1993/94), pp. 78–112; Barry Buzan and Gerald Segal, "Rethinking East Asian Security," *Survival*, Vol. 36, No. 2 (Summer 1994), pp. 3–21; and Aaron L. Friedberg, "Ripe for Rivalry: Prospects for Peace in a Multipolar Asia," *International Security*, Vol. 18, No. 3 (Winter 1993/94), pp. 5–33. On the general theme, see Yezid Sayigh, *Confronting the 1990s*.

148 Chou En-Lai, "Report to the Tenth National Congress of the Communist Party of China," Beijing, August 24, 1973.

political system of which the states system is only part. World order is more fundamental.[149]

Thus an orderly system of interstate relations that cannot also provide a context for addressing basic issues of well-being and justice within the human community is a system whose order is superficial and transient. It is a means to an end, not an end in itself.

Whatever the limits or shortcomings of Bull's approach, it suffices for the purposes of this study—to illustrate the interaction between proliferation and world order. Proliferation is both a symptom and a cause of disorder in the post–Cold War system. Its implications must be weighed not just in the parochial terms of individual states, or collections of them, but also in terms of broader processes and trends in the interstate system. This type of assessment helps to underscore that there are such things as global interests. These are the interests of the majority of states—not all, perhaps—in the functioning of a system of relations among states that provides the qualities of order necessary to the achievement of societal aspirations while minimizing the frictions caused by continual adjustments within the system. In other words, states share an interest in strengthening the element of order in an anarchic system of independent states, so long as that order is not a means unto itself, that is, providing only for slavish adherence to a rigid distribution of power, but a means to an end, that is, providing for the achievement of larger aspirations, such as survival and the further development of a sustainable global economy and a viable society.

Proliferation's negative consequences for these global interests are not difficult to conceive. If states arm in ways that destabilize regional competition and increase the likelihood of conflict, and if proliferation raises the risks of engagement for outside powers when they protect allies or perform collective security missions under UN or other auspices, then proliferation is likely to increase the trend toward disorder rather than order. Developing states, perceiving the emergence of a more chaotic world, are likely to increase their reliance on national military instruments, thus compounding the proliferation problem.

---

149 Bull, *Anarchical Society*, pp. xii, 22.

A belief that order is breaking down internationally would devalue cooperative international strategies and reinforce the tendency of national decision makers to look for national means of self-preservation, increasing their interest in weapons, especially those offering high leverage. Perceptions that allies or institutions of collective security could not be relied upon to come to the aid of states at risk or to deter the nascent ambitions of potential aggressors would have a similar result. Perceptions that states themselves are under increasing stress would reinforce the tendency of vulnerable elites to acquire weapons to bolster their own claims to power and leadership.

If the effort to create more orderly relations among states falters and there is some further breakdown in the existing patterns of cooperation, the consequences for international politics could be considerable. What Bull described as a "new medievalism...[composed of] a system of overlapping authority and multiple loyalty" could well emerge.[150] Thomas Weiss defines a credible worst-case scenario:

> The international system at the dawn of the twenty-first century may well be characterized by levels of violence and unrest not even imagined when the UN Charter was drafted. The search for order may be no less quixotic as the decolonization process continues in the former Soviet Union and as ethnic particularism elsewhere comes to dominate the global and local agendas.[151]

But this is the worst case. An alternative and arguably more likely scenario is that the vast majority of states will continue over the next decade or two to see the basic institutions of international order as consistent with their national interests. It is unreasonable to expect such institutions to function perfectly; making them function sufficiently well to satisfy a large portion of the international community is the more reasonable goal. If so, the costs and risks of recourse to strategies of national self-reliance and military dominance would be weighed against the costs and risks of a functioning, albeit imperfect, system.

---

150 Bull, *Anarchical Society*, p. 254. See also Zbigniew Brzezinski, *Out of Control: Global Turmoil on the Eve of the 21st Century* (New York, N.Y.: Charles Scribner's Sons, 1993).

151 Weiss, *Collective Security in a Changing World*, p. 14.

This would help to narrow the problem of aggression and advanced proliferation to a few dissatisfied states—a significant problem in itself, but a qualitatively different one from a broader breakdown of international society and order. Such a view of world order has led Max Singer and Aaron Wildavsky to argue that "nuclear weapons will not affect the fundamental character of the next world order, but they will cause some trouble and possibly great tragedy."[152]

Under this scenario, nascent regionalism and the declining role of external powers in balancing competition among states within regions in conflict would create the mix of fear and political will among regional leaders necessary to make them seek their own accommodation and security order; this factor probably helps to account for the current spate of regional security projects in the Middle East and Asia, which policy realists did not expect. It is also noteworthy in this regard that alliances remain in areas of potential instability (within the transatlantic community and between the United States and Japan). Furthermore, the military instrument is perceived by many developing countries as either not relevant to or actually counterproductive to their developmental goals, and even where it may be perceived to have some value, unconventional weapons remain unattractive to many states.

Proliferation may well help encourage this outcome. It has already proven to be a stimulus to new forms of order, because states act on the incentives created by heightened risks to initiate security structures that diminish reliance on armaments alone and on great power freedom of maneuver. Proliferation may over time lead to the emergence of stable balances of power within regions in conflict and/or create the incentives for concerted action against the most egregious aggressors. It may even be an antidote to the instabilities of multipolarity by providing new incentives for many if not all states to find new forms of relations in an era when economics, values, and transnational problems create many new incentives for cooperative relations. It may provide the needed new roles and incentives for the United States and other states interested in playing a leading role in global affairs after the Cold War. The challenge of finding common negotiated responses to the proliferation of weapons of mass destruction may be useful in strengthening that body of regimes and norms that

---

152 Max Singer and Aaron Wildavsky, *The Real World Order: Zones of Peace/Zones of Turmoil* (Chatham, N.J.: Chatham House Publishers, 1993), p. 60.

binds the international community to common purposes, thus contributing to a more orderly future. Because achievement of such negotiated measures will require political trade-offs and a lively international debate about the legitimacy of different weapons programs and the perceptions of just and unjust relations among nations and peoples, world order issues will be at the core of the proliferation agenda.

Conclusion

In stark contrast to decades past, proliferation is no longer a problem at the margins of international security. The central conclusion of this chapter is that proliferation is having profound implications for the kind of world emerging after the Cold War. Proliferation has begun to touch on an ever larger set of interests in states of both the developed and developing worlds and to magnify many of the basic dilemmas of security and world order arising in the new era. Cold War thinking about the implications of proliferation—and about the ingredients of world order—is increasingly threadbare in this dynamic new international environment.

Some limited diffusion of weapons and weapons competence may not be so harmful. More pacific interstate relations may emerge in zones of conflict as assured destruction capabilities diffuse. Such proliferation may change some of the fundamentals of state behavior in an anarchic system by creating incentives to decrease reliance on the military approach to national security and seek a way out of the traditional security dilemma. Proliferation may thus be conducive to the emergence of a more peaceful interstate system as states seek more cooperative forms of behavior, both within their regional subsystems and in the world system generally. At the very least, it would heighten the complexity of existing military confrontations and make much more complex the calculation of the costs and benefits of using force.

But a dramatic burst of proliferation or even a steady accretion could have far-reaching negative consequences, and not just for those states that today enjoy some measure of military advantage. Crisis instabilities could be particularly high and the transition to stable deterrent relationships between traditional rivals both difficult and prolonged. As a result, the likelihood of conflict could increase significantly. The proliferation of unconventional weapons and long-range delivery systems also has the effect of expanding the scope and increasing the potential intensity of regional conflict. Proliferation also makes collective security more risky and costly for its underwriters. Further, it raises the importance of arms control while souring the political environment in which it must be pursued.

Both the positive and negative trends are in evidence today. Which trend prevails cannot be determined solely on the basis of factors identified to this point in the present study—the outcome is not preordained in the technology, economics, or politics of proliferation. Policy will thus play a critical role. The actions of governments to shape these trends emerge as central to the future of both proliferation and world order. Ineffective policy may well aggravate proliferation and deepen the forces of disorder in the post–Cold War system. But policy soundly conceived and effectively implemented may have the effect of not only preventing further proliferation but of deepening the foundations of world order for the twenty-first century.

Chapter 5

Policy and Strategy: Beyond Nonproliferation

THE FINAL CHAPTER of this book turns to the prescriptive questions: What is the role of policy in responding to weapons proliferation? How ought that response be calibrated in the light of post–Cold War realities? Does nonproliferation fully encompass the range of actions available to governments opposed to proliferation? In framing these policy questions, it is useful to review the argument to this point.

First, because of proliferation's emergence during the Cold War as a feature of the international system, the conceptual tools of the Cold War era have been employed in understanding the basic features of the phenomenon, and the public policy tools of the Cold War have been employed in trying to manage the problem. But in the 1990s, new approaches are necessary.

Second, technically defined, proliferation is an increasingly multifaceted phenomenon. The diffusion of high-leverage systems (both conventional and unconventional) and of elements of the defense industrial base have a new prominence. This has helped to create a relatively new phenomenon in international affairs—the virtual weapon state, that is, a state that has not opted to turn its weapons potential into military prowess. The nuclear proliferation problem itself is changing in a number of important ways—not least is the marked trend away from nuclear weapons in recent years. This technical view reveals proliferation also to be a step-by-step process reflecting decisions made by leaders to cross certain qualitative or quantitative thresholds, with the commensurate investments. It also reveals a fact of major political significance—the emergence of a new tier of technically empowered states whose orientations to the international system are uncertain. The general picture of a technologically permissive environment also strikes fundamentally at the assumption underlying strategies of technology denial that heretofore have essentially been synonymous with nonproliferation policy.

Third, economic and political factors will be as important as technical factors in shaping the future rate and character of proliferation. It is unreasonable to predict a wildfire-like spread of weapons through the international system at this time. It is also unreasonable to predict that trends related to economic development and democratization preclude such proliferation in a future decade. Key determinants of the balance among these trends will be the viability and perceived credibility of existing institutions of international order. At this time, states of the new tier display a wide variety of orientations to those institutions.

Fourth, the implications of proliferation touch on a broad set of security and political issues. Proliferation is both symptom and cause of instability in the international system. It magnifies both the traditional dilemmas of achieving national security in an anarchic system and the new dilemmas of sustaining world order institutions in a world where the sources of order and disorder are uncertain. The proliferation dynamic generates many new incentives for states to cooperate in stemming its tide or minimizing its consequences. Policy well conceived will capitalize on these incentives to craft a more stable and secure international environment.

Thus, what governments do matters. This chapter offers a way of thinking about the policy challenges of the 1990s. Its purpose is *not* to delineate a detailed, highly specific set of policy recommendations. Rather, it is to identify the constituent parts of strategy, assess their approximate fit with one another, and give some idea of priorities among them. It begins with the identification of the primary tasks of policy, of which four are identified. It continues with a discussion of the various instruments of policy and of the harmony that must be achieved among them. It concludes with a review of the progress of the international community in meeting these policy challenges and an assessment of the prospects for future success.

The Tasks of Policy

In calibrating policy, it is necessary to begin with goals: What are the goals toward which policy in this area should work? Historically, nonproliferation has had one primary goal and one secondary goal: to prevent the spread of weapons and, where that is not possible, to slow their spread. These goals remain salient in the 1990s, but they no longer encompass the full range of possibilities. Reasonable and legitimate goals of policy include far more than prevention.

One new goal is the reversal of proliferation through the partial or complete removal of weapons. This goal might be termed deproliferation, although this is a term that has acquired a special usage among a few military specialists who use it to describe the denuding of a proliferant state's military capability through preemptive armed attack. Argentina, Brazil, South Africa, Belarus, Kazakhstan, and Ukraine are examples of states that have abandoned nuclear weapons in recent years. Iraq is an example of another kind, of a state compelled by the international community to abandon its advanced military programs. Especially in the domain of conventional weapons, such rollbacks are prominent. In Europe, for example, force structures continue to shrink with the implementation of the treaty on Conventional Forces in Europe (CFE). In the Middle East, the Arab–Israeli peace process portends a decline in defense spending and an increased willingness to trade military programs for the advantages of regional cooperation and international development assistance.

A second new goal is the capping of programs in places where the shedding of military capacity cannot be expected. South Asia provides the best example of a region where disarmament is at this time unrealistic but where avoiding large buildups in deployed nuclear arsenals seems to be in the interests of both Pakistan and India. Thus freezing current weapon developments or channeling them in ways that contribute to stable relations has emerged as a priority. A useful analogy can be found in the early arms control efforts of the United States and the Soviet Union, the results of which were agreements such as the Strategic Arms Limitation Treaty (SALT I) that fell far short of the ambitions of the professional disarmament community but nonetheless contributed to the stabilization of the armaments competition while providing a forum for dialogue among archenemies.

A third new goal is preventing the weapons-capable states from exploiting their potential for weapons purposes. This will be a goal of growing prominence as the number of states capable of producing high-leverage weapons continues to increase in the years and decades ahead. For many of these states, this restraint will require that they perceive their international security environments to be sufficiently secure and stable to preclude weapons-derived hedges against long-term possibilities. This points also to the salience of making it politically, economically, and militarily costly for states to make the transition from virtual to actual weapons status.

Even the narrow goal of nonproliferation deserves some rethinking in the 1990s. Rarely in the past have policymakers carefully addressed the subsidiary goal of delaying weapons programs. If the purpose of such efforts is to buy time, it is critical that the time be used effectively to ameliorate the consequences of acquisition. "Buying time for what?" emerges as a basic policy question in places like North Korea, Iraq, and South and Central Asia.

Achievement of these goals requires focusing increasingly on the will of leaders to acquire and use advanced weaponry rather than simply their country's ability to do so. Traditional nonproliferation policy has, of course, focused on both will and capability, as policy must continue to do; the point is simply that the balance is shifting from one to the other. Dealing with questions of will requires that policymakers look at a broad range of measures, including both the punitive and the cooperative, as well as a comprehensive set of political, economic, and military factors.

Achievement of any one of these goals should be counted as a success in the effort to stem weapons proliferation. They do not, of course, all meet the criteria of the nonproliferation purist. But policy is pursued in a less than perfect world and must sometimes embody a grudging acceptance that the best can be the enemy of the good. In this case, the best—the goal of zero weapons presence in places like South Asia—sometimes works against the good—capping those programs or otherwise channeling their development in stabilizing directions. Thus this chapter uses the term "positive nonproliferation outcome" to encompass those results that are not precisely preventive in character.

This chapter also adopts the term "antiproliferation" as a rubric for a strategy aiming at all of these goals. A new nomenclature is necessary to convey the new substance and focus of the policy agenda. The term "antiproliferation" connotes a break with the nonproliferation past, when the goals of reversing, capping, or channeling proliferation were less prominent. It sustains the notion that proliferation is potentially dangerous to regional peace and prosperity and deleterious to the community of nations. And it permits a broad strategy encompassing a comprehensive set of political, economic, military, and diplomatic policies aimed not at just halting the spread of weapons but also at coping with the consequences of their proliferation, shaping the will as much as the means to acquire them, and working toward rollback or disarmament where these are serious prospects.

What, then, are the means to these antiproliferation ends? What must policy do to achieve these goals? Four tasks in particular stand out:

Managing the flow of technology: At a time when technology is diffusing around the world because of a rapidly globalizing economy, that flow must be shaped in ways conducive to positive nonproliferation outcomes. Policy must build barriers to the uses of this technology for purposes inconsistent with security interests. But the extant diffusion of militarily sensitive technology and the emergence of new sources of supply on the global market pose fundamental challenges to traditional approaches to flow management.

Formalizing restraint: Patterns of restraint with regard to weapons potential are well established and the incentives to more wide-reaching constraint are numerous. Policy must capitalize on these factors by strengthening existing mechanisms of restraint, and formalizing new structures that offer some promise of durability and predictability is an increasingly important priority. Arms control has important new roles in the post–Cold War era and a variety of new purposes related to threat control, transparency, and confidence-building.

Reassuring the insecure: The so-called "demand side" of the proliferation problem requires renewed attention. The task of policy is to help to prevent the self-help rule from coming to predominate in an anarchic international system among those states of the newly empowered tier that do not face a military threat to their existence, but that also look upon the uncertainties and instabilities of the post–Cold War world with apprehension.

Deterring aggression: If an expectation is created that military force can be used for purposes of aggrandizement or territorial acquisition, the incentives for states to acquire more and higher leverage military capabilities are likely to multiply. How to establish the possibility if not also the expectation that such aggression will be met with some sort of response is one of the enduring dilemmas of an anarchic interstate system—but it is directly relevant to the future rate and character of proliferation.

The Instruments of Policy

Managing Technology Flows: Beyond Technology Denial

The cornerstone of the traditional nonproliferation policy approach has been the effort to constrain the supply of weapons and critical weapons technologies. These remain relevant, but not quite as before.

Policy Context. As the proliferation problem began to change in the 1980s with the emergence of areas of concern in addition to the nuclear, policymakers sought to extend the approaches first put in place in the nuclear domain. Those approaches emphasize so-called strategies of denial, whereby nonproliferation goals are secured through the actions of some states to deny others access to weapons or technologies. In the nuclear domain, these strategies were embodied first in the effort to control technologies and later also in the NPT.

But further treaty-based nonproliferation strategies have proven not replicable in other domains. In neither the chemical nor biological weapons areas could treaties be crafted (or recrafted) that would establish an unequal set of rights between possessors and nonpossessors. Instead, global disarmament regimes that differ fundamentally from the NPT but also offer nonproliferation benefits have been pursued, as discussed in more detail later in this chapter. So the nonproliferation effort has focused instead on expanding export controls by supplier states into an ever broader set of technologies and, in some instances, substituting supplier cartels for international treaty structures.

Because advanced technologies are widely distributed among developed countries, a failure to coordinate export controls can result in only a small impact on proliferation as well as significant imbalance in the constraints and opportunities of commercial firms in different countries. Thus the pursuit of strategies of denial has required international coordination among supplier states in the application of export controls.

In the nuclear domain, export controls on approximately 65 dual-use commodities are coordinated under the aegis of the London-based Nuclear Suppliers' Group and the so-called Zangger Committee under the NPT.[1]

---

1   David Fischer and Paul Szasz, ed. Jozef Goldblat, *Safeguarding the Atom: A Critical Appraisal* (London: Taylor and Francis for the Stockholm International Peace Research Institute, 1985),

In the chemical and biological domain, export controls on sensitive materials and technologies are coordinated under the aegis of the Australia Group, which has met biannually since 1985.

In the missile domain, export controls are coordinated under the aegis of the Missile Technology Control Regime (MTCR), established in 1987. The MTCR focuses on those missiles deemed capable of carrying nuclear warheads sufficient distances to strike deep into neighboring states, defined as missiles with a payload of 500 kg and a range of at least 300 km.

In the domain of supercomputers, the United States and Japan have cooperated informally to prevent supercomputer exports to problem countries. Efforts have been discussed to create a broader multilateral framework.[2]

The innovations in supplier coordination of the 1980s and 1990s were stimulated in part by the waning utility and ultimate collapse of the Coordinating Committee on export controls (CoCom). CoCom was a Cold War–vintage effort to prevent the flow of critical technologies to the Soviet Union and its allies. CoCom ceased to exist in 1994 amid efforts to create a successor regime aimed at controlling proliferation-sensitive technologies generally.

Between 1985, when the Cold War began to wind down, and the revelations in 1992 and 1993 about Iraq's weapons programs, such strategies of denial enjoyed a notable boost. The end of the Cold War created widespread hopes for bringing erstwhile adversaries into the export control project. The Persian Gulf War provided a major political boost to these efforts to constrain proliferation, by providing a vivid demonstration of the ways in which proliferation creates tangible military threats. The discovery that so many Western firms had been deeply involved in Iraq's armaments programs, and the political backlash it generated throughout the transatlantic community, has compelled governments to pursue the export control agenda with great vigor.

---

chapter 13, "Trigger Lists, the London Club and INFCE," pp. 101–108; and Carlton E. Thorne, "The Nuclear Suppliers Group: A Major Success Story Gone Unnoticed," in Kathleen Bailey, ed., *Director's Series on Proliferation*, No. 3 (Livermore, Calif.: Lawrence Livermore National Laboratory, 1994), 3, pp. 29–39.

2   John Markoff, "U.S. Seeks Broad Ban on Computers," *New York Times*, March 11, 1991, pp. D–1, 16.

New Challenges. But in the 1990s this strategy faces a number of significant challenges as well. The first is the increasing number of suppliers. No longer is it the case that agreement among a few industrialized countries can effectively prevent the trade in militarily significant technologies or products. No longer does the United States dominate high-technology sectors in the way it did until the 1970s. Defense cooperation between developing countries further complicates the picture. The cumulative effect of the appearance of new suppliers in the international weapons and technology markets is the undercutting of the leverage of the traditional suppliers; witness Saudi Arabia's purchase of Chinese intermediate-range ballistic missiles immediately after the U.S. Senate opted not to sell it advanced aircraft.

In the nuclear domain, an entire category of second-tier states has emerged engaged in the trade in nuclear technologies.[3] In the chemical and biological area, the vast majority of countries in the world are engaged in trade in related materials or technologies for legitimate commercial or health purposes. In the missile domain, cooperation among programs in the developing world is considerable.[4] One of the best examples of the declining dominance of the advanced states is in the computer domain. A protracted debate within the U.S. government about the prudence of licensing a Cray supercomputer for export to India led India to design and build an equivalent computer of its own, one that may well now be marketed internationally, presumably outside the control arrangements agreed between the United States and Japan.[5] New suppliers of spare parts and of service and training for military hardware have been particularly important to changing defense relationships.[6]

Some of the technology suppliers, such as Russia, can perhaps be brought into existing ad hoc mechanisms such as the Australia Group and MTCR when they are not already present, while others cannot, such as China at this time. Each of

---

3   William C. Potter, "The New Nuclear Suppliers," *Orbis*, Vol. 36, No. 2 (Spring 1992), pp. 199–210.

4   U.S. Congress, Office of Technology Assessment, *Global Arms Trade: Commerce in Advanced Military Technology and Weapons*, OTA–ISC–460 (Washington, D.C.: GPO, June 1991)

5   Stuart Auerbach, "Cray Deal a Casualty of Atomic Weapon Fears," *Washington Post*, March 19, 1993, pp. C–1, 3.

6   Ralph Sanders, *Arms Industries: New Suppliers and Regional Security* (Washington, D.C.: National Defense University, 1990), p. 20.

the regimes cited above faces a significant task in getting these suppliers to play by rules they did not help define. Some suppliers have agreed to abide by existing standards (such as China's commitment not to engage in missile sales prohibited by the MTCR, of which it is not a member); others refuse to do so. The diffusion of sources of supply also increases the opportunity to acquire relevant materials by illicit means, following the example of the Soviet Union in its theft of Western technologies.

A second challenge is the sharpening economic competition among the advanced industrialized countries. Maintaining the vitality of their export sectors is a top priority for each country as economies continue to languish within a framework of ever deeper interdependence. In an era of sharpening competition between advanced economies and domestic political pressures for job creation, export controls are criticized as imposing undue burdens on national economies. One study by the U.S. National Academy of Sciences concluded that controls on high technology cost the U.S. economy $9 billion and close to 200,000 jobs in just one year (1985).[7] Export licensing delays can impair a firm's market standing significantly.[8] A study conducted in 1993 raised questions, however, about the costs of export controls, noting that the value of exports requiring validated licenses is a relatively small percentage of total exports.[9] In years past, the Cold War provided the political incentive to play down competing economic interests in the name of solidarity against the Soviet military threat. In the 1990s, no dominant and abiding threat exists to sustain past cooperation. In the United

---

7   Committee on Science, Engineering and Public Policy, National Academy of Sciences, *Balancing the National Interest: U.S. National Security Controls and Global Economic Competition* (Washington, D.C.: National Academy Press, 1988), p. 264.

8   A Stanford University study of personal computers (PCs) illustrates this point. The study found that Taiwanese producers of PC clones "tend to be only 120 days behind U.S. manufacturers in introducing comparable product lines. Export licensing delays can thus reduce 'first to market' advantages for U.S. producers and create competitive advantages for foreign competitors." John Harvey, "Common Sense About High-Technology Export Controls" (Unpublished research paper prepared for the Center for International Security and Arms Control, Stanford University, Stanford, Calif., August 9, 1994), p. 10.

9   U.S. Congress, Office of Technology Assessment, *Export Controls and Nonproliferation Policy,* OTA–ISS–596 (Washington, D.C.: GPO, May 1994). The report recommended that the U.S. government gather (and analyze) better data about the economic costs of export controls and their utility in stopping or slowing different types of proliferation.

States, the easing of controls on computer and telecommunications technologies in 1994 in an effort to revive U.S. competitiveness in these sectors in the light of changing technology and international availability attracted much criticism from the traditional nonproliferation community.[10]

A third challenge is the pressure for advanced conventional weaponry generated by its vivid successes in the Persian Gulf War. Many countries of the developing world are pressing for exports of many of the weapons that performed so well there, including not just Patriot missile systems, cruise missiles, and stealth aircraft but also command and control systems. This demand is difficult to resist for defense industries in the developed world, coming as they do at a time of contraction in those industries and prolonged recession generally.

Another challenge is the growing number of technologies with both civilian and military applications, so-called dual-use technologies. These are in increasing abundance the more advanced the technology. The incremental incorporation of civilian technology into the military sphere has been a marked phenomenon in recent decades.[11] This tends to make list-based export controls ever less manageable, to sharpen disagreements among suppliers, and to stoke the grievances of developing countries who view such controls as anathema to the global commitment to economic development. It is one thing, after all, to try to prevent the sale of completed weapon systems and quite another to try to prevent the sale of all of the relevant subsystems and technologies that might be used in the design and production of legitimate commercial goods. As Seth Carus has argued:

> Export controls can prevent missile proliferation only if close attention is given to the range of technologies and components that can be exploited by a creative engineer seeking to make a missile. In essence, it is much easier to prevent exports of complete missiles than it is to stop transfers of technology needed to design and manufacture a missile.[12]

---

10   Michael Ledeen and Stephen Bryen, "Decontrol Freaks," *American Spectator*, June 1994, pp. 20–23, and Philip Finnegan, "Clinton Export Plan Draws Fire," *Defense Week*, October 4–10, 1993, pp. 1, 36.

11   Michael Moodie, "Beyond Proliferation: The Challenge of Technology Diffusion," *The Washington Quarterly*, Vol. 18, No. 2 (Spring 1995), pp. 186–187.

Moreover, governments have shown themselves to be both inept and fickle at applying their own export rules. The incompetence of Western governments in cutting off the flow of military hardware and technology to Iraq during its war with Iran provides a powerful example of the results of relying exclusively on government supervision of exports. Competitive commercial objectives have sometimes crept into the way nations have used the multilateral coordinating mechanisms. The unwillingness of some governments to apply rules to prevent weapons acquisition by favored friends has contributed rage and a sense ire and unfairness in the targeted states, which sometimes see export controls as being in the service not of global security but of the parochial, even misperceived, interests of a few technologically endowed and politically powerful states.[13]

Lastly, export controls bear the stigma of economic warfare, a stigma that is difficult to sustain politically without a clear and present threat from the targeted country or countries. Export controls have a collateral effect of keeping targeted states economically weak, something that was deemed by many to be an acceptable cost during the Cold War but is widely seen today as not desirable; indeed, economic growth is understood to be one of the primary means to generate the political pressures within societies to upset authoritarian systems and move toward more open forms of governance. This stigma is particularly strong in those countries of the developing world that see access to the technology and investment of the developed world as being the surest means to their economic development and improved living standards. They view such controls and the coordinating mechanisms as both unfair and counterproductive.

The Emerging Policy Agenda. With this list of challenges, shortcomings, and problems, why not jettison export controls altogether? The answer is simple: they

---

12 W. Seth Carus, *Cruise Missile Proliferation in the 1990s* (New York, N.Y.: Praeger with the Center for Strategic and International Studies, 1992), p. 90.

13 Hua Di, "The Proliferation of Advanced and Mass-Destruction Weapons: Mess, Unfairness, and Harness," in W. Thomas Wander, Eric H. Arnett, and Paul Bracken, eds., *The Diffusion of Advanced Weaponry: Technologies, Regional Implications, and Possible Responses* (Washington, D.C.: American Association for the Advancement of Science, 1994), pp. 283–296. See also K. Subrahmanyam, "Export Controls and the North–South Controversy," *The Washington Quarterly*, Vol. 16, No. 2 (Spring 1993), pp. 135–144, and Brahma Chellany, "Non-proliferation: An Indian Critique of U.S. Export Controls," *Orbis*, Vol. 38, No. 3 (Summer 1994), pp. 439–456.

serve some important purposes, and they are better than the alternative of doing without them.

Export controls support the nonproliferation goal in a number of ways. They help to build consensus among technologically advanced states about the proliferation problem and to dampen competitive commercial pressures among them as regards militarily sensitive items. They keep threshold-relevant technologies out of the hands of states with weapons programs; denial of a few key capabilities can cripple for military purposes an entire weapon system or force structure element. For example, the Brazilian missile program was forced into a redesign and a significant delay of the initial launch as a result of pressure brought by the United States on France and the French company Arianespace to curtail assistance.[14] They increase the costs of achieving self-reliance.[15] and the visibility of development programs to external monitoring. They also limit the speed and sophistication of weapons development programs. Such controls may, for example, have added a decade to the nuclear weapons development programs of Iraq and Pakistan. They are also valuable as stopgap measures pending completion of more rigorous global treaty regimes, as in the chemical and biological areas.

Their continuing utility relates to the fact that the appearance of some new suppliers of defense hardware has not yet deprived the traditional suppliers of the leverage they exert because of their dominance of some key technologies or of larger markets. Much leverage accrues from the continued reliance of industrializing states on the advanced design and production expertise of the industrialized states, or on fiscal largess in the form of foreign military assistance or arms sales or transfers below concessionary rates. Market dominance also translates into substantial leverage over militarily relevant programs in the

---

14 Proliferation Study Team, *The Emerging Ballistic Missile Threat to the United States,* Report Washington, D.C.: Proliferation Study Team, February 1993), p. 17. India's missile development program has reportedly been stymied by its difficulties in designing guidance systems and nose cones for its missiles. See Zafar Iqbal Cheema, "Nuclear Diplomacy in South Asia During the Eighties," *Regional Security* (Quarterly Journal of the Institute of Regional Studies, Islamabad), Vol. 10, No. 3 (Summer 1992), p. 64.

15 Geoffrey Kemp, "Arms Transfer and the 'Back-End' Problem in Developing Countries," in Stephanie G. Neuman and Robert E. Harkavy, eds., *Arms Transfers in the Modern World* (New York, N.Y.: Praeger, 1979), pp. 270–273.

developing world, such as missile programs, that depend upon commercial revenues for their feasibility. Because many missile programs will not survive without commercial revenues generated by associated space launches, this may prove a significant point of leverage where missile proliferation is concerned.[16]

Perhaps above all, export controls are important symbols of political will. They give meaning to the norms that have been agreed to govern state behavior in these areas.

Proposals to strengthen the export control regime are numerous. Some focus on unrealistic or undesirable schemes to bring the various formal and informal regimes into a single entity; such proposals ignore the very different political bargains embodied in each of the regimes and would lead to little better than the lowest common denominator of membership and enforcement.[17] Others emphasize political commitment, corporate responsibility, and public scrutiny as essential to the national implementation of controls.[18] The highest payoff will result from the least grandiose—piecemeal expansion of membership and more effective harmonization of the administration of existing measures, such as improved coordination of list review and notification of license awards and denials, more focus on end-use, and the achievement of common standards of effective enforcement—what has been called putting "higher fences around fewer goods."[19]

---

16 Brian G. Chow, *Emerging National Space Launch Programs: Economics and Safeguards*, RAND Report R–4179–USDP (Santa Monica, Calif.: RAND, July 1993), p. v.

17 For a description of one proposal to unify the regimes and a realistic appraisal of what can be done to better coordinate them, see Leonard S. Spector and Virginia Foran, *Preventing Weapons Proliferation: Should the Regimes Be Combined?* (Report of the Thirty-Third Strategy for Peace, U.S. Foreign Policy Conference, The Stanley Foundation, Muscatine, Iowa, October 22, 1992).

18 These proposals are drawn from the experience of Germany when it remade its export controls in the wake of revelations about its sales to Libya and Iraq. Hans Günter Brauch et al., eds., *Controlling the Development and Spread of Military Technology: Lessons from the Past and Challenges for the 1990s* (Amsterdam: VU University Press, 1992).

19 See Janne E. Nolan, *Trappings of Power: Ballistic Missiles in the Third World* (Washington, D.C.: Brookings Institution, 1991), especially chapter 6, "Toward an International Technology Security Regime." For a discussion of these and other proposals, see Gary K. Bertsch and Richard T. Cupitt, "Nonproliferation in the 1990s: Enhancing International Cooperation on Export Controls," *The Washington Quarterly*, Vol. 16, No. 4 (Autumn 1993), pp. 53–70; Ad Hoc Working Group on Non-Proliferation and Arms Control, *Non-Proliferation and Arms Control:*

But preserving the effectiveness of export controls will require more than tinkering with the export control regimes themselves. New forms of technology flow management are needed that complement the strengths and weaknesses of export controls if future dividends are to be reaped.

One new departure relates to the role of the firm. Transnational private enterprises are increasingly dominant in the international movement and application of advanced technology. Their business is driven as much by investment and joint R&D as by traditional forms of state-to-state trade of finished products. Integrating these firms into the technology management task is an urgent priority. Export controls are relevant for this task because they provide a structure of self-policing, under which firms do not solicit contracts or seek export licenses for deals with states intending to make illicit use of their products. The absence of such self-policing was a major factor in the Iraqi buildup of the 1980s. Without such self-policing, commercial pressures would likely supplant restraint, and competition could contribute to a rapid deterioration of security relations in regions in conflict as states struggle to match or outdo one another. Such self-policing will probably last only so long as firms believe that others are being as restrained in their behavior and not seeking to reap a commercial advantage—a problem that governments attempt to address through the coordinating mechanisms.

New forms of transparency must also be created. The flow of technology is simply too substantial to police in any traditional sense. Of the approximately 38,000 licenses issued by the United States for dual-use technologies in 1991, only 728 were subject to prelicensing checks and 314 to postshipment checks by personnel from the Office of Export Enforcement of the U.S. Department of Commerce or by U.S. embassies.[20] The total volume of sales approved by all members of the various coordinating mechanisms far overshadows the technology flows limited by export controls. A model for other regions may be

---

Issues and Options for the Clinton Administration, Washington, D.C., January 1993; Project on Export Controls in a Changing World, *Breaking Down the Barricades: Reforming Export Controls to Increase U.S. Competitiveness,* Final Report (Washington, D.C.: Center for Strategic and International Studies, 1994); and Advisory Council on Peace and Security, *Towards A Multifaceted Non-Proliferation Policy,* Report (The Hague, The Netherlands, Advisory Council on Peace and Security, December 1992).

20   Information provided by the U.S. Department of Commerce.

found in Europe, where a license-free zone has been created under the auspices of the European Union in exchange for complete openness. As Wolfgang Reinicke has argued:

> In a cooperative system that promoted transparency, the emphasis on supply controls and protectionism would give way on a selective basis to a control strategy stressing much freer availability of technology to all states if such states agreed to free disclosure of technology's disposition and application.[21]

Creating the conditions of openness and transparency that expose destabilizing transfers to the spotlight of public and government scrutiny is a new priority.[22]

Finally, it is increasingly important to conceive of export controls not as ends in themselves but as means to an end. In a highly dynamic and globalizing trading system, export controls cannot serve to prevent trade in technology. Rather, their purpose must be understood as facilitating trade generally and in sensitive technologies specifically. They are the tools for establishing which particular instances of technology trade are legitimate, and which not. They must be conceived as trade-empowering, not trade-restricting tools. To conceive of them otherwise is to turn a blind eye to ambitious steps taken by the international community to broaden and deepen international trade by global measures such as the General Agreement on Tariffs and Trade (GATT) and regional ones such as the North American Free Trade Agreement (NAFTA). Post-communist states generally have conceived of such controls in precisely such a way.

In sum, just because strategies of denial worked relatively well during the Cold War does not mean that they will work as well in the years and decades ahead, especially as their purview is expanded to cover an ever broader array of technologies. Strategies of denial are a wasting asset so long as they address only the technology and not the politics of proliferation. As Jed Snyder has argued:

---

21 Wolfgang H. Reinicke, "Cooperative Security and the Political Economy of Nonproliferation," in Janne E. Nolan, ed., *Global Engagement: Cooperation and Security in the 21st Century* (Washington, D.C.: Brookings Institution, 1994), pp. 175–234.

22 See Moodie, "Beyond Proliferation."

> A technological approach to stalling weapons proliferation will
> never by itself be an effective retardant, because it does not treat the
> incentives to proliferate....The proliferation threat is no longer
> susceptible—if indeed it ever was—to either the corrective or the
> preventive measures embodied in the controls established in the
> 1970s.[23]

Because a state's decision whether or not to pursue a specific weapons
program will hinge at least as much if not more on its will to do so than its
ability, proliferation must be understood as fundamentally a political process.
Strategies of denial are at best interim measures.

In an era of rapid global economic change, expanding economic activity, and
nearly universal access to technology, material, and expertise, there cannot be a
narrowly supply-side nonproliferation "fix" to the proliferation problem.[24] This
would presage an ever declining return on every new investment of political and
bureaucratic capital in strengthening export controls or expanding the ad hoc
cooperation approach to ever larger categories of weapons and technologies. The
point is not that such investments do not pay off—rather, it is that new
investments will reap declining returns, especially in the non-nuclear areas. The
bureaucratically simple adjustments to these treaties or control systems have
already been tackled. Now comes the harder and more politically taxing
challenge of making them politically viable.

Unless pursued as part of a larger strategy, strategies of denial may prove not
only ineffective but actually counterproductive. Inherent in such strategies is the
effort to put in place a permanent division between the seekers and the
possessors of advanced technologies. By suggesting a desire among the "haves" to
permanently keep the "have-nots" from getting something to which they have a

---

23 Jed C. Snyder, "Weapons Proliferation and the New Security Agenda," in Andrew W. Marshall,
    J. J. Martin, and Henry S. Rowen, eds., *On Not Confusing Ourselves: Essays on National Security
    Strategy in Honor of Albert and Roberta Wohlstetter* (Boulder, Colo.: Westview Press, 1991), pp. 271,
    280.

24 Janne E. Nolan, "Ballistic Missile Proliferation in the Third World: The Limits of
    Nonproliferation," *Arms Control Today*, November 1989, pp. 9-14. See also Brad Roberts,
    Chemical Disarmament and International Security, Adelphi Paper No. 267 (London: Brassey's for
    the International Institute for Strategic Studies, 1992).

right so long as any state does, an aggressive nonproliferation agenda undermines the political foundations of global treaty regimes that have been joined by many states in the developing world not just because of the security benefits they offer but also because of the increased access they would bring to specific technologies with economic benefits. The inherently discriminatory character of nonproliferation can actually be a stimulus to proliferation.

Formalizing Restraint: The New Arms Control Agenda

With the end of the Cold War, arms control has lost its prominence in the public mind. But its relevance for international security has only grown as it takes on new tasks and an expanding conception in the 1990s. The traditional arms control agenda, with its focus on East–West and U.S.–Soviet / Russian controls, has taken new shape in the 1990s with an emphasis not on negotiation but on implementation. Safe and secure dismantlement of excess nuclear weapons and the control of fissile materials are essential tasks of post–Cold War peacemaking; they are also relevant to the challenge of minimizing the proliferation-related effects of the breakup of the Soviet Union. But the new frontiers of arms control in the 1990s relate to the global treaty regime and regional arms control.

The Global Treaty Regime. Three major multilateral arms control treaties, backed by a number of complementary measures, today comprise a global treaty regime that binds the vast majority of states into a set of rights and obligations with regard to unconventional weapons. The 1990s will be a watershed decade for this regime. Whether it will emerge at the end of the decade strengthened or eviscerated by events remains an open question. Continuation of the status quo in the form of a weak regime with large gaps and imperfections appears untenable.

The evolution of this regime has taken decades. Negotiations to eliminate chemical and biological weapons can be traced back to the post–World War I disarmament effort that resulted in, among other products, the 1925 Protocol for the Prohibition of the Use in War of Asphyxiating, Poisonous, and Other Gases and of Bacteriological Methods of Warfare (the Geneva Protocol). The protocol remains in force today with over 130 signatories. It outlaws the use of chemical and biological weapons but permits their possession. Because 25 signatories have reserved the right to use chemical weapons if others use them first, the protocol is often described as a no-first-use agreement. A more comprehensive agreement was under negotiation at the failed Disarmament Conference in the 1930s. After

World War II, diplomats returned to the task under the aegis of the Eighteen Nation Disarmament Conference, which under various guises has remained affiliated with the UN until the present.

As described earlier, the NPT was concluded in 1968 and entered into force in 1970. The treaty is part of a larger set of institutions, including the safeguards system operating under the IAEA and the Nuclear Suppliers' Group, that together comprise the nuclear nonproliferation regime.

Building on this foundation, the UN disarmament community and the arms control community more broadly have sought to create a more far-reaching set of commitments. In the late 1960s, a long-standing stalemate was broken with the decision to separate the problems of chemical and biological weapons from one another, in the belief that the biological problem was more susceptible to rapid negotiation. Facilitated significantly by a Nixon administration decision to disarm unilaterally in this area, a bilateral agreement with the Soviet Union was rapidly concluded, which was adopted as the framework for the multilateral Biological and Toxin Weapons Convention (BTWC) that entered into force in 1975.

Notably, the multilateral regime is built on the foundation of a superpower commitment to disarm and to cease all activities oriented toward an offensive biological warfare program. This contrasts, of course, with the unequal obligations in the NPT. The fact that both superpowers retained their nuclear arsenals probably influenced their decision to abandon biological weapons. Because of the relatively low priority both attached (or appeared to attach) to these weapons at the time, comprehensive compliance provisions such as those included in the broad nuclear regime were deemed unnecessary. Over the decades since its conclusion, doubts about the efficacy of the regime have lingered.

With conclusion of the BTWC, the international effort to create a regime for the abolition of chemical weapons resumed in the mid-1970s. Again, the basic political bargain entailed in the NPT proved not to be replicable. States of the Third World were unwilling to forswear a category of weapons retained by the superpowers. Moreover, neither the Soviet Union nor the United States considered it prudent to abandon its chemical warfare arsenal given the exigencies of deterrence and military need in the Cold War standoff.

These negotiations on chemical weapons only reached their conclusion in 1992 with the adoption by the UN of a Chemical Weapons Convention (CWC) prepared by the Conference on Disarmament, and its opening for signature in January 1993. Treaty provisions dictate that it will enter into force six months after 65 states have deposited their instruments of ratification. The treaty goes beyond the Geneva Protocol in that it bans not just the use but also the possession of chemical weapons and is backed by extensive compliance provisions.

Thus, strictly speaking, the NPT is the only true nonproliferation treaty. It is the only global treaty that codifies unequal rights and obligations among possessors and nonpossessors of specific weapons—between the so-called haves and have-nots—for the specific purpose of preventing the further spread of weapons. This basic political bargain has not been replicable in other weapons areas where, instead, global disarmament agreements are being implemented that achieve nonproliferation benefits by destroying existing arsenals and rendering illegal among states parties the construction or use of new ones.

Also strictly speaking, none of these treaties is genuinely global. The basic political compromise in the NPT was not universally accepted. China and France, for example, chose not to join the regime until recently; India, Pakistan, and Israel remain non-parties. Nor does the BTWC enjoy universal membership, because some important states have either not signed the treaty or signed but not ratified (Iraq, for example).

Each of the elements of this structure faces significant challenges in the 1990s. Revelations about Iraq's nuclear program, an increasing appreciation of the limits of the safeguards system operated by the IAEA, and a general concern about the future of nuclear proliferation in the post–Cold War era have combined to generate a widespread debate about the effectiveness and future of the NPT. Some believe, as does Ted Galen Carpenter, that "the recent crisis...is merely the latest evidence that the global nonproliferation regime, symbolized by the nuclear Non-Proliferation Treaty (NPT), is inexorably breaking down."[25] A more widespread view is that some strengthening of the nuclear nonproliferation

---

25   He goes on to argue that it "is not merely breaking down, it is breaking down asymmetrically. The regimes that seem most determined to develop their own arsenals are in many cases precisely the ones that are most likely to contemplate using them." Ted Galen Carpenter, "Closing the Nuclear Umbrella," *Foreign Affairs*, Vol. 73, No. 2 (March/April 1994), pp. 8, 11.

regime is essential if the effort to prevent widespread nuclearization is to be sustained.

Since the Persian Gulf War, primary focus has fallen on improving the capacity of the IAEA to detect clandestine nuclear weapons programs. The Achilles' heel of the IAEA system has been its practice of relying on declarations of nuclear-related facilities by the state party itself when the agency conducts inspections and exercises other oversight in an effort to monitor that state's compliance with some parts of its NPT commitments. But as Lawrence Scheinman reports, the IAEA has itself now clarified the scope of its special inspection authority,

> in particular reaffirming that the agency's right of special inspection extended to locations and facilities other than those of which the IAEA had been formally notified by the state. It was made clear that plausible non-safeguards information could serve as a basis for invoking special inspections; that acceptance of such inspections was not a matter of state discretion, but of state obligation; and that in cases of dilatory response to a request, the board of governors could apprise the United Nations Security Council.[26]

Scheinman concludes that this reaffirmation puts the agency on the proper track but that more must be done if its credibility and effectiveness are to be ensured.[27]

These steps to strengthen the NPT are being supplemented by others.[28] The Persian Gulf War produced some steps in the direction of a stronger NPT

---

26 Lawrence Scheinman, *Assuring the Nuclear Non-Proliferation Safeguards System,* Occasional Paper (Washington, D.C.: Atlantic Council of the United States, October 1992), p. vi.

27 "While substantial progress has been made in seeking to come to grips with handling clandestine or undeclared activity, there is still more to be done, and...it is not self-evident that all of the aspects of the problem have yet been identified. Nor is it evident that the best institutional arrangements for meeting non-proliferation expectations in the post–Cold War, post–Gulf War world have been identified." Ibid., p. 18.

28 James F. Leonard, *Strengthening the Non-Proliferation Treaty in the Post–Cold War World,* Working Paper No. 1 (Washington, D.C.: Washington Council on Non-Proliferation, 1992). See also United Nations Institute for Disarmament Research, "The Non-Proliferation Treaty: How to Remove the Residual Threats," UNIDIR Research Paper No. 13 (New York, 1992).

system, with a reinvigoration of the role of the UN Security Council as the ultimate authority responsible for the stewardship of the nonproliferation interests of the international community. The war also reminded NPT members of the importance of investing the nuclear nonproliferation regime with both the fiscal means and intelligence support necessary to its effective functioning. Additional members are being enlisted; the recent decisions by France and China to join as nuclear-weapon states and Argentina, Brazil, and Ukraine as non-nuclear-weapon states are encouraging.

Many proposals have been offered to strengthen the nuclear nonproliferation regime, including the creation of an intelligence analysis unit within the IAEA and strengthened inspection procedures.[29] A shift of focus and inspection resources from the nuclear industries in the non-weapon states of the developed world to states suspected of acquiring weapons should also be anticipated.[30]

The spring 1995 NPT review and extension conference proved a focal point of debate about the future of the NPT system. As provided in article X of the treaty, that conference was called to "decide whether the Treaty shall continue in force indefinitely, or shall be extended for an additional fixed period or periods."[31] The conference undertook a comprehensive review of the treaty's functions and

---

29 See for example David Fischer, Ben Sanders, Lawrence Scheinman, and George Bunn, *A New Nuclear Triad: The Non-Proliferation of Nuclear Weapons, International Verification and the International Atomic Energy Agency* (Southampton, U.K.: Mountbatten Centre for International Studies, University of Southampton, September 1992); Anthony Fainberg, *Strengthening IAEA Safeguards: Lessons from Iraq* (Stanford, Calif.: Center for International Security and Arms Control, Stanford University, 1993); United Nations Institute for Disarmament Research, "The Implications of IAEA Inspections under Security Council Resolution 687," UNIDIR Research Paper No. 11 (New York, 1992); and Harald Müller, "Das nukleare Nichtverbreitungsregime im Wandel. Konsequenzen aus einem stürmischen Jahr," *Europa Archiv*, Vol. 47, No. 2 (January 25, 1992), pp. 51–58.

30 David Kay emphasizes efforts to change an IAEA organizational culture and management ethos that he deems too timid in addition to shifting the focus of time and money away from policing compliant countries in the direction of those where doubts arise. David Kay, "The IAEA: How Can It Be Strengthened?" in Mitchell Reiss and Robert S. Litwak, eds., *Nuclear Proliferation after the Cold War* (Washington, D.C.: Woodrow Wilson Center Press, 1994), pp. 309–333.

31 See George Bunn, Charles N. Van Doren, and David Fischer, *Options and Opportunities: The NPT Extension Conference of 1995*, PPNN Study No 2 (Southampton, U.K.: Mountbatten Centre for International Studies, University of Southampton, Programme for Promoting Nuclear Non-Proliferation, November 1991).

purposes, and resulted in a decision to extend the treaty indefinitely and unconditionally. This outcome was surprising to many, given the weaknesses of the regime and the desire of some leading non-nuclear states to maintain leverage over the nuclear-weapon states as a way to bring about general nuclear disarmament. Conferees committed themselves to a process of interim enhanced review, permitting a more substantive and less procedural form of assessment than heretofore has been possible of the performance of states on their treaty obligations. The broad-based renewal of the treaty provides a valuable political foundation to the future of the nonproliferation effort. Its strength and durability will be important determinants of the future of the broader treaty regime.

The BTWC, on the other hand, has never enjoyed a reputation as a particularly strong or effective treaty. The source of this reputation is the fact that it succeeded rather than stimulated disarmament commitments by the superpowers, labored under continuous doubts about Soviet compliance, and lacked verification or significant compliance provisions.[32]

The limitations of the BTWC have been well recognized and on three occasions states party to the treaty have met together in review conferences to consider the performance of the convention and possible measures to strengthen it. One such conference occurred in 1991, shortly after the near brush with Iraq's biological weapons, confessions by Russian President Boris Yeltsin of sustained Soviet and subsequently Russian noncompliance with the treaty, and reports in both Britain and the United States of a growing number of states in the Middle East and elsewhere engaged in programs to create or produce biological weapons. In prior review conferences, states parties had focused on how to increase their confidence that their partners were complying with their commitments, but by 1991, the focus had shifted to catching and punishing noncompliant states.

The focal point in the debate about strengthening the regime has been its verification provisions—or rather, their absence. It was no accident that such provisions were not included in the treaty when it was drafted over two decades

---

32 This discussion draws on Brad Roberts, "New Challenges and New Policy Priorities for the 1990s," in Roberts, ed., *Biological Weapons: Weapons of the Future?* (Washington, D.C.: Center for Strategic and International Studies, 1993). See also Graham Pearson, "Prospects for Chemical and Biological Arms Control: The Web of Deterrence," *The Washington Quarterly*, Vol. 16, No. 2 (Spring 1993), pp. 145–162.

ago. The challenge of detecting militarily significant activity in the biological area is far more difficult than in the nuclear or conventional areas. The technology to create and manufacture biological weapons is virtually all dual-use in character, unlike nuclear technology, which requires large, dedicated facilities for weapons programs. This problem is complicated by the fact that R&D is permitted—and necessary—under the BTWC for defensive purposes. Thus, even if a facility is identified as producing some biological warfare agent and inspections confirm this fact, there is no guarantee of determining a violation. But given the new challenges to the biological regime, some strengthening of the treaty is a political necessity. An experts group has met to consider means to strengthen ability to detect and deter states violating their BTWC commitments, and its recommendations are likely to lead to the addition to the convention of an assurance and compliance protocol.

A third global treaty is in the making—the Chemical Weapons Convention. It provides for the declaration of all existing chemical weapons and their production facilities by states parties and their destruction over a 10-year period. Performance of these obligations will be monitored by an Organization for the Prohibition of Chemical Weapons (OPCW, akin to the IAEA but without the charge to promote the civilian use of related technologies) that will enjoy rights to both systematic, on-site inspection of declared facilities and challenge inspections of undeclared sites.

Bringing the CWC quickly into force and ensuring its effective implementation through universal adherence are proving difficult. The period between opening for signature and entry into force is being used to build up the OPCW by defining its methods and procedures, hiring and training its staff, and acquiring the requisite scientific and technical base. This work is being performed by a Preparatory Commission, meeting in The Hague. Its work has proven far less polemical than the previous 20 years of negotiations in the Geneva-based and UN-affiliated Conference on Disarmament, but hardly less difficult. Timely entry into force has been cast in doubt by the political turmoil in Russia and Moscow's inability to put together a credible plan for the destruction of its 40,000 tons of chemical warfare agent. The cost and politics of destroying a slightly lesser amount of agent stored at a number of places in the United States has raised similar questions about the U.S. destruction program.

Changes on the international scene and the increasing focus on domestic politics in many European, North American, and Asian capitals have worked against timely ratification of the CWC and a start on the difficult project of national implementation. Expectations remain high that ultimately the regime will be near global in its reach, given that 150 states had signed the treaty before the end of 1993, but there are significant hold outs among countries like North Korea and in the Middle East, where some Arab states have refused to abandon their right to chemical weapons without some Israeli concessions on the nuclear side.

Whether the CWC emerges as an effective instrument of chemical disarmament and international security more generally will be a function of many factors: the number of states that accede to its terms by both signing and ratifying; the commitment of leading states to implementation of the treaty; and the ability of the OPCW to conduct its work effectively and build confidence in the results.[33] If it does so emerge, its impact on the international security agenda may be substantial, not just for its contributions to chemical disarmament, but for its precedents in challenge inspections, industry involvement, and strengthened compliance mechanisms beyond that found in either the NPT or the BTWC.

Looking to the future, some evolution of this basic treaty system should be expected. In the first major arms control initiative of the post–Cold War era, two significant supplements to the NPT have been proposed. The first is a comprehensive ban on nuclear tests, a ban that has been under discussion for much of the nuclear era. This would go well beyond the limited test ban treaty that continues to define the permitted size and location of such tests. Formal negotiations for a Comprehensive Test Ban Treaty (CTBT) began at the Conference on Disarmament in Geneva in January 1994, with the expectation that they would be completed by September 1996. A CTBT would constitute a significant step by the nuclear powers in honoring their commitment under article VI of the NPT to take steps toward disarmament. It would also increase the difficulty for new nuclear powers of building weapons that could be stored and used with confidence by compelling them to refrain from testing or by forcing them to test infrequently, surreptitiously, or only in laboratory settings.

---

33 Parts of this section are drawn from Brad Roberts, *Chemical Disarmament and International Security,* and from Brad Roberts, ed., *The Chemical Weapons Convention: Implementation Issues* (Washington, D.C.: Center for Strategic and International Studies, 1992). See also "Chemical Weapons Convention," UNIDIR Newsletter No. 20 (Geneva: United Nations Institute for Disarmament Research), December 1992.

The second supplement is a cutoff in the production of fissile materials. It would be helpful in constraining the buildup of nuclear fuels in South Asia, the Middle East, and East Asia and thus contribute to a capping or prevention of nuclear arms races there. In fact, it would offer a way for new nuclear powers in those regions to participate in global nuclear controls without also abandoning their capabilities (as required if they were to join the NPT). Such a cutoff might also be useful in demonstrating article VI compliance by the nuclear powers if they also agree to put existing fissile materials under international inspections.

This review underscores the difficult diplomatic agendas associated with strengthening these different pieces of the global treaty structure. In a basic sense, however, the issues confronting these treaties are generic. Most of the technical issues come down to one basic problem: how to secure compliance by states with their treaty commitments. This is an old issue in arms control. The expert community shows a marked tendency to debate the compliance issue in terms of verification issues. There is a widespread conviction that intrusive inspections on demand of facilities both declared and not declared as treaty-relevant are the missing ingredient in an effective compliance system. As the foregoing review suggests, improvements to the monitoring and inspection provisions of these treaties are a distinct priority.

But getting it right on inspections is not easy. Highly intrusive inspections that go anywhere at any time have been possible only in the case of enforcing a cease-fire on an aggressor state (Iraq) defeated militarily by the international community. The work of the UN Special Commission (UNSCOM) to police Iraq's compliance with the UN-mandated destruction of its unconventional weapons and their delivery systems and means of production has met with only partial success, underscoring that "smoking guns" proving noncompliance in one stroke are rare, and that inspections work best over a long period and many sites, thus allowing patterns of activity to emerge. Less intrusive inspections that also preserve some ability to inspect undeclared facilities and to conduct inspections with little or no advance notice are in the offing under the CWC, to a lesser extent under the NPT, and perhaps under the BTWC in the future. Carrying out such inspections while also protecting legitimate commercial or military secrets is a balancing act unique to each technology area. This underscores the importance of treaty implementation mechanisms that are carefully crafted so as to assure a low rate of false alarms and a high rate of detection of militarily significant behavior. After decades of experience at the IAEA, in the bilateral arms control process, and UNSCOM, a great deal has been learned about how to design such mechanisms—and about their intrinsic limits. The synergies arising from the implementation of various verification mechanisms in multiple international treaties may help to contribute to an alleviation of the basic problem.[34]

Moreover, getting it right on inspections is only part of the task of compliance policy. Verification is only an instrument of that policy. Inspections themselves are only a part of the larger verification task, they provide information supplemental to that gained through national or other international means. Verification itself encompasses not just information gathering; it includes also information processing, analysis, and evaluation in a political context.[35]

Furthermore, once noncompliant behavior has been verified, states parties face the separate task of restoring compliance or coping with the consequences of noncompliance. States should react strongly to violations of treaty commitments because often in the past such violations have been precursors to war.[36] Fred Iklé

---

34 Patricia Bliss McFate et al., *Constraining Proliferation: The Contribution of Verification Synergies*, Arms Control Verification Studies No. 5 (Report prepared for the Non-Proliferation, Arms Control and Disarmament Division, Department of External Affairs, Ottawa, Canada, March 1993).

35 Heinz Gaertner, *Challenges of Verification: Smaller States and Arms Control*, Occasional Paper Series 12 (New York, N.Y.: Institute for East–West Security Studies, 1989), p. 4.

36 The problem of noncompliance has been neatly summarized by William R. Harris: "A material breach [defined as an act that defeats the object or purpose of the obligation] is a warning of disequilibrium, a challenge to the rule of law and to the ethos of self-restraint, even if the specific gains to the violator would appear modest....Detection of one or more material breaches of arms control obligations is a warning that the stake of the breaching party in the agreement is insufficient to deter acts that deprive other parties of a share in the benefits of the undertaking, and the *quid pro quo* that gave rise to the original mutuality of commitment. Unless the violator of an arms control agreement is confident that violators will remain covert and undetected, a *deliberate* material breach or an *inadvertent* material breach that remains uncorrected after inquiry signifies a phenomenon even more disturbing than the abandonment of a commitment to reciprocal benefits: the violator's indifference to detection signifies the violator's anticipation of a failure of will or capability on the part of victim-states." Harris, "Breaches of Arms Control Obligations and Their Implications," in Richard F. Staar, *Arms Control: Myth Versus Reality* (Stanford, Calif.: Hoover Institution Press, 1984), p. 135. Harris goes on to clarify the requirements of compliance intelligence. "Compliance intelligence should encompass not only verification of the fact of compliance or noncompliance, but also the assessment of the materiality of the breach, the motives and causes of the breach if known, and the likely consequences of responsive measures and other actions to implement a strategy that would

framed this issue more than three decades ago in a famous article, "After Detection, What?"[37] Each of the global treaties provides for final recourse to the UN Security Council in the event of material breaches. Some, such as the CWC, also contain specific provisions for assistance to victims of noncompliance as well as penalties for the noncompliant. Iklé's own answer points to the military consequences of breaking an arms control commitment and the necessity for the other parties to a treaty to have a military option for protecting their interests and, if necessary, restoring the status quo ante. Within the diplomatic community there is a widespread sense that providing too specific and definitive an answer to this question is neither feasible nor desirable. Its impracticality relates to the unwillingness of states to be bound to specific sanctions against others in advance and without reference to political context. Its undesirability relates to the wish to create uncertainty about the level of response by the international community, so as to leave open the possibility in the cheater's mind of a decisive enforcement action by that community.

The history of arms control suggests that the most difficult problems of noncompliance are those in which the evidence is ambiguous. The history of Soviet noncompliance with its arms control treaty obligations was dominated by a long and sharp controversy about specific episodes, such as those associated with the Krasnoyarsk radar or the alleged use of chemical and/or biological warfare agents by Soviet forces in Afghanistan or Soviet proxy forces in Southeast Asia (the so-called Yellow Rain debate). Ambiguity about nuclear programs in North Korea and Iran illustrates that this problem continues after the Cold War. Dealing with ambiguous compliance problems puts a special premium on the political will of key interested states.

There is a second problem of compliance that commands less attention but is equally important to the long-term viability of these treaties—not the problem posed by the dropouts who cheat on their commitments, but that posed by the holdouts who opt not to join these treaties in the first place. The NPT, for example, struggles above all with the problem posed by the existence of a handful of new nuclear powers that can neither be easily brought into the treaty

---

restore compliance" (page 136).

37 Fred Charles Iklé, "After Detection, What?" *Foreign Affairs*, Vol. 39, No. 2 (January 1961), pp. 208–220. Reprinted in E. Lefever, ed., *Arms and Arms Control* (New York, N.Y.: Praeger, 1962).

nor left comfortably aside. Policymakers may have to settle for less than perfect solutions here, either complementary measures, such as the Treaty of Tlatelolco in Latin America, or interim measures, such as the pursuit of regional confidence-building measures in places like the Middle East or South Asia that do not also entail formal treaty membership.

Dealing with noncompliance requires above all a political commitment by a core group of interested states. The ultimate impact of intrusive verification measures will depend almost entirely on whether the political will can be mustered when noncompliance is detected or, which will be more difficult, when doubts about noncompliance remain unresolved. For both the NPT and the BTWC, more intrusive verification measures are often discussed as if they were a quick fix for each treaty. They are not. They are a part of the solution, but not the whole solution.

These global treaties have been weak in the past not just or even primarily because they lacked certain specific provisions; rather, they were not invested with the fiscal resources, intelligence assets, and above all the political will of the leading powers. The experience in the nuclear domain is instructive: nuclear proliferation has been constrained since the NPT came into force not so much by the effective functioning of the nuclear nonproliferation regime as by the political will of the superpowers to avoid the risks of proliferation. The NPT failed in the case of Iraq not so much because it lacked the rights or means to police compliance but because none of the major powers thought it important or necessary to rely on the IAEA to contend with Iraq's nuclear program. Similarly in the biological domain, the BTWC has suffered not so much from weak compliance measures as from a general sense that biological weapons are not very important and therefore problems of noncompliance do not require states to expend much political capital. If these global treaties are to function well in the decades ahead, reinvigorated political commitment and leadership will be as important as clear and agreed mechanisms for carrying out that commitment. The CWC, too, is struggling with tepid political support from countries that saw chemical disarmament as centrally relevant to managing Cold War risks but now see it as tangential (or not worth the risks to industry).

Whether a group of key interested states can be brought together in support of these treaties remains an open question. Given the challenges to the great powers and the global balance of power enumerated earlier, it is reasonable to question whether a self-selected group will enjoy the necessary coherence within itself or the acquiescence of the rest of the states parties to its role.

Moreover, the issue of political commitment is not an issue for the advanced countries alone. They may reinvigorate their commitments to the global treaty structure but fail in making that structure effective or in securing its survival through the 1990s if they do not also regenerate or integrate the political commitment of those many countries in the rest of the world that increasingly find nuclear, biological, and chemical weapons within their technological reach.

Key to reaching out to both dropouts and holdouts is the challenge of revitalizing these treaties as political bargains among nations with disparate interests and ambitions. These treaties represent trade-offs among those interests and ambitions, not their resolution. Piecemeal tinkering with the provisions of these treaties will not do enough to strengthen them. Ensuring the survival of a robust global treaty system in the 1990s requires not merely getting the legal or technical details right but also a careful nurturing of the political consensus that gives them their weight. The problem with focusing on verification issues is that it provides bureaucratic answers to what is essentially a political problem.

If these global treaties are understood above all as embodying political bargains, they can be understood as much more than legal instrumentalities. They are regimes that operate singly and together to moderate the behavior of states in an anarchic system. A regime is a set of explicit and implicit principles, norms, rules, and decision-making procedures around which actors' expectations converge. As Stephen Krasner has written, "It is the infusion of behavior with principles and norms that distinguishes regime-governed activity in the international system from a more conventional activity guided exclusively by narrow calculations of interest."[38] Whether such regimes can survive changes in basic relations of power in the international system and exhibit durability in the face of challengers are questions hotly debated today in the academic world.[39]

---

38   See Stephen D. Krasner, "Structural Causes of Regime Consequences: Regimes as Intervening Variables," in Krasner, ed., *International Regimes* (Ithaca, N.Y.: Cornell University Press, 1983), p. 2. See also Robert O. Keohane, *After Hegemony: Cooperation and Discord in the World Political Economy* (Princeton, N.J.: Princeton University Press, 1984).

39   John J. Mearsheimer, "The False Promise of International Institutions," *International Security*, Vol. 19, No. 3 (Winter 1994/95), pp. 5–49; Charles L. Glaser, "Realists as Optimists: Cooperation as Self-Help," *International Security*, Vol. 19, No. 3 (Winter 1994/95), pp. 50–90; and

The view adopted here is that the regimes operating in the realm of unconventional weapons have a foundation in the international community that transcends the end of the Cold War but that their long-term viability requires tending by states and cannot be taken for granted.

Each of these treaties embodies such an agreed set of principles and norms. Given the increasing focus in policy on the will to acquire weapons, as opposed to the ability, such principles and norms must be at the center of the effort to constrain weapons proliferation in the post–Cold War era. In an era of ever greater technical independence, the articulation, preservation, and defense of such norms offers the greatest hope of shaping the will of states to acquire and use weapons—and of mustering collective action to deter their use or defend against them.[40] Norms may also operate on the propensity of non-state actors to exploit unconventional weapons capabilities in decaying states, whenever such actors might be seeking to establish a claim to sovereign legitimacy.

These principles and norms are not for the powerful nations to claim for themselves; nor can they arrogate to themselves the right to define them—rather, they arise from the international community writ large. Only in the case of the MTCR have a few countries been able to establish a norm of sufficient breadth among the suppliers of advanced missiles to severely constrain their diffusion. It is useful to recall that some norms and principles have been articulated by the international community in which some advanced countries do not participate, such as the view that the deep seabed is the common heritage of humankind. The task of reinforcing these norms must be balanced with the preservation of long-standing norms about the right to individual and collective self-defense and about the place of just wars in relations among states. Speaking to the politics of these norms requires a diplomacy that ranges far beyond the technicalities of verification instrumentalities.

These norms are in doubt today because the sweeping changes of recent years have revealed cracks in the political consensus underlying the regime. The sharp North–South clash in the lead-up to the NPT extension conference is one

---

William C. Wohlforth, "Realism and the End of the Cold War," *International Security*, Vol. 19, No. 3 (Winter 1994/95), pp. 91–129.

40 James A. Schear, "The Diffusion of Advanced Weaponry in the Developing World: Existing Norms, Agreements, and Modes of Control," in Wander, Arnett, and Bracken, *The Diffusion of Advanced Weaponry*, pp. 329–341.

symptom of this doubt.[41] So too is the burgeoning transpacific debate about human rights and a view often expressed in parts of Asia that the norms embodied in current international treaties and the UN Charter merely reflect the dominance of the international system by the European and transatlantic community at a particular phase of its development. Rare in history are there examples of treaties that have survived major changes in the balance of power or order in the system; more frequent are examples of treaties that collapse under the weight of new strategic realities.[42] As Yohanan Cohen has observed:

> A realistic analysis of historical events underscores the fact that bilateral and multilateral agreements and treaties earn their strength and validity not from the festive signatures they bear. They remain in effect as long as this is in their signatories' political, strategic, and economic interest, and as long as the balance of forces and the international constellation that brought the arrangements into existence continue to prevail.[43]

How might the elements of this regime be expected to fare in the new circumstances? Those that gave rise to the CWC are not remote and the political bargain within the international community about chemical disarmament is still in the making; the norm against the possession and use of chemical weapons appears to be growing stronger. The BTWC is more closely tied to an era now past—the first blush of détente between the superpowers and their mutual hope to extend bilateral agreement into global frameworks; the norm against the possession of biological weapons and their use appears strong but, having gone

41 David Fischer, *Towards 1995: The Prospects for Ending the Proliferation of Nuclear Weapons* (Aldershot, U.K.: Dartmouth Publishing Company for the United Nations Institute for Disarmament Research, 1993); Gary T. Gardner, *Nuclear Nonproliferation: A Primer* (Boulder, Colo.: Lynne Rienner Publishers, 1994); John Simpson and Darryl Howlett, "The NPT Renewal Conference: Stumbling toward 1995," *International Security*, Vol. 19, No. 1 (Summer 1994), pp. 41–71; and Archelaus R. Turrentine, "The Dynamics of the NPT Extension Decision," in Bailey, *Director's Series on Proliferation*, No. 2, pp. 1–28.

42 B.J.C. McKercher, *Arms Limitation and Disarmament: Restraints on War, 1899–1939* (Westport, Conn.: Praeger, 1992).

43 Yohanan Cohen, *Small Nations in Times of Crisis and Confrontation* (New York, N.Y.: State University of New York Press, 1989), p. 341.

untested, may not be resilient. The NPT stands out above all as a regime most firmly rooted in a strategic reality now past; despite the indefinite extension of the NPT in May 1995, the norm that establishes disparate rights and obligations has weakened even as the norm against the use of nuclear weapons appears to remain high. Thus the difference between brushing up a legal instrument and refashioning the underlying political consensus that made it possible, between proliferation as a technical problem and proliferation as a political one, is most evident in the nuclear domain. Indeed, the nuclear nonproliferation regime is not likely to survive the extension debate unless that debate also occasions a revitalization of the broad international commitment to the political bargain of 25 years past. The successful extension decision will be weighed ultimately on the basis of what it made possible in the way of future international nuclear diplomacy, and not as an extension of the old politics of nuclear disarmament.[44]

Is it mere inertia, combined perhaps with an inability to perceive the true outlines of the substantial changes in the international system of the 1990s, that leads to a recommendation to strengthen and refine this global regime rather than abandon it and move down an altogether different path? What are the benefits that make further investments of political and fiscal capital worthwhile?

To be sure, these treaties are no panacea. None is perfectly verifiable or universally subscribed to. Each faces real challenges in the 1990s that will not be met on the basis of business as usual. None can function on the basis of a diktat from one or two superpowers or a handful of great powers—technology diffusion has changed all of that, because each regime has to cope with the emergence of new suppliers of technology and the declining leverage of the advanced military powers, whether it lies in their power of example or the power to coerce.[45] Treaty implementation issues are usually not high politics and rarely generate substantial public or media attention; they are thus unlikely to capture the attention of senior political leaders. None of these treaties makes sense without associated safeguards—whether the IAEA system of the NPT, the

---

44 Joseph F. Pilat and Robert E. Pendley, eds., *Beyond 1995: The Future of the NPT Regime* (New York, N.Y.: Plenum Press, 1990); and John Simpson and Darryl Howlett, "Nuclear Non-proliferation: the Way Forward," *Survival,* Vol. 33, No. 6 (November/December 1991), pp. 483–499.

45 For a discussion of the implications of the emergence of second-tier nuclear supplier states, see Avner Cohen and Benjamin Frankel, "Opaque Nuclear Proliferation," in Frankel, ed., *Opaque Nuclear Proliferation: Methodological and Policy Implications* (London: Frank Cass, 1991), p. 31.

research for defensive purposes under both the BTWC and the CWC, or the spending on intelligence resources necessary to anticipate when proliferation translates into tangible military threats—that are expensive and sometimes unpopular.

Moreover, each regime has its critics who advocate its abandonment.[46] Especially in the chemical and biological areas, there are calls to abandon the disarmament project and replace it with a nonproliferation regime, usually by individuals who little understand the diplomatic histories of these negotiations or the technical realities of proliferation.

How important is an imperfect regime? Scheinman's evaluation of the NPT is germane to this larger question:

> If a country believes that its vital security interests or national integrity require the acquisition of nuclear weapons, it will make that decision. What is more interesting is the extent to which its evaluation of all the political, economic, diplomatic, and security considerations that enter such decisions are shaped, influenced, and tempered by the more general environment and especially by its normative content. The argument presented here is that the impact is more than we might be ready to admit, but less than we might dare to hope. Neither the NPT medium, nor its normative message

---

46   A strong critique of continued U.S. support for the NPT is made by Ted Galen Carpenter, who argues that "Instead of regarding non-proliferation and extended deterrence as useful (or at least tolerable) policies under a peculiar set of conditions, they assumed that both policies had enduring value to the point of being sacrosanct. Thus the Bush administration's insistence on preserving and strengthening the NPT in a vastly different post–Cold War era....The final adjustment to the reality of proliferation is to change the focus of Washington's non-proliferation policy, substituting discrimination for uniformity of treatment. U.S. policymakers must rid themselves of the attitude that all instances and forms of proliferation are equally bad....The United States needs to move beyond the 'one size fits all' philosophy symbolized by the NPT. Indeed, Washington should decline to support an extension of the NPT when it comes up for renewal in 1995. To the extent that the United States continues to pursue a non-proliferation strategy, it should concentrate instead on making it difficult for aggressive or unstable regimes to acquire the technology and fissionable material needed to become nuclear powers." Carpenter, "A New Proliferation Policy," *National Interest,* No. 28 (Summer 1992), pp. 64, 71.

alone, can prevent a determined nation from acquiring nuclear weapons. In no case has it been, nor is it in the future likely to be, the decisive factor. But as part of the environment in which states operate, to which decision-makers respond, and in which decisions ultimately are taken, it plays an unquantifiable but meaningful role. It tints the lenses through which the world, both its opportunities and its restraints, are seen. In this sense, at least, the NPT has made a difference, and its demise would be felt far more profoundly than some of its critics would like to think.[47]

These regimes are only tools of policy, to be used in conjunction with other tools. With meaningful political commitment they can be used to ameliorate proliferation. Used badly or not at all, they can make the problem much more severe. They appear to be better than any alternatives proposed until now, although this is not to argue against experimenting with new forms or structures that achieve like results. They are better than the alternative because each makes a tangible contribution to slowing, halting, or reversing the proliferation of specific weapons and to the national security of many states. They are also valuable for giving expression to the international will and purpose to prevent changes that destabilize internationally, creating and enforcing agreed norms of behavior, reinforcing international standards of statecraft, demonstrating the possibility and efficacy of negotiated measures bridging international divisions, and laying the basis for states in the fluid post–Cold War world to work together and take risks in pursuit of larger goals.

That they are not perfectly verifiable or universally subscribed to is not quite the point; whether they are adequately verifiable or adequately broad in their adherence is for states parties to decide among themselves. Perfect treaties are important in times, such as the Cold War, when cheating by either superpower could have upset the strategic balance and substantially increased the risk of cataclysmic global war. Where such perfection remains necessary, regional or other local measures can be depended upon to provide the necessary rigor. But imperfect treaties on unconventional weapons help to give force to prevailing

---

47   Lawrence Scheinman, "Does the NPT Matter?" in Pilat and Pendley, *Beyond 1995*, p. 62.

norms, to narrow and channel the problems of military planning posed by proliferation trends, and to provide a framework for reinvigorating those norms.

In speculating about the future of this global regime, its exclusive focus on unconventional weapons is increasingly exposed by the growing importance of conventional weapons on the global proliferation agenda. Proposals have been made for new multilateral treaties banning both intermediate-range missiles and landmines.[48] But most of the political dialogue has focused on new control mechanisms for the global trade in conventional weapons generally.

Why does conventional arms control even belong on the global proliferation control agenda? Keith Krause and David Mutimer identify four reasons. First, conventional arms and weapons of mass destruction are inextricably linked in regions of instability such as the Middle East. Second, conventional arms acquisitions consume more resources than do those for unconventional weapons. Third, measures to control weapons of mass destruction increase the desire for sophisticated conventional weapons. Fourth, the so-called military-technical revolution is blurring the line of distinction between conventional and unconventional weapons in terms of their potential destructiveness.[49]

Expectations ran high after the Persian Gulf War and the end of the Cold War for some breakthrough on the conventional arms transfers subject, perhaps in the form of another informal, ad hoc arrangement whereby the major exporters would band together to direct their exports according to agreed rules. These expectations were nourished by the dialogue among the permanent members of the UN Security Council and in the United States by the return to the White House of the political party most strongly associated with the effort to control such trade.[50]

---

48   On a global missile ban, see Alton Frye, "Zero Ballistic Missiles," *Foreign Policy*, No. 88 (Fall 1992), pp. 3–20. See also Lora Lumpe, "Zero Ballistic Missiles and the Third World," Project on Rethinking Arms Control, Paper No. 3 (College Park, Md.: Center for International and Security Studies at Maryland, School of Public Affairs, University of Maryland at College Park, March 1993). On a landmine ban, see Arms Project of Human Rights Watch and Physicians for Human Rights, *Landmines: A Deadly Legacy* (New York, N.Y.: Human Rights Watch, 1993).

49   Keith Krause and David Mutimer, "The Proliferation of Conventional Weapons: New Challenges for Control and Verification," in Mutimer, ed., *Control But Verify: Verification and the New Non-Proliferation Agenda* (Toronto: Centre for International and Strategic Studies at York University, 1994), pp. 39–55.

But the consensus necessary to achieve such a new regime is missing at this time among the major suppliers, to say nothing of the new suppliers. There is a general sense that the trade in destabilizing weapons should be curtailed but stabilizing sales should be allowed. But it is very difficult to distinguish one from the other in the absence of clear criteria. The failure to define agreed criteria recalls the failure of the ambitious effort to control arms production and transfers in the years between World Wars I and II and the repeated failures in the decades since to achieve similar results in the Middle East, including the Bush administration's plan crafted after the Persian Gulf War.[51]

It reflects also the view that a complete cessation of the conventional arms trade is neither desirable nor feasible. Preservation of the security of allies by cushioning them during periods of transition in military relations with their neighbors remains a legitimate concern, especially as they are brought under increasing pressure not to resort to unconventional weapons. So, too, does the need to build up patterns of military cooperation between allies and to provide components of the infrastructure necessary to implement alliance guarantees in time of conflict.

A permanent cutoff would also disadvantage those who have not heretofore developed indigenous production capabilities. Further, it would conflict with the economic exigencies facing the manufacturers of military hardware to sustain some production and R&D despite sharply declining procurement budgets.[52] It is

---

50 President Jimmy Carter made a serious effort to impose such restraint. In May 1977 he declared that "the United States will henceforth view arms transfers as an exceptional foreign policy implement, to be used only in instances where it can be clearly demonstrated that the transfer contributes to our national security interest." This was followed by bilateral Conventional Arms Transfer Talks (CATT) with the Soviet Union. A particular effort was made to constrain the trade in "weapons of ill-repute" such as napalm, fuel-air explosives and other incendiary devices, and wide-area cluster bombs. See U.S. Congress, House of Representatives, Committee on Foreign Affairs, *Changing Perspectives on U.S. Arms Transfer Policy*, Report by the Congressional Research Service to the Subcommittee on International Security and Scientific Affairs (Washington, D.C.: GPO, 1981).

51 Thomas Ohlson, ed., *Arms Transfer Limitations and Third World Security* (Oxford: Oxford University Press for the Stockholm International Peace Research Institute, 1988), pp. 2–3.

52 For some individual products, some overseas sales may be critical to affordability. In the case of the United States, these include for example the M1A1 main battle tank, the Blackhawk helicopter, the HAWK surface-to-air missile, and Boeing 707s. Cited in U.S. Department of State

doubtful, however, that overseas sales can sustain the broad base of military manufacturing in the United States, Europe, and Asia that was long sustained by Cold War-level defense budgets, given the relatively small number of states able to afford significant arms purchases and the limited utility of those purchases in generating the profits to sustain innovation.[53]

The more promising avenue at this time is an incremental expansion of controls on conventional arms transfers[54] and a serious effort to use the newly created conventional arms transfer registry of the UN to good effect in generating regional dialogues on the ingredients of national security and stable regional force balances.[55] The long-term goal of this registry is to prevent excessive and destabilizing accumulations of conventional armaments. The medium-term goal is to provide the understanding necessary to define what is stabilizing and destabilizing in the way of specific arms sales. In the short term,

---

and U.S. Defense Security Assistance Agency, *Congressional Preparation for Security Assistance Programs,* fiscal year 1992 (Washington, D.C.), p. 6.

53 Stephanie Neuman, "Controlling the Arms Trade: Idealistic Dream or Realpolitik?" *The Washington Quarterly,* Vol. 16, No. 3 (Summer 1993), pp. 53–75. For the impact of overseas sales on budgets, see Office of Technology Assessment, *Global Arms Trade,* chapter 1, "Global Defense Business and Arms Proliferation," pp. 3–34. Its authors conclude that "expanding international business may increase profits for individual U.S. companies, but for U.S. industry overall the benefits are not so clear-cut" (page 13).

54 John M. Lamb and Jennifer L. Moher, *Conventional Arms Transfers: Approaches to Multilateral Control in the 1990s,* Aurora Papers No. 13 (Ottawa: The Canadian Centre for Arms Control and Disarmament, 1992). For an overview of the debate about arms trade controls, see Ian Anthony, *Arms Export Regulations* (Oxford: Oxford University Press with the Stockholm International Peace Research Institute, 1991).

55 Ian Anthony, "Assessing the UN Register of Conventional Arms," *Survival,* Vol. 35, No. 4 (Winter 1993–94), pp. 113–129; Michael Moodie, "Transparency in Armaments: A New Item for the New Security Agenda," *The Washington Quarterly,* Vol. 15, No. 3 (Summer 1992), pp. 75–82; Edward J. Laurance, "The UN Register of Conventional Arms: Rationales and Prospects for Compliance and Effectiveness," *The Washington Quarterly,* Vol. 16, No. 2 (Spring 1993), pp. 163–172; United Nations, Department for Disarmament Affairs, "Transparency in Armaments," Topical Papers 3 (New York, N.Y., 1990); and Edward J. Laurance, Siemon T. Wezeman, and Herbert Wulf, *Arms Watch: SIPRI Report on the First Year of the UN Register of Conventional Arms* (Oxford: Oxford University Press for the Stockholm International Peace Research Institute, 1993).

the registry serves to promote increased transparency, which is seen as valuable in its own terms and useful for building confidence among regional competitors.[56]

Unilateral restraint by the major suppliers will also be an important determinant of the success of these efforts. A few of them continue to enjoy substantial dominance in key regions or technology markets, especially the United States.[57] As Steven Mussington has argued, regulation of the arms trade must proceed

> through a supply management approach. Rather than concentrating on traditional non-proliferation measures, dominated as they are by sanctions and proscribed items lists, this approach calls for the informal coordination of arms-transfer policies among suppliers. In addition, the inclusion of positive incentives in arms-transfer agreements would give recipients an incentive to "buy-in" to a system of supply management in conventional arms.[58]

The global arms control agenda of the 1990s is thus a wide-ranging one, offering new promise for formalizing restraint among nations with regard to their weapons potential, but also offering new political challenges.

Regional Arms Control. The second area of innovation and priority identified above as central to formalizing restraint is regional arms control. In the 1990s, interest in this regional arms control agenda has grown substantially, not just in Latin America where it is well advanced, but in East Asia, South Asia, and even the Middle East.[59] In each of these regions there is active exploration of the various

---

56   United Nations, *Study on Ways and Means of Promoting Transparency in International Transfers of Conventional Arms,* UN General Assembly document A/47/301 (New York, N.Y.: September 9, 1991), p. 37. See also Frederic S. Pearson and Michael Brzoska, "The Register as an Early Warning System," in Malcolm Chalmers et al., *Developing the UN Register of Conventional Arms* (Bradford, U.K.: Department of Peace Studies, University of Bradford, 1994), pp. 225–250.

57   Office of Technology Assessment, *Global Arms Trade,* p. 27.

58   David Mussington, *Understanding Contemporary International Arms Transfers,* Adelphi Paper No. 291 (London: Brassey's for the International Institute for Strategic Studies, 1994), p. 5.

59   By authors from within these regions, see for example Oluyemi Adeniji, "Africa and Nuclear Nonproliferation," in Bailey, *Director's Series on Proliferation,* No. 6, pp. 5–14; Jayantha

concepts, methods, theories, and models of arms control developed over recent decades and an assessment of their applicability to national and regional security problems. Moreover, regional arms control has been embraced by the UN and features prominently in the foreign policies of countries like the United States.[60]

As noted in chapter 1, the modern theory of arms control was sketched out in a flurry of writings in the United States in the late 1950s and early 1960s.[61] To

Dhanapala, ed., *Regional Approaches to Disarmament: Security and Stability* (Geneva: United Nations Institute for Disarmament Research, 1993); Efraim Inbar, "Israel and Arms Control," *Arms Control*, Vol. 13, No. 2 (September 1992), pp. 214–221; Mahmoud Karem, *A Nuclear-Weapon-Free Zone in the Middle East: Problems and Prospects* (Westport, Conn.: Greenwood Press, 1988); Chung Min Lee, "The Future of Arms Control in the Korean Peninsula," *The Washington Quarterly*, Vol. 14, No. 3 (Summer 1991), pp. 181–197; Shireen M. Mazari, "Nuclear Weapons and Structures of Conflict," in Wander, Arnett, and Bracken, *The Diffusion of Advanced Weaponry*, pp. 183–192; John J. Redick, Julio C. Carasales, and Paulo S. Wrobel, "Nuclear Rapprochement: Argentina, Brazil, and the Nonproliferation Regime," *The Washington Quarterly*, Vol. 18, No. 1 (Winter 1995), pp. 107–122; Yahya M. Sadowski, *Scuds or Butter? The Political Economy of Arms Control in the Middle East* (Washington, D.C.: Brookings Institution, 1993); Jasjit Singh, "Security in a Period of Strategic Uncertainty," in Singh, ed., *Asian Strategic Review, 1991–92* (New Delhi: Institute for Defence Studies and Analyses, New Delhi, India, August 1992, pp. 7–26; Augusto Vargas, "Regional Arms Control in the South American Context," in Ohlson, *Arms Transfer Limitations and Third World Security*, pp. 175–185; and Maocheng Zhang, "Arms Control and Disarmament in the Asia–Pacific Region," in James Brown, ed., *Challenges in Arms Control for the 1990s* (Amsterdam: VU University Press, 1992), pp. 213–220. See also Michael Moodie, "Regional Arms Control: Overlooked No Longer?" in James Brown, ed., *New Horizons and Challenges in Arms Control and Verification* (Amsterdam: VU University Press, 1994), pp. 45–58; Joseph F. Pilat, "Regional Non-Proliferation Strategies," in Tariq Rauf, ed., *Regional Approaches to Curbing Nuclear Proliferation in the Middle East and South Asia*, Aurora Papers No. 16, (Ottawa: Canadian Centre for Global Security, 1992), pp. 57–66; and Sharon A. Squassoni, "Arms Control, Confidence Building, and Other Regional Responses," in W. Thomas Wander and Eric H. Arnett, *The Proliferation of Advanced Weaponry: Technology, Motivations, and Responses* (Washington, D.C.: American Association for the Advancement of Science, 1992), pp. 301–314.

60 Boutros Boutros-Ghali, *New Dimensions of Arms Regulation and Disarmament in the Post–Cold War Era* (New York, N.Y.: United Nations, York, 1992).

61 See for example Thomas C. Schelling and Morton H. Halperin, *Strategy and Arms Control* (New York, N.Y.: Twentieth Century Fund, 1961); Hedley Bull, *The Control of the Arms Race: Disarmament and Arms Control in the Missile Age* (London: Weidenfeld and Nicolson, 1961); Bernard Brodie, *Strategy in the Missile Age* (Princeton, N.J.: Princeton University Press, 1959); Donald Brennan, ed., *Arms Control, Disarmament and National Security* (New York, N.Y.: George

specialists on arms control whose focus was the Cold War, the striking aspect of the current exploration and assessment is what it reveals about how rooted in the strategic realities of the Cold War so much of the understanding of arms control is. Among these specialists there is a marked tendency to dismiss the wealth of experience in negotiating restraints on the behavior of states that predates the Cold War, including especially the naval arms control agreements of the interwar years, other constraints on war enacted in the wake of World War I, such as the Geneva Protocol, and the myriad diplomatic initiatives prior to World War I.[62] There is also a tendency to view the superpower experience through the filter of its most recent forms, overlooking the fact that the formal force structure measures on conventional and strategic forces were preceded by less formal ones, especially the interim confidence-building measures of the 1960s and 1970s.

Moreover, much of what passes for fixed and hard truths about arms control is revealed as little more than conventional wisdom. One of the first of these false notions is that there has been little or no arms control experience outside of the East–West context. In fact, developing countries have participated in substantial numbers in the global treaty regimes. They also have some experience with regional measures. Latin America enjoys its own nuclear arms control measure, the Treaty of Tlatelolco. In the Middle East, a number of states have participated in demilitarization and confidence-building measures agreed during the shuttle diplomacy of U.S. Secretary of State Henry Kissinger. In South Asia, a series of confidence-building measures has been implemented as a way to cope with the nuclearization of the conflict there, including pledges not to attack each other's nuclear facilities in an effort to diminish the pressure to strike first in time of crisis.

Braziller, 1961); and Albert Wohlstetter, "The Delicate Balance of Terror," *Foreign Affairs*, Vol. 37, No. 2 (January 1959).

62   Caroline F. Ziemke, "Peace Without Strings? Interwar Naval Arms Control Revisited," *The Washington Quarterly*, Vol. 15, No. 4 (Autumn 1992), pp. 87–106; McKercher, *Arms Limitation and Disarmament*; Harry B. Hollins, Averill L. Powers, and Mark Sommer, eds., *The Conquest of War: Alternative Strategies for Global Security* (Boulder, Colo.: Westview Press, 1989); Serge Sur, ed., *Disarmament and Limitation of Armaments: Unilateral Measures and Policies*, UNIDIR/92/60 (Geneva: United Nations Institute for Disarmament Research, 1992); and Richard Dean Burns, ed., *Encyclopedia of Arms Control and Disarmament* (New York, N.Y.: Charles Scribner's Sons, 1993).

A fresh look at arms control in the light of regional security concerns points to a number of departures in arms control theology.

First, the tradition of superpower arms control is built around the notion that participants in arms control are locked in adversarial relationships seeking only to make their competition more manageable and less risky. As Thomas Schelling and Morton Halperin put it, arms control is "all forms of military cooperation between potential enemies in the interest of reducing the likelihood of war, its scope and violence if it occurs, and the political and economic costs of being prepared for it."[63] In some regional situations, a different challenge exists, namely to work within an essentially cooperative framework that threatens to be overtaken by the destabilizing effects of weapons development and deployment. The arms control challenge is to formulate structures of security relations that make regional relations predictable, stable, and controlled and that work to prevent differences from erupting into conflicts. Latin America offers perhaps the best example of a region where arms control offers the prospect of advancing a significantly more expansive agenda of regional cooperation.[64] Southeast Asia is another such region, where larger military arsenals threaten to create fears and magnify instabilities, drawing the region into unintended and undesired wars, much as the armaments programs of the European powers of a century ago complicated relations among the states and helped tip the balance toward a war that no one seems to have wanted.[65]

Thus regional measures might best be understood as security arrangements with arms control aspects and possible nonproliferation benefits. In this sense, they are consistent with efforts of earlier eras to combine elements of national self-reliance through military preparation with cooperative measures, whether informally with other states or formally in negotiated agreements that limit a state's war-making options or create instruments for the management of sources

---

63   Schelling and Halperin, *Strategy and Arms Control*, p. 2.

64   This theme about cooperative arms control has been well delineated in Ivo H. Daalder, *Cooperative Arms Control: A New Agenda for the Post–Cold War Era*, Paper No. 1 (College Park, Md.: Center for International Security Studies at Maryland School of Public Affairs, University of Maryland at College Park, October 1991). For the discussion of Latin America in particular, see page 42.

65   Gerald Segal, "Managing New Arms Races in the Asia/Pacific," *The Washington Quarterly*, Vol. 15, No. 3 (Summer 1992), pp. 83–102.

of conflict (such as boundary disputes) that decrease (while perhaps not eliminating) reliance on the threat of the use of force.

The impact of arms control may be considerable. One might anticipate a growing interest in confidence-building measures, such as unilateral steps to limit weapons deployments or other military capabilities,[66] increased use of transparency measures such as the exchange of observers or advance notification of exercises, or the redeployment of forces so as to create larger keep-out zones. Indeed, confidence-building measures have emerged at the top of the regional arms control agenda in both the Middle East and South Asia.[67] This also suggests that the arms control of most immediate promise is informal arms control, a form that relies more on the process of dialogue than on legal documents that formalize negotiated measures.

This drift toward more cooperative security regimes evokes memories of the debate in the West in the 1970s and 1980s about the sources of its own security. The Cold War establishment by and large rejected the arguments of the political left that it was important to look beyond collective military preparations and its security benefits to comprehensive security (emphasizing the nonmilitary dimensions of stability) and common security (emphasizing the need to reduce the insecurity of adversaries). In addressing the regional arms control agenda, these various concepts of security are brought again into sharp relief and deserve the scrutiny of policy specialists.[68]

---

66   As the United Nations has noted, "The advantage of unilateral measures, as positive demonstrations of political will, especially in times of uncertainty, and as a momentum activator for disarmament, are indisputable. They also reduce the time spent on bilateral or multilateral negotiations. They could constitute a valuable confidence-building measure. Most importantly, today they can be implemented outside the confrontational bipolar context of the past. A series of unilateral measures can form a solid foundation for negotiated multilateral disarmament agreements." Sur, *Disarmament and Limitation of Armaments*, p. vii.

67   Geoffrey Kemp, *The Control of the Middle East Arms Race* (Washington, D.C.: Carnegie Endowment for International Peace, 1991); Alan Platt, ed., *Arms Control and Confidence Building in the Middle East* (Washington, D.C.: United States Institute of Peace, 1992); and C. Raja Mohan, "Crisis Management and Confidence-Building in South Asia" (Research paper prepared for the United States Institute of Peace, Washington, D.C., 1993).

68   See for example the Palme Commission report that was outspoken in its criticism of the attainment of security through the pursuit of relative power and pressed for arms control and disarmament in Europe and elsewhere. Palme Commission, *Common Security: A Programme for*

Second, the superpower tradition emphasizes the control of weapons modernization and accumulation; freezes were deemed destabilizing and deep cuts or the wholesale elimination of categories of weapons were, with rare exceptions, deemed too risky. Today, however, in some regions there is an opposite challenge: to cap existing programs or to manage falling levels of defense spending and declining military arsenals in ways that reap benefits rather than sow doubts. This pattern is pronounced in Europe, where the force ratios agreed in the days of NATO–Warsaw Pact confrontation are not sustained by the defense spending of the erstwhile adversaries. It is evident in Latin America, where the expansion of military institutions of the 1960s and 1970s has been replaced by austerity and contraction in the 1980s and 1990s. It may soon become evident in the Middle East, when and if sufficient progress on the Arab–Israeli peace agenda is made to enable the moderate Arab states to shift resources away from military preparedness to social problems.

The arms control result may be agreements, whether formal or informal, to forswear certain capabilities, cap weapons programs at existing thresholds, or take modest steps toward smaller force structures. Some such agreements are already in evidence. Under the Mendoza Agreement, a growing number of states in Latin America are forswearing the right to chemical and biological in addition to nuclear weapons.[69] In South Asia, India and Pakistan appear to have made informal assurances to each other limiting the future disposition of their nuclear weapons capabilities.[70] Capping Israel's nuclear weapons capability and rolling back South Africa's capability under international supervision are examples of related goals.[71]

Disarmament: The Report of the Independent Commission on Disarmament and Security Issues (London: Pan Books, 1982).

69   The so-called Mendoza agreement of September 1991 commits Argentina, Chile, and Brazil to create and police among themselves a zone free of nuclear, chemical, and biological weapons. For a full text see *Chemical Weapons Convention Bulletin* (Harvard–Sussex Program on CBW Armament and Arms Limitation), No. 14 (December 1991), p. 19. For discussion of its possible expansion, see Daalder, *Cooperative Arms Control*, pp. 43–44.

70   Mohan, "Crisis Management and Confidence-Building in South Asia."

71   Lewis A. Dunn, *Containing Nuclear Proliferation*, Adelphi Paper No. 263 (London: Brassey's for the International Institute for Strategic Studies, 1991), pp. 35–45.

Creating arms control instruments to manage the challenges of falling defense spending and shrinking forces skirts close to a set of issues long treated as anathema by superpower arms control specialists—disarmament. Disarmament has generally been viewed as an entirely separate, and especially foolish, form of arms control. As Schelling stated, "A fairly sharp distinction came to be drawn between 'arms control' and 'disarmament.' The former seeks to reshape military incentives and capabilities with a view to stabilizing mutual deterrence; the latter, it is alleged, eliminates military incentives and capabilities." As he went on to observe, "Disarmament does not eliminate military potential; it changes it. The essential requirement is for some stable situation of rearmament parity."[72]

If disarmament is to be durable, it must be so designed that the disadvantages of being behind in case an arms race should resume are not too great and so that, in the face of ambiguous evidence of clandestine rearmament or overt evidence of imminent rearmament, nations can react without haste. The straightforward elimination of so-called "military production facilities" might, by sheer coincidence, provide the stability; but stability is more likely if there is a deliberately designed system of

> stable equal readiness for rearmament....It is not certain that maximizing the time required to rearm is a way to deter it....The argument here is not that disarmament would be especially unstable, or less stable than the present world of armaments. It is that disarmament could be *either* more stable *or* less stable militarily than an armed world, according to how the existing military potential loaded the dice in favor of speed, surprise, and initiative or instead made it safe to wait, safe to be second in resuming an arms race or second in launching attack, or on whether the easiest directions of rearmament tended toward stable or unstable armaments.[73]

---

72   Thomas C. Schelling, *Arms and Influence* (New Haven, Conn.: Yale University Press, 1966), p. 248.

73   Ibid., pp. 257–258. Hedley Bull made a similar argument. "Even the most drastic disarmament system must leave some states with greater capacity for war than others; a nation's war potential does not reside simply in its 'armaments', but in the whole complex of its economic, technological, and demographic resources, strategic position, political leadership, military

The challenges of achieving rearmament parity, of coping with uncertainty, of buying time, of deliberately designing systems of stability, of diminishing the incentive to preemption are at the core of creating workable arms control regimes in regions in conflict. Free of the Cold War and especially of the political battles between Left and Right over the sources of Cold War security, some reconnection with the disarmament tradition and conceptual base would contribute to regional peacemaking.

This would be particularly useful on the subject of qualitative disarmament—the effort to focus on eliminating destabilizing weapons or capabilities while permitting a sufficiency of stabilizing ones. The experience of the disarmament conference of the interwar years, "when control efforts failed in part because of the inability of the Powers to equate different types and numbers of weapons"[74] created a predisposition among diplomats against such distinctions. The attributes of Cold War strategic stability reinforced this predisposition, because few weapons counted clearly as stabilizing or destabilizing in the absence of some idea of the intentions of those who possessed them.

But this began to change with the Soviet deployment of large intercontinental missiles capable of carrying numerous independently targetable warheads with sufficient accuracy to threaten the elimination of even those U.S. weapons previously deemed likely to survive a first strike and be used in retaliation. Western appreciation of especially destabilizing weapons accelerated with the proliferation of chemical weapons and crude ballistic missiles in the 1980s. A more concentrated effort to identify weapons and developmental steps that are especially destabilizing—and to build international consensus about the deleterious effects of such actions—would advance the regional arms control project.[75] The failure to do so has stymied the effort of the five permanent

---

experience and ingenuity, morale, and so on....A disarmed world...is still a world in which the capacity for organized violence exists and must play its part in human affairs. It is still a world divided into sovereign states and subject to the political conflicts by which such a world has always been characterized." Bull, *The Anarchical Society: A Study of Order in World Politics* (New York, N.Y.: Columbia University Press, 1977), pp. 236–237.

74 McKercher, *Arms Limitation and Disarmament*, p. 192.

75 See chapter 6, "Qualitative Disarmament: Eliminating the War-Making Capability of Nations," in Hollins, Powers, and Sommer, *The Conquest of War*, pp. 64–77.

members of the UN Security Council to slow the flow of weapons into the Middle East.

Third, the superpower tradition emphasizes arms control as essentially a bilateral process or something conducted between two blocs of nations. Rare, however, is the regional circumstance in which bilateral or bloc-to-bloc relations dominate the strategic environment. Even in South Asia, where India and Pakistan stand in nuclear confrontation, China and Iran loom as important to regional strategic calculations. Thus regional arms control promises to be more multilateral than the arms control of the past. Yet over the years little attention has been given to the multilateral process and its special difficulties.

Aside from the increased complexity of negotiating acceptable trade-offs among large numbers of states and of engaging influential outside powers on a continuing basis (where desirable),[76] multilateral arms control measures present special challenges with regard to their verification and compliance provisions. The small states that populate regions in conflict cannot bring to arms control the national technical means or other intelligence resources of the large powers to monitor compliance or the political influence in the international system to generate responses to noncompliant behavior. This places special importance on multilateral treaties backed by effective organizations, staffed by talented individuals, and enjoying the support of influential states.[77]

The search for arms control measures in the developing world is likely to lead to new forms and types that go beyond the experience of the East–West conflict. One such innovation is already evident in the Persian Gulf, where a universal, global regime has been focused on one state—Iraq—and backed by the toughest possible inspection and compliance mechanisms.[78] So-called coercive arms control has gained considerable currency.[79] Achievement of local political

---

76 Michael Tucker, *Non-Nuclear Powers and the Geneva Conference on Disarmament: A Study in Multilateral Arms Control*, Occasional Paper No. 7 (Ottawa: Canadian Institute for International Peace and Security, 1989).

77 Gaertner, *Challenges of Verification*.

78 There are antecedents to this effort. See Fred Tanner, ed., *From Versailles to Baghdad: Post-War Armament Control of Defeated States*, UNIDIR/92/70 (Geneva: United Nations Institute for Disarmament Research and the Graduate Institute of International Studies, 1992).

79 William H. Lewis and Christopher C. Joyner, "Proliferation of Unconventional Weapons: The Case for Coercive Arms Control," *Comparative Strategy*, Vol. 10, No. 4 (October–December

accommodation may combine with changing budgetary priorities to create conventional disarmament or build-down agreements, which might be termed deproliferation measures. States will be challenged to monitor and manage these processes while promoting defense conversion in ways that bring the benefits of cooperation rather than sow doubt. Or a group of like-minded states, responding to the concerns of the developed countries about dual-use technologies, might band together to intensively police end-use and retransfer in exchange for special consideration within the ad hoc export control coordinating entities. Especially in Latin America, where the drive to develop free trade and democracy is strong, such special undertakings might seem worth the effort. There is also an increasing interest within regions in learning from the experience of other regions.[80]

Utilizing an expansive conception of regional arms control measures, the inventory of possible subglobal security arrangements with arms control benefits appears to be truly comprehensive. Tom Farer has identified six broad categories:

> providing a framework for negotiating and implementing confidence-building measures; promoting the peaceful settlement of disputes; appraising the claims of members that they are entitled to vindicate by force legal rights violated by other member states (i.e., a claimed right to engage in self-help); authorizing and coordinating peacekeeping measures; authorizing and coordinating the application of coercive measures against members or nonmembers that threaten collective security interests whether by armed attack or otherwise; and encouraging latent belligerents to alter the ricocheting mutual perceptions of interest and identity that underlie their hostility.[81]

In whatever way the regional arms control agenda may compel a rethinking of the tradition of arms control, regional arms control must also confront some enduring truths. First, preferring negotiated measures and achieving them with

---

1991), pp. 299–309.

80 Karem, *A Nuclear-Weapon-Free Zone in the Middle East.*

81 Farer, "The Role of Regional Collective Security Arrangements," in Thomas G. Weiss, ed., *Collective Security in a Changing World* (Boulder, Colo.: Lynne Rienner Publishers, 1993), p. 171.

one's neighbors are two quite different matters. The architects of regional arms control confront many significant challenges beyond the different security orientations of regional actors. These include, for example, the integration of regional measures into existing global frameworks—a problem especially in the nuclear domain, where there is a widespread desire that formal regional measures not be seen to undercut the NPT and that a two-tiered system of verification not emerge.[82] There is the necessity of dealing with the myriad sources of insecurity in each of these regions.[83] Of course, the very process itself of talking and negotiating may be as beneficial for regional security as the creation of formal treaty regimes—as was frequently the case in East–West relations.

Moreover, having an agreement on paper is rarely the same as having effective arms control. Even among the best intentioned of parties to a treaty, there is the always difficult task of implementing treaty commitments and managing the inevitable uncertainties that arise and the complications caused by the passage of time. Tending to such implementation issues requires a steadiness of purpose not always found in governments and an ability to capture the attention of senior political figures even when they see few or no benefits to be reaped.[84]

The challenges of securing effective arms control are especially acute, however, among parties not equally intentioned to honor their commitments. Regional arms controllers are likely to face the same intellectual debates about the place of arms control in national strategy and the same challenges of building effective regimes with credible compliance mechanisms that have long bedeviled the East–West experience.[85]

---

82   See Scheinman, "Assuring the Nuclear Non-Proliferation Safeguards System," pp. 36–37.

83   It has been argued, for example, that the confidence-building agendas cannot be implemented regionally if they are focused on military measures alone. "The debate on confidence-building measures should not be guided solely by the criteria of the balance of military power. It has to go beyond the question of shaping stability and preserving the *status quo*. It has to incorporate other interlocking qualitative aspects of inter-State relations and the perceptions and policies of all countries, great and small." Fernando Simas Magalhaes, "The Impact of East–West Confidence-building Measures on Global Security: A View from the South," *Disarmament*, Vol. 13, No. 1 (1990), pp. 158–161.

84   Charles C. Flowerree, "On Tending Arms Control Agreements," *The Washington Quarterly*, Vol. 13, No. 1 (Winter 1990), pp. 199–214. For a contemporary example see Nathaniel C. Nash, "Argentina Lagging on Missile Pledge; Years After Condor II Project, Some Parts Appear Intact and Some Are Missing," *New York Times*, August 19, 1992.

There are two schools of thought on this problem in the West. One sees arms control as "overrated as a path to peace"[86] because it does not resolve underlying conflicts and lulls complacent democratic publics into a false perception of peace and as "subordinated to, not substituted for, enough strength and clarity to protect our interests and values....The most disturbing aspects of the arms control approach to international affairs are not the problems of verification—difficult as they are—but the absence of penalties for noncompliance."[87] The other sees arms control as the sine qua non of peaceful relations among competitive powers.[88] It is noteworthy that the Cold War ended and the Soviet Union collapsed before the arms control community in the West finally came to terms with Soviet cheating and the means of compelling Soviet compliance. Hence these two schools of thought continue to shape thinking about arms control even after the Cold War.

---

85 See for example Patrick Glynn, *Closing Pandora's Box: Arms Races, Arms Control, and the History of the Cold War* (New York, N.Y.: Basic Books, 1992); Colin S. Gray, *Weapons Don't Make War: Policy, Strategy, and Military Technology* (Lawrence, Kan.: University of Kansas Press, 1993); and a book review by Gideon Rose, "A Farewell to Arms Control," *National Interest,* No. 30 (Winter 1992/93), pp. 93–100.

86 Steven E. Miller, "Is Arms Control a Path to Peace?" in W. Scott Thompson and Kenneth M. Jensen with Richard N. Smith and Kimber M. Schraub, eds., *Approaches to Peace: An Intellectual Map* (Washington, D.C.: United States Institute of Peace, 1991), pp. 46–63.

87 Jeane J. Kirkpatrick, *The Withering Away of the Totalitarian State...And Other Surprises* (Washington, D.C.: American Enterprise Institute, 1990), pp. 101, 103. Kirkpatrick also criticizes "a tendency to legalism in the conduct of foreign policy [by which] we have attempted to outlaw war by contract" (p. 102).

88 One recent study has also sought to establish a connection between arms control and conflict, concluding that "agreements that restrict the level of arms tend to be introduced in periods of military buildup decelerations, but fail to be accompanied by lower military spending patterns beyond the short run; and that agreements are followed by a significant decrease in the frequency of international conflict." Vally Koubi, "Military Buildups and Arms Control Agreements," *International Studies Quarterly,* Vol. 38, No. 4 (December 1994), p. 605. Another study cites nearly three dozen instances since the end of World War II when arms control has been used as an instrument in conflict settlement. Fred Tanner, *Arms Control in Times of Conflict: A Contribution to Conflict Management in the Post–Cold War World,* Paper No. 7 (College Park, Md.: Project on Rethinking Arms Control, Center for International and Security Studies at Maryland, October 1993).

But, as argued above, dealing with problems of compliance is at the heart of making an arms control strategy serve national security interests. Given the failure of the West to resolve these issues and the many regional security challenges, skepticism about the future of regional arms control is warranted. Whether such measures will ultimately prove effective or ineffective remains an open question and contingent on those issues of effectiveness and compliance outlined above. Arms control qua comprehensive disarmament and major force-structuring agreements akin to CFE or the Strategic Arms Reduction Treaty (START) appears today to be a remote possibility in most regions. However, at this time, more fruitful endeavors are being found in the areas of confidence-building measures and the codification of arms deployments at existing thresholds of force levels or capabilities.

Arms control measures that go beyond modest confidence-building measures and existing commitments to bilateral, regional, or global regimes will not be possible in these regions without some willingness by leaders of states in unstable circumstances to gamble on cooperative strategies rather than continue to rely on the military instrument of national security. Most Western security experts seem to be fairly doctrinaire in their belief that this is unlikely if not impossible. This skepticism is well founded in history but does not account for the reality confronting many of those leaders today.

As noted in chapter 3, the number of states that pursue high-leverage military capability for purposes of urgent and immediate self-defense or deterrence are relatively few in the international system. The vast majority pursuing such capabilities are states whose commitment to advanced weapons programs should be understood as contingent upon whether these programs advance or detract from national security, sovereignty, or ambitions. The leaders of such states may perceive some benefits in unconventional weapons or other military capabilities of significant leverage, but also some risks. Foremost among these risks is the possibility that a war with unacceptable consequences for the state and/or the regime may be unleashed in an era in which weapons of strategic impact have proliferated widely. As argued earlier, the familiar habit of engaging in brinkmanship as a form of crisis management may be passing as the stakes of failure go up. States currently enjoying a preponderance of power may also find reason in the difficulty and cost of maintaining that advantage to seek a more permanent basis for their security. States unable to sustain defense spending in support of strategic weapons or weapons development programs may find in arms control a strategy for extracting concessions from a competitor for something that would be relinquished in any case (this pattern became familiar in the superpower arms control experience). This creates an array of incentives and disincentives related to the pursuit of specific programs.

Some such states might be willing to trade off the narrow, specific military benefits of certain desired capabilities with other enhancements such as improved relations with influential members of the international system, access to the global trading and financial systems, or a legitimate claim to call upon the collective security functions of regional alliances or the UN. Or they might be enticed to freeze capabilities at current thresholds in exchange for other security enhancements, such as reciprocal behavior by an opponent.

In speculating about the likelihood that regional arms control measures will be adopted, some variables directly linked to the proliferation subject merit particular attention. One is the increasing incentive to avoid war with potentially cataclysmic consequences. No better example of the effect of proliferation in changing perceptions of the stakes of conflict exists than in the Middle East, where negotiations have some significant new hope today because of the perceived growing disutility of interstate war for national purposes among each of the major protagonists.

A second factor is the growing complexity of force balances and perceptions of stability in regions where the proliferation of conventional and unconventional capabilities is advanced.[89] In the Middle East in particular, some states have pointed to the increasingly complex linkages among different factors of a military and nonmilitary nature to argue that there is an operative linkage requiring comprehensive, wide-ranging measures. This is principally an Arab argument linking abandonment of their unacknowledged chemical arsenals to controls on Israel's nuclear capabilities. The connections are real, but the linkage argument is not fully persuasive. Such interconnections were to be found in abundance in Cold War Europe, but these did not preclude piecemeal approaches resulting in separate measures on conventional, intermediate-range nuclear, and strategic forces that over time stabilized the military competition while minimizing its undesirable side effects. The Arab argument would be more potent

---

89   Frankel, *Opaque Nuclear Proliferation;* Brahma Chellany, "South Asia's Passage to Nuclear Power," *International Security,* Vol. 16, No. 1 (Summer 1991), pp. 43–72.

diplomatically were there not a history of the use of chemical weapons by Arab governments against other Arabs and Iranians and their own peoples.[90]

A third variable is the fate of the UN's efforts to destroy Iraq's existing arsenal of unconventional weapons and to prevent the reconstruction of that arsenal. If Iraq is widely perceived as able to circumvent the UN's demands over the long term, some renegade states might decide to join existing or new regimes with the full expectation of cheating. Similarly, if the international community is seen to be unwilling to enforce its will over the long term, few states are likely to take serious national security risks by opting for negotiated agreements rather than armaments programs.

The integration of regional and global mechanisms is a major new challenge as the former gain prominence on the global security agenda. In some cases, global measures seem necessary as the foundation for regional measures, as in the case of arms registers. If, for example, greater transparency is to be achieved in Southeast Asia, where conventional arms acquisitions are occurring in large numbers, it will happen only on the basis of the beginnings made with the UN register. In other cases, regional measures may be a substitute for what is not possible in the global arena. If, for example, a regional arms control agreement is created in the Middle East it is likely to have inspection provisions far more rigorous than those embodied in the existing nuclear nonproliferation regime.

Supporters of the global regimes have been opposed to the creation of regional regimes that are less thorough in their obligations or rigorous in their enforcement. This sentiment has contributed to the absence of regional measures in South Asia and to continued frustration with Latin America's separate nuclear regime. But especially in regions such as South Asia and the Middle East, where comprehensive disarmament appears impossible at this time, regional measures offer decided advantages and some tailoring of global regimes to the divergent security requirements of the world's regions.[91] To the extent the commitment to comprehensive disarmament prevents the achievement of more proximate short-term goals that would also contribute to stability and security, such sentiments are likely to prove less dominant in policymaking circles in the future.

---

90   See Roberts, *Chemical Disarmament and International Security*, pp. 6–7.

91   David Fischer, "Innovations in IAEA Safeguards to Meet the Challenges of the 1990s," in Fischer, *A New Nuclear Triad*, p. 31.

Supporting regional peace and arms control initiatives may sometimes require compromise of nonproliferation aspirations—at least in the short term. But the benefits may well outweigh these costs.

The core argument that regional arms control merits new prominence in policy will read to some as a paean to arms control. In the Cold War, many arms control advocates little appreciated the limited utility of such measures in the absence of felicitous externalities or the dangers accompanying arms control measures badly conceived or implemented. Similarly, many arms control critics little appreciated its virtues both as a process of dialogue among adversaries and as a product that usually worked to ease the military burden by narrowing the range of options for which it was necessary to prepare. Whatever the truth or half-truth of these viewpoints during the Cold War, in today's new strategic realities it is useful to revisit what might be done to decrease reliance on military means alone and increase the role of cooperative negotiated measures in providing national and regional security.

This discussion of arms control answers one of the fundamental questions posed in the opening chapter about the instruments of post–Cold War strategy and especially about the utility of arms control. In Washington and elsewhere in the developed world there is a tendency to view arms control primarily as an instrument of security during the Cold War, one whose central importance lay not so much in the specific measures it produced as the process of dialogue it made possible, and one that has ever less to contribute to U.S. and global security as Cold War challenges recede. In fact, there is a large and growing arms control agenda for the 1990s. It entails not just strengthening the global regimes for the control of unconventional weapons or the implementation of existing measures, both of which will have significant implications for proliferation; but also this expansive new agenda of regional measures. Thus the end of the Cold War has altered the place of arms control in the strategies of the developed countries, but has not eliminated it. Arms control will remain a focus of interest and energy in the decades ahead, but not as before, at least for the United States and others for whom arms control played such a central security and political role during the Cold War.[92]

---

92   For a general discussion of the future of regional, multilateral, and global arms control measures, see Brad Roberts, "Arms Control and the End of the Cold War," *The Washington*

Reassurance and Deterrence: The Future of Security Policy

A third set of policies revolves around the tasks of providing reassurance to the insecure and achieving deterrence of those with aggressive intentions.

Reassurance entails convincing leaders of states facing an uncertain strategic environment or a potentially threatening armed neighbor that current and future threats will not overwhelm them and that the risks of not relying on an armaments program and security measures narrowly defined can be safely borne. The reassurance function is especially significant for states in regions of instability or facing hostile neighbors that are also uncertain of their own ability to fund, build, or effectively use advanced military capabilities. Some may simply prefer not to pursue national security strategies based on national self-reliance in the military domain but require some reassurance if they are to gamble on cooperative measures. Military preparations by their friends and allies or by collective security institutions are a prerequisite for encouraging them to depend on outside military support, whether by the United States, some other advanced military power, or an international grouping, in combination with their own conventional forces, rather than to seek nuclear weapons or other strategic capabilities of their own. The principle of collective security signals them that they will not stand alone.

Deterrence entails convincing leaders of potentially aggressive states that the costs of aggression will outweigh its benefits. More specifically, it entails persuading an adversary to choose peaceful means to achieve his goals by

---

Quarterly, Vol. 15, No. 4 (Autumn 1992), pp. 39–56 (from which portions of this chapter have been drawn). See also U.S. Department of State, *New Purposes and Priorities for Arms Control* (A Report to Sherman M. Funk, Inspector General of the United States Arms Control and Disarmament Agency, December 14, 1992); Ronald F. Lehman II, "Arms Control: Passing the Torch as Time Runs Out," *The Washington Quarterly*, Vol. 16, No. 3 (Summer 1993), pp. 37–52; Michael Moodie, "Multilateral Arms Control: Challenges and Opportunities," in Brown, *Challenges in Arms Control for the 1990s*, pp. 71–82; *The Future of Arms Control*, Report prepared for the Subcommittee on Arms Control, International Security and Science of the Committee on Foreign Affairs, U.S. House of Representatives, April 1992; Ivo Daalder, "The Future of Arms Control," *Survival*, Vol. 34, No. 1 (Spring 1992), pp. 51–73; and John Hawes, *Arms Control: A New Style for a New Agenda*, Paper No. 2 (College Park, Md.: Center for International and Security Studies at Maryland School of Public Affairs, University of Maryland at College Park, January 1993).

convincing him that aggressive acts will not succeed, that the costs associated with aggression are too high, that any gains will be reversed, that indirect costs (particularly retaliation) will be too great, and that transgressing agreed international norms will irreversibly alter the nature of the conflict to the adversary's disadvantage. The focus is on the leaders of states planning or carrying out the exploitation of their military capabilities for purposes of aggression.

The means of deterring such individuals is a matter of much speculation after the Cold War. There is a tendency toward overconfidence among some, who argue that because the Cold War collapsed and never went hot the fundamentals of deterrence have been proven and can be readily applied to any potential adversary. Elsewhere there is a tendency toward hysteria and the view that deterrence in the Cold War functioned because leaders in both East and West had few genuine non-ideological sources of conflict and were adequately rational decision makers capable of clearly communicating and understanding each other's intentions; surveying renegade states in the developing world, some commentators find there dogma rather than rationality, and rhetoric rather than communication.[93] In thinking about a potential conflict transregional conflict under the shadow of nuclear weapons, experts in the West bring with them a good deal of conceptual baggage from the East–West context. During the debate about the Persian Gulf War, it was evident that the strategies, doctrines, and assumptions about the politics of conflict, and especially deterrence, were rooted firmly in a world of which Saddam Hussein appears not to have been a part—especially in his apparent desire to fight a war he would be certain to lose, and to shed a great deal of his compatriots' blood along the way. This bodes ill for the future ability to deter aggression. Much homework needs to be done in to

---

93   This argument is often used by those who believe strategic defenses are an urgent military priority for the United States. Keith Payne argues that lower confidence in the reliability of deterrence in a multipolar world "is not because Third World leaders should be considered irrational, but because a high level of mutual understanding and effective communication is unlikely to characterize Western relations with many of the developing countries now acquiring advanced military technology." Keith B. Payne, "Proliferation: Implications for U.S. Security Policy," in Bailey, *Director's Series on Proliferation,* No. 1, p. 7. See also Keith B. Payne, "Proliferation, Deterrence, Stability and Missile Defense," *Comparative Strategy,* Vol. 13, No. 1 (1994), pp. 117–130.

explore the assumptions underpinning the use of force in the developing world by states of the developed and about the political dynamics of such conflicts. Particularly relevant is the question of retaliation and the dependence of current thinking on expectations of escalation ladders and in-kind deterrents.[94]

Doubts about the ability to successfully deter overarmed autocrats in the developing world are heightened with the growing appreciation of the willingness of such leaders to take risks in the face of what they perceive to be an untenable status quo and to pursue asymmetric strategies that pitch their strengths, usually the indiscriminate use of force, against the weaknesses of the deterring states, usually developed democracies with low tolerance for shedding blood for foreign causes. Credible deterrence requires also a reputation for delivering on the threat to use force when deterrence has failed and aggression has been committed so as to compel the undoing of the act that was not deterred; such reputations are noteworthy for their perishability. It also requires strong signals of intent, signals most evident in objective long-term ties (which by definition cannot be given quickly or promiscuously). If both reputation and historical commitment are absent, credibility devolves to the capacity to respond quickly and early in time of crisis with powerful military capabilities.[95]

Policies that help to both reassure and deter include, for example, alliances. NATO is an example of an alliance that during the Cold War provided reassurance to its members and deterrence of possible aggression by the Warsaw Pact. NATO's continued viability is germane to the question of future nuclear competence among many European countries, not least Germany, just as the U.S. alliance with Japan serves a similar function in East Asia. The continued credibility of the guarantees embodied in those alliances is an important determinant of the future of proliferation in those regions.

Security assurances are another type of policy intended to reassure and deter. Such assurances may be offered formally but not as guarantees, as in the case of

---

94   George Quester and Victor Utgoff, "U.S. Arms Reductions and Nuclear Nonproliferation: The Counterproductive Possibilities," *The Washington Quarterly*, Vol. 16, No. 1 (Winter 1993), pp. 129–140. Patrick J. Garrity and Steven A. Maaranen, eds., *Nuclear Weapons in the Changing World: Perspectives from Europe, Asia, and North America* (New York, N.Y.: Plenum Press for the Center for National Security Studies at the Los Alamos National Laboratory, 1992).

95   Dean Wilkening and Kenneth Watman, *Deterring Nuclear Threats From Regional Adversaries*, DRR–544/2–A/AF (Santa Monica, Calif.: RAND, February 1994).

those given to Ukraine in exchange for its commitment to join the NPT as a non-nuclear-weapon state. Or they may be offered in the context of a joint declaration, such as that of the nuclear-weapon states not to use those weapons against non-nuclear-weapon states. Guarantees may also be extended but not taken as sufficiently credible, as in the case of U.S. guarantees to Israel.

Moreover, for those states that face uncertainty in the form of doubts about long-term trends but not a strong immediate security threat, some reassurance is probably also derived from deepening patterns of economic cooperation and political dialogue, such that strong relationships are built with other states, especially influential ones within the region or beyond.

The focus of this analysis is on collective security. The future credibility of collective security is one of the core issues raised by weapons proliferation, as noted in chapter 4.

Collective Security After the Cold War. Collective security had its genesis in the effort to solve the problem created by militarily ambitious states in an anarchic international system, that is, one lacking a central authority. Conceived, crafted, and recrafted by diplomats during the first half of the twentieth century, it represents a conscious rejection of the balance of power approach to interstate relations and historically has operated in tension with it. Collective security depends on "a preponderance of power wielded by a combination of states acting as agents of international society as a whole that will deter challenges to the system or deal with them if they occur."[96] It reflects a reliance on armed responses to aggression as the ultimate recourse of the international community to the unlawful effects of power.[97] As Inis Claude has argued, collective security is more properly defined as a policy of selective collective reaction:

---

96 Bull, *The Anarchical Society,* p. 239. See also Lincoln P. Bloomfield et al., *Collective Security in a Changing World,* Occasional Paper No. 10 (Providence, R.I.: Thomas J. Watson Jr. Institute for International Studies, Brown University, 1992), p. 9.

97 As Robert Tucker has written, "War—or the meaningful threat of war—has been the only reliable response to undoing the unlawful effects of power, above all in the case of strong states. In the absence of that response, international law could adjust to the new situation, however unlawful its origins, only by recognizing its validity....In a system governed by self-help, rights will tend to be coextensive with power." Robert W. Tucker, *The Inequality of Nations* (New York, N.Y.: Basic Books, 1977), p. 13.

> The choice of selectivity is not altogether reassuring.
> Discrimination among cases is always likely to appear arbitrary,
> inviting charges of double standards, hypocrisy, and invidious
> favoritism....The real choice, however, is not between "sometimes"
> and "always" but between "sometimes" and "never."[98]

The UN Security Council acts as the final arbiter of the use of collective security instruments. With regard to weapons proliferation, it has specific functions under the global treaties as the final recourse for dealing with material and egregious noncompliance with nuclear, chemical, and biological disarmament commitments (under article 39 enforcement measures governed by chapter VII of the Charter and actions undertaken to eliminate threats to the peace).[99] The UN system as a whole—defined as including the Security Council, General Assembly, secretary general, and the organizations formally under control of either the Assembly or the Economic and Social Council and the autonomous specialized agencies—plays a wide variety of roles relevant to proliferation, ranging from articulation of norms and negotiations of mechanisms to compliance enforcement, crisis management, and dialogue about the political content of the proliferation agenda.

Collective security operates not just as a military factor in time of war; indeed, it has operated in this fashion only rarely, as in the effort to expel North Korea from South Korea and Iraq from Kuwait. Ideally it operates to both reassure states at risk of aggression and to deter the instigators of aggression.

The challenge of creating military instruments of policy that offer *credible* reassurance and deterrence requires that nations work together as much as

---

98   Inis L. Claude, Jr., "Collective Security After the Cold War," in Gary L. Guertner, ed., *The Search for Strategy: Politics and Strategic Vision* (Westport, Conn.: Greenwood Press for the Strategic Studies Institute of the U.S. Army War College, 1993), pp. 267–268. See also Inis L. Claude, Jr., "The New International Security Order: Changing Concepts," *Naval War College Review,* Vol. 47, No. 1, Sequence 345 (Winter 1994), pp. 9–17. For a critique of collective security in the post–Cold War era, see Richard Betts, "Systems for Peace or Causes of War: Collective Security, Arms Control, and the New Europe," *International Security,* Vol. 17, No. 1 (Summer 1992).

99   Jonathan Dean, "Expanding the Security Council Role in Blocking the Spread of Nuclear Weapons," in Jonathan Dean and David Koplow, eds., "World Security and Weapons Proliferation," a symposium in *Transnational Law and Contemporary Problems,* Vol. 2, No. 2 (Fall 1992), pp. 587–604.

possible in crafting those instruments. Because the use of military force is today so politicized internationally and among the democratic publics, the threat of armed responses to aggression is likely to be taken as more credible if some collective framework exists to review, endorse, and perhaps execute the operation. It is essential also to alleviate the fear of some states of the developing world that preservation of military instruments for potential conflicts in their regions will nourish the ambitions of the erstwhile colonial powers to make war against or otherwise dominate them.

These functions face a number of significant new challenges in the 1990s, including the following. First, the UN finds itself badly overextended and underfunded as it has taken on new tasks after the Cold War, especially in the peacekeeping and peacemaking domain; such overextension casts significant doubt on its ability to act collectively to restore security through the remainder of the decade.[100]

Second, there is a growing awareness of the important distinctions between the use of force to defeat an enemy on the battlefield and the use of force to intervene in response to instability. The latter use is intended to bring about political changes that lead to regime transformation and a fundamental reorientation toward armaments and international security. This awareness raises further doubt about the use of UN-led forces to deal with proliferation-related threats to the peace for anything other than short-term deproliferation through preemptive elimination.[101]

---

100 Thomas G. Weiss and Meryl A. Kessler, eds., *Third World Security in the Post–Cold War Era* (Boulder, Colo.: Lynne Rienner Publishers, 1991). See also Weiss, "Intervention: Whither the United Nations?" *The Washington Quarterly*, Vol. 17, No. 1 (Winter 1994), pp. 109–128; and Gene M. Lyons, "A New Collective Security: The United Nations and International Peace," *The Washington Quarterly*, Vol. 17, No. 2 (Spring 1994), pp. 173–199.

101 See Ariel E. Levite, Bruce W. Jentleson, and Larry Berman, eds., *Foreign Military Intervention: The Dynamics of Protracted Conflict* (New York, N.Y.: Columbia University Press, 1992), especially their concluding chapter, "Foreign Military Intervention in Perspective," pp. 301–325. "The utility of any policy instrument (military, foreign, or domestic) to achieve an objective does not necessarily imply its utility for the achieving of some other and very different objective...there is a fundamental different in the nature of the central objectives to be achieved through classical warfare (defeat of the armed forces of an adversary) and through foreign military intervention (remake the internal political order of another state)" (p. 308).

Third, in the societies of many leading members of the Security Council there is a profound rejection of the military instrument of policy, what some have termed not mere pacifism but the comprehensive debellicization of Western societies. As argued above, proliferation reinforces the public perception of risk associated with the use of force abroad. Such societal divisions about using force in support of collective goals may impair the ability of the UN to react even to clear threats to the peace and may actually embolden ambitious hegemons, as appears to have been the case with Saddam Hussein.

The chief challenge, however, to collective security relates to the growing tension within the UN on questions of international peace and security, a tension manifest in the competing authority of an assertive Security Council, a secretary general capable of action independent of the Council, and a General Assembly eager not to have its participatory roles coopted by the Council. Proliferation is deepening these tensions. As Carpenter has argued,

> If the Security Council arrogates to itself the right to judge these matters, the fact that the five permanent members are also the five openly declared nuclear weapons states is not going to be lost on nations seeking to acquire such weapons. From their perspective it will be the verdict of a kangaroo court, however much the Council might invoke noble sounding principles, and the United States, as the leader of an international program of coercive non-proliferation, would be the principal target of their wrath.[102]

Of special concern at the UN after the collapse of the Soviet Union is the possibility that the United States may misuse its newfound status as the sole remaining superpower, in Mohammed Ayoob's words, "to extend the duration of its unipolar moment by persuading the international community to underwrite a world order largely manufactured in Washington principally to serve US interests. In other words, it could be seen as an exercise in promoting US hegemony under UN auspices."[103] Ayoob goes on to argue that:

---

102 Carpenter, "New Proliferation Policy," p. 68. See also Jose E. Alvarez, "The Once and Future Security Council," *The Washington Quarterly*, Vol. 18, No. 2 (Spring 1995), pp. 5–22.

103 Mohammed Ayoob, "Squaring the Circle: Collective Security in a System of States," in Weiss, *Collective Security in a Changing World*, p. 52.

> If a major power was able to appropriate the authority to define
> the content of collective security on behalf of the international
> community and to implement its military strategy without any
> supervision (let alone control) on the part of the UN, then the
> question arises whether it is possible to make the idea of collective
> security successfully operational in an international context marked
> by both tremendous inequalities in the distribution of power and
> the total concentration of military and political decisionmaking at
> the national level. The answer has to be negative.[104]

Differences of opinion on these issues, and a failure to restore some coherence
to the international community's thinking about collective security, may coalesce
to significantly impair the ability of the UN to act in support of that security. On
the Security Council itself, differences of opinion may become more pronounced.
Russia's tenuous support of U.S. and Western policy initiatives in the Council
may not survive the turmoil associated with the post-Soviet transformation.
China's traditional defense of the sovereignty of weak states combined with its
own deep, historical uncertainty about whether to participate in or isolate itself
from global affairs casts doubt on its active support of collective security
functions.[105] Widening Security Council membership, while desirable in terms of
deepening the stake of other major powers in the functioning of the UN, also
casts doubt on the ability to create an ever wider consensus on the use of force in
diplomacy, especially if those new members find the use of force antithetical or
sharply contest the distribution of power and authority embodied in the UN
structure, and especially in the Security Council.

At issue today is how the international community will negotiate a new
bargain about this distribution of power and authority to find mutual
accommodation on an uneven distribution that to some looks like the
"hegemony of the Five"[106] permanent members of the Security Council or the
hegemony of the one, the United States. The Charter can be understood after all

---

104 Ibid., p. 54.

105 R. Bates Gill, *Chinese Arms Transfers: Purposes, Patterns, and Prospects in the New World Order*
   (Westport, Conn.: Praeger, 1992), pp. 8–11, 187.

106 Lincoln P. Bloomfield et al., *Collective Security in a Changing World*, p. 26.

as reflecting the post–World War II balance of power and order. It is not surprising that, with the passing of the superpower era and the rising power and weight of powers not represented among the permanent members of the Security Council, there is a growing resentment of the special responsibilities and privileges reserved by the great powers and a desire to update the UN for a world now half a century removed from its founding. As Avi Beker has observed:

> The Charter is to a very large extent a multilateral treaty dedicated to maintain the status quo of the postwar international order and balance of power. In providing special responsibilities and privileges to the great powers, the Charter exempts them from some of the restrictions upon sovereignty that ordinary states theoretically accepted in ratifying it.[107]

A UN empowered again to act on behalf of the global good will require more than a resolution of this particular political problem, however. The passing of the Cold War has revealed an institution confronting profound political problems. As Rosemary Righter has argued:

> A genuine revival of the UN would imply the successful addressing of a wide array of deeply embedded institutional ills, putting the UN organizations on a soundly managed basis and rendering them properly accountable. There are political diseases to be cured too; debates that have only the most tenuous grip on reality, manufactured confrontations, absurdly swollen agendas. Beyond that, purely governmental clubs that have habitually treated voluntary organizations with disdain, and commerce with hostility, have the smell of decay in a world where events are increasingly shaped by forces outside government. The UN, finally, has to learn to weave itself a place in the modern textures of multilateral cooperation, which are far richer and more complex than could have been envisaged in 1945....the UN has reached a watershed, and that is why the changed political conditions of the 1990s will not

---

107 Avi Beker, *Disarmament Without Order: The Politics of Disarmament at the United Nations* (Westport, Conn.: Greenwood Press, 1985), p. 89.

alone guarantee the future of the massively complicated global enterprise the UN has become.[108]

The full range of measures that might be considered to strengthen the collective security functions of the international community is a large subject beyond the scope of this inquiry.[109] With regard specifically to the proliferation aspects of this problem, a number of priorities stand out. First, in anticipation of that time when a collective security operation of the UN faces the threat of nuclear use by the state being coerced, some degree of preparation would be useful, covering not just joint declaratory statements by the nuclear members of the Council but some broader understanding of the implications of nuclear use.[110] Second, the Security Council must attend not only to deterring the spread of nuclear and other weapons by the threat of sanction but should also remember the task of inducing nonproliferation by the promise of security. Third, the many limitations of the UN point to the desirability of increasing the capacity of regional collective security organizations.[111]

Counterproliferation and International Security. The credibility of the UN's willingness to use force in support of collective security is also held hostage to the military competence of the major powers on the Security Council. If it is believed that the permanent members of the Security Council face special proliferation-related military vulnerabilities and thus might not choose to act in time of need, few will be either reassured or deterred, whatever mandate is delivered by the UN.

Proliferation poses a number of generic challenges for military planners in countries dispensing armed forces on behalf of collective security operations. The most basic challenge is establishing the ability of military forces to carry out their designated missions in an increasingly sophisticated threat environment,

---

108 Rosemary Righter, *Utopia Lost: The United Nations and World Order* (New York, N.Y.: Twentieth Century Fund Press, 1995), pp. 4–5, 16.

109 Lyons, "A New Collective Security: The United Nations and International Peace."

110 George H. Quester and Victor A. Utgoff, "No-First-Use and Nonproliferation: Redefining Extended Deterrence," *The Washington Quarterly*, Vol. 17, No. 2 (Spring 1994), pp. 103–114.

111 Farer, "The Role of Regional Collective Security Arrangements," in Weiss, *Collective Security in a Changing World*, pp. 153–186.

one that offers especially the growing specter of attack by unconventional weapons. Development of a capability to fight for an extended period in an environment contaminated by chemical and/or biological weapons has never been a high priority for the advanced military powers (with the exception of the Soviet Union, now Russia) but it should become one if they expect to deter the use of such weapons by those possessing them in the developing world.

The character and requirements of nuclear contingencies in North–South conflict have hardly begun to command attention.[112] A 1984 study on military preparations required by the proliferation of small nuclear forces noted the following as important:

> protective gear and equipment hardening, appropriate tactical doctrine, and conditioning personnel to protect themselves against nuclear effects. But also important are the mobility, firepower, operational software, and military intelligence requirements of adequate force protection during high-intensity operations under nuclear conditions. The first set of elements relates more to passive defense against small nuclear forces, while the second set implies active or preemptive defense.[113]

A decade later, these questions have become much more complicated with the military build-down and pattern of nuclear deemphasis prevailing after the Cold War. For each of the nuclear-weapon states there are critical questions today about how far to go in reducing the nuclear overhang of the Cold War and about how proliferation interests influence those decisions. The NPT reflects a certain way of thinking on these questions, to the effect that nuclear reductions and disarmament could make a significant impact on limiting nuclear weapons proliferation by establishing a more equitable balance of power.[114] Russia and the

---

112 There have been some important exceptions. See Roger C. Molander and Peter A. Wilson, *The Nuclear Asymptote: On Containing Nuclear Proliferation* (Santa Monica, Calif.: RAND/UCLA Center for Soviet Studies, 1993).

113 Rodney W. Jones, *Small Nuclear Forces* (New York, N.Y.: Praeger with the Center for Strategic and International Studies, 1984), p. 120.

114 Dunn, *Containing Nuclear Proliferation*, p. 70. See also Washington Council on Non-Proliferation, *Nuclear Arms Control: The U.S. and India*, A Report of the Study Group on U.S. Policy Options for

United States have charted a course of deep reductions under bilateral agreements, which presumably will be reinforced by the denuclearization of Ukraine. The other nuclear-weapon states—France, Britain, and China—look at proliferation rather differently, as a reason not to rush into reductions and disarmament, although pressure on them to participate in the nuclear build-down after the Cold War is likely to increase.[115]

As Lawrence Freedman has observed, "[Nuclear] weapons have ceased to serve as active instruments of strategy."[116] Post–Cold War nuclear deemphasis has caused questions about whether or not a nuclear-weapons-free world is possible or desirable to reemerge after decades of neglect, and they are likely to be much debated for what they have to say about the credibility of the great powers to use force in the face of blackmail by lesser powers and of the institution of collective security.[117] This fact has also given rise to a debate about whether extended deterrence and actual punishment of aggression can be secured through reliance on conventional weapons alone or still requires the threat of a nuclear component.[118] Among the nuclear-weapon states this also generates concerns

---

Constraining Proliferation in South Asia, Working Paper No. 2 (Washington, D.C.: Washington Council on Non-Proliferation, May 1993).

115 John C. Hopkins and Weixing Hu, eds., *Strategic Views from the Second Tier: The Nuclear Weapons Policies of France, Britain, and China* (La Jolla, Calif.: University of California Institute on Global Conflict and Cooperation, 1994).

116 Freedman, "Foreword," Garrity and Maaranen, *Nuclear Weapons in the Changing World*, p. x.

117 Joseph Rotblat, Jack Steinberger, and Bhalchandra Udgaonkar, eds., and Frank Blackaby, executive ed., *A Nuclear-Weapon-Free World: Desirable? Feasible?* (Boulder, Colo.: Westview Press, 1993); Barry M. Blechman and Cathleen S. Fisher, "Phase Out the Bomb," *Foreign Policy*, No. 97 (Winter 1994/95), pp. 79–95; Seth Cropsey, "The Only Credible Deterrent," *Foreign Affairs*, Vol. 73, No. 2 (March/April 1994), pp. 14–20; Michael McGwire, "Is There a Future for Nuclear Weapons?" *International Affairs*, Vol. 70, No. 2 (1994), pp. 211–228; Wolfgang K. H. Panofsky and George Bunn, "The Doctrine of the Nuclear-Weapon-States and the Future of Non-Proliferation," *Arms Control Today*, July/August 1994, pp. 3–9; Quester and Utgoff, "U.S. Arms Reductions and Nuclear Nonproliferation: The Counterproductive Possibilities," pp. 129–140; and Michael Quinlan, "The Future of Nuclear Weapons: Policy for Western Possessors?" *International Affairs*, Vol. 69, No. 3 (1993), pp. 485–596.

118 Gary L. Guertner, "Deterrence and Conventional Military Forces," *The Washington Quarterly*, Vol. 16, No. 1 (Winter 1993), pp. 141–152; Marc Dean Millot, "Facing the Emerging Reality of Regional Nuclear Adversaries," *The Washington Quarterly*, Vol. 17, No. 3 (Summer 1994), pp. 41–71; and Charles T. Allan, "Extended Conventional Deterrence: In from the Cold and Out of

about how to maintain the skills necessary for sustained nuclear competence when nuclear weapons remain but are essentially at the margins of the international system.[119]

Defensive preparations are useful for helping to narrow the range of conventional weaponry that will have strategic applications against the military forces of advanced countries. For example, theater ballistic or cruise missiles will have diminished military salience if effective theater missile defenses can be deployed. Shallow-water submarine forces will be deprived of their surprise attack capabilities if guarantor militaries master the art of shallow-water anti-submarine warfare (deep-water tactics having been the focus of Cold War concern).[120] The reassurance and deterrence functions of military preparations put a premium on forces that are sufficiently visible or ready to be immediately available in time of crisis but not so visible as to provoke overmatching responses or preemptive strikes against them.

In a more general sense, in a world in which weapons of significant strategic leverage are proliferating, military forces must be crafted in such a way that they can be used quickly at long range and with minimal collateral damage—especially in terms of civilian casualties—while maintaining control of the escalation process and minimizing repercussions within and beyond the region of use. Because such forces are often likely to be outnumbered on the battlefield (and because there will always be a political premium on keeping casualties among guarantor forces to an absolute minimum), there will also be a premium on extremely high kill ratios through technological superiority. The very high cost of building and maintaining large, mobile, and cutting edge technology weapons suggests that the advanced countries will have a difficult time sustaining such a conventional deterrent force and will fall back, as they did in the Cold War, on the supposed leverage found in nuclear weapons.

---

the Nuclear Fire?" *The Washington Quarterly*, Vol. 17, No. 3 (Summer 1994), pp. 203–233.

119 Nuclear stockpile stewardship supports a variety of missions: to survey and maintain the stockpile of weapons, retain and replenish weapons expertise, support assessment of proliferation and changing military threats, assure safe dismantlement, provide adequate capability for remanufacture and/or replacement, provide capability for limited technology options, and provide a credible basis for reconstitution.

120 Henry D. Sokolski, "Nonapocalyptic Proliferation," *The Washington Quarterly*, Vol. 17, No. 2 (Spring 1994), pp. 115–128.

These planning parameters are relevant to any state planning to use military forces in regions where weapons have proliferated and to international organizations such as the UN that might marshal those forces. But they are particularly germane to the United States, given its key role as security guarantor in Europe, the Middle East, and East Asia and the salience of its preponderance of military power in the collective security functions of the UN. Only a few advanced militaries have the capacity to conduct theaterwide operations and to employ sophisticated strike-complex systems with high-precision weapons over extended periods so as to meet the criteria of decisive effect with minimal collateral damage. Fewer yet possess the nuclear weapons that might be necessary in a confrontation with a nuclear-armed aggressor state bent on rewriting regional borders or conducting a holy war against the developed world.

But in the United States, little thought was given to the military requirements created by weapons proliferation during the Cold War. For the United States and its militarily advanced European allies, the military capabilities of regional states generally were conceived as a "lesser-included" threats, for which Western forces were deemed adequately prepared by virtue of their preparation for East–West conflict.[121] With the end of the Cold War and the wake-up call in the Persian Gulf War, U.S. military planners have begun to take seriously the special tasks of coping militarily with the consequences of weapons proliferation. Their efforts have coalesced in a counterproliferation initiative emphasizing protection against proliferation's effects, as well as some prevention.[122] This strategy was presented at a briefing by then Secretary of Defense Les Aspin on December 7, 1993. Figure

---

121 But their ability to plan for regional contingencies was significantly constrained by the fear of diverting forces that might be needed in East-West confrontation at exactly those moments of insecurity generated by regional crises. Commission on Integrated Long-Term Strategy, *Discriminate Deterrence*, (Washington, D.C.: GPO, January 1988).

122 The counterproliferation strategy was presented by Secretary of Defense Les Aspin to a public meeting of the National Academy of Sciences on December 7, 1993. For further discussion, see Thomas W. Lippman, "If Nonproliferation Fails, Pentagon Wants 'Counterproliferation' in Place," *Washington Post*, May 15, 1994, p. A–11; Joseph F. Pilat and Walter L. Kirchner, "The Technological Promise of Counterproliferation," *The Washington Quarterly*, Vol. 18, No. 1 (Winter 1995), pp. 153–166; Michael Rühle, "NATO and the Coming Proliferation Threat," *Comparative Strategy*, Vol. 13, No. 3 (July–September 1994), pp. 313–320; and Jennifer Sims, "The Intelligence Requirements for Nonproliferation Policy," in Wander and Arnett, *The Proliferation of Advanced Weaponry*, pp. 271–281.

Figure 5–1
Responding to the Proliferation Threat

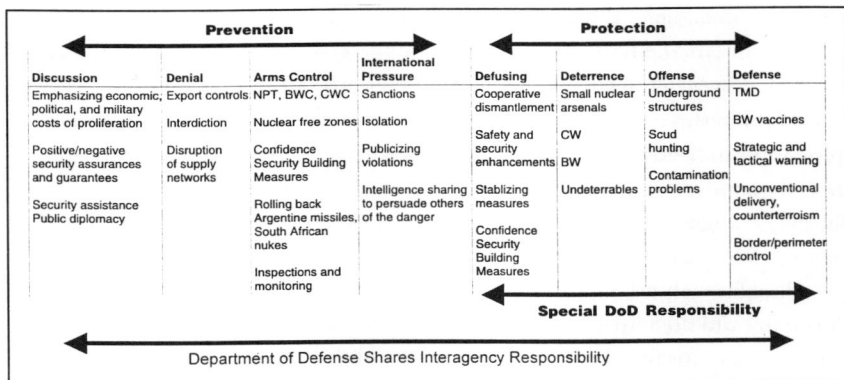

Prevention				Protection			
Discussion	Denial	Arms Control	International Pressure	Defusing	Deterrence	Offense	Defense
Emphasizing economic, political, and military costs of proliferation	Export controls	NPT, BWC, CWC	Sanctions	Cooperative dismantlement	Small nuclear arsenals	Underground structures	TMD
Positive/negative security assurances and guarantees	Interdiction	Nuclear free zones	Isolation	Safety and security enhancements	CW	Scud hunting	BW vaccines
Security assistance Public diplomacy	Disruption of supply networks	Confidence Security Building Measures	Publicizing violations	Stablizing measures	BW	Contamination problems	Strategic and tactical warning
		Rolling back Argentine missiles, South African nukes	Intelligence sharing to persuade others of the danger		Undeterrables		Unconventional delivery, counterterrorism
		Inspections and monitoring		Confidence Security Building Measures			Border/perimeter control

Special DoD Responsibility

Department of Defense Shares Interagency Responsibility

Source: Annual Report to the President and the Congress, Les Aspin, Secretary of Defense, 1994.

5-1 is the chart used by the secretary to define the purview of the strategy. Deputy Secretary of Defense John M. Deutch subsequently identified 14 priority areas of technology development requiring approximately $400 million per year in defense expenditures.[123] This strategy is a prudent departure from the neglect of the past. But military planning alone cannot serve as a substitute for a broader antiproliferation strategy combining political, economic, and military elements. Yet evidence suggests that counterproliferation is conceived by many to be just that.[124] As discussed further below, counterproliferation may well prove counterproductive to its intended goal.

---

123 U.S. Department of Defense, *Report on Nonproliferation and Counterproliferation Activities and Programs* (Washington, D.C.: Office of the Deputy Secretary of Defense, May 1994). The report identified existing (fiscal year 1994) funding of approximately $1 billion for programs that are unique to non- and counterproliferation and another $3 billion for programs that are strongly related.

124 Harald Müller and Mitchell Reiss, "Counterproliferation: Putting New Wine in Old Bottles," *The Washington Quarterly*, Vol. 18, No. 2 (Spring 1995), pp. 143–154. See also Reiss and Müller, eds., *International Perspectives on Counterproliferation*, Working Paper 99, (Washington, D.C.: Division of International Studies, Woodrow Wilson Center for Scholars, January 1995).

In this discussion of the future military competence of the underwriters of collective security, it is important to take note of a current of thought to the effect that the capacity of the great powers to intervene unilaterally should be narrowly circumscribed if not forsworn or eliminated. Prior to his appointment as Bill Clinton's secretary of defense, William Perry, for example, argued that U.S. forces should be redefined so that they would best be used in cooperation with others—for the specific purpose of both bolstering deterrence of potential aggressors by underscoring the indivisibility of the guaranteeing states and of strengthening reassurance that no state would be threatened by a larger military establishment seeking unilateral advantage.[125] Former Secretary of Defense Robert S. McNamara has called for the great powers to renounce unilateral action in dealing with regional conflicts.[126]

To underscore the importance of collective security in the overall antiproliferation strategy is not also to offer it as a panacea. Its limitations are obvious. But so, too, are the consequences of reverting to an international system in which collective security does not operate as a factor.

There will, of course, be times when collective deliberation in an international forum will act as a brake on collective action rather than its generator. In such instances, states will have to decide whether their national interests are sufficiently at risk to warrant unilateral action. For the permanent members of the Security Council, as for many other states, some capacity to act unilaterally is certain to remain. Arguably, this is also necessary and useful in a time when collective security is not guaranteed, only held out as a possibility, as a promise to be made real if circumstances warrant. So long as these states define their interests in collective terms and so long as their independent action serves purposes other than those of aggrandizement or aggression, their friends and allies will benefit from their continued if limited autonomy.

It is essential not to misjudge the scale or character of the collective security challenge after the Cold War. Only on the Korean peninsula and in the Middle

---

125 William J. Perry, "Military Action: When to Use It and How to Ensure Its Effectiveness," in Nolan, *Global Engagement*, pp. 235–242.

126 Robert S. McNamara, "The Post–Cold War World and Its Implications for Military Expenditures in the Developing Countries," in Brian Urquhart and Robert S. McNamara, *Toward Collective Security: Two Views*, Occasional Paper No. 5 (Providence, R.I.: Thomas J. Watson Jr. Institute for International Studies, Brown University, 1991), pp. 21–42.

East do interstate wars of aggression or annihilation appear even remotely possible. These are problems of deterrence (and reassurance) for which bilateral U.S. relationships play an equally if not more important role than the vague promises of collective security. The potential for collective response must remain as an operative concern for those contemplating aggression, even if its certainty is not guaranteed. It is important to tend to its credibility but not to mistake it for fully addressing the security dilemma of states in the post–Cold War era, most of which find themselves not threatened by an aggressive neighbor but simply confronting uncertainty and long-term trends of questionable impact.

For this security concern, other security strategies, such as comprehensive and cooperative security, are germane. The question today is not which strategy is best but how to proceed with a broad mix of security strategies that deepen the security of states of different orientations and capacities. Comprehensive security, as noted earlier, focuses on those elements of political and economic community that deepen the sense of stability and security among nations. Cooperative security has a somewhat different orientation. Ashton B. Carter, William J. Perry, and John D. Steinbruner describe it as follows.

> The new threats cannot be met solely with readiness and deterrence. The new security problems require more constructive and more sophisticated forms of influence that concentrate more on the initial preparation of military forces than on the final decisions to use them....The appropriate principle for dealing with these new security problems is that of cooperative engagement—in essence a commitment to regulate the size, technical composition, investment patterns, and operational practices of all military forces by consent for mutual benefit....Cooperative security is designed to ensure that organized aggression cannot start on any large scale. Collective security, however, is an arrangement for deterring aggression through counterthreat and defeating it if it occurs.[127]

Antonia and Abram Chayes put it somewhat differently:

---

127 Ashton B. Carter, William J. Perry, John D. Steinbruner, *A New Concept of Cooperative Security*, Occasional Paper (Washington, D.C.: Brookings Institution, 1992), pp. 6–7.

The central strategic problem for a cooperative security regime is not deterrence, as in the Cold War, but reassurance. For deterrence to be effective, the actors must be convinced that any attack will be met by a response sufficient to erase any potential gains by the aggressor. In a cooperative security system, by contrast, the actors must have confidence that the other participants are abiding by the applicable restrictions on force structures and capabilities. Unlike deterrence, which relies on strategic interactions between opposed states, the key to reassurance is a reliable normative and institutional structure.[128]

Strategies of cooperative and comprehensive security merit new prominence at a time when proliferation is creating new incentives for states to move to new forms of cooperative behavior and when a globalization of economic and political values is deepening the sense of community among peoples. If these strategies are successful, they will further marginalize those instances where collective security must work.

Diplomacy: The Linchpin

The policy agenda discussed so far underscores the expanding nature of the proliferation challenge in the post–Cold War era, when action is required on a broad array of political, military, and economic fronts. If this agenda is to be carried forward, it must be supported by a substantial diplomatic commitment. A much more activist diplomacy is necessary, starting with the United States but ranging far and wide.

That diplomacy ought to reflect an integration of proliferation concerns into the patterns of relations among states and groupings of states, so that proliferation interests are not merely an adjunct to the large pattern of diplomatic activity. It ought also to reflect a sustained effort to deepen coordination among states on antiproliferation through a careful manipulation of the new incentives for cooperation described in earlier chapters. Three different categories of states merit specialized strategies.

---

128 Antonia Handler Chayes and Abram Chayes, "Regime Architecture: Elements and Principles," in Nolan, *Global Engagement,* p. 65.

The Weapons-Disinterested States. One category of states consists of those most frequently overlooked in the diplomacy of proliferation—those countries with no interest in acquiring weapons of mass destruction or engaging in arms races with neighbors. This group constitutes in fact the majority of countries of the world—witness the absence of significant armaments competition in Latin America and Africa, for example.

These countries should be a focus of diplomatic energy for two reasons. First, they are the recipients and conduits of militarily sensitive technologies. Advanced technology flows to many of these countries from the technologically advanced world, and it is frequently reexported to countries that pose serious proliferation threats. Second, they must be active in the promulgation of international norms about weapons and war and the functioning of the multilateral regimes reflecting those norms. Without such participation, the international political consensus in support of antiproliferation and arms control enforcement will be limited to a few countries, mostly those of the developed world.

Among this category of states are two especially important subcategories whose practices and strategic orientations deserve broader understanding. The first consists of those states that have prospered even in an insecure international environment without resort to armaments programs; Costa Rica is perhaps the best example here. The second consists of the "repentant proliferants,"[129] those states that have abandoned strategic weapons or their development programs after lengthy debate about what national options best serve the national interest; South Africa, Argentina, Brazil, Ukraine, Belarus, and Kazakhstan are perhaps the prime examples here. The international community should not miss the opportunity to hold these states up as models. The creative and forceful diplomacy shown by many of these states at the NPT extension conference, where they played a valuable role in building the consensus for extension, is indicative of the type of role that such states might play more generally in post–Cold War world politics. Greater study of the domestic determinants of their policies and of the lessons for others could make a significant contribution to an understanding of the proliferation subject.

---

129 Leonard S. Spector, "Repentant Nuclear Proliferants," *Foreign Policy*, No. 88 (Fall 1992), pp. 3–20.

The Weapons-Committed State. The second category consists of those states unwilling to relinquish major armaments or development programs. The historical tendency to view all proliferation in negative terms results in a complementary tendency to lump all such recalcitrant states into a single category, branded with the name renegade.[130] They are then treated to a general strategy of ostracism and deterrence. In fact, specialized strategies must be crafted for each.[131]

Circumstances in which weapons combine with national ambitions to constitute a tangible and significant threat to international security pose challenges different from those in which proliferant states are essentially defensive in their strategic orientations. When the threat of war appears high, aggressive states might be turned into pariahs, as with North Korea.

The diplomatic instrument best suited to isolating states is the economic sanction. Sanctions have a mixed reputation. Historically, they have not worked as well as their advocates have hoped, largely because few governments have been prepared to sacrifice short-term national interests over a sustained period of time for long-term goals and the punishment of wrongdoing that does not also appear to present a threat of imminent war. By 1994, the UN had mandated sanctions six times: against Rhodesia in 1966, South Africa in 1977 (an arms embargo), Iraq in 1990, Libya in 1992, Yugoslavia in 1992, and Haiti in 1993. In no instance did such sanctions have the immediately desired effect of curtailing behavior deemed unacceptable by the international community. They are sometimes necessary largely for purposes of domestic politics in the sanctioning countries, however, as a way to demonstrate resolve and to act when public opinion demands it.[132] Nevertheless, sanctions sometimes backfire, helping leaders of targeted states to generate support for the regime and opposition to the sanctioning states,

---

130 Anthony Lake, "Confronting Backlash States," *Foreign Affairs*, Vol. 73, No. 2 (March/April 1994), pp. 45–55.

131 For the argument that there are increasing benefits to be reaped from tailoring policy to specific proliferation cases, see William C. Potter, "On Nuclear Proliferation," in Edward A. Kolodziej and Patrick M. Morgan, eds., *Security and Arms Control*, Vol. 2, *A Guide to International Policymaking* (New York, N.Y.: Greenwood Press, 1989), pp. 319–355.

132 Margaret P. Doxey, *International Sanctions in Contemporary Perspective* (New York, N.Y.: St. Martin's Press, 1987), pp. 143–144.

although this is an advantage that seems to accrue more in authoritarian states than democratic ones.[133]

On the other hand, the end of the Cold War has increased the room for maneuver of the international community in isolating such states, now that these states no longer enjoy the ability to play one side off against the other. An increasingly global economy and the transparency of economic activity have also strengthened the hand of the international community.[134] In the case of Iran, for example, the chief form of leverage enjoyed by the international community over the future of Iranian nuclear programs is the huge debt Iran owes to other countries. The United States holds approximately $12 billion in Iranian debt, which has given the Department of the Treasury an unprecedented nonproliferation role.

This potential leverage is suggested by those sanctions that have had an effect. Sanctions pursued by certain coalitions of nations against Libya, Cuba, and North Korea have had a clear long-term effect on the economic standing of those countries. Unilateral sanctions targeted under U.S. law against individual firms trading in banned items used for chemical and biological warfare purposes have proven highly effective in halting such trade. The sanctions subject is yet another that deserves a broad reassessment in the 1990s. Many of the assumptions about sanctions derive from experience in an international context now past. Where sanctions have not worked, it is important to understand why and how they did not work, or in what ways or phases they may have been quite significant. A case in point can be found in Iraq, where sanctions failed to compel Saddam Hussein to abandon his annexation of Kuwait but where for at least four years since the war, sanctions have moderated the behavior of his regime on some issues of key interest to the coalition that defeated him, such as the disposition of Iraq's weapons development programs.

Not all states unwilling to relinquish their weapons can be treated as renegades, however, because not all such states have aggressive purposes or

---

133 Etel Solingen, *The Domestic Sources of Nuclear Postures: Influencing "Fence-sitters" in the Post–Cold War Era,* Policy Paper No. 8 (La Jolla, Calif.: Institute on Global Conflict and Cooperation, University of California, October 1994). See also Solingen, "The Political Economy of Nuclear Restraint," *International Security,* Vol. 19, No. 2 (Fall 1994), pp. 126–169.

134 Chayes and Chayes, "Regime Architecture," pp. 65–130; and Reinicke, "Cooperative Security and the Political Economy of Nonproliferation," pp. 175–234.

object to the status quo. If Israel, for example, chooses to retain its nuclear weapons for an interim period while the peace process takes root, it can hardly be treated in the same fashion as a country seeking weapons for purposes of hegemony or aggrandizement. Where the threat of war is low because the motives are defensive, selective engagement might be more appropriate.[135] Such a strategy could pay dividends in rewarding positive behavior, as arguably in the cases of South Africa and China. It might also stimulate some movement toward political change. But the history of the Western effort to reach out to Iraqi leadership in the 1980s in the hope of balancing Iranian influence while also moderating Iraqi ambitions illustrates the folly of a policy of selective engagement wrongly pursued.

It is noteworthy that many of the states of most concern in the weapons proliferation area—Iraq, North Korea, Cuba, Syria, and, arguably, China—are led by an individual or cadre of leaders not likely long to survive. Their successors may well opt to take some steps, modest in some cases and considerable in others, to rejoin the international community.

The Contingent Proliferator. The third category of states consists of those in the middle—those with weapons or weapons development programs but with strategic purposes that fall outside the category of immediate national survival or aggression. This category may include states with ambitious weapons development programs as well as those that have paused at certain thresholds related to weaponization, serial production, or declaratory policy and that face new questions about the continued evolution of national military capabilities. The future of their weapons programs depends fundamentally on choices made by national leaders and thus is contingent on political perceptions and external factors.

The diplomatic strategies best suited to this category of states are those that look for solutions to the security problems that give rise to the proliferation concern. This requires a level of political commitment by friendly powers to

---

135 For a discussion of ways to integrate nonproliferation concerns into a broader diplomatic engagement with Iran, see Geoffrey Kemp, *Forever Enemies? American Policy and the Islamic Republic of Iran* (Washington, D.C.: Carnegie Endowment, 1994), and with India, see Selig S. Harrison and Geoffrey Kemp, *India and America After the Cold War* (Washington, D.C.: Carnegie Endowment for International Peace, 1993).

addressing security problems that goes well beyond the traditional rhetorical commitment to regional peace. As noted earlier, in the Middle East and in South and East Asia, changing perceptions brought by the end of the Cold War, the Persian Gulf War, and by the proliferation process itself have generated interest in new approaches to insecurity. Dialogues have sprung up in each region, of varying degrees of intensity and seriousness, about regional peacemaking and security. They have also brought into focus the varying degrees of readiness or urgency to begin more cooperative approaches to common problems.

What can diplomacy do in support of this dialogue? Historically, the role of the international community in support of regional security has been largely to grant or deny security assurances or guarantees to insecure states. In some instances, these have worked to prevent or forestall proliferation, as in the cases of Germany, Japan, and South Korea. An unwillingness to extend special security guarantees to some states has contributed to their decisions to acquire nuclear weapons capabilities, as in Israel[136] and Pakistan,[137] for example. The declining credibility of superpower guarantees has in the past contributed to proliferation, as in South Korea after U.S. withdrawal from Southeast Asia, as did doubts that alliance guarantees would cater sufficiently to specifically national security interests, as in the case of France.[138]

As noted earlier, the end of the Cold War is having ambiguous effects on such guarantees. In a certain sense, it would seem to have increased their credibility, because the risks for security guarantors would seem to have declined with the passing of the superpower nuclear confrontation. On the other hand, such guarantees may not enjoy deep public support in the guaranteeing state, where there is substantial uncertainty about the costs of international obligations, and thus might not survive periods of tension. Over the last two centuries the guarantees of large powers to smaller ones have proven to be "clear and adequate" in less than half of the cases.[139] This augurs badly for new security

---

136 Avner Cohen and Marvin Miller, "How to Think About—and Implement—Nuclear Arms Control in the Middle East," *The Washington Quarterly*, Vol. 16, No. 2 (Spring 1993), pp. 101–113.

137 Cheema, "Nuclear Diplomacy in South Asia During the Eighties," pp. 53–66.

138 Snyder, "Weapons Proliferation and the New Security Agenda," p. 268.

139 "The historical examples...prove that at the moment of trial, when the friendly superpower is supposed to meet its commitment—not only to warn and deter, but to come to the small nation's aid—reluctance often outweighs commitment....Of 115 guarantee arrangements signed

guarantees offered solely on the basis of deterring regional proliferants rather than on the basis of deep, shared national interests beyond the nonproliferation ones.

But this hardly exhausts the subject of the leverage of the international community in supporting regional security dialogues and arms control. That community should not underestimate its ability to exploit its economic and political influence to manipulate the balance of incentives and disincentives. Economic aspects have been insufficiently studied. The international financial institutions could play a prominent role here, as suggested in 1989 by the heads of the International Monetary Fund and the World Bank when they began to speak out against imbalances between security spending and development resources. Their initiative resulted in approval in December 1993 by the Development Assistance Committee of the Organization for Economic Cooperation and Development (OECD) of a statement on "Orientations on Participatory Development and Good Governance," which, among other things, "underscores the links between excessive military spending, politically active armed forces and conflict, and outlines specific actions that bilateral aid donors can take to strengthen civilian control over the military and reduce military spending in recipient countries."[140]

Another approach emphasizes bilateral development assistance. The reduction of military expenditures is an objective for which a growing number of donors are willing to make aid conditional. The goal of such conditionality is to condition behavior on adherence to norms without also compromising genuine security interests.[141]

---

since 1815, only 45 (48 percent) were clearly both reliable and adequate." Cohen, *Small Nations in Times of Crisis and Confrontation,* pp. 338–339, citing Alan Dowty, *The Role of Great Power Guarantees in International Peace Agreements* (Jerusalem: Hebrew University, 1974), pp. 15–21.

140 OECD, "DAC Orientations on Participatory Development and Good Governance," OECD/GD (93)191 (OECD, Paris, 1993). For a general discussion see David A. Koplow and Philip G. Schrag, "Linking Disarmament and Development," *SAIS Review,* Vol. 11, No. 2 (Summer/Fall 1991), pp. 95–112.

141 Joan M. Nelson and Stephanie J. Eglinton, *Global Goals, Contentious Means: Issues of Multiple Aid Conditionality,* Policy Essay No. 10 (Washington, D.C.: Overseas Development Council, 1993); Nicole Ball, "Demilitarizing the Third World," in Michael T. Klare and Daniel C. Thomas, *World Security: Challenges for a New Century,* 2d ed. (New York, N.Y.: St. Martin's Press, 1994), pp. 216–235; and Jacques Fontanel and Jean-François Guilhaudis, "Arms Transfer Control and

In the past, well-orchestrated diplomatic campaigns have brought sufficient pressure to bear on some states to lead them to abandon steps in the direction of a nuclear-weapons capability, as in Taiwan and South Korea.[142] In the future, more might be done to build on the self-restraint of states that have halted at certain thresholds in their weapons development programs, perhaps by advertising that restraint and reinforcing its sources.[143] A decision to award new seats on the UN Security Council might also be contingent upon a commitment by candidate states not to acquire or further develop nuclear or mass destruction weapons; the choice between a larger political stake in the system and a larger nuclear weapons program would be especially difficult for India.[144]

More generally, there are new roles for the international community in support of the arms control agenda spelled out above. Influential states have roles as facilitator, monitor, or guarantor of specific measures. This is especially true of the United States, with its extensive political influence, sophisticated verification capabilities, and military strength, which will enable it to cushion some of the risks for states involved in negotiations.

Active diplomacy in support of regional security and arms control measures will sometimes take a back seat to other priorities in bilateral relations. In the Middle East, for example, formal arms control measures can emerge—if they ever do in substantial form—only as a result of successful work on the diplomacy of regional peace, combined with the economics of regional development. In South Asia, the strong nonproliferation interests of the United States have had to reach a compromise with the desire to take advantage of the opportunity afforded by the end of the Cold War to improve relations with India. The challenge, as always in diplomacy, is to integrate new concerns and priorities into the larger fabric of bilateral and multilateral relations.

Proposals to Link Disarmament and Development," in Ohlson, *Arms Transfer Limitations and Third World Security*, pp. 215–226.

142 Lewis Dunn, *Controlling the Bomb* (New Haven, Conn.: Yale University Press, 1982), pp. 110–111.

143 Carnegie Task Force on Non-Proliferation and South Asian Security, *Nuclear Weapons and South Asian Security* (Washington, D.C., Carnegie Endowment for International Peace, 1988), pp. 68–74.

144 Stephen Philip Cohen, "A Way Out of the South Asia Arms Race," *Washington Post*, September 28, 1992.

This discussion of the diplomatic agenda would not be complete without underscoring the antiproliferation value of diplomatic strategies aimed at supporting those long-range trends identified in chapter 3 as relevant to moderating proliferation risks. For example, support for the development of stable democratic processes and institutions in developing countries will pay dividends for antiproliferation.

An Assessment of Progress to 1995

By the mid-point in the 1990s, a decade after the Cold War began to thaw, the efforts of states opposed to proliferation can best be described as piecemeal and incomplete when measured against the foregoing policy agenda.

There are successes of note. The May 1995 decision to extend the NPT indefinitely and unconditionally stands out as one of the most important. Some successes are the work of leaders in the developing world who have sought to build new, more cooperative relations with their neighbors. The peace process in the Middle East, the Argentine-Brazilian nuclear accord, and the regional security dialogue in Southeast Asia all reflect departures in traditional ways of thinking about security for leaders in those regions and a new willingness to take some risks for cooperation rather than just the risks of strategies emphasizing military strength alone. The diplomacy of key outside states and individuals has been important in facilitating these dialogues and working toward the creation of regional security mechanisms with antiproliferation benefits.

Some successes also belong to the crisis managers in Western governments and particularly the United States, who have, by and large, dealt with the proliferation-related crises of recent years with energy and determination. Ukraine's ultimate commitment to the NPT, Iraq's continued supervision by UNSCOM, and the framework agreement with North Korea constitute important milestones toward antiproliferation. Failure on any of those fronts would have cast doubt on the utility of the nuclear nonproliferation regime.

There are other successes as well. Good progress has been made in limiting the proliferation-related consequences of the breakup of the Soviet Union through the process of safe and secure dismantlement. Membership of some of the ad hoc coordinating mechanisms for export controls has expanded. Efforts to tighten controls on excess plutonium have also had positive results.[145] Experts have also made good progress in elaborating a post-CoCom technology control regime, in building the infrastructure of the Chemical Weapons Convention, and in defining compliance mechanisms for the Biological and Toxin Weapons Convention.

But despite these successes, large gaps remain between the needs of policy and performance to date.

With regard to new approaches to technology flow management, a basic defensiveness on the part of the technology-exporting states has played into the arguments of states such as Pakistan and Indonesia that Western states desire to keep the developing world both insecure and poor. They have gained wide sympathy for the argument that the rich are willing to trade off the development aspirations of the poor in order to protect their own security and wealth. Adherents of this viewpoint tend to see the global treaty regime as being about the security interests of the North and the development aspirations of the developing countries. These critics of the traditional strategies of denial are numerous among the states of the newly empowered tier and will be vigilant to prevent greater reliance on export controls and discriminatory measures in the years ahead. Unless the developed countries can begin to perceive and defend export controls as trade-empowering regimes, this corrosive element in North–South relations is likely to grow in importance.

With regard to formalizing restraint, the progress in pursuing regional measures stands in marked contrast to what has happened to the global regime. Only at the beginning of 1995 have major Western governments begun to focus on the political tasks necessary to ensure indefinite and unconditional extension of the NPT in May 1995. The effort to bring the Chemical Weapons Convention into force has languished because of delays in the ratification process.

Especially in the United States, arms control policy has collapsed into disarray at a critical time in the global agenda, with debates about whether arms control has any role at all in the post–Cold War era and whether or not the U.S. Arms Control and Disarmament Agency (ACDA) continues to serve any useful function. Ad hoc approaches have reinforced the view, widespread among U.S. experts today, that proliferation is a problem separate and distinct from arms control. The ad hoc nature of U.S. arms control diplomacy has combined with the seeming inability of senior political leadership in the Clinton administration

---

145 Brian G. Chow and Kenneth A. Solomon, *Limiting the Spread of Weapon-Usable Fissile Materials,* RAND Report MR–346–USDP (Santa Monica, Calif., RAND, 1993).

to articulate the issues involved in preventing proliferation. Nonproliferation is praised as a civic virtue but its value as an instrument of national security for nations other than the United States is rarely noted. This has nurtured a concern among both friends and potential adversaries that the United States is simply going through the motions, unaware of the stakes, unconcerned about the breakdown of existing treaties, and unmindful of the insecurities that might be generated.

With regard to security policy, the picture is even more bleak. The UN is beset by myriad political and economic problems arising from its new peacemaking agenda and its stark failures in some recent collective security operations, as in Bosnia and Somalia. The capacity of the Security Council to act on any but the most tangential of issues is in doubt, given the apparent unwillingness of the major powers to expend national blood and treasure to solve the conflicts of others.

The U.S. counterproliferation policy has aggravated this problem. Designed to sustain the credibility of the threat to use U.S. force and intended to support collective security principles, counterproliferation came instead to be seen as an alternative to nonproliferation, or as a successor. This suggested that the United States was abandoning the nonproliferation effort in the wake of the unsettling discoveries about the weakness of the regime. To many in the developing world, the counterproliferation strategy suggests that the United States intends to make war upon them, perhaps for the very purpose of denuding them of weapons deemed unacceptable by the United States. It suggests to them a United States moving in its unipolar moment to aggressively police rules of its own making. Among friends and allies of the United States are many who are unsure of its actual willingness or ability to perform such a role, given its history as a fickle great power, uncertain of its interests overseas and unwilling to consistently use its power even for stated purposes. Among potential adversaries, the fear of an overarmed and aggressive United States may well have accelerated the search for asymmetric strategies.

With regard to the diplomatic agenda, the record of the major powers is very poor. Again, the problems are most stark in the United States, where post–Cold War diplomacy is widely criticized for its lack of energy and vision and for its crisis-driven agenda. The United States has not been good at multilateral diplomacy, other than in NATO, and has made little progress in this area. Its engagement is in doubt in places where that engagement is a major factor in long-range calculations about the balance of power among great powers—as in the Asia-Pacific and Europe.

The cornerstone of the effort to broaden the global treaty regime is the effort to strengthen the nuclear nonproliferation regime. This is a task that began with the review and extension conference in spring 1995 but continues well beyond that point. The prospects for revitalization of the nuclear regime are uncertain. Its prospects are clouded by a certain hubris among the nuclear states and a certain ambition among some other states.

The hubris has its source in the legacy of global preeminence and the Cold War balance of nuclear terror. It is evident in the inability of the nuclear states to articulate a new post–Cold War vision of a global nuclear order that is both desirable and politically sustainable; instead, they defend nonproliferation as an abstract value shared by civilized peoples but seem to have lost the ability to defend it as a concrete necessity for regional and global security (and not just the security of the nuclear-weapon states). Their failure to propound a new nuclear order effectively cedes the terms of debate to those who cast it in terms of an illegitimate differentiation of rights.

The ambition has its source in opposition to the rigid allocation of status embodied in the NPT's unequal obligations, tied as it was to a distribution of power in the international system at the end of World War II that was codified in the subsequent nuclear realities of the mid-1960s. The ambition is evident in the effort of some states in the developing world, such as Iran, Pakistan, and Algeria, to use the NPT review process to contest the status quo.

The nuclear-weapon states and particularly the United States, as the leading nuclear power with the most far-flung international obligations and entanglements of any major state after the Cold War, must take the lead in articulating and pursuing a vision of international politics and of an allocation of nuclear rights and responsibilities that is politically sustainable in the period ahead—for another 10 or 25 years. There will be many pressures from developing countries to move toward a system of more equal rights and obligations, toward global nuclear disarmament. But the NPT is not itself an instrument of general nuclear disarmament, only a narrowing of differences. Only to the extent that the nuclear powers can make a persuasive case that their retention of nuclear weapons as the sole nuclear-weapon states remains relevant to the solution of new, post–Cold War problems of international security, might some basis for a continued inequality of obligations be sustained.

Prospects

Widespread throughout the Western community of international security specialists is a sense that the post–Cold War era will linger in its current shape for years if not decades to come. Especially in the United States, people seem to have been lulled by a sense that the nation's status as "the sole remaining superpower" cushions it from disruptions from abroad. This view permits a continued drift and anomie in policy.[146]

It is a view also significantly at odd with the facts. The decade of the 1990s is proving to be a period of trial and decision for states of the newly empowered tier. On trial are the institutions of world order inherited from recent decades and, by implication, those states that purport or aspire to lead those institutions. The decisions will be made as major milestones are reached in this decade with regard to a broad set of multilateral mechanisms. They include arms control decisions, such as whether to strengthen the NPT, ratify and promote entry into force of the CWC, amend the BTWC, participate in the UN register, and/or carry forward progress on regional measures. Also included are trade-related decisions, such as whether or not to promote the World Trade Organization, expand regional free trade zones, and participate in the post-CoCom entity. Further decisions are related to security, such as whether or not to restructure the membership, rights, and responsibilities of the Security Council, a question arising in conjunction with the fiftieth anniversary of the founding of the UN. For this new tier of states, the 1990s mark the end of an era. A new era will begin, characterized by the effects of their own diplomacy and national actions.

In making these decisions, leaders in the newly empowered countries can be expected to invoke their own intellectual inheritance. This casts doubt on a positive outcome. Nations must begin to reconcile profoundly differing views of security and stability. On the proliferation subject itself, there could hardly be a sharper contrast between Western concerns and the concerns of those who dismiss them as "a moralistic stand akin to drug pushers shedding tears about the weaknesses of drug addicts."[147]

---

146 This section draws heavily on Brad Roberts, "1995 and the End of the Post–Cold War Era," *The Washington Quarterly*, Vol. 18, No. 1 (Winter 1995), pp. 5–25.

147 C. Raja Mohan and K. Subrahmanyam, "High-Technology Weapons in the Developing World," in Eric Arnett, ed., *New Technologies for Security and Arms Control: Threats and Promise*

Among political elites in some leading states of the developing world, old political dogmas stand in the way of a fresh rethinking of the international security agenda. Some leaders decry the sins of the developed world while also voraciously consuming weapons and building unconventional arsenals of their own.[148] But the problem runs deeper than hypocrisy. For many leaders in the developing world, public rhetoric on international security has served as an escape from responsibility and as an exercise in scapegoating through the manipulation of international issues for domestic political benefit with little regard for the content of the issues. Developing countries are right to demand equitable international measures, but are foolish when they push the logic of eliminating inequalities to an extreme that sows the seeds of their own instability and eviscerates collective security principles.

A number of factors in particular stand out in the politics of proliferation in the developing world. The first is the long-term dominance of the North–South security agenda by a few states whose views are unrepresentative of the rest. The near nuclear states such as India and others with major investments in weapons and military capability have joined up with many states of the developing world to crusade for independence and global equality. Iran has pressed a more aggressive agenda in the 1990s, tying efforts to strengthen existing mechanisms to its own view of a corrupt and unjust world. But these crusades appear more oriented to the legitimization of Indian and Iranian national choices than to the broad interests of the vast majority of states of the developing world, which have no interest in unconventional weapons or in military solutions to problems of national development and security. A Singaporean diplomat identified the problem clearly two decades ago:

(Washington, D.C.: American Association for the Advancement of Science, 1989), p. 230. It should be noted that the authors, in scoring this strong rhetorical point, are seeking to confront Western predispositions in a search for common understanding.

148 In 1987, among the 20 largest importers of conventional weapons in the Third World, 18 belonged to the non-aligned movement. See S. D. Muni, "Third World Arms Control: Role of the Non-aligned Movement," in Ohlson, *Arms Transfer Limitations and Third World Security*, pp. 198–211. Avi Beker chronicles the "double standard" evident in the Third World's disarmament agenda, which has focused on the "global arms race and balance of terror" while carefully avoiding its obligations in the conventional domain. Beker, *Disarmament Without Order*, especially chapter 7, "The Conventional Arms Race: The Third World's Double Standard," pp. 147–171.

> The Third World's contribution to the cause of arms control and
> disarmament should not be confined to delivering moral sermons
> to the super-powers and to the other nuclear-weapon states....We
> must not allow this special session of disarmament to become yet
> another United Nations exercise in propaganda and collective
> hypocrisy.[149]

Second, many diplomats of the developing world who are working today on
regional and global arms control issues received their training during postings at
the Conference on Disarmament (CD) in Geneva, a UN-affiliated organization.
The mantras of non-alignment have been particularly powerful there, and they
include especially a pervasive anti-Americanism, the portrayal of disarmament in
near messianic terms, and the propensity to view interstate conflict in
value-neutral terms, unless it has clear Western involvement, which is decried as
imperialism. There has also been a tendency to categorize the security benefits of
the global treaty regimes as salient primarily for the developed countries, while
the developing ones look primarily for economic benefits from those regimes.
The easy resort to dogma at the CD has faded in recent years with the passing of
the Cold War and the completion of its major piece of work, the drafting of the
Chemical Weapons Convention, which required these countries to grapple with
their interests vis-à-vis the convention in non-ideological terms. But for decades
the CD and the related UN machinery have served as a training ground for
diplomats who came to see in arms control a political rather than a security
instrument, and the result has been that they approach global and regional
security issues from a primarily ideological viewpoint.[150]

---

149 Ambassador T. T. Koh, June 1978, cited in Beker, *Disarmament Without Order*, p. 147.

150 "During the three-year period 1974–1976...a total of fifteen disarmament bodies...met for 46
sessions; in the three-year period 1979–1981, about forty committees, commissions, conferences,
expert groups held approximately 140 sessions....The result is an endless, vicious cycle of
bureaucratic activities aimed apparently at compensating for the lack of real influence of the
United Nations in the field of disarmament....The proliferation and expansion of the United
Nations machinery of disarmament and the new North–South type of confrontation in
disarmament debates were the culmination of a revolutionary process that took place within the
United Nations over two decades....Disarmament became a corollary of their NIEO [New
International Economic Order] politics." Beker, *Disarmament Without Order*, pp. 52, 59–60. See
also Beker's useful taxonomy "On Terminology," pp. 179–185.

A third factor is the fragile role of the non-governmental sector in many developing countries. In the United States and the developed world generally, institutions and individuals outside government have usefully served to generate and test strategic concepts and especially arms control ideas without the bureaucratic stake of governmental agencies or the vow of silence imposed upon those with access to classified information. In the Middle East and East Asia, a few such institutions are beginning to appear, but their continued ability to contribute to the security debate is uncertain, as is the willingness of their governments to open that debate. In South Asia too, the non-governmental sector holds out similar promise of offering fresh contributions to the policy debate.[151]

Finally, for decades the publics in most countries of the developing world have been fed state dogma on questions of international conflict and security through a compliant media and academe. A frequent private lament of diplomats from both the Middle East and South Asia is that decades of controlled debate and the resulting ideological blinkers among elites have robbed policymakers of the room for maneuver they need in the new environment to take new risks and establish new international relations.

These factors will be important in shaping the ability of policymakers in the developing world to look to the consequences of their choices, to weigh the risks associated with alternatives, and to debate trade-offs in terms of national and international interests. This bodes ill for a refashioning of their national security debates and especially for arms control, which necessarily entails the acceptance

---

151 The quasi-independent Institute for Defence Studies and Analyses in Delhi is one example. In presenting its first annual survey of the Asian security scene in 1992, its director, Jasjit Singh, offered the following significant departures in regional thinking: "International security in the past has been constructed essentially on a competitive and autonomous basis. As we move towards the desirable goal of cooperative security for all, it is necessary to enhance mutual political understanding and trust. Transparency in strategic and military posture becomes a prerequisite for this: and a regional framework more relevant." In his introduction to Singh, ed., *Asian Strategic Review, 1991–92*, p. 6. In Pakistan, where the discriminatory practices of the great powers are often decried, one analyst concluded a study of arms control in the Third World as published in a Pakistani journal as follows: "If it is...in the interests of security to with-hold certain weapons or certain armament patterns from certain regions of the world, then one must simply stand up to the charge of discrimination and paternalism." A. Z. Hilali, "Arms Control in the Third World," *Strategic Studies*, Vol. 14, No. 3 (Spring 1991), p. 73.

of risk, debates about competing priorities, and decisions to limit or relinquish military instruments otherwise available.

Nor will these factors pass quickly from the scene. But the refashioning of conventional wisdoms about security issues can be accelerated by leaders committed to serious pursuit of negotiated restraints. As has been so often demonstrated in the last decade of dramatic change, leaders can redefine political reality. The rethinking of national strategies within governments and a willingness to look at arms control in new ways can be stimulated as well. A useful model for this purpose is ACDA. Established in 1961 as a separate agency within the U.S. government and charged with advocacy in the interagency process for policy approaches emphasizing negotiated restraints, ACDA proved instrumental in rethinking the U.S. approach to the Cold War and became a primary vehicle for the pursuit of U.S. strategy. Although its voice in the policy process has waxed and waned with the interest of senior policymakers, its record as a catalyst for more cooperative approaches to questions of international security suggests that it might be a useful model for other governments interested in improving their competence on these matters.

The task of "de-ideologizing" the international security agenda (to borrow a term from the Gorbachev era) is central to managing the proliferation problem. In a basic sense, proliferation provides a large incentive to many states of the developing world to narrow the ideological divide between South and North for the purpose of sustaining collective security principles.

Long-term political and economic trends are encouraging, as noted earlier. Democratization in the developing world is having a major impact on security choices made by its governments by facilitating a modernization of civil-military relations, broadening the role of the non-governmental sector, strengthening the role of the independent media, and stimulating public education on global issues. Economic factors are also important, because the debt crisis has brought into sharper relief the choices between weapons programs and other national priorities, while generally reinforcing the notion that military instruments are less important than in previous decades to achieving and sustaining sovereignty in the developing world. Cultural factors are also operative, as ideas and values related to state behavior, such as arms control and cooperative security, are transmitted across borders and reach into constituencies struggling to meet diplomatic and security challenges.[152]

The NPT extension conference hinted at the remaking of the international security orientations of developing countries that may further unfold in future years. That hint can be found in the virtual abandonment by the Non-Aligned Movement of its radical leadership and the assumption of places of authority within the politics of developing countries by post-nuclear states like South Africa. The more moderate orientation of such states, combined with their strong interest in participating more fully in existing international institutions and processes, suggests the coalescence of a new set of states not opposed to the international status quo but ambitious to play a more active and leading role in it.

In making decisions about the global regimes, leaders in the states of the developing world will weigh the expected functioning of the regimes in terms of their own national interests and of their security, development, political stability—and aspirations. They will question whether these regimes are led sufficiently well to offer meaningful promise of future efficacy; they will also question whether there is room at the table to exert some leadership of their own. They will, in essence, look through these regimes to the great powers and the leadership they offer.

They will focus necessarily on the United States. As the purported leader of the international community, its credentials are under review. As the world's sole remaining superpower, it generates both hope and fear—while harboring some suspicion of those who would check its credentials. The developing world will hardly need a microscope to detect the broad themes of U.S. foreign policy at this time. Their concerns about export controls and counterproliferation will resonate with recognition that the Clinton administration and its Republican opponents have abandoned multilateralism as a guiding principle. Among the newly empowered tier are many who share the concern of U.S. voters about "the vision thing." Among those who fear a rudderless America are both friends and potential foes—friends because uncertainty about the international role of the

---

152 Emmanuel Adler describes this process of "evolutionary epistemology" by which nations diffuse concepts that condition state behavior, particularly in the arms control domain. "New concepts may end up affecting the practices of governments, not only because they offer a superior or even a new understanding of the situation but also because they carry political clout as a collective interpretation of the national interest and of international stability." Adler, "'Opaque Nuclear Proliferation' and the Political Selection of Arms Control Concepts," in Frankel, *Opaque Nuclear Proliferation*, p. 193.

United States casts doubts on the credibility of its commitments, and foes because the world's only superpower has tremendous room to use its power to its sole advantage.

Janne Nolan attributes the inability of policymakers everywhere to articulate a new view of the United States in a changing international system to ways of thinking rooted in the Cold War:

> In the end, the failure to recognize and to adapt successfully to new international imperatives may result from a stubborn reluctance to consider the interests of regional powers as a compelling determinant of U.S. policy and a new international order. Credible international norms cannot be designed by those who are not persuaded that other countries are worthy of equality or that their amity is important in crafting new rules for the international system. In the United States, in particular, this intellectual impediment is especially difficult to dislodge. It is the product of years of studied indifference to all but a narrow set of technical security issues and a proud embrace of ignorance about and rejection of politics, culture, and regional dynamics as legitimate influences on national policy.[153]

On proliferation in particular, leaders in the developing world will note that the United States enshrines nonproliferation as a centerpiece of its international policies in the 1990s. Many view this position as a form of "nonproliferation imperialism"[154] that is counterproductive of the intended goal because it suggests that the United States little understands the security concerns or political realities in the developing world.[155] These leaders will also note the emphasis on nonproliferation at a time when the United States also seeks to preserve its own conventional and nuclear preponderance. This ambiguous stance reinforces global fears of the nation as a capricious great power, especially when it has been freed of an opponent that some valued as a balance to U.S. power and ambitions.

---

153 Janne E. Nolan, "Cooperative Security in the United States," in Nolan, *Global Engagement*, p. 537.

154 Müller and Reiss, "Counterproliferation," p. 147.

155 Shahram Chubin, "The South and the New World Order," *The Washington Quarterly*, Vol. 16, No. 4 (Autumn 1993), pp. 87–107.

Such fears are well grounded in the history of the interstate system, with its ample evidence of the tendency of powerful states to exercise their will over others. But they also reflect a serious misreading of a United States that, so far at least, has met the challenges and opportunities of the new era with timidity and renewed isolationism.

If the United States seeks continued international engagement and a measure of leadership of global affairs, it will be necessary to address these perceptions—and misperceptions. Achieving positive nonproliferation outcomes will require of the United States a willingness to take steps to harness its power more firmly to collective goals. Today, instead, it advertises its efforts to preserve its military advantages in perpetuity. Some Americans fear that this implies abandoning a significant proportion of those advantages; it need not. Although such advantages are not politically sustainable at a global level on their own terms, meaningful military superiority may be preserved for a long time if the United States rearticulates the purposes of American power—and especially its nuclear weapons—in the changed global context.

Until the United States takes on this challenge, the accusation that it is an essentially conservative, status quo-oriented power that holds on to its nuclear preponderance in order to perpetuate its moment of preeminence after World War II will continue to find their mark. This will have a direct impact on the effort to extend and strengthen global controls on weapons of mass destruction and to make the most of the new opportunities for the UN. For many developing countries, as for many developed ones, these treaties and institutions are essentially security instruments embodying an agreed allocation of rights, responsibilities, and power in the world. They are reluctant to codify a set of rules for a new era without some revitalized consensus about the nature of the international security agenda now that the Cold War is over, and of the utility of those instruments for new purposes. The United States makes achievement of a new consensus more difficult by turning a deaf ear to the concerns of other states about its own uncertain role, thereby reinforcing their fears that the United States really has little or no idea of how to use its power on behalf of the larger international community.

Of course, some will look beyond the global role and responsibilities of the United States to its regional roles. Appreciation of an essentially benign United States, whose stable commitment, military presence, and security guarantees make a tangible contribution to positive regional dynamics can be found among many states in the Middle East and Far East. The same may be true in many states in Latin America. Yet in South Asia, Central Asia, and Africa, the regional role of the United States may do less to restore luster to its global credentials.

The widely varied strategic orientations of states of the new tier may be brought into rapid convergence if questions about the world role of the United States sufficiently crystallize to act as a lightning rod. If the United States comes to be perceived as a status quo power unable to look after anything but its own narrow self-interests, or the interests of like-minded wealthy and secure states, international institutions will suffer. If the United States cannot craft with others a vision of progress toward a more pacific and prosperous future, the views of opponents of that status quo will surely gain broader currency. If a split between status quo and dissatisfied powers emerges, a North–South political dynamic will coalesce that will interfere with the accomplishment of major shared purposes. At least one leading intellectual in the developing world has defended the desirability of "a new international military order" as the only means of securing a more just distribution of wealth.[156] In the lead-up to the major decisions of the coming years, it appears unlikely that many states among the new tier want to abandon existing modalities of international order. But others will join their cause if through a failure to revitalize the consensus about the means and ends of international security the United States helps to precipitate a confrontation between states resentful of U.S. power and those fearful of change.

This is not to argue that a complete convergence of views among and between developed and developing countries on questions of national, regional, and global security is necessary in order to preserve significant elements of international order and carry forward the antiproliferation strategy. The question is, rather, whether a sufficient degree of *congruence* can be created and/or sustained to permit this. As Farer has argued:

> The principal determinants of whether effective global or localized collective security arrangements can be built and maintained include the following: congruent worldviews; a recent or ongoing experience of cooperation in some field; satisfaction with the

---

156 Ali Mazrui, "The Barrel of the Gun and the Barrel of Oil in the North–South Equation," *World Order Models Project*, No. 5 (New York, N.Y.: Institute for World Order, 1978), p. 24.

territorial status quo; and the cost-benefit ratio of military action as a means for achieving greater national power. On the whole the trajectory of these determinants is favorable. Congruent worldviews do not mean coincident worldviews.[157]

M. Granger Morgan and Mitchel B. Wallerstein have made a similar point in a study of militarization in the developing world:

> If the great powers are not sensitive to the legitimate needs of developing states, if they are not acting collectively, if they are not taking steps to limit their own arms (particularly their nuclear weapons), and if they appear to be motivated only by narrow national interest, then the developing world can be expected to object strenuously with charges of exploitation, arrogance, elitism, and paternalism. If, however, a diplomatic context can be developed in which a genuine concern for cooperative security emerges as the dominant motivation for collective action, then wide (though certainly not universal) acceptance, even in the developing world, should be possible.[158]

But what would failure mean? Failure to achieve a new global political bargain could have the effect of driving the proliferation problem well beyond the capacity of the United States or the Security Council to cope using only existing mechanisms and the military forces likely to be preserved in an era of fiscal restraint and strategic retreat. Dramatic failure, meaning collapse of the NPT, would certainly doom the other treaties and would probably bring with it gridlock at the UN and major problems in the free trade movement. Not every new state among the new tier is likely to move quickly to build weapons; but many would probably decide that it would be prudent to hedge their bets by assembling the ingredients of a virtual arsenal. Whether proliferation might also lead to more, and more lethal, wars is an open question. What new arsenals do

---

157 Farer, "The Role of Regional Collective Security Arrangements," p. 159.

158 M. Granger Morgan and Mitchel B. Wallerstein, "Controlling the High-Technology Militarization of the Developing World," in Wander and Arnett, *The Proliferation of Advanced Weaponry*, pp. 285–299.

emerge should be seen as hedges against uncertainty and thus in some sense as symptoms of a deeper malady in the international system, and not just as problems in and of themselves.

A less dramatic form of failure but failure nonetheless would be the continued functioning of these treaties and institutions in form but not substance. The decision to extend the NPT unconditionally may yet contribute to a weakening of the regime if steps are not taken to redress the concerns of the states most disgruntled by the decision to abandon conditionality. If some leading members of the new tier opt to begin to put together a virtual nuclear arsenal while standing in the way of the CWC and a strengthened BTWC and developing an arsenal of biological or chemical weapons as an interim measure, NPT extension will have contributed little. It would be a tragedy indeed if the nuclear era were to be succeeded by an era dominated by biological weapons. If the process of strengthening the global treaty regime grinds to a halt but does not also bring about its collapse, the international community will have lost the benefits of the openness and transparency and confidence these regimes are creating among long-time adversaries. Enforcement operations are also likely to emerge as sources of sharp acrimony in the international system. If all of this happens, the North–South dynamic will certainly replace the East–West confrontation as a barrier to a more just, pacific, and prosperous world order. The United States will not have lost its place at the head table, but it might well find itself overruled by erstwhile friends or squandering scarce capital to regain its seat at the center.

If the coming years bring success in meeting these challenges, credit will be due to many: to those states in the developing and developed world playing key roles in strengthening the NPT, building up the CWC, and improving the BTWC; to those international civil servants who keep international mechanisms functioning; and to those national leaders who sustain a staunch commitment to free trade in the face of persistent domestic opposition. A successful revitalization of the global order cannot be delivered by any one state, even with the most visionary and assertive leadership.

But the converse is also true: success cannot be achieved without U.S. leadership. Many will despair that the United States is so impaired at this critical moment, when it should exercise such leadership. But the leadership required here is not the leadership for which students of the Cold War plead. The attempted restoration of U.S. dominance of international events would be inappropriate in an era when so many newly empowered states seek to play a larger world role. It would indeed be counterproductive, driving them away from cooperation with the United States. Moreover, such a restoration is beyond the reach of the United States at this time—not least because of the nation's success in creating an international political and economic order along liberal lines in the context of global stability.

Between anomie and hegemony is a middle ground well suited to American characteristics, resources, and competence. On each of the agenda items cited above, rules are to be negotiated, debates to be led, decisions to be enforced collectively. The United States is well suited to cooperative engagement on these terms, to offering stewardship of common interests, to serving as a catalyst to generate change, to building on the investments of the past to derive new dividends in the future. As David Koplow has argued:

> America's real comparative advantage...lies with invocation of law. We are the foremost maker of, and the foremost beneficiary of, international law. We depend upon treaties, custom, and international institutions more than any other country, and we are certain to have the most to lose if these phenomena are undercut.[159]

This is a notion of leadership born of the idea that for one to lead, others must want to follow. The United States can only lead on arms control, nuclear diplomacy, collective security, and the international economy if it is working from a position accorded it by others to safeguard shared interests. The more simpleminded leadership that asserts narrowly defined U.S. interests aggressively and pursues them dogmatically is bound to prove counterproductive in an era when other states no longer need to tolerate a perfidious great power. This is also a type of leadership that it can offer in full partnership with other democratic states from all parts of the world.

---

159 David A. Koplow, "The Jurisprudence of Non-Proliferation: Taking International Law Seriously," in Jonathan Dean and Koplow, "World Security and Weapons Proliferation," p. 382.

Conclusion

This chapter began with the proposition that what governments do matters to the future rate and character of weapons proliferation. Its conclusion is that what governments do matters more than ever before.

Proliferation cannot be treated as a problem at the margins of the international security agenda, as it was during the Cold War. If in the 1990s and succeeding years positive nonproliferation outcomes are to be achieved, policymakers must look beyond traditional nonproliferation to a more comprehensive antiproliferation strategy. Such a strategy embraces a broader set of goals and a more complex set of policy instruments.

Effective policy requires both continuity and change. Effective export controls, sound arms control, meaningful security policies, and purposeful diplomacy are cornerstones of the policy agenda. But innovation is necessary if future antiproliferation benefits are to be reaped from each.

Effective strategy requires infusing these policies with a renewed political commitment and a reinvigorated international political consensus. In an era of profound doubt about the international roles of the great powers, especially the United States, and of a nascent split between status quo and dissatisfied powers, these political challenges loom far larger than the instrumental problems associated with finding technical policy adjustments.

Failure to implement a comprehensive antiproliferation strategy may not prove especially costly in the short term. The global treaty regime remains in place and is growing stronger and more far-reaching. Global norms regarding the use of force were reinforced by the collective response to Iraq's annexation of Kuwait. Democratization in the developing world and the growth of the private sector may work to undermine the power and/or ambitions of leaders. Proliferation itself is creating incentives in many parts of the world for countries to pursue more cooperative relations with their neighbors. In short, the world might muddle through for a while without benefit of a comprehensive strategy.

But in the longer term, coasting on the nonproliferation instruments of the past backed by the quixotic use of collective or U.S. power will not work to constrain the further militarization of regional relations and a sharpening of conflict within the developing world—a conflict that also threatens to engage and engulf the developed world. Until some form of new world order is achieved that, like the Cold War before it, acts as a significant brake on the ambitions of aggressive leaders and states, the pursuit of an antiproliferation strategy may be the best means to promote stable relations among nations in an era of rapid industrial innovation, rapidly expanding trade, and nearly universal access to at least some weapons of strategic leverage.

Lastly, the 1990s will be critical in determining what follows. Over this decade, the patterns likely to prevail in the ensuing decades will take shape. That we live in a period of transition is evident from a glance at the technology base, where many trends will reach fruition as research, development, or acquisition strategies either collapse or culminate in major new military capabilities. It is also evident in the politics of international security, where expectations about the future functioning of global institutions and norms will be firmly entrenched. Choices made in the 1990s about how to deal with proliferation are determinants of the kind of order (or disorder) that will prevail well into the next century.

Chapter 6

Conclusion

THIS STUDY BEGAN with two main purposes: first, to better understand the nature of the weapons proliferation subject as it exists today and, second, to assess its impact on the post–Cold War world order. What has been learned?

Weapons proliferation is indeed a subject whose basic features and dynamics are at odds with conventional wisdom. The growing salience of non-nuclear elements is an important new feature, as is the diffusion of the defense industrial base. The nuclear element, nevertheless, remains paramount and has given rise to new concerns about the availability of plutonium and so-called instant proliferation by theft or sale. But the nuclear element is noteworthy above all for the reversal of proliferation in recent years and the growing number of states that are not turning what now stands as their weapons potential into deployed weapons. Furthermore, the proliferation subject is taking on important political dimensions in addition to its military components. Above all, proliferation is creating a new tier of states technically capable of producing military instruments of high leverage, a tier whose political emergence in world affairs is coterminous with the end of the Cold War. Proliferation is also adding to demands on scholars to rethink basic tenets and to look beyond Cold War experience to understand and predict what factors lead states to turn weapons potential into weapons prowess, and the effects of such actions.

What about proliferation's impact on world order? The disrupting consequences of proliferation are obvious: the increased risk of war, whether through heightened pressures to strike preemptively in time of crisis or through simple miscalculation; the increased insecurity of states in regions of intense armaments competition; the aggressions of aspring hegemons fueled by more powerful arsenals and perceptions of superiority; the potential breakdown of collective security principles, of global norms about the use of force, and of consensus about the distribution of power and authority; and the possibility that states will evolve toward a different, far less cooperative pattern of international relations that will have tremendous opportunity costs generally for global political and economic developments.

The contributions of proliferation to order are equally important, if perhaps less evident. The new risks and instabilities encountered by states acquiring advanced weaponry are compelling some to seek alternative routes to security that also decrease their reliance on military instruments. Proliferation is also creating new incentives to revitalize the global bargain about the distribution of power and authority in the service of more effective world order institutions.

What then does proliferation suggest about the future of world order? It demonstrates the contingent character of that future—its emergence not just as a result of basic trends of a technical, military, economic, or political character, but also as a result of the decisions and actions of leaders in states large and small. Leaders of the technically capable states will be able to insert new demands into the global agenda. The new prominence of these states may accelerate the decline of the traditional institutions of world order, or it may lead to their revitalization, or to the creation of new institutions and instruments of order. In short, the primary world order task of the 1990s is not isolating and deterring the new tier of technically empowered states but integrating them deeper into the existing patterns and processes of cooperation and assurance, while also building new ones.

Proliferation presents the traditional great powers with a set of choices about their international roles, which might range from activist guarantors, through field judges or referees, to isolated, declining powers who like sleeping giants, wait to be roused only at the last minute (if then). The fact of proliferation compels these states to make choices, but it by no means preordains what they will choose. Leaders in these states should recognize the impossibility of bringing the new tier more firmly into existing world order institutions if they themselves remain aloof. The engagement of the new tier is unlikely if they perceive what they believe to be status quo powers withdrawing from the world and isolating themselves behind a curtain of military power, economic combativeness, and political condescension. Such engagement is particularly required of the United States: engagement not solely or even primarily of its military or economic power, but of the political standing it derives from its democratic credentials, capacity for vision, and reputation as a benign power with a sometimes willingness to contribute its advantages of power, wealth, and political energy in the service of common global purposes. No other state brings this mix of assets to the world order challenge.

Beyond engagement, leadership is needed. Or perhaps it is merely inevitable: some state or group of states will come forward to catalyze the fractious global debate about the means and ends of international security policy. The seemingly ineluctable diffusion of weapons of mass destruction must nourish the hope that such leadership will be oriented toward cooperative and not divisive goals. Proliferation has fundamentally altered the nature of leadership that is necessary and possible in the world today. In the post–Cold War era, leadership does not automatically devolve onto states disposing of the weight of great powers. Rather, in a permissive technology environment, leadership must spring from a political consensus that enables certain states to lead the international community, or at least large coalitions within the interstate system. To put it simply: for one to lead, others must want to follow. No single power, as in the United States in its so-called unipolar moment, or group of powers, as in the developed world, can lead on questions of arms control, nuclear diplomacy, collective security, and the international economy unless it is working from a position accorded it by others to safeguard their shared interests; others will want to follow only if they have played a role in defining a basic direction and the rules of the game.

Such leadership will be accorded only to that state (or group of states) that takes on the challenge of striving to create a broad measure of international consensus about the means and ends of international security policy. The challenge of pursuing traditional nonproliferation interests in the context of a comprehensive antiproliferation strategy will help to carry forward this task of consensus building. It will take political courage to begin a debate about world order that encompasses all the new circumstances. This is especially so at a time when so many people in the developed world are gripped by the illusion that they can remain isolated from instability in the developing world. But that courage may well prove to be the beginning point of new legitimacy.

Bibliography

Books and Monographs

Acharya, Amitav. *A New Regional Order in South-East Asia: ASEAN in the Post–Cold War Era.* Adelphi Paper No. 279. London: Brassey's for the International Institute for Strategic Studies, 1993.

Adams, James. *Engines of War: Merchants of Death and the New Arms Race.* New York: Atlantic Monthly Press, 1990.

Adler, Emanuel, ed. *The International Practice of Arms Control.* Baltimore, Md.: Johns Hopkins University Press, 1992.

Alves, Dora, ed. *Evolving Pacific Basin Strategies.* Washington, D.C.: National Defense University Press, 1990.

Anthony, Ian. *Arms Export Regulations.* Oxford: Oxford University Press with the Stockholm International Peace Research Institute, 1991.

———. *The Naval Arms Trade.* Oxford: Oxford University Press with the Stockholm International Peace Research Institute, 1990.

Arms Project of Human Rights Watch and Physicians for Human Rights. *Landmines: A Deadly Legacy.* New York: Human Rights Watch, 1993.

Arnett, Eric H. *Gunboat Diplomacy and the Bomb: Nuclear Proliferation and the U.S. Navy.* New York: Praeger, 1989.

———, ed. *New Technologies for Security and Arms Control: Threats and Promise.* Washington, D.C.: American Association for the Advancement of Science, 1989.

———. *Science and International Security: Responding to a Changing World.* Washington, D.C.: American Association for the Advancement of Science, 1990.

———. *Science and Security: Technology Advances and the Arms Control Agenda.* Washington, D.C.: American Association for the Advancement of Science, 1989.

Arnett, Eric H., Elizabeth J. Kirk, and W. Thomas Wander, eds. *Critical Choices: Setting Priorities in the Changing Security Environment.* Washington, D.C.: American Association for the Advancement of Science, 1991.

Asia's International Role in the Post–Cold War Era, Part II. Adelphi Paper No. 276. London: Brassey's for the International Institute for Strategic Studies, 1993.

Baek, Kwang-Il, Ronald D. McLaurin, and Chung-in Moon. *The Dilemma of Third World Defense Industries: Supplier Control or Recipient Autonomy?* Boulder, Colo.: Westview Press, 1989.

Bibliography

Bailey, Kathleen. *Doomsday Weapons in the Hands of the Many: The Arms Control Challenge of the '90s.* Urbana, Ill.: University of Illinois Press, 1991.

———. *Strengthening Nuclear Nonproliferation.* Boulder, Colo.: Westview Press, 1993.

———, ed. *Director's Series on Proliferation.* Livermore, Calif.: Lawrence Livermore National Laboratory. Various from 1993.

Ball, Desmond, Richard L. Grant, and Jusuf Wanandi. *Security Cooperation in the Asia–Pacific Region.* Washington, D.C.: Center for Strategic and International Studies, 1993.

Ball, Nicole. *Security and Economy in the Third World.* Princeton, N.J.: Princeton University Press, 1988.

Beker, Avi. *Disarmament Without Order: The Politics of Disarmament at the United Nations.* Westport, Conn.: Greenwood Press, 1985.

Blair, Bruce G. *The Logic of Accidental Nuclear War.* Washington, D.C.: Brookings Institution, 1993.

Blix, Hans, et al. *Probleme der nuklearen Nichtverbreitungspolitik* (Problems of the politics of nuclear nonproliferation). Arbeitspapiere zur Internationalen Politik 83. Bonn: Europa Union Verlag für die Fortschungsinstitut der Deutschen Gesellschaft für Auswärtige Politik, 1994.

Bloomfield, Lincoln P., Tom J. Farer, Leon Gordenker, Ernst B. Haas, John MacKinlay, Oscar Schachter, James S. Sutterlin, and Thomas G. Weiss. *Collective Security in a Changing World.* Occasional Paper No. 10. Providence, R.I.: Thomas J. Watson Jr. Institute for International Studies, Brown University, 1992.

Booth, Ken, and Eric Herring. *Keyguide to Information Sources in Strategic Studies.* London: Mansell Publishing Ltd., 1994.

Brauch, Hans Guenter, Henny J. Van der Graaf, John Grin, and Wim A. Smit, eds. *Controlling the Development and Spread of Military Technology: Lessons from the Past and Challenges for the 1990s.* Amsterdam: VU University Press, 1992.

Brito, Dagobert, et al. *Strategies for Managing Nuclear Proliferation.* Lexington, Mass.: Lexington Books, 1983.

Brodgen, Peter, and Walter Dorn, eds. *Controlling the Global Arms Threat.* Aurora Paper No. 12. Ottawa: The Canadian Centre for Arms Control and Disarmament, 1992.

Brodie, Bernard, ed. *The Absolute Weapon.* New York: Harcourt, Brace, 1946.

Brodie, Bernard, Michael D. Intriligator, and Roman Kolkowicz, eds. *National Security and International Stability.* Cambridge, Mass.: Oelgeschlager, Gunn & Hain for the Center for International and Strategic Studies, 1983.

Brown, James, ed. *Challenges in Arms Control for the 1990s.* Amsterdam: VU University Press, 1992.

———. *New Horizons and Challenges in Arms Control and Verification.* Amsterdam: VU University Press, 1994.

Brzezinski, Zbigniew. *Out of Control: Global Turmoil on the Eve of the 21st Century.* New York: Charles Scribner's Sons, 1993.

Brzoska, Michael, and Thomas Ohlson, eds. *Arms Production in the Third World.* London: Taylor & Francis for the Stockholm International Peace Research Institute, 1986.

Brzoska, Michael, and Frederic S. Pearson. *Arms and Warfare: Escalation, De-escalation, and Negotiation.* Columbia, S.C.: University of South Carolina Press, 1994.

Carl H. Builder. *The Prospects and Implications of Non-nuclear Means for Strategic Conflict.* Adelphi Paper No. 200. London: International Institute for Strategic Studies, 1985.

Bull, Hedley. *The Anarchical Society: A Study of Order in World Politics.* New York: Columbia University Press, 1977.

———. *The Control of the Arms Race: Disarmament and Arms Control in the Missile Age.* London: Weidenfeld and Nicolson, 1961.

Bundy, McGeorge, William J. Crowe, Jr., and Sidney D. Drell. *Reducing the Nuclear Danger: The Road Away From the Brink.* New York: Council on Foreign Relations, 1993.

Bunn, George, Charles N. Van Doren, and David Fischer. *Options and Opportunities: The NPT Extension Conference of 1995.* Southampton, U.K.: Programme for Promoting Nuclear Non-Proliferation, Mountbatten Centre for International Studies, University of Southampton, November 1991.

Burns, Richard Dean, ed. *Encyclopedia of Arms Control and Disarmament.* New York: Charles Scribner's Sons, 1993.

Burt, Richard. *Nuclear Proliferation and Conventional Arms Transfers: The Missing Link.* Discussion Paper No. 76. Los Angeles, Calif.: California Seminar on Arms Control and Policy, September 1977.

Buzan, Barry. *People, States and Fear: An Agenda for International Security in the Post–Cold War Era.* 2d ed. New York: Harvester Wheatsheaf, 1991.

Carr, E. H. *The Twenty Years' Crisis: 1919–1939.* London: Macmillan Press, Ltd., 1939.

Carter, Ashton B., William J. Perry, and John D. Steinbruner. *A New Concept of Cooperative Security.* Occasional Paper. Washington, D.C.: Brookings Institution, 1992.

Carus, W. Seth. *Ballistic Missiles in Modern Conflict.* New York: Praeger with the Center for Strategic and International Studies, 1991.

———. *Cruise Missile Proliferation in the 1990s.* New York: Praeger with the Center for Strategic and International Studies, 1992.

———. *The Genie Unleashed: Iraq's Chemical and Biological Weapons Production.* Policy Paper No. 14. Washington, D.C.: Washington Institute for Near East Policy, 1989.

Bibliography

Chalmers, Malcolm, Owen Greene, Edward J. Laurance, and Herbert Wulf, eds. *Developing the UN Register of Conventional Arms.* Bradford, U.K.: Department of Peace Studies, University of Bradford, 1994.

Chow, Brian G. *Emerging National Space Launch Programs: Economics and Safeguards.* RAND Report R–4179–USDP. Santa Monica, Calif.: RAND, July 1993.

Chow, Brian G., and Kenneth A. Solomon. *Limiting the Spread of Weapon-Usable Fissile Materials.* RAND Report MR–346–USDP. Santa Monica, Calif.: RAND, 1993.

Chubin, Shahram. *Iran's National Security Policy: Capabilities, Intentions, and Impact.* Washington, D.C.: Carnegie Endowment for International Peace, 1994.

Clark, Asa A., and John F. Lilley, eds. *Defense Technology.* New York: Praeger, 1989.

Cohen, Stephen. *Nuclear Proliferation in South Asia: The Prospects for Arms Control.* Boulder, Colo.: Westview Press, 1990.

Cohen, Yohanan. *Small Nations in Times of Crisis and Confrontation.* New York: State University of New York Press, 1989.

Cossa, Ralph A., ed. *The New Pacific Security Environment: Challenges and Opportunities.* Washington, D.C.: National Defense University Press, 1993.

Daalder, Ivo H. *Cooperative Arms Control: A New Agenda for the Post–Cold War Era.* Paper No. 1. College Park, Md.: Center for International Security Studies at Maryland, School of Public Affairs, University of Maryland at College Park, October 1991.

Dando, Malcolm. *Biological Warfare in the 21st Century: Biotechnology and the Proliferation of Biological Weapons.* London: Brassey's, 1994.

Dannreuther, Roland. *The Gulf Conflict: A Political and Strategic Analysis.* Adelphi Paper No. 264. London: Brassey's for the International Institute for Strategic Studies, Winter 1991/92.

Dauber, Cori Elizabeth. *Cold War Analytical Structures and the Post Post-War World.* Westport, Conn.: Praeger, 1993.

Davis, Zachary S., and Benjamin Frankel, eds. *The Proliferation Puzzle: Why Nuclear Weapons Spread (and What Results).* London: Frank Cass, 1993.

Deger, Saadet. *The Economics of Disarmament: Prospects, Problems and Policies for the Disarmament Dividend.* Innocenti Occasional Papers, Economic Policy Series No. 30. Florence, Italy: UNICEF International Child Development Centre, August 1992.

DeWitt, David B., ed. *Nuclear Non-Proliferation and Global Security.* New York: St. Martin's Press, 1987.

DeWitt, David, David Haglund, and John Kirton, eds. *Building a New Global Order: Emerging Trends in International Security.* Oxford: Oxford University Press, 1993.

Dhanapala, Jayantha, ed. *Regional Approaches to Disarmament: Security and Stability.* Geneva: United Nations Institute for Disarmament Research, 1993.

Diamond, Larry, and Marc F. Plattner, eds. *The Global Resurgence of Democracy.* Baltimore, Md.: Johns Hopkins University Press, 1993.

Doxey, Margaret P. *International Sanctions in Contemporary Perspective.* New York: St. Martin's Press, 1987.

Dunn, Lewis A. *Containing Nuclear Proliferation.* Adelphi Paper No. 263. London: Brassey's for the International Institute for Strategic Studies, 1991.

———. *Controlling the Bomb.* New Haven, Conn.: Yale University Press, 1982.

———. *Fifty Years Since Stagg Field: Nuclear Non-Proliferation Challenges and Opportunities.* Prepared for a symposium at the University of Chicago, Chicago, November 24, 1992.

Dunn, Lewis A., and Sharon A. Squassoni. *Arms Control: What Next?* Boulder, Colo.: Westview Press, 1992.

Evron, Yair. *Israel's Nuclear Dilemma.* Ithaca, N.Y.: Cornell University Press, 1994.

Falk, Richard A. *A Study of Future Worlds.* New York: Free Press, 1975.

Feldman, Shai. *Israeli Nuclear Deterrence: A Strategy for the 1980s.* New York: Columbia University Press, 1982.

———, ed. *Confidence Building and Verification: Prospects in the Middle East.* Jaffee Center for Strategic Studies, Study No. 25. Jerusalem: *Jerusalem Post* and Westview Press, 1994.

Findlay, Trevor, ed. *Chemical Weapons and Missile Proliferation: With Implications for the Asia/Pacific Region.* Boulder, Colo.: Lynne Rienner Publishers, 1991.

Fischer, David. *Towards 1995: The Prospects for Ending the Proliferation of Nuclear Weapons.* Aldershot, U.K.: Dartmouth Publishing Company for the United Nations Institute for Disarmament Research, 1993.

Fischer, David, and Paul Szasz. Edited by Jozef Goldblat. *Safeguarding the Atom: A Critical Appraisal.* London: Taylor and Francis for the Stockholm International Peace Research Institute, 1985.

Fischer, David, Ben Sanders, Lawrence Scheinman, and George Bunn. *A New Nuclear Triad: The Non-Proliferation of Nuclear Weapons, International Verification and the International Atomic Energy Agency.* Southampton, U.K.: Mountbatten Centre for International Studies, University of Southampton, September 1992.

Frankel, Benjamin, ed. *Opaque Nuclear Proliferation: Methodological and Policy Implications.* London: Frank Cass, 1991.

Gaertner, Heinz. *Challenges of Verification: Smaller States and Arms Control.* Occasional Paper Series 12. New York: Institute for East–West Security Studies, 1989.

Gallois, Pierre. *The Balance of Terror, Strategy for the Nuclear Age.* Boston: Houghton Mifflin, 1961.

Gardner, Gary T. *Nuclear Nonproliferation: A Primer.* Boulder, Colo.: Lynne Rienner Publishers, 1994.

Bibliography

Garrity, Patrick J. *Does the Gulf War Still Matter? Foreign Perspectives on the War and the Future of International Security.* Report No. 16. Los Alamos, N.Mex.: Center for National Security Studies, Los Alamos National Laboratory, May 1993.

Garrity, Patrick J., and Steven A. Maaranen, eds. *Nuclear Weapons in the Changing World: Perspectives from Europe, Asia, and North America.* New York: Plenum Press, 1992.

George, Alexander L. *Bridging the Gap: Theory and Practice in Foreign Policy.* Washington, D.C.: United States Institute of Peace, 1993.

Gill, R. Bates. *Chinese Arms Transfers: Purposes, Patterns, and Prospects in the New World Order.* Westport, Conn.: Praeger, 1992.

Gilpin, Robert, and Christopher Wright, eds. *Scientists and National Policy-Making.* New York: Columbia University Press, 1964.

Gizewski, Peter, ed. *Minimum Nuclear Deterrence in a New World Order.* Aurora Paper No. 23. Ottawa: Canadian Centre for Global Security, 1994.

Glynn, Patrick. *Closing Pandora's Box: Arms Races, Arms Control, and the History of the Cold War.* New York: Basic Books, 1992.

Gray, Colin S. *Weapons Don't Make War: Policy, Strategy, and Military Technology.* Lawrence, Kan.: University of Kansas Press, 1993.

Grimmett, Richard F. *Conventional Arms Transfers to the Third World, 1983–1990.* Washington, D.C.: Congressional Research Service Report, August 2, 1991.

Guertner, Gary L., ed. *The Search for Strategy: Politics and Strategic Vision.* Westport, Conn.: Greenwood Press for the Strategic Studies Institute of the U.S. Army War College, 1993.

Halperin, Morton H., and David J. Scheffer with Patricia L. Small. *Self-Determination in the New World Order.* Washington, D.C.: Carnegie Endowment for International Peace, 1992.

Hammond, Grant T. *Plowshares into Swords: Arms Races in International Politics, 1840–1991.* Columbia, S.C.: University of South Carolina Press, 1993.

Harrison, Selig G., and Geoffrey Kemp. *India and America: After the Cold War.* Washington, D.C.: Carnegie Endowment for International Peace, 1993.

Harvey, John R., Cameron Binkley, Adam Block, and Rick Burke. *A Common-Sense Approach to High-Technology Export Controls.* Stanford, Calif.: Center for International Security and Arms Control, Stanford University, March 1995.

Hawes, John. *Arms Control: A New Style for a New Agenda.* Paper No. 2. College Park, Md.: Center for International Security Studies at Maryland, School of Public Affairs, University of Maryland at College Park, January 1993.

Hollins, Harry B., Averill L. Powers, and Mark Sommer, eds. *The Conquest of War: Alternative Strategies for Global Security.* Boulder, Colo.: Westview Press, 1989.

Hopkins, John C., and Weixing Hu, eds. *Strategic Views from the Second Tier: The Nuclear Weapons Policies of France, Britain, and China.* La Jolla, Calif.: University of California Institute on Global Conflict and Cooperation, 1994.

Hughes, Barry B. *International Futures: Choices in the Creation of a New World Order.* Boulder, Colo.: Westview Press, 1993.

Imai, Ryukichi. "Nuclear Proliferation in the Post–Cold War World." In *Asia's International Role in the Post–Cold War Era, Part II.* Adelphi Paper No. 276, pp. 31–41. London: Brassey's for the International Institute for Strategic Studies, 1993.

Ion, A. Hamish, and E. J. Errington, eds. *Great Powers and Little Wars: The Limits of Power.* Westport, Conn.: Praeger, 1993.

Jervis, Robert. *The Meaning of the Nuclear Revolution: Statecraft and the Prospect of Armageddon.* Ithaca, N.Y.: Cornell University Press, 1989.

———. *Perception and Misperception in International Politics.* Princeton, N.J.: Princeton University Press, 1976.

Jesuran, C., ed. *Arms Production and Trade in South East Asia.* Singapore: ISEAS, 1990.

Jones, R. V. *Future Conflict and New Technology.* Washington Paper No. 88. Beverly Hills and London: Sage Publications for the Center for Strategic and International Studies, Georgetown University, 1981.

Jones, Rodney W. *Proliferation of Small Nuclear Forces.* Washington, D.C.: Center for Strategic and International Studies, Georgetown University, 1983.

———. *Small Nuclear Forces.* Washington Paper No. 103. New York: Praeger with the Center for Strategic and International Studies, 1984.

Jones, Rodney W., and Steven A. Hildreth, eds. *Emerging Powers: Defense and Security in the Third World.* New York: Praeger with the Center for Strategic and International Studies, 1986.

———. *Modern Weapons and Third World Powers.* CSIS Significant Issues Series, Vol. 6, No. 4. Boulder, Colo.: Westview Press with the Center for Strategic and International Studies, 1984.

Kaplan, Morton A. *System and Process in International Politics.* New York: John Wiley, 1975.

Karem, Mahmoud. *A Nuclear-Weapon-Free Zone in the Middle East: Problems and Prospects.* Westport, Conn.: Greenwood Press, 1988.

Karp, Aaron. *Controlling Weapons Proliferation in the 1990s: The Role of Export Controls.* SWP–AP2766. Ebenhausen, Germany: Stiftung Wissenschaft und Politik, September 1992.

Karsh, Efraim, Martin S. Navias, and Philip Sabin, eds. *Non-Conventional Weapons Proliferation in the Middle East.* Oxford: Clarendon Press, 1993.

Katz, James Everett, ed. *Arms Production in Developing Countries: An Analysis of Decision Making.* Lexington, Mass.: Lexington Books/D.C. Heath and Co., 1984.

Kemp, Geoffrey. *The Control of the Middle East Arms Race*. Washington, D.C.: Carnegie Endowment for International Peace, 1991.

———. *Forever Enemies? American Policy and the Islamic Republic of Iran*. Washington, D.C.: Carnegie Endowment for International Peace, 1994.

Kirkpatrick, Jeane J. *The Withering Away of the Totalitarian State...And Other Surprises*. Washington, D.C.: American Enterprise Institute, 1990.

Kissinger, H. A. *Nuclear Weapons and Foreign Policy*. New York: Harper and Row, 1957.

Klare, Michael T., and Daniel C. Thomas. *World Security: Challenges for a New Century*. 2d ed. New York: St. Martin's Press, 1994.

Knorr, Klaus. *On the Uses of Military Power in the Nuclear Age*. Princeton, N.J.: Princeton University Press, 1966.

———, ed. *Power, Strategy, and Security*. Princeton, N.J.: Princeton University Press, 1983.

Kolodziej, Edward A., and Patrick M. Morgan, eds. *Security and Arms Control*, Vol. 2, *A Guide to International Policymaking*. New York: Greenwood Press, 1989.

Krasner, Stephen D., ed., *International Regimes*. Ithaca, N.Y.: Cornell University Press, 1983.

Krause, Joachim, ed., *Kernwaffenverbreitung und internationaler Systemwandel* (Nuclear weapons, proliferation, and a changing international system). Baden-Baden, Germany: Nomos Verlagsgesellschaft für die Stiftung Wissenschaft und Politik, 1994.

Krause, Keith. *Arms and the State: Patterns of Military Production and Trade*. Cambridge: Cambridge University Press, 1992.

Krepon, Michael, Peter D. Zimmerman, Leonard S. Spector, and Mary Umberger, eds. *Commercial Observation Satellites and International Security*. New York: St. Martin's Press with the Carnegie Endowment for International Peace, 1990.

Kuhn, Thomas S. *The Structure of Scientific Revolutions*. 2d ed. Chicago: University of Chicago Press, 1970.

Labbé, Marie-Hélène. *La Prolifération Nucléaire*. Paris: Jacques Bertoin, 1992.

Lamb, John M., and Jennifer L. Moher. *Conventional Arms Transfers: Approaches to Multilateral Control in the 1990s*. Aurora Paper No. 13. Ottawa: The Canadian Centre for Arms Control and Disarmament, 1992.

Laurance, Edward J. *The International Arms Trade*. Lexington, Mass.: Lexington Books, 1992.

Laurance, Edward J., Siemon T. Wezeman, and Herbert Wulf. *Arms Watch: SIPRI Report on the First Year of the UN Register of Conventional Arms*. Oxford: Oxford University Press for the Stockholm International Peace Research Institute, 1993.

Leonard, James F. *Strengthening the Non-Proliferation Treaty in the Post–Cold War World*. Working Paper No. 1. Washington, D.C.: Washington Council on Non-Proliferation, October 1992.

Levine, Robert A. *Uniform Deterrence of Nuclear First Use.* Santa Monica, Calif.: RAND, 1993.

Levite, Ariel E., Bruce W. Jentleson, and Larry Berman, eds. *Foreign Military Intervention: The Dynamics of Protracted Conflict.* New York: Columbia University Press, 1992.

Luck, Edward C. *Arms Control: The Multilateral Alternative.* New York and London: New York University Press, 1983.

Lynn-Jones, Sean M., Steven E. Miller, and Stephen Van Evera, eds. *Nuclear Diplomacy and Crisis Management.* Cambridge, Mass.: MIT Press, 1990.

Mack, Andrew, and Paul Keal, eds. *Security and Arms Control in the North Pacific.* Boston: Allen and Unwin, 1988.

Maldifassi, José O., and Pier A. Abetti. *Defense Industries in Latin American Countries: Argentina, Brazil, and Chile.* Westport, Conn.: Praeger, 1994.

Mandelbaum, Michael. *The Nuclear Revolution: International Politics Before and After Hiroshima.* New York: Cambridge University Press, 1981.

Martel, William C., and William T. Pendley. *Nuclear Coexistence: Rethinking U.S. Policy to Promote Stability in an Era of Proliferation.* Air War College Studies in National Security No. 1. Montgomery, Ala.: Air University, Maxwell Air Force Base, 1993.

Marshall, Andrew W., J. J. Martin, and Henry S. Rowen, eds. *On Not Confusing Ourselves: Essays on National Security Strategy in Honor of Albert and Roberta Wohlstetter.* Boulder, Colo.: Westview Press, 1991.

Mastny, Vojtech. *The Helsinki Process and the Reintegration of Europe 1986–1991.* New York: New York University Press for the Institute for East–West Security Studies, 1992.

Mataija, Steven, ed. *Non-Proliferation and Multilateral Verification: The Comprehensive Nuclear Test Ban Treaty.* Toronto: Centre for International and Strategic Studies at York University, 1994.

Mataija, Steven, and Lyne C. Bourque, eds. *Proliferation and International Security: Converging Roles of Verification, Confidence Building and Peacekeeping.* Toronto: Centre for International and Strategic Studies at York University, 1993.

Mazarr, Michael J., and Alexander T. Lennon, eds. *Toward a Nuclear Peace: The Future of Nuclear Weapons.* New York: St. Martin's Press with the Center for Strategic and International Studies, 1994.

McClean, Andrew. *Security, Arms Control, and Conflict Reduction in East Asia and the Pacific: A Bibliography, 1980–1991.* Westport, Conn.: Greenwood Press, 1993.

McDaniel, Douglas E. *United States Technology Export Control: An Assessment.* Westport. Conn.: Praeger, 1993.

McKercher, B.J.C. *Arms Limitation and Disarmament: Restraints on War, 1899–1939.* Westport, Conn.: Praeger, 1992.

Meiers, Franz-Josef. *From START I to START II: Arms Control Under Uncertainty*. PSIS Occasional Paper 2/1994. Geneva: Programme for Strategic and International Security Studies, 1994.

Millot, Marc Dean, Roger Molander, and Peter A. Wilson. *"The Day After..." Study: Nuclear Proliferation in the Post–Cold War World*. Santa Monica, Calif.: RAND, 1993. Three volumes.

Miskel, James F. *Buying Trouble? National Security and Reliance on Foreign Industry*. Lanham, Md.: University Press of America, 1993.

Molander, Roger C., and Peter A. Wilson. *The Nuclear Asymptote: On Containing Nuclear Proliferation*. Santa Monica, Calif.: RAND/UCLA Center for Soviet Studies, 1993.

Morel, Benoit, and Kyle Olson, eds. *The Chemical Weapons Convention: Shadow and Substance*. Boulder, Colo.: Westview Press, 1993.

Morgenthau, Hans J. *Politics Among Nations: The Struggle for Power and Peace*. 5th ed. rev. New York: Alfred A. Knopf, 1973.

Moss, Kenneth B., ed. *Technology and the Future Strategic Environment*. Washington, D.C.: Wilson Center Press, 1990.

Mueller, John. *Retreat from Doomsday: The Obsolescence of Major War*. New York: Basic Books, 1989.

Müller, Harald. *Die Chance der Kooperation: Regime in den Internationalen Beziehungen*. Darmstadt, Germany: Wissenschaftliche Buchgesellschaft, 1993.

Mullins, A. F., Jr. *Born Arming: Development and Military Power in New States*. Stanford, Calif.: Stanford University Press, 1987.

Mussington, David. *Understanding Contemporary International Arms Transfers*. Adelphi Paper No. 291. London: Brassey's for the International Institute for Strategic Studies, 1994.

———. *United States Counter-Proliferation Policy in the 1990s: From Prohibition to Stabilization and Management*. Ottawa: Department of Foreign Affairs and International Trade, 1994.

Mutimer, David, ed. *Control But Verify: Verification and the New Non-Proliferation Agenda*. Toronto: Centre for International and Strategic Studies at York University, 1994.

Nelson, Joan M., and Stephanie J. Eglinton. *Global Goals, Contentious Means: Issues of Multiple Aid Conditionality*. Policy Essay No. 10. Washington, D.C.: Overseas Development Council, 1993.

Neuman, Stephanie G., ed. *Defense Planning in Less-Industrialized States: The Middle East and South Asia*. Lexington, Mass.: Lexington Books, 1984.

Neuman, Stephanie G., and Robert E. Harkavy, eds. *Arms Transfers in the Modern World*. New York: Praeger, 1979.

Nolan, Janne E. *Trappings of Power: Ballistic Missiles in the Third World*. Washington, D.C.: Brookings Institution, 1991.

———, ed. *Global Engagement: Cooperation and Security in the 21st Century*. Washington, D.C.: Brookings Institution, 1994.

Ohlson, Thomas, ed. *Arms Transfer Limitations and Third World Security.* Oxford: Oxford University Press for the Stockholm International Peace Research Institute, 1988.

Pelletiere, Stephen C., Douglas V. Johnson II, and Leif R. Rosenberger. *Iraqi Power and U.S. Security in the Middle East.* Carlisle Barracks, Pa.: Strategic Studies Institute, U.S. Army War College, 1990.

Pilat, Joseph F., and Robert E. Pendley, eds. *Beyond 1995: The Future of the NPT Regime.* New York: Plenum Press, 1990.

Platt, Alan, ed. *Arms Control and Confidence-Building in the Middle East.* Washington, D.C.: United States Institute of Peace, 1992.

Potter, William C. *Nuclear Profiles of the Soviet Successor States.* Monterey, Calif.: Monterey Institute of International Studies, 1993.

The Problem of Chemical and Biological Warfare, Vol. 2, *CB Weapons Today.* Stockolm: Almqvist & Wiksell for the Stockholm International Peace Research Institute, 1973.

Ramburg, Bennet, ed. *Arms Control Without Negotiation: From the Cold War to the New World Order.* Boulder, Colo.: Lynne Rienner Publishers, 1993.

Rauf, Tariq, ed. *Regional Approaches to Curbing Nuclear Proliferation in the Middle East and South Asia.* Aurora Paper No. 16. Ottawa: Canadian Centre for Global Security, 1992.

———. *Strengthened IAEA Safeguards and Regional Non-Proliferation Strategies.* Aurora Paper No. 23. Ottawa: Canadian Centre for Global Security, 1994.

Reiss, Mitchell. *Bridled Ambition: Why Countries Constrain Their Nuclear Capabilities.* Washington, D.C.: Woodrow Wilson Center Press, 1995.

Reiss, Mitchell, and Robert S. Litwak, eds. *Nuclear Proliferation After the Cold War.* Washington, D.C.: Woodrow Wilson Center Press, 1994.

Richter, Andrew. *Reconsidering Confidence and Security Building Measures: A Critical Analysis.* Toronto: Centre for International and Strategic Studies at York University, 1994.

Righter, Rosemary. *Utopia Lost: The United Nations and World Order.* New York: Twentieth Century Fund Press, 1995.

Roberts, Brad. *Chemical Disarmament and International Security.* Adelphi Paper No. 267. London: Brassey's for the International Institute for Strategic Studies, 1992.

———, ed. *Biological Weapons: Weapons of the Future?* Washington, D.C.: Center for Strategic and International Studies, 1993.

———. *Chemical Disarmament and U.S. Security.* Boulder, Colo.: Westview Press for the Center for Strategic and International Studies, 1992.

Rochester, J. Martin. *Waiting for the Millennium: The United Nations and the Future of World Order.* Columbia, S.C.: University of South Carolina Press, 1993.

Bibliography

Rotblat, Joseph, Jack Steinberger, and Bhalchandra Udgaonkar, eds., and Frank Blackaby, executive ed. *A Nuclear-Weapon-Free World: Desirable? Feasible?* Boulder, Colo.: Westview Press, 1993.

Rummel, R. J. *Death by Government.* New Brunswick, N.J.: Transaction Publishers, 1994.

Russett, Bruce. *Controlling the Sword: The Democratic Governance of National Security.* Cambridge, Mass.: Harvard University Press, 1990.

———. *Grasping the Democratic Peace: Principles for a Post–Cold War World.* Princeton, N.J.: Princeton University Press, 1993.

Sadowski, Yahya M. *Scuds or Butter? The Political Economy of Arms Control in the Middle East.* Washington, D.C.: Brookings Institution, 1993.

Sagan, Scott D., ed. *Civil-Military Relations and Nuclear Weapons.* Stanford, Calif.: Center for International Security and Arms Control, Stanford University, 1994.

——— and Kenneth N. Waltz. *The Spread of Nuclear Weapons: A Debate.* New York: W. W. Norton & Company, 1995.

Sanders, Ralph. *Arms Industries: New Suppliers and Regional Security.* Washington, D.C.: National Defense University, 1990.

Sarkesian, Sam C. *Unconventional Conflicts in a New Security Era.* Westport, Conn.: Greenwood Press for the Strategic Studies Institute of the U.S. Army War College, 1993.

Sayigh, Yezid. *Arab Military Industry: Capability, Performance and Impact.* London: Brassey's, 1992.

———. *Confronting the 1990s: Security in the Developing Countries.* Adelphi Paper No. 251. London: Brassey's for the International Institute for Strategic Studies, 1990.

Schear, James A., ed. *Nuclear Weapons Proliferation and Nuclear Risk.* London: St. Martin's Press for the International Institute for Strategic Studies, 1984.

Schechterman, Bernard, and Martin Slann, eds. *The Ethnic Dimension in International Relations.* Westport, Conn.: Praeger, 1993.

Scheinman, Lawrence. *Assuring the Nuclear Non-Proliferation Safeguards System.* Occasional Paper. Washington, D.C.: Atlantic Council of the United States, October 1992.

Schelling, Thomas C. *Arms and Influence.* New Haven, Conn.: Yale University Press, 1966.

Schelling, Thomas C., and Morton H. Halperin. *Strategy and Arms Control.* New York: Twentieth Century Fund, 1961.

Schlesinger, James R. "The International Implications of Third-World Conflict: An American Perspective." In Christoph Bertram, ed., *Third-World Conflict and International Security, Part I.* Adelphi Paper No. 166. London: International Institute for Strategic Studies, Summer 1981.

Schoultz, Lars, William C. Smith, and Augusto Varas, eds. *Security, Democracy, and Development in U.S.-Latin American Relations.* Miami, Fla.: North–South Center of the University of Miami, distributed by Transaction Publishers, 1994.

Segal, Gerald. "The Consequences of Arms Proliferation in Asia: II." In *Asia's International Role in the Post–Cold War Era, Part II.* Adelphi Paper No. 276, Conference Papers, pp. 50–61. London: Brassey's for the International Institute for Strategic Studies, 1993.

Shultz, Richard, Roy Godson, and Ted Greenwood, eds. *Security Studies for the 1990s.* Washington, D.C.: Brassey's (US), 1993.

Singer, Max, and Aaron Wildavsky. *The Real World Order: Zones of Peace/Zones of Turmoil.* Chatham, N.J.: Chatham House Publishers, 1993.

Singh, Jasjit, ed. *Asian Strategic Review, 1991–92.* New Delhi: Institute for Defence Studies and Analyses, 1992.

Singh, Jasjit, and Thomas Bernauer, eds. *Security of Third World Countries.* Geneva: United Nations Institute for Disarmament Research, 1993.

Sivard, Ruth Leger. *World Military and Social Expenditures, 1982.* Leesburg, Va.: World Priorities, 1982.

Small, Melvin, and J. David Singer, eds. *International War: An Anthology.* Chicago, Ill.: Dorsey Press, 1989.

Smith, Chris. *India's Ad Hoc Arsenal: Direction or Drift in Defence Policy?* Oxford: Oxford University Press for Stockholm International Peace Research Institute, 1994.

Snyder, Jed C., and Samuel F. Wells, eds. *Limiting Nuclear Proliferation.* Cambridge, Mass.: Ballinger, 1985.

Sokolski, Henry. "Nonapocalyptic Proliferation: A New Strategic Threat?" In *Proliferationsrisiken SASVP IV*, pp. 25–40. Ebenhausen, Germany: Stiftung Wissenschaft und Politik, Winter 1993.

Spector, Leonard S. *Nuclear Ambitions.* Washington, D.C.: Carnegie Endowment for International Peace, 1990.

Speed, Roger D. *The International Control of Nuclear Weapons.* Stanford, Calif.: Center for International Security and Arms Control, Stanford University, 1994.

Spiers, Edward M. *Chemical and Biological Weapons: A Study of Proliferation.* London: Macmillan Press, 1994.

Staar, Richard F. *Arms Control: Myth Versus Reality.* Stanford, Calif.: Hoover Institution Press, 1984.

Stahl, Shelley A., and Geoffrey Kemp, eds. *Arms Control and Weapons Proliferation in the Middle East and South Asia.* New York: St. Martin's Press for the Carnegie Endowment for International Peace, 1992.

Sur, Serge, ed. *Disarmament and Limitation of Armaments: Unilateral Measures and Policies.* UNIDIR/92/60. Geneva: United Nations Institute for Disarmament Research, 1992.

Tanham, George K. *Indian Strategic Thought: An Interpretive Essay.* R–4207–USDP. Santa Monica, Calif.: RAND, 1992.

Tanner, Fred, ed. *From Versailles to Baghdad: Post-War Armament Control of Defeated States.* UNIDIR/92/70. Geneva: United Nations Institute for Disarmament Research and Graduate Institute of International Studies, 1992.

Taylor, William J., Jr. *The Future of Conflict: U.S. Interests.* Washington Paper No. 94. New York: Praeger for the Center for Strategic and International Studies, Georgetown University, 1983.

Thomas, Raju C. G. *South Asian Security in the 1990s.* Adelphi Paper No. 278. London: Brassey's for the International Institute for Strategic Studies, 1993.

Thompson, W. Scott, and Kenneth M. Jensen with Richard N. Smith and Kimber M. Schraub, eds. *Approaches to Peace: An Intellectual Map.* Washington, D.C.: United States Institute of Peace, 1991.

Tucker, Michael. *Non-Nuclear Powers and the Geneva Conference on Disarmament: A Study in Multilateral Arms Control,* Occasional Paper No. 7. Ottawa: Canadian Institute for International Peace and Security, 1989.

Tucker, Robert W. *The Inequality of Nations.* New York: Basic Books, 1977.

Ungar, Sheldon. *The Rise and Fall of Nuclearism: Fear and Faith as Determinants of the Arms Race.* University Park, Pa.: Penn State Press, 1992.

Urquhart, Brian, and Robert S. McNamara. *Toward Collective Security: Two Views.* Occasional Paper No. 5. Providence, R.I.: Thomas J. Watson Jr. Institute for International Studies, Brown University, 1991.

Van Benthem van den Bergh, Godfried. *Forced Restraint: The Nuclear Revolution and the End of the Cold War.* London: Macmillan, 1992.

Van Creveld, Martin. *Nuclear Proliferation and the Future of Conflict.* New York: Free Press, 1993.

———. *Technology and War: From 2000 BC to the Present.* New York: Free Press, 1989.

Van Ham, Peter. *Managing Non-Proliferation Regimes in the 1990s: Power, Politics and Policies.* London: Pinter Publishers, 1993.

Waltz, Kenneth N. *The Spread of Nuclear Weapons: More May Be Better.* Adelphi Paper No. 171. London: International Institute for Strategic Studies, 1981.

———. *Theory of International Politics.* Reading, Mass.: Addison–Wesley, 1979.

Wander, W. Thomas, and Eric H. Arnett. *The Proliferation of Advanced Weaponry: Technology, Motivations, and Responses.* Washington, D.C.: American Association for the Advancement of Science, 1992.

Wander, W. Thomas, Eric H. Arnett, and Paul Bracken, eds. *The Diffusion of Advanced Weaponry: Technologies, Regional Implications, and Possible Responses.* Washington, D.C.: American Association for the Advancement of Science, 1994.

Watman, Kenneth, and Dean Wilkening. *U.S. Regional Deterrence Strategy.* DRR–544/1–A/AF. Santa Monica, Calif.: RAND, February 1994.

Weiss, Thomas G., ed. *Collective Security in a Changing World*. Boulder, Colo.: Lynne Rienner Publishers, 1993.

Weiss, Thomas G., and Meryl A. Kessler, eds. *Third World Security in the Post–Cold War Era*. Boulder, Colo.: Lynne Rienner Publishers, 1991.

Wight, Martin. *Power Politics*. Edited by Hedley Bull and Carsten Holbraad. London: Penguin Books and the Royal Institute of International Affairs, 1979.

Wilkening, Dean, and Kenneth Watman. *Deterring Nuclear Threats From Regional Adversaries*. DRR–544/2–A/AF. Santa Monica, Calif.: RAND, February 1994.

Winham, Gilbert R. *New Issues in International Crisis Management*. Boulder, Colo.: Westview Press, 1988.

Winkler, Theodore H., and Peter Ziegler, eds. *The World of Tomorrow* (Die Welt von morgen). Stuttgart: Paul Haupt Berne, 1994.

Wohlstetter, Albert. *The Spread of Nuclear Bombs: Predictions, Premises, and Policies*. Los Angeles, Calif.: Pan Heuristics, 1977.

Wohlstetter, Albert, et al. *Moving Toward Life in a Nuclear Armed Crowd?* Report Prepared for the U.S. Arms Control and Disarmament Agency by Pan Heuristics, ACDA/PAB–263, Los Angeles, Calif., April 22, 1976.

Wulf, Herbert, ed. *Arms Industry Limited*. Oxford: Oxford University Press for the Stockholm International Peace Research Institute, 1993.

Journal Articles

Aftab, Mariam. "The New World Order: A Critical Evaluation." *Strategic Studies*, Vol. 14, No. 3 (Spring 1991), pp. 48–56.

Allan, Charles T. "Extended Conventional Deterrence: In from the Cold and Out of the Nuclear Fire?" *The Washington Quarterly*, Vol. 17, No. 3 (Summer 1994), pp. 203–233.

Alvarez, Jose E. "The Once and Future Security Council." *The Washington Quarterly*, Vol. 18, No. 2 (Spring 1995), pp. 5–22.

Anthony, Ian. "Assessing the UN Register of Conventional Arms." *Survival*, Vol. 35, No. 4 (Winter 1993–94), pp. 113–129.

Atkeson, Edward B. "The Middle East: A Dynamic Military Net Assessment for the 1990s." *The Washington Quarterly*, Vol. 16, No. 2 (Spring 1993), pp. 115–133.

Ball, Desmond. "Arms and Affluence: Military Acquisitions in the Asia–Pacific Region." *International Security*, Vol. 18, No. 3 (Winter 1993/94), pp. 78–112.

Barzilai, Gad, and Efraim Inbar. "Do Wars Have an Impact? Israeli Public Opinion After the Gulf War." *Jerusalem Journal of International Relations*, Vol. 14, No. 1 (March 1992), pp. 48–64.

Benedict, John. "There Is a Sub Threat." *Proceedings* (U.S. Naval Institute) (August 1990), p. 57.

Berkowitz, Bruce D. "Proliferation and the Likelihood of War." *Journal of Conflict Resolution* (March 1985), pp. 57–82.

Bertsch, Gary K., and Richard T. Cupitt. "Nonproliferation in the 1990s: Enhancing International Cooperation on Export Controls." *The Washington Quarterly*, Vol. 16, No. 4 (Autumn 1993), pp. 53–70.

Bitzinger, Richard A. "Arms to Go: Chinese Arms Sales to the Third World." *International Security*, Vol. 17, No. 2 (Fall 1992), pp. 84–111.

——. "The Globalization of the Arms Industry: The Next Proliferation Challenge." *International Security*, Vol. 19, No. 2 (Fall 1994), pp. 170–198.

Blechman, Barry M., and Cathleen S. Fisher. "Phase Out the Bomb." *Foreign Policy*, No. 97 (Winter 1994/95), pp. 79–95.

Blix, Hans. "Verification of Nuclear Nonproliferation: The Lesson of Iraq." *The Washington Quarterly*, Vol. 15, No. 4 (Autumn 1992), pp. 57–66.

Bracken, Paul. "The Military After Next." *The Washington Quarterly*, Vol. 16, No. 4 (Autumn 1993), pp. 157–174.

——. "Nuclear Weapons and State Survival in North Korea." *Survival*, Vol. 35, No. 3 (Autumn 1993), pp. 137–153.

Brodie, Bernard. "Why Were We So (Strategically) Wrong?" *Foreign Policy*, No. 5 (Winter 1971–72), pp. 151–162.

Buzan, Barry, and Gerald Segal. "Rethinking East Asian Security." *Survival*, Vol. 36, No. 2 (Summer 1994), pp. 3–21.

Carpenter, Ted Galen. "Closing the Nuclear Umbrella." *Foreign Affairs*, Vol. 73, No. 2 (March/April 1994), pp. 8–13.

——. "A New Proliferation Policy." *National Interest*, No. 28 (Summer 1992), pp. 63–72.

Carus, W. Seth. "Missiles in the Third World: The 1991 Gulf War." *Orbis*, Vol. 35, No. 2 (Spring 1991), pp. 253–257.

——. "Proliferation and Security in Southwest Asia." *The Washington Quarterly*, Vol. 17, No. 2 (Spring 1994), pp. 129–139.

Chan, Steve. "Mirror, Mirror on the Wall...Are Freer Countries More Pacific?" *Journal of Conflict Resolution*, Vol. 28, No. 4 (December 1984), pp. 617–648.

Cheema, Zafar Iqbal. "Nuclear Diplomacy in South Asia During the Eighties." *Regional Security* (Quarterly Journal of the Institute of Regional Studies, Islamabad), Vol. 10, No. 3 (Summer 1992), pp. 53–66.

Chellany, Brahma. "Non-proliferation: An Indian Critique of U.S. Export Controls." *Orbis*, Vol. 38, No. 3 (Summer 1994), pp. 439–456.

———. "South Asia's Passage to Nuclear Power." *International Security*, Vol. 16., No. 1 (Summer 1991), pp. 43–72.

Chipman, John. "The Future of Strategic Studies: Beyond Even Grand Strategy." *Survival*, Vol. 34, No. 1 (Spring 1992), pp. 109–131.

———. "Third World Politics and Security in the 1990s: 'The World Forgetting, By the World Forgot'?" *The Washington Quarterly*, Vol. 14, No. 1 (Winter 1991), pp. 151–168.

Chubin, Shahram. "Does Iran Want Nuclear Weapons?" *Survival*, Vol. 37, No. 1 (Spring 1995), pp. 86–104.

———. "The South and the New World Order." *The Washington Quarterly*, Vol. 16, No. 4 (Autumn 1993), pp. 87–107.

Clancy, Tom, and Russell Seitz. "Five Minutes Past Midnight—and Welcome to the Age of Proliferation." *National Interest*, No. 26 (Winter 1991/92), pp. 3–12.

Claude, Inis L., Jr. "The New International Security Order: Changing Concepts." *Naval War College Review*, Vol. 47, No. 1, Sequence 345 (Winter 1994), pp. 9–17.

Cohen, Avner, and Marvin Miller. "How to Think About—and Implement—Nuclear Arms Control in the Middle East." *The Washington Quarterly*, Vol. 16, No. 2 (Spring 1993), pp. 101–113.

Cohen, Eliot A. "Distant Battles: Modern War in the Third World." *International Security*, Vol. 10, No. 4 (Spring 1986), pp. 143–171.

Cohen, Stuart A. "Israel's Changing Military Commitments, 1981–1991." *Journal of Strategic Studies*, Vol. 15, No. 3 (September 1992), pp. 330–350.

Cropsey, Seth. "The Only Credible Deterrent." *Foreign Affairs*, Vol. 73, No. 2 (March/April 1994), pp. 14–20.

Cupitt, Richard T. "Export Controls, Technology Transfer, and Nonproliferation: Learning from the Polish Experience." *Eye on Supply*, No. 7 (Fall 1992), pp. 40–42.

Cusack, Thomas R., and Richard J. Stoll. "Collective Security and State Survival in the Interstate System." *International Studies Quarterly*, Vol. 38, No. 1 (March 1994), pp. 33–59.

Daalder, Ivo. "The Future of Arms Control." *Survival*, Vol. 34, No. 1 (Spring 1992), pp. 51–73.

———. "What Vision for the Nuclear Future?" *The Washington Quarterly*, Vol. 18, No. 2 (Spring 1995), pp. 127–142.

David, Steven R. "Why the Third World Matters." *International Security*, Vol. 14, No. 1 (Summer 1989), pp. 50–85.

Dean, Jonathan, and David Koplow, guest editors. "Symposium on World Security and Weapons Proliferation." *Transnational Law and Contemporary Problems*, Vol. 2, No. 2 (Fall 1992).

Bibliography

Dessouki, Ali E. Hillal. "Globalization and the Two Spheres of Security." *The Washington Quarterly*, Vol. 16, No. 4 (Autumn 1993), pp. 109–117.

Deutch, John M. "The New Nuclear Threat." *Foreign Affairs*, Vol. 71, No. 4 (Fall 1992), pp. 120–134.

Diehl, Paul, and Jean Kingston. "Messenger or Message: Military Buildups and the Initiation of Conflict." *Journal of Politics*, Vol. 49, No. 3 (1987), pp. 801–813.

Dowty, Alan. "Sanctioning Iraq: The Limits of the New World Order." *The Washington Quarterly*, Vol. 17, No. 3 (Summer 1994), pp. 179–198.

Dunn, Lewis A. "Four Decades of Nuclear Nonproliferation: Some Lessons from Wins, Losses, and Draws." *The Washington Quarterly*, Vol. 13, No. 3 (Summer 1990), pp. 5–18.

Ekéus, Rolf. "The Iraqi Experience and the Future of Nuclear Nonproliferation." *The Washington Quarterly*, Vol. 15, No. 4 (Autumn 1992), pp. 67–74.

Fahmy, Mohamed Nabil. "Controlling Weapons of Mass Destruction in the Middle East." *American–Arab Affairs*, No. 35 (Winter 1990–91), pp. 126–134.

Fetter, Steve. "Ballistic Missiles and Weapons of Mass Destruction." *International Security*, Vol. 16, No. 1 (Summer 1991), pp. 5–42.

Freedman, Lawrence. "Great Powers, Vital Interests, and Nuclear Weapons." *Survival*, Vol. 34, No. 4 (Winter 1994/95), pp. 35–52.

———. "Order and Disorder in the New World." *Foreign Affairs*, Vol. 71, No. 1 (America and the World, 1991/92), pp. 20–37.

Friedberg, Aaron L. "Ripe for Rivalry: Prospects for Peace in a Multipolar Asia." *International Security*, Vol. 18, No. 3 (Winter 1993/94), pp. 5–33.

Frye, Alton. "Zero Ballistic Missiles." *Foreign Policy*, No. 88 (Fall 1992), pp. 3–20.

Gaddis, John. "The Long Peace: Elements of Stability in the Postwar International System." *International Security*, Vol. 10, No. 4 (Spring 1986).

Ganguly, Sumit. "South Asia After the Cold War." *The Washington Quarterly*, Vol. 15, No. 4 (Autumn 1992), pp. 173–186.

Garrity, Patrick J. "Implications of the Persian Gulf War for Regional Powers." *The Washington Quarterly*, Vol. 16, No. 3 (Summer 1993), pp. 153–170.

Giles, Gregory F. "Safeguarding the Undeclared Nuclear Arsenals." *The Washington Quarterly*, Vol. 16, No. 2 (Spring 1993), pp. 173–189.

Goodby, James E. "Can Arms Control Survive Peace?" *The Washington Quarterly*, Vol. 13, No. 4 (Autumn 1990), pp. 93–101.

Gouré, Dan. "Is There a Military-Technical Revolution in America's Future?" *The Washington Quarterly*, Vol. 16, No. 4 (Autumn 1993), pp. 175–192.

Gray, Colin S. "Villains, Victims, and Sheriffs: Strategic Studies and Security for an Interwar Period." *Comparative Strategy*, Vol. 13, No. 4 (October–December 1994), pp. 353–370.

Gregorian, Raffi. "Global Positioning Systems: A Military Revolution for the Third World?" *SAIS Review*, Vol. 13, No. 1 (Winter–Spring 1993), pp. 133–148.

Groom, A. J. R. "Paradigms in Conflict: The Strategist, the Conflict Researcher and the Peace Researcher." *Review of International Studies*, Vol. 14, No. 2 (1988), pp. 97–116.

Guertner, Gary L. "Deterrence and Conventional Military Forces." *The Washington Quarterly*, Vol. 16, No. 1 (Winter 1993), pp. 141–152.

Gupta, Amit. "Third World Militaries: New Suppliers, Deadlier Weapons." *Orbis*, Vol. 37, No. 1 (Winter 1993), pp. 57–68.

Hagan, Joe D. "Domestic Political Systems and War Proneness." *Mershon International Studies Review* (supplement to the *International Studies Quarterly*), Vol. 38, Supplement 2 (October 1994), pp. 183–208.

Harvey, John R. "Regional Ballistic Missiles and Advanced Strike Aircraft: Comparing Military Effectiveness." *International Security*, Vol. 17, No. 2 (Fall 1992), pp. 41–83.

Heo, Man-Ho. "Confidence Building and Arms Control Negotiations in South–North High Level Talks: Issues and Prospects." *Korean Journal of International Studies*, Vol. 24, No. 1 (Spring 1993), pp. 69–96.

Hewitt, Daniel. "Controlling Military Expenditures: Military Expenditures in the Developing World." *Finance & Development*, Vol. 28, No. 3 (September 1991), pp. 22–25.

———. "What Determines Military Expenditures?" *Finance & Development*, Vol. 28, No. 4 (December 1991), pp. 22–25.

Hilali, A. Z. "Arms Control in the Third World." *Strategic Studies*, Vol. 14, No. 3 (Spring 1991), pp. 57–76.

Howlett, Darryl, and John Simpson. "Nuclearisation and Denuclearisation in South Africa." *Survival*, Vol. 35, No. 3 (Autumn 1993), pp. 154–173.

Hussain, Syed Rifaat. "The Future of Non-Aligned Movement and its Implications for Pakistan." *Strategic Studies*, Vol. 14, No. 4 (Summer 1992), pp. 43–51.

Iklé, Fred C. "Nth Countries and Disarmament." *Bulletin of the Atomic Scientists* (December 1966).

Inbar, Efraim. "Israel and Arms Control." *Arms Control*, Vol. 13, No. 2 (September 1992), pp. 214–221.

———. "Israel's Strategic Environment." *Strategic Review* (Fall 1992), pp. 34–40.

Inbar, Efraim, and Shmuel Sandler. "Israel's Deterrence Strategy Revisited." *Security Studies*, Vol. 3, No. 2 (Winter 1993/94), pp. 330–358.

Jervis, Robert. "The Political Effects of Nuclear Weapons: A Comment." *International Security*, Vol. 13, No. 2 (Fall 1988), pp. 80–90.

Johnston, Douglas M. "Anticipating Instability in the Asia–Pacific Region." *The Washington Quarterly*, Vol. 15, No. 3 (Summer 1992), pp. 103–112.

Karp, Aaron. "Controlling Ballistic Missile Proliferation." *Survival*, Vol. 33, No. 6 (November/December 1991), pp. 517–530.

Karsh, Efraim, and Yezid Sayigh. "A Cooperative Approach to Arab–Israeli Security." *Survival*, Vol. 36, No. 1 (Spring 1994), pp. 114–125.

Kellman, Barry. "Bridling the International Trade of Catastrophic Weaponry." *American University Law Review*, Vol. 43, No. 3 (Spring 1994), pp. 755–847.

Kemp, Geoffrey. "Regional Security, Arms Control, and the End of the Cold War." *The Washington Quarterly*, Vol. 13, No. 4 (Autumn 1990), pp. 33–51.

Klare, Michael T. "An Arms Control Agenda for the Third World." *Arms Control Today*, Vol. 20, No. 3 (April 1990, pp. 8–12.

———. "Growing Firepower in the Third World." *Bulletin of the Atomic Scientists* (May 1990), pp. 9–13.

———. "The Next Great Arms Race." *Foreign Affairs*, Vol. 72, No. 3 (Summer 1993), pp. 136–154.

Kolodziej, Edward A. "Renaissance in Security Studies? Caveat Lector!" *International Studies Quarterly*, Vol. 36., No. 4 (December 1992), pp. 421–438.

Koplow, David A. "Parsing Good Faith: Has the United States Violated Article VI of the Nuclear Non-Proliferation Treaty?" *Wisconsin Law Review*, Vol. 1993, No. 2, pp. 301–394.

Koplow, David A., and Philip G. Schrag. "Linking Disarmament and Development." *SAIS Review*, Vol. 11, No. 2 (Summer/Fall 1991), pp. 95–112.

Koubi, Vally. "Military Buildups and Arms Control Agreements." *International Studies Quarterly*, Vol. 38, No. 4 (December 1994), pp. 605–620.

Lake, Anthony. "Confronting Backlash States." *Foreign Affairs*, Vol. 73, No. 2 (March/April 1994), pp. 45–55.

Laurance, Edward J. "The UN Register of Conventional Arms: Rationales and Prospects for Compliance and Effectiveness." *The Washington Quarterly*, Vol. 16, No. 2 (Spring 1993), pp. 163–172.

Lavoy, Peter R. "Nuclear Myths and the Causes of Nuclear Proliferation." *Security Studies*, Vol. 2, No. 3/4 (Spring/Summer 1993), pp. 192–212.

Layne, Christopher. "Kant or Cant: The Myth of the Democratic Peace." *International Security*, Vol. 19, No. 2 (Fall 1994), pp. 5–49.

———. "The Unipolar Illusion: Why New Great Powers Will Rise." *International Security*, Vol. 17, No. 4 (Spring 1993), pp. 5–51.

Lee, Chung Min. "The Future of Arms Control in the Korean Peninsula." *The Washington Quarterly*, Vol. 14, No. 3 (Summer 1991), pp. 181–197.

Lehman, Ronald F., II. "Arms Control: Passing the Torch as Time Runs Out." *The Washington Quarterly*, Vol. 16, No. 3 (Summer 1993), pp. 37–52.

Lewis, William H., and Christopher C. Joyner. "Proliferation of Unconventional Weapons: The Case for Coercive Arms Control." *Comparative Strategy*, Vol. 10, No. 4 (October–December 1991), pp. 299–309.

Lieber, Robert J. "Existential Realism After the Cold War." *The Washington Quarterly*, Vol. 16, No. 1 (Winter 1993), pp. 155–168.

Luck, Edward C., and Toby Trister Gati. "Whose Collective Security?" *The Washington Quarterly*, Vol. 15, No. 2 (Spring 1992), pp. 43–56.

Luttwak, Edward N. "An Emerging Postnuclear Era?" *The Washington Quarterly*, Vol. 11, No. 1 (Winter 1988), pp. 5–15.

——. "Where Are the Great Powers?" *Foreign Affairs*, Vol. 73, No. 4 (July/August 1994), pp. 23–28.

MacKenzie, Donald. "Technology and the Arms Race: A Review." *International Security*, Vol. 14, No. 1 (Summer 1989), pp. 161–175.

Magalhaes, Fernando Simas. "The Impact of East–West Confidence-building Measures on Global Security: A View from the South." *Disarmament*, Vol. 13, No. 1 (1990), pp. 158–161.

Mahbubani, Kishore. "The West and the Rest." *National Interest*, No. 28 (Summer 1992), pp. 3–12.

Mahnken, Thomas G. "America's Next War." *The Washington Quarterly*, Vol. 16, No. 3 (Summer 1993), pp. 171–184.

——. "The Arrow and the Shield: U.S. Responses to Ballistic Missile Proliferation." *The Washington Quarterly*, Vol. 14, No. 1 (Winter 1991), pp. 189–203.

——. "Why Third World Space Systems Matter." *Orbis*, Vol. 35, No. 4 (Fall 1991), pp. 563–579.

Mahnken, Thomas G., and Timothy D. Hoyt. "Missile Proliferation and American Interests." *SAIS Review*, Vol. 10, No. 1 (Winter–Spring 1990), pp. 101–116.

Mazarr, Michael J. "Nuclear Weapons After the Cold War." *The Washington Quarterly*, Vol. 15, No. 3 (Summer 1992), pp. 185–201.

McCain, John. "Controlling Arms Sales to the Third World." *The Washington Quarterly*, Vol. 14, No. 2 (Spring 1991), pp. 79–90.

MccGwire, Michael. "Is There a Future for Nuclear Weapons?" *International Affairs*, Vol. 70, No. 2 (April 1994), pp. 211–228.

——. "Prospects for a Nuclear Free World." In *Brassey's Defence Yearbook 1995*. Edited by Michael Clarke. London: Brassey's (U.K.) for the Centre for Defence Studies, Spring 1995.

McNamara, Robert S. "Slowing Third World Militarization." *Issues in Science and Technology,* Vol. 9, No. 3 (Spring 1993), pp. 35–40.

Mearsheimer, John. "Back to the Future: Instability in Europe After the Cold War." *International Security,* Vol. 15, No. 1 (Summer 1990).

———. "The False Promise of International Institutions." *International Security,* Vol. 19, No. 3 (Winter 1994/95), pp. 5–49.

Millot, Marc Dean. "Facing the Emerging Reality of Regional Nuclear Adversaries." *The Washington Quarterly,* Vol. 17, No. 3 (Summer 1994), pp. 41–71.

Molander, Roger C., and Peter A. Wilson. "On Dealing with the Prospect of Nuclear Chaos." *The Washington Quarterly,* Vol. 17, No. 3 (Summer 1994), pp. 19–39.

Moodie, Michael. "Beyond Proliferation: The Challenge of Technology Diffusion." *The Washington Quarterly,* Vol. 18, No. 2 (Spring 1995), pp. 183–202.

———. "Transparency in Armaments: A New Item for the New Security Agenda." *The Washington Quarterly,* Vol. 15, No. 3 (Summer 1992), pp. 75–82.

Morgan, M. Granger, K. Subrahmanyam, K. Sundarji, and Robert M. White. "India and the United States." *The Washington Quarterly,* Vol. 18, No. 2 (Spring 1995), pp. 155–179.

Moritan, Roberto Garcia. "The Developing World and the New World Order." *The Washington Quarterly,* Vol. 15, No. 4 (Autumn 1992), pp. 149–156.

Mueller, John. "The Essential Irrelevance of Nuclear Weapons: Stability in the Postwar World." *International Security,* Vol. 13, No. 2 (Fall 1988), pp. 55–79.

Müller, Harald. "Das nukleare Nichtverbreitungsregime im Wandel. Konsequenzen aus einem stürmischen Jahr." *Europa Archiv,* Vol. 47, No. 2 (January 25, 1992), pp. 51–58.

Müller, Harald, and Mitchell Reiss. "Counterproliferation: Putting New Wine in Old Bottles." *The Washington Quarterly,* Vol. 18, No. 2 (Spring 1995), pp. 143–154.

Neuman, Stephanie. "The Arms Market: Who's On Top?" *Orbis,* Vol. 33, No. 4 (Fall 1989).

———. "Controlling the Arms Trade: Idealistic Dream or Realpolitik?" *The Washington Quarterly,* Vol. 16, No. 3, pp. 53–75.

Nolan, Janne E. "Ballistic Missile Proliferation in the Third World: The Limits of Nonproliferation." *Arms Control Today,* November 1989, pp. 9–14.

———. "Controlling the Global Arms Market." *The Washington Quarterly,* Vol. 14, No. 3 (Summer 1991).

Nolan, Janne E., and Albert Wheelon. "Third World Ballistic Missiles." *Scientific American* (August 1990).

Nuruzzaman, M. "The Arms Race in South Asia: Some Approaches to Stability." *Strategic Studies,* Vol. 16, Nos. 1 and 2 (Autumn and Winter 1993), pp. 27–43.

Nye, Joseph S., Jr. "Arms Control After the Cold War." *Foreign Affairs*, Vol. 68, No. 5 (Winter 1989–1990).

———. "Maintaining the Non-Proliferation Regime." *International Organization*, Vol. 35, No. 1 (Winter 1981).

———. "What New World Order?" *Foreign Affairs*, Vol. 71, No. 2 (Spring 1992), pp. 83–96.

Nye, Joseph S., Jr., and Sean M. Lynn-Jones. "International Security Studies: A Report of a Conference on the State of the Field." *International Security*, Vol. 12, No. 4 (Spring 1987), pp. 5–27.

Owen, John M. "How Liberalism Produces Democratic Peace." *International Security*, Vol. 19, No. 2 (Fall 1994), pp. 87–125.

Panofsky, Wolfgang K. H., and George Bunn. "The Doctrine of the Nuclear-Weapon-States and the Future of Non-Proliferation." *Arms Control Today*, July/August 1994, pp. 3–9.

Payne, Keith B. "Proliferation, Deterrence, Stability and Missile Defense." *Comparative Strategy*, Vol. 13, No. 1 (January–March 1994), pp. 117–130.

Pearson, Graham S. "Prospects for Chemical and Biological Arms Control: The Web of Deterrence." *The Washington Quarterly*, Vol. 16, No. 2 (Spring 1993), pp. 145–162.

Perkovich, George. "The Plutonium Genie." *Foreign Affairs*, Vol. 72, No. 3 (Summer 1993), pp. 153–165.

Pilat, Joseph F., and Paul C. White. "Technology and Strategy in a Changing World." *The Washington Quarterly*, Vol. 13, No. 2 (Spring 1990), pp. 79–91.

Potter, William C. "The New Nuclear Suppliers." *Orbis*, Vol. 36, No. 2 (Spring 1992), pp. 199–210.

Quester, George H., and Victor A. Utgoff. "No-First-Use and Nonproliferation: Redefining Extended Deterrence." *The Washington Quarterly*, Vol. 17, No. 2 (Spring 1994), pp. 103–114.

———. "Toward an International Nuclear Security Policy." *The Washington Quarterly*, Vol. 17, No. 4 (Autumn 1994), pp. 5–18.

———. "U.S. Arms Reductions and Nuclear Nonproliferation: The Counterproductive Possibilities." *The Washington Quarterly*, Vol. 16, No. 1 (Winter 1993), pp. 129–140.

Quinlan, Michael. "The Future of Nuclear Weapons: Policy for Western Possessors?" *International Affairs*, Vol. 69, No. 3 (1993), pp. 485–596.

Redick, John. "Latin America's Emerging Non-Proliferation Consensus." *Arms Control Today*, Vol. 24, No. 2 (March 1994), pp. 3–9.

Reiss, Mitchell. "The Last Nuclear Summit?" *The Washington Quarterly*, Vol. 17, No. 3 (Summer 1994), pp. 5–15.

Revelle, Daniel J., and Lora Lumpe. "Third World Submarines." *Scientific American*, August 1994, pp. 26–31.

Bibliography

Rimanelli, Marco. "The Rationale, Evolution, and Future of Arms Control." *Comparative Strategy*, Vol. 11, No. 3 (July–September 1992), pp. 307–329.

Roberts, Adam. "The United Nations and International Security." *Survival*, Vol. 35, No. 2 (Summer 1993), pp. 3–30.

Roberts, Brad. "Arms Control and the End of the Cold War." *The Washington Quarterly*, Vol. 15, No. 4 (Autumn 1992), pp. 39–56.

———. "Controlling Chemical Weapons." In Jonathan Dean and David Koplow, guest editors. "Symposium on World Security and Weapons Proliferation." *Transnational Law and Contemporary Problems*, Vol. 2, No. 2 (Fall 1992), pp. 435–452.

———. "From Nonproliferation to Antiproliferation." *International Security*, Vol. 18, No. 1 (Summer 1993), pp. 139–173.

———. "1995 and the End of the Post–Cold War Era." *The Washington Quarterly*, Vol. 18, No. 1 (Winter 1995), pp. 5–25.

Rose, Gideon. "A Farewell to Arms Control." *National Interest*, No. 30 (Winter 1992/93), pp. 93–100.

Rosh, Robert M. "Third World Arms Production and the Evolving Interstate System." *Journal of Conflict Resolution*, Vol. 34, No. 1 (March 1990), pp. 57–73.

Ross, Andrew L. "Do-it-yourself Weaponry." *Bulletin of the Atomic Scientists*, Vol. 46, No. 4 (May 1990), p. 20.

Rothstein, Robert L. "Democracy, Conflict, and Development in the Third World." *The Washington Quarterly*, Vol. 14, No. 2 (Spring 1991), pp. 43–63.

Rühle, Michael. "NATO and the Coming Proliferation Threat." *Comparative Strategy*, Vol. 13, No. 3 (July–September 1994), pp. 313–320.

Sagan, Scott D. "The Perils of Proliferation: Organization Theory, Deterrence Theory, and the Spread of Nuclear Weapons." *International Security*, Vol. 18, No. 4 (Spring 1994), pp. 66–107.

Schneider, Barry R. "Nuclear Proliferation and Counter-Proliferation: Policy Issues and Debates." *Mershon International Studies Review* (supplement to the *International Studies Quarterly*), Vol. 38, Supplement 2 (October 1994), pp. 209–234.

Schroeder, Paul W. "Historical Reality vs. Neo-realist Theory." *International Security*, Vol. 19, No. 1 (Summer 1994), pp. 108–148.

———. "The New World Order: A Historical Perspective." *The Washington Quarterly*, Vol. 17, No. 2 (Spring 1994), pp. 25–43.

Segal, Gerald. "Managing New Arms Races in the Asia/Pacific." *The Washington Quarterly*, Vol. 15, No. 3 (Summer 1992), pp. 82–102.

Simpson, John, and Darryl Howlett. "The NPT Renewal Conference: Stumbling toward 1995." *International Security*, Vol. 19, No. 1 (Summer 1994), pp. 41–71.

———. "Nuclear Non-proliferation: The Way Forward." *Survival,* Vol 33, No. 6 (November/December 1991), pp. 483–499.

Slocombe, Walter B. "Technology and the Future of Arms Control." In *New Technology and Western Security Policy, Part II,* pp. 39–47. Adelphi Paper No. 198. London: International Institute for Strategic Studies, 1985.

Sloss, Leon. "U.S. Strategic Forces After the Cold War: Policies and Strategies." *The Washington Quarterly,* Vol. 14, No. 4 (Autumn 1992), pp. 145–156.

Snider, Don M., and Gregory Grant. "The Future of Conventional Warfare and U.S. Military Strategy." *The Washington Quarterly,* Vol. 15, No. 1 (Winter 1992), pp. 203–228.

Sokolski, Henry. "Fighting Proliferation with Intelligence." *Orbis,* Vol. 38, No. 2 (Spring 1994), pp. 245–260.

———. "Nonapocalyptic Proliferation: A New Strategic Threat?" *The Washington Quarterly,* Vol. 17, No. 2 (Spring 1994), pp. 115–128.

Solingen, Etel. "The Political Economy of Nuclear Restraint." *International Security,* Vol. 19, No. 2 (Fall 1994), pp. 126–169.

Spector, Leonard S. "Neo-Nonproliferation." *Survival,* Vol. 37, No. 1 (Spring 1995), pp. 66–85.

———. "Repentant Nuclear Proliferants." *Foreign Policy,* No. 88 (Fall 1992), pp. 3–20.

Spiro, David E. "The Insignificance of the Liberal Peace." *International Security,* Vol. 19, No. 2 (Fall 1994), pp. 50–86.

Steinberg, Gerald M. "Middle East Arms Control and Regional Security." *Survival,* Vol. 36, No. 1 (Spring 1994), pp. 126–141.

———. "Non-proliferation: Time for Regional Approaches?" *Orbis,* Vol. 38, No. 3 (Summer 1994), pp. 409–423.

Stremlau, John. "Clinton's Dollar Diplomacy." *Foreign Policy,* No. 97 (Winter 1994/95), pp. 18–35.

Subrahmanyam, K. "Export Controls and the North–South Controversy." *The Washington Quarterly,* Vol. 16, No. 2 (Spring 1993), pp. 135–144.

Terrill, W. Andrew. "The Gulf War and Ballistic Missile Proliferation." *Comparative Strategy,* Vol. 11, No. 2 (April–June 1992), pp. 163–176.

Wallace, Michael D. "Arms Races and Escalation." *Journal of Conflict Resolution,* Vol. 23 (March 1979), pp. 3–16.

Wallensteen, Peter, and Karin Axell. "Conflict Resolution and the End of the Cold War, 1989–93." *Journal of Peace Research,* Vol. 31, No. 3 (August 1994), pp. 333–349.

Walt, Stephen M. "The Renaissance of Security Studies." *International Studies Quarterly,* Vol. 35 (June 1991), pp. 211–239.

Waltz, Kenneth N. "The Emerging Structure of International Politics." *International Security*, Vol. 18, No. 2 (Fall 1993), pp. 44–79.

Watts, Barry. "The Conventional Utility of Strategic-Nuclear Forces." *The Washington Quarterly*, Vol. 14, No. 4 (Autumn 1991), pp. 173–202.

Weigley, Russell F. "War and the Paradox of Technology." *International Security*, Vol. 14, No. 2 (Fall 1989), pp. 192–202.

Weiss, Thomas G. "New Challenges for UN Military Operations: Implementing an Agenda for Peace." *The Washington Quarterly*, Vol. 16, No. 1 (Winter 1993), pp. 51–66.

Welch, Thomas J. "Technology Change and Security." *The Washington Quarterly*, Vol. 13, No. 2 (Spring 1990), pp. 111–120.

Weltman, John J. "Managing Nuclear Multipolarity." *International Security*, Vol. 6, No. 3 (Winter 1981–82).

———. "Nuclear Devolution and World Order." *World Politics*, Vol. 32, No. 2 (January 1980), pp. 169–193.

Wohlforth, William, C. "Realism and the End of the Cold War." *International Security*, Vol. 19, No. 3 (Winter 1994/95), pp. 91–129.

Wohlstetter, Albert. "The Delicate Balance of Terror." *Foreign Affairs*, Vol. 37, No. 2 (January 1959), pp. 211–234.

———. "Nuclear Sharing: NATO and the N+1 Country." *Foreign Affairs*, Vol. 39, No. 3 (April 1961), pp. 355–387.

Zagare, Frank C., and D. Marc Kilgour. "Asymmetric Deterrence." *International Studies Quarterly*, Vol. 37, No. 1 (March 1993), pp. 1–28.

Zakaria, Fareed. "Is Realism Finished?" *National Interest*, No. 30 (Winter 1992/93).

Ziemke, Caroline F. "Peace Without Strings? Interwar Naval Arms Control Revisited." *The Washington Quarterly*, Vol. 15, No. 4 (Autumn 1992), pp. 87–108.

Zimmerman, Peter D. "Proliferation: Bronze Medal Technology Is Enough." *Orbis*, Vol. 38, No. 1 (Winter 1994), pp. 67–82.

Reports

Ad Hoc Working Group on Non-Proliferation and Arms Control. *Non-Proliferation and Arms Control: Issues and Options for the Clinton Administration*. Ad Hoc Working Group on Non-Proliferation and Arms Control, January 1993.

Advisory Council on Peace and Security. *Towards A Multifaceted Non-Proliferation Policy.* The Hague, The Netherlands: Advisory Council on Peace and Security, December 1992.

———. *What Is Peace Worth to Us? The United Nations After the Cold War.* The Hague, The Netherlands: Advisory Council on Peace and Security, May 1992.

ANSER. *Decision Maker's Guide to International Space.* STDN 92–12. Arlington, Va.: ANSER, August 1992.

Aspen Strategy Group. *New Threats: Responding to the Proliferation of Nuclear, Chemical and Delivery Capabilities in the Third World.* Lanham, Md.: University Press of America, 1990.

Aspin, Les. *From Deterrence to Denuking: Dealing with Proliferation in the 1990s.* Statement by the chairman, House Armed Services Committee, February 18, 1992.

Bermudez, Joseph S., Jr. *Proliferation for Profit: North Korea in the Middle East.* Research Memorandum No. 27. Washington, D.C.: The Washington Institute, July 1994.

Biddle, Stephen, and Robert Zirkle. "Technology, Civil-Military Relations, and Warfare in the Developing World." Alexandria, Va.: Institute for Defense Analyses, January 28, 1993.

Bitzinger, Richard A. *The Globalization of Arms Production: Defense Markets in Transition.* Washington, D.C.: Defense Budget Project, December 1993.

Boutin, J. D. Kenneth. "Structural Changes in the International Technology Order and Their Impact on the Strategic Environment of the 21st Century." Paper presented to the ISSS and ISA/West Conference, Phoenix, Arizona, November 5-7, 1992.

Boutros-Ghali, Boutros. *An Agenda for Peace: Preventive Diplomacy, Peacemaking and Peace-keeping.* New York: United Nations, 1992.

Brassey's Defence Yearbook 1995. Edited by Michael Clarke. London: Brassey's (U.K.) for the Centre for Defence Studies, Spring 1995.

Browne & Shaw Research Corporation. *The Diffusion of Combat Aircraft, Missiles, and Their Supporting Technologies.* Report prepared for the Office of the Assistant Secretary of Defense for International Security Affairs, Washington, D.C., October 1966.

Bunn, George, Roland M. Timerbaev, and James F. Leonard. *Nuclear Disarmament: How Much Have the Five Nuclear Powers Promised in the Non-Proliferation Treaty?* Washington, D.C.: The Lawyers Alliance for World Security, the Committee for National Security, and the Washington Council on Non-Proliferation, 1994.

Butterworth, Robert L. *Space Systems and the Military Geography of Future Regional Conflicts.* Report No. 14. Los Alamos, N.Mex.: Center for National Security Studies, Los Alamos National Laboratory, January 1992.

Carnegie Endowment for International Peace. *Nuclear Successor States of the Soviet Union: Nuclear Weapon and Sensitive Export Status Report.* No. 1. A cooperative project of the Carnegie Endowment for International Peace and the Monterey Institute of International Studies, distributed in English and Russian. Washington, D.C.: Carnegie Endowment for International Peace, 1994.

Bibliography

Carnegie Task Force on Non-Proliferation and South Asian Security. *Nuclear Weapons and South Asian Security.* Washington, D.C.: Carnegie Endowment for International Peace, 1988.

Center for International Security and Arms Control. *Assessing Ballistic Missile Proliferation and Its Control.* Stanford, Calif.: Center for International Security and Arms Control, Stanford University, November 1991.

Center for Naval Analyses. *Weapons Proliferation and U.S. National Security.* Symposia Series. Alexandria, Va.: Center for Naval Analyses, 1990.

Center for Strategic and International Studies. *Breaking Down the Barricades: Reforming Export Controls to Increase U.S. Competitiveness.* Final report of the Project on Export Controls in a Changing World. Washington, D.C.: Center for Strategic and International Studies, 1994.

———. *Dynamic Net Military Assessment of the Middle East.* Washington, D.C.: Center for Strategic and International Studies, 1992.

———. *Negotiating a U.S.–EURATOM Successor Agreement: Finding Common Ground in Nuclear Cooperation.* A Consensus Report of the CSIS U.S.–EURATOM Senior Policy Panel. Washington, D.C.: Center for Strategic and International Studies, October 1990.

———. *Toward a Nuclear Peace: The Future of Nuclear Weapons and U.S. Foreign and Defense Policy.* Report of the CSIS Nuclear Strategy Study Group. Washington, D.C.: Center for Strategic and International Studies, June 1993.

Center for Strategic Studies. *The Defense of Small and Medium-Sized Countries.* Paper No. 17. Tel Aviv, Israel: Tel Aviv University, August 1982.

Chafetz, Glenn, and Suzette Grillot. "National Role Conception and Nuclear Proliferation: Comparing Belarus and Ukraine." Unpublished Conference Paper, Athens, Ga., Autumn 1994.

Cohen, Avner. "Nuclear Weapons, Opacity, and Democracy: Understanding the Israeli Case." Unpublished Conference Paper, March 1992.

Commission on Integrated Long-Term Strategy. *Discriminate Deterrence.* Washington, D.C.: GPO, January 1988.

Cordesman, Anthony H. "After the Gulf War: The World Arms Trade and Its Arms Races in the 1990s." Working draft released by the office of Senate John McCain, Washington, D.C., May 1991.

———. "Current Trends in Arms Sales and Proliferation in the Middle East." Paper released by the office of Senator John McCain, Washington, D.C., January 1992.

———. "Regional Security Options in the Middle East: The Politics of Reality versus the Politics of Hope." Paper released by the office of Senator John McCain, Washington, D.C., July 25, 1991.

———. *U.S. Defense Policy: Resources and Capabilities.* Working Paper No. 98. Washington, D.C.: Woodrow Wilson International Center for Scholars, December 1993.

Deger, Saadet. "The Economics of Disarmament: Prospects, Problems and Policies for the Disarmament Dividend." Innocenti Occasional Papers, Economic Policy Series No. 30. Florence, Italy: UNICEF, International Child Development Centre, August 1992.

Fainberg, Anthony. *Strengthening IAEA Safeguards: Lessons from Iraq.* Stanford, Calif.: Center for International Security and Arms Control, Stanford University, 1993.

"Final Statement of the Palme Commission on Disarmament and Security Issues." *Disarmament*, Vol. 13, No. 1 (1990), pp. 165-186.

Graybeal, Sidney, and Patricia McFate. *GPALs and Foreign Space Launch Vehicle Capabilities.* A report of the Science Applications International Corporation, McLean, Va., prepared for the Strategic Defense Initiative Organization, February 1992.

Harvey, John. "Common Sense About High-Technology Export Controls." Unpublished research paper prepared for the Center for International Security and Arms Control, Stanford University, Stanford, Calif., August 9, 1994.

Hazlett, James A. "Low Intensity Conflict and Anti-Submarine Warfare." Unpublished research paper prepared for the Center for Strategic and International Studies, Washington, D.C., June 1, 1992.

Inbar, Efraim, and Shmuel Sandler. "Israeli Deterrence Revisited." Paper prepared for the Bar-Ilan Center for Strategic Studies, 1992.

Kober, Avi. "Deterrence, Early Warning and Strategic Decision: The Israeli Security Conception in the Wake of the Gulf War." Depaartment of International Relations, Hebrew University of Jerusalem, Israel, n.d.

Krepon, Michael, Amy E. Smithson, and James A. Schear. *The U.S. Arms Control and Disarmament Agency: Restructuring for the Post–Cold War Era.* Washington, D.C.: Henry L. Stimson Center, 1992.

Mahnken, Thomas G. "Shiva's Trident: Prospects for India's Acquisition of Advanced Military Technologies." Unpublished Research Paper, July 19, 1993.

Mazarr, Michael J. *The Military Technical Revolution: A Structural Framework.* Final Report of the CSIS Study Group on the MTR. Washington, D.C.: Center for Strategic and International Studies, March 1993.

McFate, Patricia Bliss, Sidney N. Graybeal, George Lindsey, and D. Marc Kilgore. *Constraining Proliferation: The Contribution of Verification Synergies.* Arms Control Verification Studies No. 5. Report prepared for the Non-Proliferation, Arms Control and Disarmament Division, Department of External Affairs, Ottawa, March 1993.

McMahon, K. Scott, and Dennis M. Gormley. *Controlling the Spread of Land-Attack Cruise Missiles.* Report prepared by the American Institute for Strategic Cooperation, Marina del Rey, Calif., September 1994.

Mohan, C. Raja. "Crisis Management and Confidence-Building in South Asia." Research paper prepared for the United States Institute of Peace, Washington, D.C., 1993.

Müller, Harald, Matthias Dembinski, Alexander Kelle, and Annette Schaper. *From Black Sheep to White Angel? The New German Export Control Policy.* Report No. 32. Frankfurt, Germany: Peace Research Institute, 1994.

National Academy of Sciences, Committee on International Security and Arms Control. *Management and Disposition of Excess Weapons Plutonium.* Washington, D.C.: National Academy Press, 1994.

North Atlantic Assembly, Defence and Security Committee. *1990 Reports.* Brussels, Belgium: North Atlantic Assembly, November 1990.

——, Special Committee on Alliance Strategy and Arms Control. *1991 Report.* Brussels, Belgium: North Atlantic Assembly, October 1991.

Palme Commission. *Common Security: A Programme for Disarmament: The Report of the Independent Commission on Disarmament and Security Issues.* London: Pan Books, 1982.

Palme Commission on Disarmament and Security Issues. *A World At Peace: Common Security in the Twenty-first Century.* Stockholm: The Palme Commission, 1989.

Pilat, Joseph. "Consolidating Nonproliferation Regimes." Unpublished Paper, October 1992.

Primakov, Y. "A New Challenge After the Cold War: The Proliferation of Weapons of Mass Destruction." Report prepared by the Foreign Intelligence Service of the Russian Federation, Moscow, 1993, translated by U.S. Foreign Broadcast Information Service in February 1993. Summary and excerpts made available by U.S. Committee on Government Affairs, U.S. Senate, February 24, 1993, and subsequently published in *Proliferation Threats of the 1990's,* Hearing Before the Committee on Governmental Affairs, U.S. Senate, 103rd Cong., 1st Sess., February 24, 1993. Washington, D.C.: GPO, 1993.

Proliferation Study Team. *The Emerging Ballistic Missile Threat to the United States.* Washington, D.C.: Proliferation Study Team, February 1993.

Reiss, Mitchell, and Harald Müller, eds. *International Perspectives on Counterproliferation.* Working Paper No. 99. Washington, D.C.: Woodrow Wilson International Center for Scholars, January 1995.

Rosen, Stephen Peter. "Lessons from the 1991 U.S.-Iraq War: Hypothetical Nuclear Weapons Use." Draft.

Simon Wiesenthal Center. *Weapons of Mass Destruction: The Cases of Iran, Syria, and Libya.* Los Angeles, Calif.: Simon Wiesenthal Center, August 1992.

Sokolski, Henry. "The Greatest Proliferation Threat: Our Outmoded Thinking." Presentation to Defense Policy Board, Washington, D.C., May 1, 1991.

Solingen, Etel. *The Domestic Sources of Nuclear Postures: Influencing "Fence-sitters" in the Post–Cold War Era.* Policy Paper No. 8. La Jolla, Calif.: Institute on Global Conflict and Cooperation, University of California, October 1994.

Spector, Leonard S., and Virginia Foran. *Preventing Weapons Proliferation: Should the Regimes Be Combined?* Report of the Thirty-Third Strategy for Peace, U.S. Foreign Policy Conference, The Stanley Foundation, Muscatine, Iowa, October 22–24, 1992.

Stanley Foundation. *State of the United Nations: Decline or Regeneration for the Next Fifty Years.* Report of the Twenty-Ninth United Nations of the Next Decade Conference, The Stanley Foundation, Muscatine, Iowa, June 19–24, 1994.

———. *The United Nations and Multilateral Sanctions: New Options for US Policy?* Report of the Thirty-Third Strategy for Peace, U.S. Foreign Policy Conference, The Stanley Foundation, Muscatine, Iowa, October 22–24, 1992.

Stockholm International Peace Research Institute. *SIPRI Yearbook, 1991, World Armaments and Disarmament.* Oxford: Oxford University Press for the Stockholm International Peace Research Institute, 1992.

———. *SIPRI Yearbook, 1992, World Armaments and Disarmament.* Oxford: Oxford University Press for the Stockholm International Peace Research Institute, 1993.

———. *SIPRI Yearbook, 1993, World Armaments and Disarmament.* Oxford: Oxford University Press for the Stockholm International Peace Research Institute, 1993.

———. *SIPRI Yearbook, 1994, World Armaments and Disarmament.* Oxford: Oxford University Press for the Stockholm International Peace Research Institute, 1994.

Swaine, Michael D. *The Modernization of the Chinese People's Liberation Army: Prospects and Implications for Northeast Asia.* Vol. 5, No. 3. Seattle, Wash.: National Bureau of Asian Research, October 1994.

Tanham, George K. *Indian Strategic Thought: An Interpretive Essay.* RAND Report R–4207–USDP. Prepared for the Under Secretary of Defense for Policy, Washington, D.C., 1992.

Tanner, Fred. *Arms Control in Times of Conflict: A Contribution to Conflict Management in the Post–Cold War World.* Paper No. 7. College Park, Md.: Project on Rethinking Arms Control, Center for International and Security Studies at Maryland, School of Public Affairs, University of Maryland at College Park, October 1993.

United Nations, Report of the Secretary General. *Chemical and Bacteriological (Biological) Weapons and the Effects of Their Possible Use.* A/7575/Rev. 1, S/9292/Rev. 1. New York, 1969.

———, Department of Disarmament Affairs. "Transparency in Armaments." Topical Papers 3. New York, 1990.

———, Institute for Disarmament Research. "Chemical Weapons Convention." UNIDIR Newsletter No. 20. Geneva, December 1992.

———. "The Conference on Disarmament." UNIDIR Newsletter No. 1. Geneva, April 1992.

———. *Disarmament, Environment, and Development and Their Relevance to the Least Developed Countries.* UNIDIR Research Paper No. 10. UNIDIR/91/83. New York, 1991.

———. *Economic Aspects of Disarmament.* UNIDIR/92/94. Geneva, 1993.

———. "The Implications of IAEA Inspections under Security Council Resolution 687." UNIDIR Research Paper No. 11. New York, 1992.

———. "The Non-Proliferation Treaty: How to Remove the Residual Threats." UNIDIR Research Paper No. 13. New York, 1992.

U.S. Arms Control and Disarmament Agency. *Arms Control and Disarmament Agreements: Texts and Histories of the Negotiations.* 1990 ed. Washington, D.C.: Arms Control and Disarmament Agency, 1990.

———. *World Military Expenditures and Arms Transfers, 1972–1982.* ACDA Publication 117. Washington, D.C.: Arms Control and Disarmament Agency, April 1984.

———. *World Military Expenditures and Arms Transfers, 1990.* Washington, D.C.: Arms Control and Disarmament Agency, November 1991.

U.S. Congress, Congressional Research Service. *Analysis of Six Issues About Nuclear Capabilities of India, Iraq, Libya, and Pakistan.* Prepared for the Subcommittee on Arms Control, Oceans, and International Operations and Environment of the Committee on Foreign Relations, U.S. Senate, January 1982.

———. *Conventional Arms Transfers to the Third World, 1983–1990.* Prepared by Richard F. Grimmett. Washington, D.C., August 2, 1991.

———. *Iraq's Nuclear Achievements: Components, Sources, and Structure.* Prepared by Peter Zimmerman. Washington, D.C., February 18, 1993.

———. *Middle East Arms Control and Related Issues.* Washington, D.C., May 1, 1991.

———. *Missile Proliferation: A Discussion of U.S. Objectives and Policy Options.* Washington, D.C., February 21, 1990.

———. *Non-Proliferation Regimes: A Comparative Analysis of Policies to Control the Spread of Nuclear, Chemical and Biological Weapons and Missiles.* Washington, D.C., April 1, 1991.

———. *Nuclear, Biological, and Chemical Weapon Proliferation: Potential Military Countermeasures.* Washington, D.C., June 28, 1994.

———. *The United States and the Use of Force in the Post–Cold War World: Toward Self-Deterrence?* Prepared by Stanley R. Sloan. Washington, D.C., July 20, 1994.

———. *U.S. Counterproliferation Doctrine: Issues for Congress.* Prepared by Zachary Davis and Mitchell Reiss. Washington, D.C., September 21, 1994.

———. *Weapons Nonproliferation Policy and Legislation.* Report of the Foreign Affairs and National Defense Division. Washington, D.C., July 3, 1991.

U.S. Congress, House of Representatives, Committee on Armed Services. *Countering the Chemical and Biological Weapons Threat in the Post-Soviet World.* Report of the Special Inquiry Into the Chemical and Biological Threat, February 23, 1993. Washington, D.C.: GPO, 1993.

———. Testimony by the director of U.S. naval intelligence, Rear Admiral Thomas A. Brooks, to the Subcommittee on Seapower, Strategic, and Critical Materials, March 7, 1991.

———, Committee on Foreign Affairs. *Changing Perspectives on U.S. Arms Transfer Policy.* Report Prepared for the Subcommittee on International Security and Scientific Affairs, September 25, 1981.

———. *The Future of Arms Control.* Report Prepared for the Subcommittee on Arms Control, International Security and Science, April 1992.

———. *Proliferation and Arms Control.* Hearings before the Subcommittee on Arms Control, International Security, and Science, May 17 and June 11, 1990.

U.S. Congress, Office of Technology Assessment. *Export Controls and Nonproliferation Policy.* OTA–ISS–596. Washington, D.C.: GPO, May 1994.

———. *Global Arms Trade: Commerce in Advanced Military Technology and Weapons.* OTA–ISC–460. Washington, D.C.: GPO, June 1991.

———. *Proliferation and the Former Soviet Union.* OTA–ISS–605. Washington, D.C.: GPO, September 1994.

———. *Proliferation of Weapons of Mass Destruction: Assessing the Risks.* OTA–ISC–559. Washington, D.C.: GPO, August 1993.

———. *Technologies Underlying Weapons of Mass Destruction.* OTA–BP–ISA–115. Washington, D.C.: GPO, December 1993.

U.S. Congress, Senate, Committee on Foreign Relations. *Implications of President Carter's Conventional Arms Transfer Policy.* Report by the Subcommittee on Foreign Assistance, December 1977.

———, Committee on Governmental Affairs. *Proliferation Threats of the 1990's.* Hearings, 103rd Cong., 1st Sess., February 24, 1993. Washington, D.C.: GPO, 1993.

———, Committee on Governmental Affairs and its Permanent Subcommittee on Investigations. *Global Spread of Chemical and Biological Weapons.* Hearings, February 9, 10 and May 2, 17, 1989.

U.S. Defense Nuclear Agency. *Proceedings of the Defense Nuclear Agency's International Conference on Controlling Arms,* Richmond, Va., June 7–9, 1993, August 1994.

U.S. Department of Defense. *Report on Nonproliferation and Counterproliferation Activities and Programs.* Washington, D.C.: Office of the Deputy Secretary of Defense, May 1994.

———. *Technology Proliferation and U.S. Technological Superiority.* Joint Strategy Review Plan, Key Judgment Paper, Final Draft (unclassified). Washington, D.C., April 13, 1993.

U.S. Department of Energy. *DOE Guide to Technology Security.* Prepared for the U.S. Department of Energy, Office of Nonproliferation Technology Support, May 1992.

Bibliography

U.S. Department of State. *New Purposes and Priorities for Arms Control.* Department of State Publication 10023. Report to Sherman M. Funk, Inspector General of the U.S. Arms Control And Disarmament Agency, Washington, D.C., December 14, 1992.

Washington Council on Non-Proliferation. *Nuclear Arms Control: The U.S. and India.* A Report of the Study Group on U.S. Policy Options for Constraining Proliferation in South Asia. Working Paper No. 2. Washington, D.C.: Washington Council on Non-Proliferation, May 1993.

Wheeler, Michael. *Positive and Negative Security Assurances.* Paper No. 9. College Park, Md.: Project on Rethinking Arms Control, Center for International and Security Studies at Maryland, School of Public Affairs, University of Maryland at College Park, February 1994.

Wolf, Barry. "When the Weak Attack the Strong: Failures of Deterrence." RAND Note N–3261–A. Santa Monica, Calif.: RAND, 1991.